The Steinsaltz Mishne Torah

SEFER HAMADDA

INTRODUCTION TO RAMBAM

Steinsaltz Center

KOREN

משנה תורה לרמב"ם שטיינזלץ

THE STEINSALTZ MISHNE TORAH

ספר המדע

SEFER HAMADDA

INTRODUCTION TO RAMBAM

COMMENTARY BY

Rabbi Adin Even-Israel
Steinsaltz

STEINSALTZ CENTER
KOREN PUBLISHERS JERUSALEM

The Steinsaltz Mishne Torah
Volume 1A: *Sefer HaMadda*, Introduction to Rambam

Paperback edition, ISBN 978-965-583-163-4

First Hebrew/English Edition, 2026

Koren Publishers Jerusalem Ltd.
PO Box 4044, Jerusalem 9104001, ISRAEL
PO Box 8531, New Milford, CT 06776, USA
www.korenpub.com

Steinsaltz Center
Steinsaltz Center is the parent organization
of institutions established by Rabbi Adin Even-Israel Steinsaltz
PO Box 45187, Jerusalem 91450 ISRAEL
Telephone: +972 2 646 0900, Fax +972 2 624 9454
www.steinsaltz-center.org

This book was published in cooperation with the Israel Institute for Talmudic Publications.

First printing, 2026

Printed in ROT

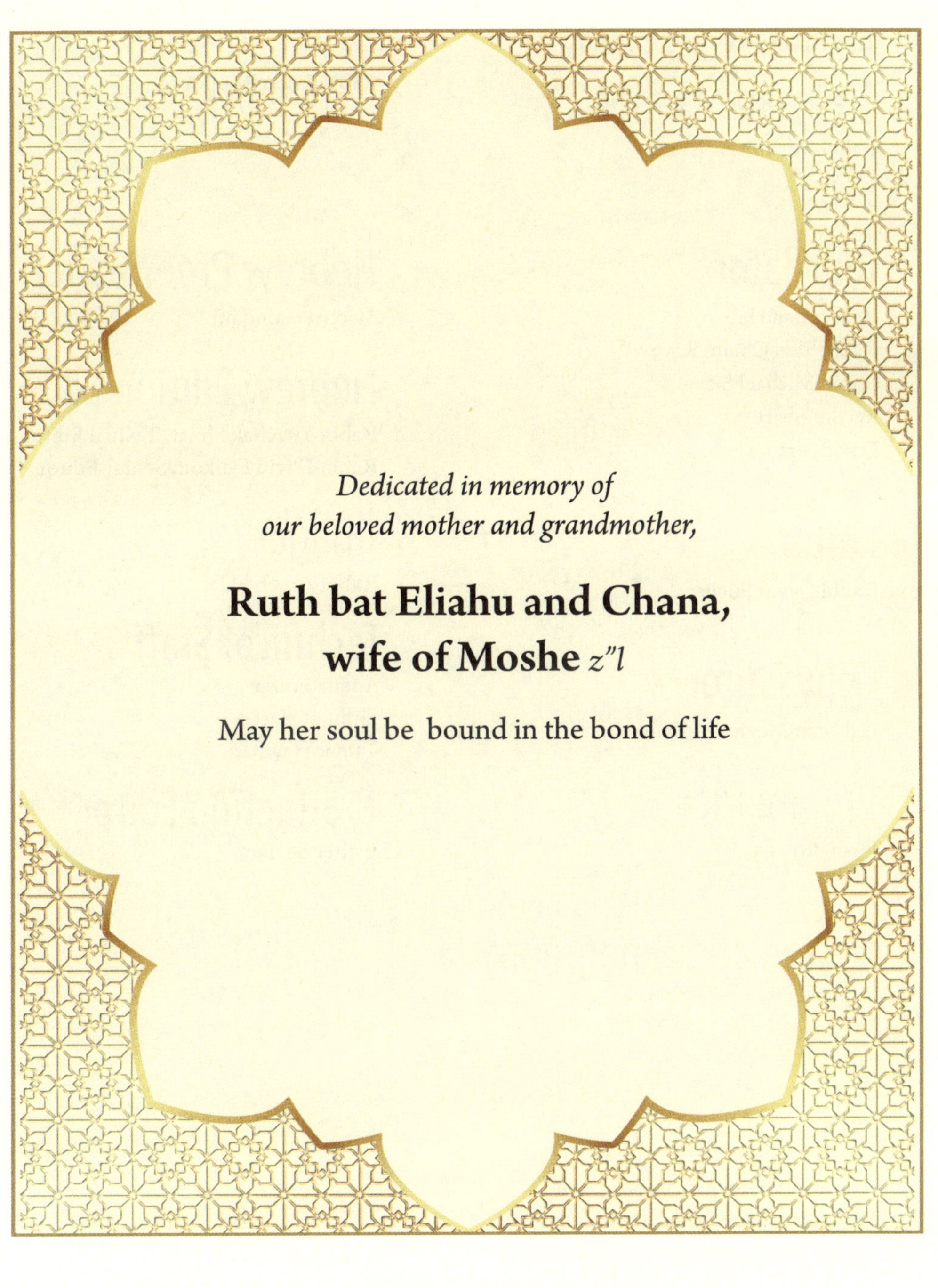

Dedicated in memory of
our beloved mother and grandmother,

Ruth bat Eliahu and Chana,
wife of Moshe *z"l*

May her soul be bound in the bond of life

Executive Director, Steinsaltz Center
Rabbi Meni Even-Israel

Editor-in-Chief
Rabbi Jason Rappoport

Translators
Rabbi Alan Haber
Rabbi Tzvi Chaim Kaye
Rabbi Michael Siev
Avi Steinhart
David Strauss

Editor
Rabbi David Fuchs

Copy Editor
Deborah Meghnagi Bailey

Proofreader
Dvora Rhein

Hebrew Proofreader
Avichai Gamdani

Hebrew Edition Editors
Rabbi Yitzchak Shilat, Textual Editor
Rabbi David Fialkoff, Senior Editor

Images
Rabbi Aryeh Sklar

Technical Staff
Adena Frazer
Shmuel Hart
Tamar Hayman

Production Editor
Esther Shafier

Design and Typography
Raphaël Freeman MISTD

Editor-in-Chief, Avishai Magence
Production Manager, Caryn Meltz
Typesetting, Rina Ben Gal and Tomi Mager
Cover Design, Eliyahu Misgav and Shmooel Lasry

Contents

Preface to This Edition of the *Mishne Torah*

The *Mishne Torah* is the most all-encompassing work of Jewish law ever written. It benefits from a clear style, and is arranged in an impressively orderly and logical manner. This enables the students of the book, whether or not they have a Torah background, to gain a distinct and comprehensive picture of the halakha on any given topic.

With that said, the contemporary reader may still find it somewhat difficult to study this work, due to changes in language and culture since the Rambam's time, which necessitate clarifications of many words and terms. Furthermore, although the Rambam provided the reasoning for a large number of his rulings, there are still numerous laws that lack explanations, with regard to both their rationales and their underlying principles.

From the perspective of the practical halakha, many important factors are absent from the *Mishne Torah*, such as dissenting opinions that have been accepted as halakha by a majority of Jews (or in specific communities), certain halakhic topics that are not addressed by the Rambam at all, customs and enactments that are omitted, and areas of concern that did not exist in the Rambam's day. Consequently, although the *Mishne Torah* was initially designed to serve as a work of practical halakha, and despite the fact that the vast majority of the Rambam's rulings have indeed been accepted as halakha, one who studies the book nowadays cannot rely on it to such an extent that he will know, in every situation, how to act in practice.

The aim of this edition of the *Mishne Torah* is to bridge these gaps. It renders the book accessible to everyone with the addition of study tools which allow readers to use the book as a means of understanding the halakha in practice. The different sections of this edition have been specifically adapted for this purpose, and were prepared with great care, in order that the book would be elegant, professional, useful, and accessible to all.

Many thanks to the team at Koren Publishers, Jerusalem, who worked hard on the design and preparation of the edition.

Some Observations on this Edition

The text of the *Mishne Torah*

Due to the importance of the *Mishne Torah* to the Torah world, it has been copied, printed, and edited many times, in many different generations and, as a result, the text has fallen prey to numerous changes and corruptions, unconsciously or otherwise. This edition is based on the precise text edited by Rabbi Yitzḥak Sheilat, the *Rambam HaMeduyak* [*The Precise Rambam*], which he prepared through consultation with Mizrahi and Yemeni manuscripts of the *Mishne Torah*, considered the most reliable. Foremost among these is the manuscript approved with the signature of the Rambam himself for *Sefer HaMadda* and *Sefer Ahava* (see Rabbi Sheilat's introduction to his text, where his method of establishing the most accurate version is clarified in detail). The sketches and diagrams that appear in the *Mishne Torah* itself have been precisely arranged, based on the images that appear in the manuscripts of the *Mishne Torah*, as in Rabbi Sheilat's edition.

The division into Halakhot

The Rambam divides every chapter of the *Mishne Torah* into Halakhot. In the manuscripts of the *Mishne Torah*, including those with Rambam's own handwriting, in his drafts of the work, the Halakhot were not numbered. The numbering of the Halakhot was added in the printed editions, but these divisions are often corrupt and do not correspond to the original division of the Rambam. In certain cases, the alternative division stemmed from publishers' errors of comprehension; there are even instances where a Halakha is interrupted in the middle of a sentence. In this edition, the paragraphs have been separated in accordance with the Rambam's original division of the Halakhot, but the standard numbering of the Halakhot of the printed editions was preserved, as an aid to the reader.

Vowels and punctuation

The vowels and punctuation in this edition have been prepared in a meticulous, precise manner. The spelling has been adjusted so that the word is fully spelled out when that is required by the rules of grammar, while the spelling of the biblical verses quoted by the Rambam follows the Masoretic tradition. Aside from this, the verses are presented as they were written in the manuscripts, and it is noted when they deviate from the Masoretic text. Where there is a gap in a quotation, and the manuscripts read וכו׳, "etc.," the Hebrew text states likewise, and where such an indication is missing, an ellipsis [...] has been added instead. In the translation, there is either an ellipsis replacing the "etc." or the verse has been completed. As for the vowels, there are many cases where the vowels were likely added by the Rambam himself in his *Commentary on the Mishna*. In most instances, these vowels are accepted, even if they reflect a tradition of pronunciation that differs slightly from the one in use today, but the vowels of several words have been adjusted to follow the customary contemporary pronunciation. Since the vowels accord with the spelling that appears in the manuscripts, certain words might sometimes appear unusual to the eye.

The glosses of the Raavad

The Raavad was a contemporary of the Rambam, and is considered his greatest critic. Throughout the *Mishne Torah* the Raavad comments on the Rambam's statements. Sometimes he disagrees with the Rambam outright, while on other occasions he clarifies his meaning or provides a source. Over the generations, the glosses of the Raavad have been studied together with the text of the Rambam itself, and many of the ruling authorities have assumed that if the Raavad does not take issue with the Rambam on a particular matter, this can be taken as a sign of his agreement with the Rambam's rulings. The text of the Raavad's glosses on *Sefer Zemanim* are based on the text of the Raavad's glosses on Sefer Zemanim in this edition is based on *Yad Peshuta* by Rabbi Naḥum Eliezer Rabinovitch. We thank him for granting us permission to use his edition.[1]

From the Lubavitcher Rebbe

This section features commentaries on the *Mishne Torah* by the Lubavitcher Rebbe, Rabbi Menachem Mendel Schneerson, who instituted a program for the daily study of the *Mishne Torah* and devoted much attention to Rambam's teachings. The Rebbe's commentaries address both the plain meanings of the laws and their spiritual, esoteric message. The commentaries presented here have been gathered from across the Rebbe's extensive teachings. From among the Rebbe's numerous observations on the *Mishne Torah*, those cited here illuminate the Rambam's distinctive approach and the unique wording of his formulations.

Daily study schedule

The *Mishne Torah* is studied by many as part of a regular daily learning schedule. The daily study of the Rambam was proposed by the Lubavitcher Rebbe in the year 5744 (1984). The Rebbe explained that because the *Mishne*

1 Sadly, Rabbi Rabinovitch passed away before the publicationof this volume.

Torah is the only halakhic work that encompasses the entire Torah, studying it gives a person the opportunity to acquire comprehensive knowledge of all parts of the Torah. Studying the *Mishne Torah* daily study can unite the entire Jewish people in shared learning of all the parts of the Torah.

In order to make the daily study suitable for as broad an audience as possible, including people with Torah background and those without, the Rebbe proposed three study tracks:

1. Three chapters per day – In this framework, the entire *Mishne Torah* is completed in slightly under a year.
2. One chapter per day – In this framework, the entire *Mishne Torah* is completed once every three years and three months.
3. Study of the Rambam's *Sefer HaMitzvot* – In this framework the daily content is coordinated with the topics being studied in the three-chapter track. Students in this track complete the *Sefer HaMitzvot* each year.

All frameworks include studying the entire work, beginning with the Rambam's introduction to the *Mishne Torah*. To assist the learner, in this current edition, there are markings for the one-chapter-per-day and three-chapters-per-day tracks as follows:

A symbol of three triangles (◂⁝) at the beginning of the introduction serves as the starting point for both tracks. For those studying three chapters per day, the three-triangle symbol marks the transition point from day to day. Throughout the introduction and *Sefer HaMitzvot* (and also later in the book in "*Seder Tefillot*"), for those studying one chapter per day, in addition to the three-triangle marking, they should also stop at the single triangle symbol (◂).

The introductions

To every *Sefer* of the *Mishne Torah*, as well as each of its halakhic units, we have added an introduction. The introductions present basic descriptions of the topics of that section, highlighting the main points of each topic. They also include general references to the rabbinic sources that deal with that subject, while addressing the structure of the book as a whole and the position of that section of Halakhot within the entire work.

The headings

At the beginning of each section of Halakhot, we have offered titles for the topics of the chapters and their laws. These serve as a kind of table of contents for the section, while also outlining a general picture of how the unit is organized as a whole. The titles are presented again at the start of each chapter, to help the reader understand its structure and development.

The commentary

The commentary is presented in a concise form. It explains difficult words and halakhic terms, as well as the principles and rationales that underlie the Rambam's decisions. The commentary is based on an in-depth study of the relevant passages in the rabbinic sources and their commentaries, comparisons with other sections of the *Mishne Torah* and different works of the Rambam, the opinions of the early authorities on the work, as well as newer commentaries from recent generations, up to and including our own. This is all part of an effort to establish the true meaning of the Rambam's words. Special note should be made of Rabbi Yosef Kapaḥ's translation of the Rambam's *Commentary on the Mishna*, and his commentary to the *Mishne Torah*, as well as the *Yad Peshuta* commentary by Rabbi Naḥum Eliezer Rabinovitch, of which we have made extensive use. The commentary also provides images and diagrams that clarify and illustrate the Rambam's statements.

Halakhic discussion

This edition notes the opinions of the *Shulḥan Arukh* and the Rema, when they refer to the rulings of the Rambam. It also cites the views of authorities who disagree with the Rambam, or who add details to the halakha, beginning with the *Shulḥan Arukh* and its commentaries, through the later authorities, down to contemporary rabbis. This tells the reader when the Rambam's opinion has been accepted as law, and in which instances the halakha has been decided differently. In those Halakhot that are not discussed in the *Shulḥan Arukh*, such as laws that are not practiced in this age, the main opinions of the early and later authorities over the generations have been referenced, where they take issue with or add to the Rambam's statements.

The appendices

The appendices, which form an independent unit at the end of each book, offer analyses of halakhically complex topics. They present a comprehensive overview of the subject matter, from the sources of the halakha to rulings by contemporary authorities, while referencing the historical, social, and technological changes that have occurred over the generations, as well as the degree of their influence on the halakhic reality as practiced today. This section thus complements the "Halakhic Discussion" notes on subject matters that include, among other issues, various topical questions that arise in the modern world.

Introduction to the *Mishne Torah*

The purpose of the book: To provide a comprehensive summary of the Oral Torah

The *Mishne Torah*, by Rabbi Moses ben Maimon (Maimonides, or the Rambam), is his greatest work and one of the most important books in all of Jewish history. The grand plan of the book, as the Rambam outlined in his introduction, was for it to serve as a compilation of the entire Oral Torah, so much so that one who is well-versed in the Bible and this book of the Rambam would have the entire Torah in his grasp and would not require any other book. For this reason, he called his book *Mishne Torah* ("restatement of the Torah," or "second to the Torah"). Although the book was ultimately not accepted as an exclusive authority, it has been one of the foundational texts of the Torah from the time it was written until this day, and a pillar of halakha for the entire Jewish people.

The work provides a distillation of the entire Oral Torah. Accordingly, it incorporates areas of law that other halakhic works do not address. The Rambam does not distinguish, in the manner of the great Sages who preceded him, between halakhot that apply in the present time and those that can be fulfilled only when the people of Israel are residing in their land in full strength. He even deals with matters that pertain solely to the days of the Messiah. Although the Talmud did not rule on such laws, and some have contended that these "halakhot for the messianic period" should perhaps be left for future generations to adjudicate, the Rambam did not shy away from them. He thus issues rulings in all realms of halakha, both practical and otherwise, those which are relevant today together with mitzvot that have no current application. This is a clear expression of his comprehensive vision, for he views the Oral Torah as a unified whole, all of whose parts are interconnected organically.

In addition, unlike other halakhic works, the Rambam does not deal exclusively with "halakha" in the narrow sense of the term. Rather, he addresses everything that, in his view, is binding upon every Jew, whether in terms of religious-halakhic practice, matters of faith, worthy character traits, or even basic principles of health. Conversely, areas of the Oral Torah that are not binding are omitted. Thus, the Rambam, following the example of his teacher, the Rif, omits the dialectical discussions of the Oral Torah and the opinions of the Sages that were ultimately rejected as halakha. He includes very few interpretations of biblical verses and their midrashic explanations, rarely recounts historical events, and is sparing when it comes to philosophical reflections, poetic passages, and inspirational teachings from the "aggadic" literature, including the *aggadot* of the Talmud. Nevertheless, he does occasionally, especially at the conclusions of certain *Hilkhot* sections, add words of inspiration and ethical exhortations.

The Style of the Book: Language, Structure, and Conciseness

The *Mishne Torah* is written entirely in Hebrew, in a style very similar to that of the Mishna. In his introduction to *Sefer HaMitzvot*, where the Rambam essentially presents his design for the *Mishne Torah*, he explains that he did not choose the style of the Bible due to its limited vocabulary which is unsuitable for a work of this kind. He did not wish to use the language of the Talmud either, because it contains many words that are not universally understood. The Mishna, by contrast, served for the Rambam as a model of the clear, concise, and unembellished style that he sought for the material included in this work.

Although the Rambam wrote most of his books in Arabic (including commentaries and legal rulings), the *Mishne Torah* is written entirely in Hebrew. He likely made this choice to ensure that the book could reach a Jewish audience that did not speak Arabic. He may also have been thinking ahead to times when Arabic would no longer be commonly spoken among Jews. In other words, the very decision to write in Hebrew is part of his broader plan to compose a work that would serve the entire Jewish people across all generations.

In general, the Rambam allows himself the liberty to rephrase traditional materials and provide them with new forms and expressions. At the same time, however, he also cites numerous sources, especially the Mishna and related works, in their original language and formulations. It should also be noted that although the Rambam's language is basically the same as that of the Mishna, his syntax and word usage do not always match those of his sources. This can lead to slight variations stemming from differences between the original texts and the Rambam's individual style. Nevertheless, the elegance of the Rambam's language, and his exceptional ability to clarify complex ideas, render the *Mishne Torah* a literary masterpiece as well, and one of the greatest achievements in Hebrew in all generations.

There are several other important characteristics of the *Mishne Torah* which the Rambam touches upon in his introduction to *Sefer HaMitzvot*, and which are foundational to his work. The most prominent feature, one that in many ways makes the book exceptional, perhaps in all of Jewish literature, is the extraordinary degree of order it exhibits. First and foremost, there is the new organizational structure that the Rambam creates in his book. Unlike the traditional division of the Mishnah and Talmud into six Orders, which some earlier halakhic works, such as that of the Rif, also followed, the Rambam introduces a new thematic division. The work is divided into fourteen books, each of which is further subdivided into sections called *Hilkhot*, which focus on more specific topics.

Beyond this broad restructuring, the internal organization of the book is also highly methodical. The Rambam provides an introduction for each subject, both for broader topics that span entire books or sets of *Hilkhot*, and for more minor and specific issues. These introductions provide a general definition of the subject, and sometimes also definitions of key terms and relevant concepts. After these definitions, the Rambam proceeds to the specific laws, all of which are likewise presented in a consistent order: Each subject appears in its proper place, is explained in detail, and is logically connected to the ensuing topic.

Despite the exceptional organization of this work, there are certain subjects that do not fit neatly into the framework of main and secondary topics. As a result, their placement is somewhat forced. From a different perspective, the very logical order that characterizes the book can at times make it difficult to locate a specific topic and can even appear counterintuitive. For example, in the *Arbaa Turim* (the "Four Columns," a halakhic work that gained prominence after the Rambam's time and which served as the basis for the *Shulḥan Arukh*), the first section, *Oraḥ Ḥayyim*, follows the chronological flow of a person's daily life. For the laws of festivals, for instance, all the unique halakhot of the various festivals are collected in one volume, including the order of prayer on that day, its Torah reading, and so on. By contrast, in the *Mishne Torah*, the mitzvot of the festivals appear in one place (*Sefer Zemanim*), while the special prayers and Torah readings are found elsewhere (*Hilkhot Tefilla* in *Sefer Ahava*).

Another characteristic of this work is the relative scarcity of justifications for its legal rulings, as well as the fact that there are no references or citations to the Talmud or other rabbinic literature. The halakhic rulings that the Rambam records in his book are, in effect, summaries of decisions between divergent opinions of the Sages, without any explicit acknowledgment of these disputes. In his introductions to both *Sefer HaMitzvot* and the *Mishne Torah,* the Rambam explains that this is due to his pursuit of brevity and his desire not to overburden or confuse the reader with detailed halakhic debates. Presenting arguments and proofs invites discussion and lengthy elaboration, whereas the Rambam sought to present what he called the "clean, fine flour," i.e., the distilled halakhic conclusions as determined by the final redactors of the Talmud and the Sages who followed them. The absence of sources can be explained in a similar vein: Since some rulings are based on a combination of two or three different sources, quoting or detailing them could open the door to debate that would certainly disrupt the flow of the text and make it more difficult to understand.

Since the sources of the Rambam, and at times his reasoning for certain halakhic rulings, are not always entirely clear, many important commentaries on the book have sought to identify his sources and methods of halakhic decision-making. Over the generations, the consensus has emerged that in general the Rambam indeed uses clearly identifiable consistent methodologies for issuing his halakhic rulings. These are based on halakhic principles delineated in the Talmud or received from the geonim, which the Rambam uses far more frequently than other halakhic authorities. Principles such as "the halakha is in accordance with an unattributed mishna," or "the halakha is in accordance with the second version" (when the Gemara offers "another version" of a discussion) are frequently used in this work, as are other halakhic rules of a similar nature, such as those regarding the halakhic status of various rabbinic sources (the Babylonian Talmud, Jerusalem Talmud, *Tosefta,* and the halakhic midrashim) and the relationships between them. The systematic use of these rules is yet another example of the meticulous order of the *Mishne Torah.*

The Importance of the Book Across the Generations

Due to the vast scope of the *Mishne Torah,* notwithstanding the areas it does not include, it has a central place of importance, beyond its significance as a foundational text of halakha. In fact, no other book, from those written before or after the *Mishne Torah,* offers such a broad and comprehensive overview of "the entire Torah." Accordingly, there is no doubt that anyone who wishes to understand the Torah of God, not merely some of its isolated details, but as a large and complete world, has no better resource than this book. It presents the Torah in its broadest scope, encompassing all areas of Jewish law as they developed over generations.

This Edition of the *Mishne Torah*

The purpose of this edition of the *Mishne Torah* is to assist the reader, especially those who learn it on a regular basis. This refers not only to understanding the content itself, but also in terms of situating it within the broader framework of the Torah. For despite the centrality and importance of the *Mishne Torah* in the world of Jewish law, historically speaking the mainstream halakhic development did not continue directly through the Rambam's work. Although the Rambam was, and continues to be, one of the great pillars of halakhic authority, in terms of practical halakhic rulings there are other major sources that are considered equally important, namely the rulings of the Rif and the Rosh. In addition, the rulings of many other Sages are also used as sources of halakha, along with various customs that became widespread in different Jewish communities. The halakha, as it exists and is binding today, largely followed the approach of the *Arbaa Turim* and its commentaries, and the *Shulḥan Arukh* and its commentaries in its wake, and the Jewish people conduct themselves mostly in accordance with their conclusions.

For this reason, alongside the rulings of the Rambam, this edition includes a section entitled "Halakhic Discussion," which provides references to other halakhic works, particularly the *Shulḥan Arukh* and the glosses of the Rema, which relate to the Rambam's rulings. In cases where the *Shulḥan Arukh* and later halakhic authorities followed the opinion of the Rambam (sometimes to the extent that they even copied his wording verbatim), only a reference is provided. However, whenever the halakhic tradition did not follow the Rambam's position, a more detailed explanation is given. This way, in addition to learning the Rambam's view on a particular issue, the reader will also learn about the practical halakhic ruling accepted in our times.

By comparing the Rambam's rulings with contemporary halakhic practice on the same subjects, his words are presented not merely as an ancient text that was preeminent in its time, but as a work that can also serve as a guide for practical halakha today. From these comparisons, one can discern those points at which later authorities disagreed with, modified, or developed the Rambam's opinion, thereby giving his statements ongoing practical significance, rather than merely historical value.

Even in those areas of halakha that are not addressed by the *Shulḥan Arukh*, such as laws that are currently inapplicable, this edition includes the major views of the early and later authorities over the generations on those topics. Although these may not constitute halakhic rulings in the practical, everyday sense, there is certainly value in becoming familiar with the central approaches taken by other great Torah scholars, alongside those of the Rambam.

More than eight hundred years have passed since the composition of the *Mishne Torah*, and throughout these centuries the Torah of Israel has never ceased to grow, as it responds to both fresh Torah ideas and new realities of the world. The profound changes that continue to occur in our own time, both in ways of life and in the technological reality of the modern world, have created the need to update halakhic rulings beyond the decisions of the classical halakhic authorities. This includes taking into account halakhic opinions that address present-day concerns, even if they have not yet been codified in the form of binding halakhic literature in recent generations.

For this purpose, this edition includes a section of appendices, which broadens the scope and discussion of topics that have undergone changes due to social, historical, technological, and other developments. Although this section is not intended to provide practical halakhic rulings on these matters, it does attempt to review and summarize the relevant sources and halakhic approaches. This overview includes both subjects on which there is a relatively clear halakhic consensus, as well as issues regarding which there is as yet no full agreement. In such cases, the ideas are presented in a manner that signals to the reader that, should a practical ruling be needed, one must consult a knowledgeable rabbi in the field.

A different kind of problem that might arise for the modern learner involves comprehending the words of the Rambam themselves. For despite the clarity of his language, the words and terms he uses are not always familiar or commonly used by the reader of today. This is the case for native Hebrew speakers, and all the more so for those who wish to learn the Rambam through the medium of a translation. Additionally, while the Rambam often provides explanations for his rulings, certain details sometimes require further clarification. For this reason, a brief commentary has been added to this edition. This commentary does not engage in in-depth analysis of the Rambam's statements, in the manner of the classical commentaries, but rather offers concise explanations of his language, while supplementing it with clarifications and elucidations when necessary.

An additional section has been added to the English edition, titled "From the Lubavitcher Rebbe." This material is a collection of commentaries by the Lubavitcher Rebbe that shed additional light on the teachings of the Rambam, revealing their spiritual depth and profundity.

The Rambam's Introduction to the *Mishne Torah*

״בְּשֵׁם יי אֵל עוֹלָם״ (בראשית כא, לג)

"In the name of the Lord, God of the Universe" (Genesis 21:33)

״אָז לֹא אֵבוֹשׁ בְּהַבִּיטִי אֶל כָּל מִצְוֹתֶיךָ״ (תהלים קיט, ו)

"For then I would not be ashamed when looking upon all Your commandments"* (Psalms 119:6)

INSIGHTS OF THE LUBAVITCHER REBBE

***For then I would not be ashamed when looking upon all Your commandments – אָז לֹא אֵבוֹשׁ בְּהַבִּיטִי אֶל כָּל מִצְוֹתֶיךָ:** The connection between this verse and the beginning of the *Mishne Torah* can be explained in two ways: 1) The basic explanation is that after reading the Written Law, one feels ashamed due to his lack of knowledge of how to fulfill the details of the mitzvot. It is only "then," after studying the *Mishne Torah*, that one will "not be ashamed." 2) On a deeper level, the Rambam is declaring that he is not ashamed to define his work as a replacement to the study of the Oral Law, for one who is "looking upon all Your commandments," in a clear and comprehensive manner is not only allowed, but is actually obligated to publicize his knowledge to all Jews (*Torat Menaḥem*, *Hitvaaduyot*, *Parashat Kedoshim*, *Emor* [and] *Ki Tavo* 5744; *Parashat Vayak'hel* 5746).

NOTES

a. N.B. The division into paragraphs is found in early manuscripts, while their numbering and headings have been added for the reader's convenience.

כָּל הַמִּצְוֹות שֶׁנִּתְּנוּ לוֹ לְמֹשֶׁה בְּסִינַי – בְּפֵרוּשָׁן נִתְּנוּ, שֶׁנֶּאֱמַר: "וְאֶתְּנָה לְךָ אֶת לֻחֹת הָאֶבֶן וְהַתּוֹרָה וְהַמִּצְוָה" (שמות כד, יב): "תּוֹרָה" – זוֹ תּוֹרָה שֶׁבִּכְתָב, וּ"מִצְוָה" – זֶה פֵּרוּשָׁהּ, וְצִוָּנוּ לַעֲשׂוֹת הַתּוֹרָה עַל פִּי הַמִּצְוָה. וּמִצְוָה זוֹ הִיא הַנִּקְרֵאת תּוֹרָה שֶׁבְּעַל פֶּה.

All of the mitzvot[a] **given to Moses at** Mount **Sinai were given** together **with their explanations,*** **as it is stated: "And I will give you the stone tablets and the law and the commandment"** (Exodus 24: 12). **"The law," this is the Written Law; "the commandment," this is its explanation.** God thus **commanded us to perform "the Torah" in accordance with "the commandment." This "commandment" is called the Oral Law.****

כָּל הַתּוֹרָה כְּתָבָהּ מֹשֶׁה רַבֵּנוּ קֹדֶם שֶׁיָּמוּת בִּכְתַב יָדוֹ, וְנָתַן סֵפֶר לְכָל שֵׁבֶט וְשֵׁבֶט, וְסֵפֶר אֶחָד נְתָנָהוּ בָּאָרוֹן לְעֵד, שֶׁנֶּאֱמַר: "לָקֹחַ אֵת סֵפֶר הַתּוֹרָה הַזֹּאת וְשַׂמְתֶּם אֹתוֹ מִצַּד אֲרוֹן בְּרִית יי אֱלֹהֵיכֶם וְהָיָה שָׁם בְּךָ לְעֵד" (דברים לא, כו, ושם: סֵפֶר הַתּוֹרָה הַזֶּה). וְהַמִּצְוָה, שֶׁהִיא פֵּרוּשׁ הַתּוֹרָה – לֹא כְּתָבָהּ, אֶלָּא צִוָּה בָּהּ לַזְּקֵנִים וְלִיהוֹשֻׁעַ וְלִשְׁאָר כָּל יִשְׂרָאֵל, שֶׁנֶּאֱמַר: "אֵת כָּל הַדָּבָר אֲשֶׁר אָנֹכִי מְצַוֶּה אֶתְכֶם אֹתוֹ תִשְׁמְרוּ לַעֲשׂוֹת לֹא תֹסֵף עָלָיו וְלֹא תִגְרַע מִמֶּנּוּ" (שם יג, א), וּמִפְּנֵי זֶה נִקְרֵאת תּוֹרָה שֶׁבְּעַל פֶּה.

Moses, our teacher, transcribed the entire Torah before he died, in his own hand. He gave a Torah **scroll to each tribe, and placed one** other **scroll in the ark as a witness, as it is stated: "Take this book of the Torah, and place it at the side of the Ark of the Covenant of the Lord your God, and it will be there as a witness for you"** (Deuteronomy 31:26). **But** Moses **did not write down "the commandment," which is the explanation of the Torah. Instead, he commanded it to the elders, and to Joshua, and to all the rest of Israel, as it is stated: "All this matter that I command you, you shall take care to perform; you shall not add to it and you shall not subtract from it"** (Deuteronomy 13:1). **For this reason it is called the Oral Law.**

אַף עַל פִּי שֶׁלֹּא נִכְתְּבָה תּוֹרָה שֶׁבְּעַל פֶּה, לִמְּדָהּ מֹשֶׁה רַבֵּנוּ כֻּלָּהּ בְּבֵית דִּינוֹ לְשִׁבְעִים זְקֵנִים. וְאֶלְעָזָר וּפִינְחָס וִיהוֹשֻׁעַ – שְׁלָשְׁתָּם קִבְּלוּ מִמֹּשֶׁה. וְלִיהוֹשֻׁעַ, שֶׁהוּא תַּלְמִידוֹ שֶׁל מֹשֶׁה רַבֵּנוּ, מָסַר תּוֹרָה שֶׁבְּעַל פֶּה וְצִוָּהוּ עָלֶיהָ. וְכֵן יְהוֹשֻׁעַ כָּל יְמֵי חַיָּיו לִמֵּד עַל פֶּה.

Even though the Oral Law was not written down, Moses, our teacher, taught it in its entirety, in his court, to the **seventy elders. The three** leaders, **Elazar, Pinhas, and Joshua, received from Moses** the tradition of the Oral Law as the explanation of the Torah ("the commandment"). It was **to Joshua, our teacher Moses'** primary **disciple,** that he **transmitted** the **Oral Law, and** Moses **instructed him regarding it,** that he has the responsibility to hand down the Oral Torah to future generations. **Similarly, all his life Joshua taught** the Torah **orally.**

INSIGHTS OF THE LUBAVITCHER REBBE

***All of the mitzvot given to Moses... were given together with their explanations – כָּל מַעֲשָׂיו:** The Oral Law, which is the "explanation" of the Torah, enables one to know and understand it fully, and therefore it is part of the definition of the Torah itself. Accordingly, it was given a) together with the Written Law, so that the Torah would be given in complete form; and b) it was given by Moses, and therefore the Oral Law also has the status of "the Torah of Moses" (*Torat Menaḥem, Hitvaaduyot, Yud Gimmel Nisan* 5745; *Parashat Aḥarei* [*Mot*] 5749).

****The commandment," this is its explanation... the Oral Law – כָּל מַעֲשָׂיו כֻּלָּם כְּדֵי לֵידַע אֶת הַשֵּׁם:** According to the Rambam, this "explanation" consists of the details of the laws of the Oral Law, not the reasons for the halakhot. This accords with his opinion, expressed in the book, that it is permitted to issue a ruling of halakha even without knowing the reason for it. Thus, the book includes the entire "commandment" of the Torah (*Torat Menaḥem, Hitvaaduyot, Parashat Kedoshim* 5744).

וּזְקֵנִים רַבִּים קִבְּלוּ מִיהוֹשֻׁעַ, וְקִבֵּל עֵלִי מִן הַזְּקֵנִים וּמִפִּינְחָס, וּשְׁמוּאֵל קִבֵּל מֵעֵלִי וּבֵית דִּינוֹ, וְדָוִד קִבֵּל מִשְּׁמוּאֵל וּבֵית דִּינוֹ. וַאֲחִיָּה הַשִּׁילוֹנִי מִיּוֹצְאֵי מִצְרַיִם הָיָה, וְלֵוִי הָיָה, וְשָׁמַע מִמֹּשֶׁה, וְהָיָה קָטָן בִּימֵי מֹשֶׁה, וְהוּא קִבֵּל מִדָּוִד וּבֵית דִּינוֹ.

Many elders received the tradition **from Joshua. Eli received** it **from the elders*** **and from Pinhas. Samuel received** it **from Eli and his court, and David received** it **from Samuel and his court. Ahiya the Shilonite was from** among **those who left Egypt and he was a Levite,** and was therefore not included in the decree imposed on that generation that they would die in the wilderness. The tradition of the Sages is that "Ahiya the Shilonite saw Amram; Elijah saw Ahiya the Shilonite."[a] Ahiya **heard** teachings **from Moses** himself, **but** he did not receive the tradition from him, because **he was young in the days of Moses, and he** later **received** the tradition **from David and his court.**

GLOSSES OF THE RAAVAD

וַאֲחִיָּה הַשִּׁילוֹנִי וְכוּ'. אָמַר אַבְרָהָם: אֵין זֶה נָכוֹן, אֶלָּא שֶׁהָיָה אֲחִיָּה הַשִּׁילוֹנִי מִבֵּית דִּינוֹ שֶׁל דָּוִד.

"Ahiya the Shilonite . . ." Avraham says: This is not correct. Rather, the truth of the matter is **that Ahiya the Shilonite was** a member **of David's court.**

אֵלִיָּהוּ קִבֵּל מֵאֲחִיָּה הַשִּׁילוֹנִי וּבֵית דִּינוֹ, וֶאֱלִישָׁע קִבֵּל מֵאֵלִיָּהוּ וּבֵית דִּינוֹ, וִיהוֹיָדָע הַכֹּהֵן קִבֵּל מֵאֱלִישָׁע וּבֵית דִּינוֹ, וּזְכַרְיָהוּ קִבֵּל מִיהוֹיָדָע וּבֵית דִּינוֹ, וְהוֹשֵׁעַ קִבֵּל מִזְּכַרְיָה וּבֵית דִּינוֹ, וְעָמוֹס קִבֵּל מֵהוֹשֵׁעַ וּבֵית דִּינוֹ, וִישַׁעְיָהוּ קִבֵּל מֵעָמוֹס וּבֵית דִּינוֹ, וּמִיכָה קִבֵּל מִישַׁעְיָה וּבֵית דִּינוֹ, וְיוֹאֵל קִבֵּל מִמִּיכָה וּבֵית דִּינוֹ, וְנַחוּם קִבֵּל מִיּוֹאֵל וּבֵית דִּינוֹ, וַחֲבַקּוּק קִבֵּל מִנַּחוּם וּבֵית דִּינוֹ, וּצְפַנְיָה קִבֵּל מֵחֲבַקּוּק וּבֵית דִּינוֹ, וְיִרְמְיָה קִבֵּל מִצְּפַנְיָה וּבֵית דִּינוֹ, וּבָרוּךְ בֶּן נֵרִיָּה קִבֵּל מִיִּרְמְיָה וּבֵית דִּינוֹ, וְעֶזְרָא וּבֵית דִּינוֹ קִבְּלוּ מִבָּרוּךְ וּבֵית דִּינוֹ.

Elijah received the tradition **from Ahiya the Shilonite and his court. Elisha received** it **from Elijah and his court. Yehoyada the priest received** it **from Elisha and his court. Zechariah received** it **from Yehoyada and his court. Hosea received** it **from Zechariah and his court. Amos received** it **from Hosea and his court. Isaiah received** it **from Amos and his court. Micah received** it **from Isaiah and his court. Joel received** it **from Micah and his court. Nahum received** it **from Joel and his court. Habakkuk received** it **from Nahum and his court. Zephaniah received** it **from Habakkuk and his court. Jeremiah received** it **from Zephaniah and his court. Barukh son of Neriya received** it **from Jeremiah and his court. Ezra and his court received** it **from Barukh and his court.**

INSIGHTS OF THE LUBAVITCHER REBBE

*Received from Moses . . . Eli received from the elders – קִבְּלוּ מִמֹּשֶׁה...וְקִבֵּל עֵלִי מִן הַזְּקֵנִים: The Rambam is careful to use the verb "received" when dealing with transmission of the Oral Law, rather than "handed down," for the Oral Law "receives" from the Written Law, and the emphasis is on those who receive it and their ability to comprehend it (*Torat Menaḥem, Hitvaaduyot, Yom Beit DeḤag HaShavuot* 5746; *Likkutei Siḥot* 30, p. 10).

NOTES

a. *Bava Batra* 121b.

בֵּית דִּינוֹ שֶׁל עֶזְרָא הֵם הַנִּקְרָאִין אַנְשֵׁי כְּנֶסֶת הַגְּדוֹלָה, וְהֵם חַגַּי זְכַרְיָה וּמַלְאָכִי, וְדָנִיֵּאל חֲנַנְיָה מִישָׁאֵל וַעֲזַרְיָה, וּנְחֶמְיָה בֶּן חֲכַלְיָה וּמָרְדֳּכַי וּזְרֻבָּבֶל, וְהַרְבֵּה חֲכָמִים עִמָּהֶם – תַּשְׁלוּם מֵאָה וְעֶשְׂרִים זְקֵנִים. הָאַחֲרוֹן מֵהֶם הוּא שִׁמְעוֹן הַצַּדִּיק, וְהוּא הָיָה מִכְּלַל הַמֵּאָה וְעֶשְׂרִים, וְקִבֵּל תּוֹרָה שֶׁבְּעַל פֶּה מִכֻּלָּן, וְהוּא הָיָה כֹּהֵן גָּדוֹל אַחַר עֶזְרָא.

The court of Ezra are the ones called the members of the Great Assembly. They include **Haggai, Zechariah, Malachi, Daniel, Hananya, Mishael and Azarya, Nehemiah son of Hakhalya, Mordekhai, Zerubbabel and many** other **Sages with them; one hundred and twenty elders in all. The last of them is Shimon HaTzaddik** ("the Just"), **who was included in the** sum of **one hundred and twenty elders and received the Oral Law from all of them. He was** the **High Priest after Ezra.**

אַנְטִיגְנָס אִישׁ שׂוֹכוֹ וּבֵית דִּינוֹ קִבְּלוּ מִשִּׁמְעוֹן הַצַּדִּיק וּבֵית דִּינוֹ, וְיוֹסֵף בֶּן יוֹעֶזֶר אִישׁ צְרֵדָה וְיוֹסֵף בֶּן יוֹחָנָן אִישׁ יְרוּשָׁלַיִם וּבֵית דִּינָם קִבְּלוּ מֵאַנְטִיגְנָס וּבֵית דִּינוֹ, וִיהוֹשֻׁעַ בֶּן פְּרַחְיָה וְנִתַּאי הָאַרְבֵּלִי וּבֵית דִּינָם קִבְּלוּ מִיּוֹסֵף וְיוֹסֵף וּבֵית דִּינָם, יְהוּדָה בֶּן טַבַּאי וְשִׁמְעוֹן בֶּן שָׁטָח וּבֵית דִּינָם קִבְּלוּ מִיהוֹשֻׁעַ וְנִתַּאי וּבֵית דִּינָם, שְׁמַעְיָה וְאַבְטַלְיוֹן גֵּרֵי הַצֶּדֶק וּבֵית דִּינָם קִבְּלוּ מִיהוּדָה וְשִׁמְעוֹן וּבֵית דִּינָם, וְהִלֵּל וְשַׁמַּאי וּבֵית דִּינָם קִבְּלוּ מִשְּׁמַעְיָה וְאַבְטַלְיוֹן וּבֵית דִּינָם, וְרַבָּן יוֹחָנָן בֶּן זַכַּאי וְרַבָּן שִׁמְעוֹן בְּנוֹ שֶׁל הִלֵּל קִבְּלוּ מֵהִלֵּל וּבֵית דִּינוֹ.

Antigonus of Sokho and his court received the tradition **from Shimon HaTzaddik and his court. Yosef ben Yoezer of Tzereida and Yosef ben Yoḥanan of Jerusalem and their court received** it **from Antigonus and his court. Yehoshua ben Peraḥya and Nitai HaArbeli and their court received** it **from Yosef** ben Yoezer **and Yosef** ben Yoḥanan **and their court. Yehuda ben Tabbai and Shimon ben Shataḥ and their court received** it **from Yehoshua ben Peraḥya and Nitai HaArbeli and their court. Shemaya and Avtalyon,** who were **converts, and their court received** it **from Yehuda** ben Tabbai **and Shimon** ben Shataḥ **and their court. Hillel and Shammai and their court received** it **from Shemaya and Avtalyon and their court. Rabban Yoḥanan ben Zakkai and Rabbi Shimon, son of Hillel, received** the tradition **from Hillel and his court.**

חֲמִשָּׁה תַּלְמִידִים הָיוּ לוֹ לְרַבָּן יוֹחָנָן בֶּן זַכַּאי, וְהֵם גְּדוֹלֵי הַחֲכָמִים שֶׁקִּבְּלוּ מִמֶּנּוּ, וְאֵלּוּ הֵם: רַבִּי אֱלִיעֶזֶר הַגָּדוֹל, וְרַבִּי יְהוֹשֻׁעַ, וְרַבִּי יוֹסֵי הַכֹּהֵן, וְרַבִּי שִׁמְעוֹן בֶּן נְתַנְאֵל, וְרַבִּי אֶלְעָזָר בֶּן עֲרָךְ. וְרַבִּי עֲקִיבָה בֶּן יוֹסֵף קִבֵּל מֵרַבִּי אֱלִיעֶזֶר הַגָּדוֹל, וְיוֹסֵף אָבִיו גֵּר צֶדֶק הָיָה. וְרַבִּי יִשְׁמָעֵאל וְרַבִּי מֵאִיר בֶּן גֵּר הַצֶּדֶק קִבְּלוּ מֵרַבִּי עֲקִיבָה, וְגַם קִבֵּל רַבִּי מֵאִיר וַחֲבֵרָיו מֵרַבִּי יִשְׁמָעֵאל.

Rabban Yoḥanan ben Zakkai had five main **students, and they were the great Sages who received** the tradition **from him. They are as follows: Rabbi Eleazar the great; Rabbi Yehoshua, Rabbi Yosei the priest; Rabbi Shimon ben Netanel, and Rabbi Elazar ben Arakh. Rabbi Akiva ben Yosef received** the tradition **from Rabbi Eleazar the Great, and Yosef, his father, was a convert. Rabbi Yishmael and Rabbi Meir, the son of a convert, received** it **from Rabbi Akiva, and Rabbi Meir and his colleagues also received** it **from Rabbi Yishmael.**

חֲבֵרָיו שֶׁל רַבִּי מֵאִיר הֵם: רַבִּי יְהוּדָה, וְרַבִּי יוֹסֵי, וְרַבִּי שִׁמְעוֹן, וְרַבִּי נְחֶמְיָה, וְרַבִּי אֶלְעָזָר בֶּן שַׁמּוּעַ, וְרַבִּי יוֹחָנָן הַסַּנְדְּלָר, וְשִׁמְעוֹן בֶּן עַזַּאי, וְרַבִּי חֲנַנְיָה בֶּן תְּרַדְיוֹן. וְכֵן קִבְּלוּ חֲבֵרָיו שֶׁל רַבִּי עֲקִיבָה מֵרַבִּי אֱלִיעֶזֶר הַגָּדוֹל. וַחֲבֵרָיו שֶׁל רַבִּי עֲקִיבָה הֵם: רַבִּי טַרְפוֹן רַבּוֹ שֶׁל רַבִּי יוֹסֵי הַגְּלִילִי, וְרַבִּי שִׁמְעוֹן בֶּן אֶלְעָזָר, וְרַבִּי יוֹחָנָן בֶּן נוּרִי.

These **colleagues of Rabbi Meir are Rabbi Yehuda, Rabbi Yosei, Rabbi Shimon, Rabbi Neḥemya, Rabbi Elazar ben Shamua, Rabbi Yoḥanan HaSandlar, Shimon ben Azzai, and Rabbi Ḥananya ben Teradyon. Similarly, the colleagues of Rabbi Akiva received** the tradition **from Rabbi Eleazar the Great. Rabbi Akiva's colleagues are Rabbi Tarfon, the teacher of Rabbi Yosei HaGelili, and Rabbi Shimon ben Elazar, and Rabbi Yoḥanan ben Nuri.**

רַבָּן גַּמְלִיאֵל הַזָּקֵן קִבֵּל מֵרַבָּן שִׁמְעוֹן אָבִיו בְּנוֹ שֶׁל הִלֵּל, וְרַבָּן שִׁמְעוֹן בְּנוֹ קִבֵּל מִמֶּנּוּ, וְרַבָּן גַּמְלִיאֵל בְּנוֹ קִבֵּל מִמֶּנּוּ, וְרַבָּן שִׁמְעוֹן בְּנוֹ קִבֵּל מִמֶּנּוּ, וְרַבִּי יְהוּדָה בְּנוֹ שֶׁל רַבָּן שִׁמְעוֹן זֶה הוּא הַנִּקְרָא רַבֵּנוּ הַקָּדוֹשׁ, וְהוּא קִבֵּל מֵאָבִיו וּמֵרַבִּי אֶלְעָזָר בֶּן שַׁמּוּעַ וּמֵרַבִּי שִׁמְעוֹן חֲבֵרוֹ.

Rabban Gamliel the Elder received the tradition **from his father, Rabban Shimon, son of Hillel. Rabban Shimon, his son, received** the tradition from **him, and Rabban Gamliel, his son, received** it **from him and Rabban Shimon, his son, received** it **from him. Rabbi Yehuda, son of Rabban Shimon, is the one called *Rabbeinu HaKadosh*** ["Our Holy Rabbi"], **and he received** the tradition **from his father and from Rabbi Elazar ben Shamua and from Rabban Shimon his colleague.**

רַבֵּנוּ הַקָּדוֹשׁ חִבֵּר הַמִּשְׁנָה. וּמִימוֹת מֹשֶׁה וְעַד רַבֵּנוּ הַקָּדוֹשׁ לֹא חִבְּרוּ חִבּוּר שֶׁמְּלַמְּדִין אוֹתוֹ בָּרַבִּים בַּתּוֹרָה שֶׁבְּעַל פֶּה, אֶלָּא בְּכָל דּוֹר וָדוֹר רֹאשׁ בֵּית דִּין אוֹ נָבִיא שֶׁיִּהְיֶה בְּאוֹתוֹ הַדּוֹר כּוֹתֵב לְעַצְמוֹ זִכָּרוֹן בַּשְּׁמוּעוֹת שֶׁשָּׁמַע מֵרַבּוֹתָיו, וְהוּא מְלַמֵּד עַל פֶּה בָּרַבִּים.

Rabbeinu HaKadosh **composed the Mishna. From the days of Moses, our teacher, until *Rabbeinu HaKadosh*, no work had been composed for teaching the Oral Law in public. Instead, in each generation the head of the court or a prophet of that generation would write down for himself a record of the teachings that he had heard from his teachers,** in outline form,[a] **and teach** them **verbally in public.**

וְכֵן כָּל אֶחָד וְאֶחָד כּוֹתֵב לְעַצְמוֹ כְּפִי כֹּחוֹ מִבֵּאוּר הַתּוֹרָה וּמֵהִלְכוֹתֶיהָ כְּמוֹ שֶׁשָּׁמַע, וּמִדְּבָרִים שֶׁנִּתְחַדְּשׁוּ בְּכָל דּוֹר וָדוֹר בְּדִינִים שֶׁלֹּא לְמָדוּם מִפִּי הַשְּׁמוּעָה אֶלָּא בְּמִדָּה מִשְּׁלֹשׁ עֶשְׂרֵה מִדּוֹת, וְהִסְכִּימוּ עֲלֵיהֶן בֵּית דִּין הַגָּדוֹל. וְכֵן הָיָה הַדָּבָר תָּמִיד עַד רַבֵּנוּ הַקָּדוֹשׁ.

Likewise, each and every one of these leaders **would** be allowed to **write down for himself, in accordance with his ability,** some **of the explanations of the Torah and** some **of its laws, as he had heard** them from his teachers, **and** some **of the new ideas that were innovated in each generation, involving laws that were not derived by** the Oral **tradition, but rather through one of the thirteen principles of** deriving halakhot from Biblical **exegesis**[b] **and which were accepted by the High Court. This was always the case until** the days of ***Rabbeinu HaKadosh*.**

וְהוּא קִבֵּץ כָּל הַשְּׁמוּעוֹת וְכָל הַדִּינִין וְכָל הַבֵּאוּרִין וְהַפֵּרוּשִׁין שֶׁשָּׁמְעוּ מִמֹּשֶׁה רַבֵּנוּ וְשֶׁלִּמְּדוּ בֵּית דִּין שֶׁל כָּל דּוֹר וָדוֹר בְּכָל הַתּוֹרָה כֻּלָּהּ, וְחִבֵּר מֵהַכֹּל סֵפֶר הַמִּשְׁנָה, וְשִׁנְּנוֹ בָּרַבִּים, וְנִגְלָה לְכָל יִשְׂרָאֵל, וּכְתָבוּהוּ כֻּלָּם, וְרִבְּצוּ בְּכָל מָקוֹם כְּדֵי שֶׁלֹּא תִּשְׁתַּכַּח תּוֹרָה שֶׁבְּעַל פֶּה מִיִּשְׂרָאֵל.

Rabbeinu HaKadosh, also known as Rabbi Yehuda HaNasi, **collected all the teachings, all the laws, and all the explanations and the commentaries that** the leaders **had heard from Moses, our teacher, and which had been taught by the courts of every generation, concerning the entire Torah. From all these, he composed the book of the Mishna, which he taught in public and** thus **it was revealed to the Jewish people, who all wrote it down.**[c] **He spread it in all places, so that the Oral Law would not be forgotten by the Jewish people.**

NOTES

a. These notes, which were not publicized, are called *Megillat Setarim* ("concealed scrolls").

b. See *Hilkhot Mamrim* 1:2.

c. Some of the early authorities disagree, maintaining that the Mishna was only compiled in the days of Rabbi Yehuda HaNasi, and not written down until some generations later (Rashi and others; in this regard, there is a difference between textual variants of *Iggeret Rav Sherira Gaon* ["The Epistle of Rav Sherira Gaon"]).

וְלָמָּה עָשָׂה רַבֵּנוּ הַקָּדוֹשׁ כָּךְ, וְלֹא הִנִּיחַ הַדָּבָר כְּמוֹת שֶׁהָיָה? לְפִי שֶׁרָאָה שֶׁהַתַּלְמִידִים מִתְמַעֲטִים וְהוֹלְכִים, וְהַצָּרוֹת מִתְחַדְּשׁוֹת וּבָאוֹת, וּמַלְכוּת הָרִשְׁעָה פּוֹשֶׁטֶת בָּעוֹלָם וּמִתְגַּבֶּרֶת, וְיִשְׂרָאֵל מִתְגַּלְגְּלִים וְהוֹלְכִים לַקְּצָווֹת – חִבֵּר חִבּוּר אֶחָד לִהְיוֹת בְּיַד כֻּלָּם כְּדֵי שֶׁיִּלְמְדוּהוּ בִּמְהֵרָה וְלֹא יִשָּׁכַח. וְיָשַׁב כָּל יָמָיו הוּא וּבֵית דִּינוֹ וְלִמֵּד הַמִּשְׁנָה בָּרַבִּים.

Why did *Rabbeinu HaKadosh* do this, instead of leaving the matter as it was? Because he saw that the students were diminishing at ever greater rates, and new troubles were constantly arising, and the evil empire, Rome, **was spreading and growing in strength in the world, while the Jewish people were increasingly drifting to the far ends** of the globe. Accordingly, **he composed a single work that would be available to all, in order that it could be studied quickly and would not be forgotten. Throughout his entire life, he and his court sat and taught the Mishna in public.**

וְאֵלּוּ הֵם גְּדוֹלֵי הַחֲכָמִים שֶׁהָיוּ בְּבֵית דִּינוֹ שֶׁל רַבֵּנוּ הַקָּדוֹשׁ וְקִבְּלוּ מִמֶּנּוּ: שִׁמְעוֹן וְגַמְלִיאֵל בָּנָיו, וְרַבִּי אָפֵס, וְרַבִּי חֲנַנְיָה בֶּן חָמָא, וְרַבִּי חִיָּא, וְרַב, וְרַבִּי יַנַּאי, וּבֶן קַפָּרָא, וּשְׁמוּאֵל, וְרַבִּי יוֹחָנָן, וְרַבִּי הוֹשַׁעְיָה. אֵלּוּ הֵם הַגְּדוֹלִים שֶׁקִּבְּלוּ מִמֶּנּוּ, וְעִמָּהֶם אֲלָפִים וּרְבָבוֹת מִשְּׁאָר הַחֲכָמִים.

These are the great Sages who were members **of the court of *Rabbeinu HaKadosh* and who received** the tradition **from him: his sons Shimon and Gamliel, Rabbi Afes, Rabbi Ḥananya ben Ḥama, Rabbi Ḥiyya, Rav, Rabbi Yannai, bar Kappara, Shmuel, Rabbi Yoḥanan, and Rabbi Hoshaya. These are the greatest** of the Sages **who received** the tradition **from them, together with thousands and myriads of other Sages.**

GLOSSES OF THE RAAVAD

וּשְׁמוּאֵל וְרַבִּי יוֹחָנָן וְכוּ׳. אָמַר אַבְרָהָם: לֹא הָיָה שְׁמוּאֵל וְר׳ יוֹחָנָן וְר׳ הוֹשַׁעְיָא וְר׳ יַנַּאי וּבַר קַפָּרָא מִבֵּית דִּינוֹ שֶׁל רַבִּי, אֲבָל לֵוִי וְר׳ בִּיסָא וְר׳ חָמָא בְּנוֹ וְר׳ יִשְׁמָעֵאל בְּ״רַ יוֹסֵי וְר׳ יוֹסֵי בַּר לָקוּנְיָא הֵם הָיוּ מִבֵּית דִּינוֹ. וְזֶה הָרַב הַמְאַסֵּף אָסַף מִדַּעְתּוֹ וְלֹא יָדַע עַל מָה.

"Shmuel, Rabbi Yoḥanan..." Avraham says: Shmuel, Rabbi Yoḥanan, Rabbi Hoshaya, Rabbi Yannai, and bar Kappara were not from the court of Rabbi Yehuda HaNasi. **Rather, Levi, Rabbi Bisa, Rabbi Ḥama, Rabbi Yishmael son of Rabbi Yosei, and Rabbi Yosei ben Lakonya were from his court. This rabbi,** the Rambam, **who collected** this data, **collected it of his own accord, without knowing** to **what** he was referring.

אַף עַל פִּי שֶׁאֵלּוּ הָאַחַד עָשָׂר קִבְּלוּ מֵרַבֵּנוּ הַקָּדוֹשׁ וְעָמְדוּ בְּמִדְרָשׁוֹ, רַבִּי יוֹחָנָן קָטָן הָיָה, וְאַחַר כָּךְ הָיָה תַּלְמִיד לְרַבִּי יַנַּאי וְקִבֵּל מִמֶּנּוּ תּוֹרָה, וְכֵן רַב קִבֵּל מֵרַבִּי יַנַּאי, וּשְׁמוּאֵל קִבֵּל מֵרַבִּי חֲנַנְיָה בֶּן חָמָא.

Even though all of these eleven Sages **received** the tradition **from *Rabbeinu HaKadosh* and were present in his study** hall, **Rabbi Yoḥanan was young** at the time, **and he later became a disciple of Rabbi Yannai and received Torah** teachings **from him. Similarly, Rav received** the tradition **from Rabbi Yannai, and Shmuel received** it **from Rabbi Ḥananya ben Ḥama.**

GLOSSES OF THE RAAVAD

וְכֵן רַב וְכוּ׳. זֶה לֹא הָיָה וְלֹא נִבְרָא. וּשְׁמוּאֵל קִבֵּל וְכוּ׳. אָמַר אַבְרָהָם: וְגַם זֶה לֹא הָיָה, אֶלָּא מִלֵּוִי.

"Similarly, Rav..." Avraham says: This never occurred. "And Shmuel received..." Avraham says: This was also not the case; **rather,** Shmuel received the tradition **from Levi.**

רַב חִבֵּר סִפְרָא וְסִפְרֵי לְבָאֵר וּלְהוֹדִיעַ עִקְּרֵי הַמִּשְׁנָה, וְרַבִּי חִיָּא חִבֵּר הַתּוֹסֶפְתָּא לְבָאֵר עִנְיְנֵי הַמִּשְׁנָה. וְכֵן רַבִּי הוֹשַׁעְיָה וּבֶן קַפָּרָא חִבְּרוּ בָּרַיְתוֹת לְבָאֵר דִּבְרֵי הַמִּשְׁנָה. וְרַבִּי יוֹחָנָן חִבֵּר הַתַּלְמוּד הַיְרוּשַׁלְמִי בְּאֶרֶץ יִשְׂרָאֵל אַחַר חֻרְבַּן הַבַּיִת בְּקָרוֹב מִשְּׁלֹשׁ מֵאוֹת שָׁנָה.

Rav composed the ***Sifra***, the *midrash halakha* on Leviticus, **and** the ***Sifrei***, the *midrash halakha* on the books of Numbers and Deuteronomy, in order **to clarify and present the basic** Torah sources for the halakhot **of the Mishna. Rabbi Ḥiyya composed the *Tosefta*,** a collection of halakhic opinions of *tanna'im*, which serves as a kind of commentary and addendum to the Mishna, in order **to clarify the cases** discussed in **the Mishna. Similarly, Rabbi Hoshaya and ben Kappara composed *baraitot*,** additional collections of halakhot, **to clarify the statements of the Mishna. And Rabbi Yoḥanan composed the Jerusalem Talmud in the Land of Israel, approximately three hundred years after the destruction of the Temple.**

וּמִגְּדוֹלֵי הַחֲכָמִים שֶׁקִּבְּלוּ מֵרַב וּמִשְּׁמוּאֵל: רַב הוּנָא, וְרַב יְהוּדָה, וְרַב נַחְמָן, וְרַב כָּהֲנָא. וּמִגְּדוֹלֵי הַחֲכָמִים שֶׁקִּבְּלוּ מֵרַבִּי יוֹחָנָן: רַבָּה בַּר בַּר חָנָה, וְרַבִּי אַמִּי, וְרַבִּי אַסִּי, וְרַב דִּימִי, וְרָאבוּן.

Among the great Sages who received the tradition **from Rav and Shmuel** were **Rav Huna, Rav Yehuda, Rav Naḥman, and Rav Kahana. Among the great Sages who received** the tradition **from Rabbi Yoḥanan** were Rava **bar bar Ḥana, Rav Ami, Rav Asi, Rav Dimi, and Ravun,** called Ravin in the extant versions of the Babylonian Talmud.

GLOSSES OF THE RAAVAD

רַבָּה בַּר בַּר חָנָה וְכוּ'. אָמַר אַבְרָהָם: וְר' חִיָּא בַּר אַבָּא.

"Rava bar bar Ḥana…" Avraham says: And Rabbi Ḥiyya bar Abba.

וּמִכְּלַל הַחֲכָמִים שֶׁקִּבְּלוּ מֵרַב הוּנָא וּמֵרַב יְהוּדָה: רַבָּה וְרַב יוֹסֵף. וּמִכְּלַל הַחֲכָמִים שֶׁקִּבְּלוּ מֵרַבָּה וְרַב יוֹסֵף: אַבַּיֵּי וְרָבָא, וּשְׁנֵיהֶם קִבְּלוּ גַּם מֵרַב נַחְמָן. וּמִכְּלַל הַחֲכָמִים שֶׁקִּבְּלוּ מֵרָבָא: רַב אָשֵׁי וְרָבִינָא. וּמָר בֶּן רַב אָשֵׁי קִבֵּל מֵאָבִיו וּמֵרָבִינָא.

The Sages who received the tradition **from Rav Huna and Rav Yehuda include Rabba and Rav Yosef. The Sages who received** the tradition **from Rabba and Rav Yosef include Abaye and Rava, both of whom also received** the tradition **from Rav Naḥman. The Sages who received** the tradition **from Rava include Rav Ashi and Ravina. Mar ben Rav Ashi received** the tradition **from his father,** Rav Ashi, **and from Ravina.**

GLOSSES OF THE RAAVAD

רַבָּה וְכוּ'. אָמַר אַבְרָהָם: רַב חִסְדָּא וְרַבָּה בַּר רַב הוּנָא.

"Rabba…" Avraham says: Rav Ḥisda and Rabba bar Rav Huna.

נִמְצָא מֵרַב אָשֵׁי עַד מֹשֶׁה רַבֵּנוּ אַרְבָּעִים אִישׁ, וְאֵלּוּ הֵם: רַב אָשֵׁי מֵרָבָא, מֵרַבָּה, מֵרַב הוּנָא, מֵרַבִּי יוֹחָנָן וְרַב וּשְׁמוּאֵל, מֵרַבֵּנוּ הַקָּדוֹשׁ, מֵרַבָּן שִׁמְעוֹן אָבִיו, מֵרַבָּן גַּמְלִיאֵל אָבִיו, מֵרַבָּן שִׁמְעוֹן אָבִיו, מֵרַבָּן גַּמְלִיאֵל אָבִיו, מֵרַבָּן שִׁמְעוֹן אָבִיו, מֵהִלֵּל אָבִיו וְשַׁמַּאי, מִשְׁמַעְיָה וְאַבְטַלְיוֹן, מִיהוּדָה וְשִׁמְעוֹן, מִיהוֹשֻׁעַ וְנִתַּאי, מִיּוֹסֵף וְיוֹסֵף, מֵאַנְטִיגְנָס, מִשִּׁמְעוֹן הַצַּדִּיק, מֵעֶזְרָא, מִבָּרוּךְ, מִיִּרְמְיָה, מִצְּפַנְיָה, מֵחֲבַקּוּק, מִנַּחוּם, מִיּוֹאֵל, מִמִּיכָה, מִישַׁעְיָה, מֵעָמוֹס, מֵהוֹשֵׁעַ, מִזְּכַרְיָה, מִיהוֹיָדָע, מֵאֱלִישָׁע, מֵאֵלִיָּהוּ, מֵאֲחִיָּה, מִדָּוִד, מִשְּׁמוּאֵל, מֵעֵלִי, מִפִּינְחָס, מִיהוֹשֻׁעַ, מִמֹּשֶׁה רַבֵּנוּ רַבָּן שֶׁל כָּל הַנְּבִיאִים, מֵעִם יי אֱלֹהֵי יִשְׂרָאֵל.

There were **thus forty men from Rav Ashi** back **to Moses, our teacher.** In several of his glosses, the Raavad notes various inaccuracies in the Rambam's list. It seems that the Rambam is merely demonstrating here that the chain of tradition remained intact until the completion of the Talmud (and forty is a symbolic number), even if this list is not entirely precisely in accordance with the calculation of the years. **They are as follows: Rav Ashi,** who received the tradition **from Rava,** who received it **from Rabba,** and he received it **from Rav Huna,** and so on in this manner: Rav Huna **from Rabbi Yoḥanan, Rav, and Shmuel; from *Rabbeinu HaKadosh*; from Rabbi Shimon, his father; from Rabban Gamliel, his father; from Rabban Shimon, his father; from Rabban Gamliel, his father; from Rabban Shimon, his father; from Hillel, his father, and Shammai; from Shemaya and Avtalyon; from Yehuda and Shimon** ben Shataḥ; **from Yehoshua and Nitai; from Yosef** ben Yoezer **and Yosef** ben Yoḥanan; **from Antigonus; from Shimon HaTzaddik; from Ezra; from Barukh; from Jeremiah; from Zephaniah; from Ḥabakkuk; from Naḥum; from Joel; from Micah; from Isaiah; from Amos; from Hoshea; from Zechariah; from Yehoyada; from Elisha; from Elijah; from Aḥiya; from David; from Shmuel; from Eli; from Pinḥas; from Joshua; from Moses, our teacher, teacher of all the prophets,** who received the tradition **from God, Lord of Israel.**

▸ כָּל אֵלּוּ הַחֲכָמִים הַנִּזְכָּרִים הֵם גְּדוֹלֵי הַדּוֹרוֹת, מֵהֶם רָאשֵׁי יְשִׁיבוֹת, וּמֵהֶם רָאשֵׁי גָּלֻיּוֹת, וּמֵהֶם מִסַּנְהֶדְרִי גְּדוֹלָה, וְעִמָּהֶם בְּכָל דּוֹר וָדוֹר אֲלָפִים וּרְבָבוֹת שֶׁשָּׁמְעוּ מֵהֶם וְעִמָּהֶם.

All of these aforementioned Sages were **the leaders of** their **generations. Some of them were heads of academies, others were heads of the exiles,** and yet **others were members of the Great Sanhedrin. In each and every generation they were accompanied by thousands and myriads** of other scholars **who heard their** teachings **from them and** studied Torah **with them.**

רָבִינָא וְרַב אָשֵׁי הֵם סוֹף חַכְמֵי תַּלְמוּד, וְרַב אָשֵׁי הוּא שֶׁחִבֵּר הַתַּלְמוּד הַבַּבְלִי בְּאֶרֶץ שִׁנְעָר, אַחַר שֶׁחִבֵּר רַבִּי יוֹחָנָן הַתַּלְמוּד הַיְרוּשַׁלְמִי בִּכְמוֹ מֵאָה שָׁנָה.

Ravina and Rav Ashi are the last of the Sages of the Talmud. It was Rav Ashi who composed the Babylonian Talmud in the Land of Shinar, Babylonia, **approximately one hundred years after Rabbi Yoḥanan had composed the Jerusalem Talmud.**

וְעִנְיַן שְׁנֵי הַתַּלְמוּדִין הוּא פֵּרוּשׁ דִּבְרֵי הַמִּשְׁנָה וּבֵאוּר עֲמֻקוֹתֶיהָ, וּדְבָרִים שֶׁנִּתְחַדְּשׁוּ בְּכָל בֵּית דִּין וּבֵית דִּין מִימוֹת רַבֵּנוּ הַקָּדוֹשׁ וְעַד חִבּוּר הַתַּלְמוּד. וּמִשְּׁנֵי הַתַּלְמוּדִין וּמִן הַתּוֹסֶפְתָּא וּמִסִּפְרָא וּמִסִּפְרֵי וּמִן הַתּוֹסֶפְתּוֹת – מִכֻּלָּם יִתְבָּאֵר הָאָסוּר וְהַמֻּתָּר וְהַטָּמֵא וְהַטָּהוֹר וְהַחַיָּב וְהַפָּטוּר וְהַכָּשֵׁר וְהַפָּסוּל, כְּמוֹ שֶׁהֶעְתִּיקוּ אִישׁ מִפִּי אִישׁ מִפִּי מֹשֶׁה מִסִּינַי.

The objective of both of the Talmuds is to explain the statements of the Mishna, and clarify its deeper meanings, **and** to present those **novelties that were developed by each and every court from the days of *Rabbeinu HaKadosh* until the composition of the Talmud. From the two Talmuds, from the *Tosefta*, from the *Sifra*, from the *Sifrei*, and from the** other **additions,** the *baraitot* mentioned in 17 above, **from all of them the prohibited and the permitted, the ritually impure and the pure, the liable and the exempt, the valid and the invalid, are clarified in the manner** that the Torah **was received** in the tradition, **one man from another,** all the way back, **from Moses at Sinai.**

גַּם יִתְבָּאֵר מֵהֶם דְּבָרִים שֶׁגָּזְרוּ חֲכָמִים וּנְבִיאִים שֶׁבְּכָל דּוֹר וָדוֹר לַעֲשׂוֹת סְיָג לַתּוֹרָה, כְּמוֹ שֶׁשָּׁמְעוּ מִמֹּשֶׁה בְּפֵרוּשׁ "וּשְׁמַרְתֶּם אֶת מִשְׁמַרְתִּי" (ויקרא יח, ל), שֶׁאָמַר: עֲשׂוּ מִשְׁמֶרֶת לְמִשְׁמַרְתִּי. וְכֵן יִתְבָּאֵר מֵהֶם הַמִּנְהָגוֹת וְהַתַּקָּנוֹת שֶׁהִתְקִינוּ אוֹ שֶׁנָּהֲגוּ בְּכָל דּוֹר וָדוֹר כְּמוֹ שֶׁרָאוּ בֵּית דִּין שֶׁל אוֹתוֹ הַדּוֹר, לְפִי שֶׁאָסוּר לָסוּר מֵהֶם, שֶׁנֶּאֱמַר: "לֹא תָסוּר מִכָּל הַדָּבָר אֲשֶׁר יַגִּידוּ לְךָ יָמִין וּשְׂמֹאל" (דברים יז, יא, ושם: מִן הַדָּבָר).

Also clarified from these sources are those **things that were decreed by the Sages and prophets in each generation,** in order **to build a safeguard for the Torah, as they explicitly heard from Moses: "You shall keep My commission"** (Leviticus 18:30), **for he** thereby **stated: "Establish a safeguard for my** prized **possession."**[a] **Likewise, the customs and enactments that were instituted or practiced in each generation, as seen** fit by the leading **court of that generation, are clarified from them. For it is prohibited to deviate from these** decisions, **as it is stated: "You shall not deviate from the matter that they will tell you, right or left"** (Deuteronomy 17:11). The Sages have the authority to impose their enactments even when these are not designed as safeguards for Torah prohibitions, but serve to regulate interpersonal behavior or general religious conduct.[b]

וְכֵן מִשְׁפָּטִים וְדִינִין פְּלָאִים שֶׁלֹּא קִבְּלוּ אוֹתָן מִמֹּשֶׁה, וְדָנוּ בָּהֶן בֵּית דִּין הַגָּדוֹל שֶׁל אוֹתוֹ הַדּוֹר בַּמִּדּוֹת שֶׁהַתּוֹרָה נִדְרֶשֶׁת בָּהֶן, וּפָסְקוּ אוֹתָן הַזְּקֵנִים וְגָמְרוּ שֶׁהַדִּין כָּךְ הוּא – הַכֹּל חִבֵּר רַב אָשֵׁי בַּתַּלְמוּד, מִימוֹת מֹשֶׁה וְעַד יָמָיו.

The same applies to **obscure judgments and laws,** i.e., halakhot that are not explicitly stated in the Torah, **which they did not receive from Moses, but which were rather derived by the High Court of that generation through the hermeneutical principles of the Torah, and regarding which those elders ruled and concluded that this is the law: Rav Ashi compiled all** of these and included them **in the Talmud,** these rulings **from the days of Moses, our teacher, until his** own **days.**

NOTES

a. *Moed Katan* 5a; *Yevamot* 21a.

b. See Rambam's introduction to his *Commentary on the Mishna*; *Hilkhot Mamrim* 1:3, 2:2.

וְחִבְּרוּ חַכְמֵי מִשְׁנָה חִבּוּרִין אֲחֵרִים לְפָרֵשׁ דִּבְרֵי הַתּוֹרָה: רַבִּי הוֹשַׁעְיָה תַּלְמִידוֹ שֶׁל רַבֵּנוּ הַקָּדוֹשׁ חִבֵּר בֵּאוּר סֵפֶר בְּרֵאשִׁית, וְרַבִּי יִשְׁמָעֵאל פֵּרֵשׁ מֵ'אֵלֶּה שְׁמוֹת' עַד סוֹף הַתּוֹרָה, וְהוּא הַנִּקְרָא מְכִלְתָּא, וְכֵן רַבִּי עֲקִיבָה חִבֵּר מְכִלְתָּא, וַחֲכָמִים אֲחֵרִים אַחֲרֵיהֶם חִבְּרוּ מִדְרָשׁוֹת – וְהַכֹּל חֻבַּר קֹדֶם הַתַּלְמוּד הַבַּבְלִי.

The Sages of the **Mishna also composed other works** that serve **to explain the words of the Torah. Rabbi Hoshaya, a student of *Rabbeinu HaKadosh*, composed an explanation of the book of Genesis.** This is the midrash of *Bereshit Rabba*, which starts "Rabbi Hoshaya the Great began." **Rabbi Yishmael explained** all the rest of the Torah, **from: "These are the names"** (Exodus 1:1) **until the end of the Torah.**[a] **This is called** the ***Mekhilta*. Rabbi Akiva likewise composed a *Mekhilta*,** known to us as the "*Mekhilta* of Rabbi Shimon ben Yoḥai," **and other Sages** who came **after them composed *midrashim*,** interpretations of verses. **All** of these works **were composed before the Babylonian Talmud.**

נִמְצָא רָבִינָא וְרַב אָשֵׁי וְחַבְרֵיהֶם סוֹף גְּדוֹלֵי חַכְמֵי יִשְׂרָאֵל הַמַּעְתִּיקִים תּוֹרָה שֶׁבְּעַל פֶּה, וְשֶׁגָּזְרוּ גְּזֵרוֹת וְהִתְקִינוּ תַּקָּנוֹת וְהִנְהִיגוּ מִנְהָגוֹת, וּפָשְׁטוּ גְּזֵרוֹתָם וְתַקָּנוֹתָם וּמִנְהֲגוֹתָם בְּכָל יִשְׂרָאֵל בְּכָל מְקוֹמוֹת מוֹשְׁבוֹתֵיהֶם.

Thus, Ravina, Rav Ashi, and their colleagues were **the last of the great Sages of Israel who transmitted the Oral Law. They imposed decrees, instituted enactments, and established customs. Their decrees, enactments, and customs spread out among the entire Jewish people, in all of their dwelling places.**

וְאַחַר בֵּית דִּינוֹ שֶׁל רַב אָשֵׁי, שֶׁחִבֵּר הַתַּלְמוּד בִּימֵי בְּנוֹ וּגְמָרוֹ, נִתְפַּזְּרוּ יִשְׂרָאֵל בְּכָל הָאֲרָצוֹת פִּזּוּר יָתֵר, וְהִגִּיעוּ לַקְּצָווֹת וְלָאִיִּים הָרְחוֹקִים, וְרָבָת קְטָטָה בָּעוֹלָם, וְנִשְׁתַּבְּשׁוּ הַדְּרָכִים בְּגַיָּסוֹת, וְנִתְמַעֵט תַּלְמוּד תּוֹרָה, וְלֹא נִתְכַּנְּסוּ יִשְׂרָאֵל לִלְמֹד בִּישִׁיבוֹתֵיהֶם אֲלָפִים וּרְבָבוֹת כְּמוֹ שֶׁהָיוּ מִקֹּדֶם.

After the court of Rav Ashi, which composed the Talmud and completed it in the days of his son, the Jewish people became even more dispersed throughout all the lands, reaching the distant edges of the civilized world **and the far-flung islands. There was much conflict in the world, and the routes** between places **were disrupted by troops. Torah study decreased and Jews no** longer **gathered to study in their academies** in their **thousands and myriads, as they would previously.**

אֶלָּא מִתְקַבְּצִים יְחִידִים, הַשְּׂרִידִים אֲשֶׁר יי קֹרֵא, בְּכָל עִיר וָעִיר וּבְכָל מְדִינָה וּמְדִינָה, וְעוֹסְקִים בַּתּוֹרָה וּמְבִינִים בְּחִבּוּרֵי הַחֲכָמִים כֻּלָּם, וְיוֹדְעִים מֵהֶם דֶּרֶךְ הַמִּשְׁפָּט הֵיאַךְ הוּא.

Instead, individuals, the remnants to whom God **called,**[b] **would gather in each and every city and country, engage in Torah** study, and seek to **understand all the works of the Sages and learn from them the nature of the path of judgment.**

NOTES

a. Actually the end of Exodus.

b. See Joel 3:5.

וְכָל בֵּית דִּין שֶׁעָמַד אַחַר הַתַּלְמוּד בְּכָל מְדִינָה וּמְדִינָה, וְגָזַר אוֹ הִתְקִין אוֹ הִנְהִיג לִבְנֵי מְדִינָתוֹ אוֹ לִבְנֵי מְדִינוֹת – לֹא פָּשְׁטוּ מַעֲשָׂיו בְּכָל יִשְׂרָאֵל, מִפְּנֵי רֹחַק מוֹשְׁבוֹתֵיהֶם וְשִׁבּוּשׁ הַדְּרָכִים וֶהֱיוֹת בֵּית דִּין שֶׁל אוֹתָהּ הַמְּדִינָה יְחִידִים, וּבֵית דִּין הַגָּדוֹל שֶׁל שִׁבְעִים בָּטֵל מִכַּמָּה שָׁנִים קֹדֶם חִבּוּר הַתַּלְמוּד.

With regard to **every court that was established after** the conclusion of **the Talmud, in every country, and which issued** decrees, **instituted** enactments, **or established** customs **for the inhabitants of that country – or for the inhabitants of** several **countries – its practices did not spread throughout the Jewish people.** This was **due to the distances between** their various **settlements and the disruption of the** travel **routes, and because** the **court of that country** was comprised merely of **individual** judges, **and the Sanhedrin of seventy**-one judges **had been nullified many years before the composition** and completion **of the Talmud.**

לְפִיכָךְ אֵין כּוֹפִין אַנְשֵׁי מְדִינָה זוֹ לִנְהֹג בְּמִנְהַג מְדִינָה אַחֶרֶת, וְאֵין אוֹמְרִין לְבֵית דִּין זֶה לִגְזֹר גְּזֵרָה שֶׁגְּזָרָהּ בֵּית דִּין אַחֵר בִּמְדִינָתוֹ. וְכֵן אִם לָמַד אֶחָד מִן הַגְּאוֹנִים שֶׁדֶּרֶךְ הַמִּשְׁפָּט כָּךְ הוּא, וְנִתְבָּאֵר לְבֵית דִּין אַחֵר שֶׁעָמַד אַחֲרָיו שֶׁאֵין זֶה דֶּרֶךְ הַמִּשְׁפָּט הַכָּתוּב בַּתַּלְמוּד – אֵין שׁוֹמְעִין לָרִאשׁוֹן, אֶלָּא לְמִי שֶׁהַדַּעַת נוֹטָה לִדְבָרָיו, בֵּין רִאשׁוֹן בֵּין אַחֲרוֹן.

Therefore, people in one country could not be compelled to follow the customs of another country, nor is one court instructed to impose decrees that another court had decreed in its country. Likewise, if one of the geonim had learned that the path of judgment was such and such, and then **another court which arose after it understood that** their opinion **was not the path of judgment as written in the Talmud, one** need **not listen to the first** court. **Rather,** one may follow **whichever opinion logic dictates** is the correct one, **whether** it is the **first or** the **last.**

וּדְבָרִים הַלָּלוּ – בְּדִינִים וּגְזֵרוֹת וְתַקָּנוֹת וּמִנְהָגוֹת שֶׁנִּתְחַדְּשׁוּ אַחַר חִבּוּר הַתַּלְמוּד. אֲבָל כָּל הַדְּבָרִים שֶׁבַּתַּלְמוּד הַבַּבְלִי – חַיָּבִין כָּל בֵּית יִשְׂרָאֵל לָלֶכֶת בָּהֶם, וְכוֹפִין כָּל עִיר וָעִיר וְכָל מְדִינָה וּמְדִינָה לִנְהֹג בְּכָל הַמִּנְהָגוֹת שֶׁנָּהֲגוּ חֲכָמִים שֶׁבַּתַּלְמוּד וְלִגְזֹר גְּזֵרוֹתָם וְלָלֶכֶת בְּתַקָּנוֹתָם.

These principles apply **to the judgments, decrees, enactments, and customs that were newly established after the composition of the Talmud. However,** regarding **all the matters** detailed **in the Babylonian Talmud, the entire house of Israel must follow them. Each and every city and each and every country are compelled to act in accordance with all the customs that were put into practice by the Sages of the Talmud, to impose their decrees, and to follow their enactments.**

הוֹאִיל וְכָל אוֹתָן הַדְּבָרִים שֶׁבַּתַּלְמוּד הִסְכִּימוּ עֲלֵיהֶם כָּל יִשְׂרָאֵל, וְאוֹתָן הַחֲכָמִים שֶׁהִתְקִינוּ אוֹ שֶׁגָּזְרוּ אוֹ שֶׁהִנְהִיגוּ אוֹ שֶׁדָּנוּ דִּין וְלָמְדוּ שֶׁהַמִּשְׁפָּט כָּךְ הוּא הֵם כָּל חַכְמֵי יִשְׂרָאֵל אוֹ רֻבָּן, וְהֵם שֶׁשָּׁמְעוּ הַקַּבָּלָה בְּעִקְּרֵי הַתּוֹרָה כֻּלָּהּ אִישׁ מִפִּי אִישׁ עַד מֹשֶׁה.

All Jews must follow the rulings of the Babylonian Talmud, **because all the matters that are in the Babylonian Talmud were accepted by the entire Jewish people. And those** talmudic **Sages who instituted** enactments, **or decreed, or established** customs, **or derived a law and taught that the judgment is such and such, they are all the Sages of Israel, or** at least **their majority. It is they who heard the tradition regarding the fundamental principles of the entire Torah, one man from another,** all the way back **to Moses.**

כָּל הַחֲכָמִים שֶׁעָמְדוּ אַחַר חִבּוּר הַתַּלְמוּד וּבָנוּ בּוֹ וְיָצָא לָהֶם שֵׁם בְּחָכְמָתָם – הֵם הַנִּקְרָאִים גְּאוֹנִים. וְכָל אֵלּוּ הַגְּאוֹנִים שֶׁעָמְדוּ בְּאֶרֶץ יִשְׂרָאֵל וּבְאֶרֶץ שִׁנְעָר וּבִסְפָרַד וּבְצָרְפַת לִמְּדוּ דֶּרֶךְ הַתַּלְמוּד וְהוֹצִיאוּ לָאוֹר תַּעֲלוּמוֹתָיו וּבֵאֲרוּ עִנְיָנָיו, לְפִי שֶׁדֶּרֶךְ עֲמֻקָּה דַּרְכּוֹ עַד לִמְאֹד. וְעוֹד שֶׁהוּא בִּלְשׁוֹן אֲרַמִּי מְעֹרָב עִם לְשׁוֹנוֹת אֲחֵרוֹת, לְפִי שֶׁאוֹתָהּ הַלָּשׁוֹן הָיְתָה בְּרוּרָה לַכֹּל בְּשִׁנְעָר בְּעֵת שֶׁחֻבַּר הַתַּלְמוּד, אֲבָל בִּשְׁאָר הַמְּקוֹמוֹת, וְכֵן בְּשִׁנְעָר בִּימֵי הַגְּאוֹנִים – אֵין אָדָם מַכִּיר אוֹתָהּ לָשׁוֹן עַד שֶׁמְּלַמְּדִין אוֹתוֹ.

All of the Sages who arose after the composition of the Talmud and reflected upon the Talmud **and became renowned for their wisdom are called the geonim.** The Rambam calls all the leaders geonim, even those who did not live in Babylonia, despite the fact that this title was initially bestowed only upon the heads of the two great Babylonian academies. **All these geonim who arose in the Land of Israel, the Land of Babylonia, Spain, and France taught the method of the Talmud, revealing its secrets and clarifying its ideas, for its method is extremely intricate. Furthermore, it is** written **in Aramaic, mixed with other languages. For that language was clear to everyone in Babylonia in the era when the Talmud was composed, but in other places, and also in Babylonia in the era of the geonim,** when Arabic was the lingua franca, **no person understood that language unless he had been taught it.**

וּשְׁאֵלוֹת רַבּוֹת שׁוֹאֲלִין אַנְשֵׁי כָּל עִיר וָעִיר לְכָל גָּאוֹן שֶׁיִּהְיֶה בִּימֵיהֶם לְפָרֵשׁ לָהֶם דְּבָרִים קָשִׁים שֶׁבַּתַּלְמוּד, וְהֵם מְשִׁיבִים לָהֶם כְּפִי חָכְמָתָם, וְאוֹתָן הַשּׁוֹאֲלִין מְקַבְּצִין הַתְּשׁוּבוֹת, וְעוֹשִׂין מֵהֶן סְפָרִים לְהָבִין מֵהֶם.

The inhabitants of each and every city would ask many questions of every gaon who lived in their days, for him **to explain to them the difficult cases in the Talmud.** The geonim **would reply to them in accordance with their wisdom. Those who asked** the questions **would collect the responses and compile books from them, from which they could understand** the issues.

גַּם חִבְּרוּ הַגְּאוֹנִים שֶׁבְּכָל דּוֹר וָדוֹר חִבּוּרִין לְבָאֵר הַתַּלְמוּד, מֵהֶם מִי שֶׁפֵּרֵשׁ הֲלָכוֹת יְחִידוֹת, וּמֵהֶם מִי שֶׁפֵּרֵשׁ פְּרָקִים יְחִידִים שֶׁנִּתְקַשּׁוּ בְּיָמָיו, וּמֵהֶם מִי שֶׁפֵּרֵשׁ מַסֶּכְתּוֹת וּסְדָרִים.

The geonim of each generation also composed works designed **to clarify the Talmud. Some of them explained isolated halakhot, while others explained selected chapters that** people **found difficult in their time.** Yet **others explained entire tractates and orders** of the Talmud.

וְעוֹד חִבְּרוּ הֲלָכוֹת פְּסוּקוֹת בְּעִנְיַן הָאָסוּר וְהַמֻּתָּר וְהַחַיָּב וְהַפָּטוּר בִּדְבָרִים שֶׁהַשָּׁעָה צְרִיכָה לָהֶן, כְּדֵי שֶׁיִּהְיוּ קְרוֹבִין לְמַדַּע מִי שֶׁאֵינוֹ יָכוֹל לֵירֵד לְעָמְקוֹ שֶׁל תַּלְמוּד. וְזוֹ הִיא מְלֶאכֶת יי שֶׁעָשׂוּ בָּהּ כָּל גְּאוֹנֵי יִשְׂרָאֵל מִיּוֹם שֶׁחֻבַּר הַתַּלְמוּד וְעַד זְמַן זֶה, שֶׁהוּא שָׁנָה שְׁמִינִית אַחַר מֵאָה וָאֶלֶף לַחֻרְבָּן.

The geonim **also composed rulings of halakhot regarding the permitted and prohibited** items, **and** regarding **the liable and the exempt** individuals, **on topical issues, so that they would be accessible to one who could not plumb the depths of the Talmud. This is the labor of the Lord,**[a] **in which all the geonim of Israel engaged, from the day of the** final **composition of the Talmud until the present date, which is the eighth year after 1100** years **to the destruction** of the Temple, 4937 years to the creation of the world, 1176 CE.[b]

NOTES

a. See Jeremiah 48:10.

b. This is probably the year when the Rambam finished the *Mishne Torah*, which took him some ten years to complete. This introduction was written after the body of the work itself; see *Iggerot HaRambam*, Sheilat edition, p. 195 and onward.

וּבַזְּמַן הַזֶּה תָּכְפוּ צָרוֹת יְתֵרוֹת, וְדָחֲקָה שָׁעָה אֶת הַכֹּל, וְאָבְדָה חָכְמַת חֲכָמֵינוּ וּבִינַת נְבוֹנֵינוּ נִסְתַּתְּרָה. לְפִיכָךְ אוֹתָן הַפֵּרוּשִׁין וְהַתְּשׁוּבוֹת וְהַהֲלָכוֹת שֶׁחִבְּרוּ הַגְּאוֹנִים וְרָאוּ שֶׁהֵם דְּבָרִים מְבֹאָרִים – נִתְקַשׁוּ בְּיָמֵינוּ, וְאֵין מֵבִין עִנְיְנֵיהֶם כָּרָאוּי אֶלָּא מְעַט בְּמִסְפָּר, וְאֵין צָרִיךְ לוֹמַר הַתַּלְמוּד עַצְמוֹ, הַבַּבְלִי וְהַיְּרוּשַׁלְמִי, וְסִפְרָא וְסִפְרֵי וְהַתּוֹסֶפְתּוֹת, שֶׁהֵן צְרִיכִין דַּעַת רְחָבָה וְנֶפֶשׁ חֲכָמָה וּזְמַן אָרֹךְ, וְאַחַר כָּךְ יִוָּדַע מֵהֶן הַדֶּרֶךְ הַנְּכוֹחָה בַּדְּבָרִים הָאֲסוּרִין וְהַמֻּתָּרִין וּשְׁאָר דִּינֵי תּוֹרָה הֵיאַךְ הִיא.

In the present age, we are **beset by numerous troubles, everyone feels the pressure of the hour, and the wisdom of our Sages has become lost, and the insight of our wise ones has become hidden. Therefore, those explanations, responses, and halakhot which the geonim composed and viewed as clarified have become difficult** to understand **in our day, and only a select few comprehend their ideas properly.* Needless to say,** the same applies **to the Talmud itself, both the Babylonian and the Jerusalem** Talmuds, **and the *Sifra*, the *Sifrei*, and the** other **additions,** the *Tosefta* and *baraitot*. **For they require a breadth of knowledge, a wise spirit, and much** study **time,** only **after which can it be known from them** what is **the correct path regarding the prohibited and permitted items, and how the other laws of the Torah are** to be followed.

וּמִפְּנֵי זֶה נָעַרְתִּי חָצְנִי, אֲנִי מֹשֶׁה בְּרַבִּי מַיְמוֹן הַסְּפָרַדִּי, וְנִשְׁעַנְתִּי עַל הַצּוּר בָּרוּךְ הוּא, וּבִינוֹתִי בְּכָל אֵלּוּ הַסְּפָרִים, וְרָאִיתִי לְחַבֵּר דְּבָרִים הַמִּתְבָּרְרִים מִכָּל אֵלּוּ הַחִבּוּרִין בְּעִנְיַן הָאָסוּר וְהַמֻּתָּר וְהַטָּמֵא וְהַטָּהוֹר עִם שְׁאָר דִּינֵי תּוֹרָה כֻּלָּן, בְּלָשׁוֹן בְּרוּרָה וְדֶרֶךְ קְצָרָה, עַד שֶׁתְּהֵא תּוֹרָה שֶׁבְּעַל פֶּה כֻּלָּהּ סְדוּרָה בְּפִי הַכֹּל, בְּלֹא קֻשְׁיָא וְלֹא פֵּרוּק, וְלֹא זֶה אוֹמֵר בְּכֹה וְזֶה אוֹמֵר בְּכֹה, אֶלָּא דְּבָרִים בְּרוּרִים, קְרוֹבִים, נְכוֹנִים עַל פִּי הַמִּשְׁפָּט אֲשֶׁר יִתְבָּאֵר מִכָּל אֵלּוּ הַחִבּוּרִין וְהַפֵּרוּשִׁין הַנִּמְצָאִים מִימוֹת רַבֵּנוּ הַקָּדוֹשׁ וְעַד עַכְשָׁו.

For this reason, I shook out the corner of my garment,[a] i.e., I was moved to take action, **I, Moses, son of Rabbi Maimon the Sephardi.** I relied upon the Rock, blessed be He. I contemplated all of these books and saw fit to compose a text** containing **the clarified** ideas **from all these works regarding the prohibited and the permitted, the ritually impure and the pure, together with all the rest of the laws of the Torah, in a clear language and a concise manner, such that everyone would be fluent in the entire Oral Law,*** without** the raising of **difficulties and without** the ensuing need for **resolutions.** There would be **no "this** Sage **says that and that** Sage **says the other,"** but **rather clear, comprehensible, and correct statements in accordance with the judgments that can be clarified from all those works and explanations, which are extant from the days of *Rabbeinu HaKadosh* until the present.**

NOTES

a. See Nehemiah 5:13.

INSIGHTS OF THE LUBAVITCHER REBBE

*And only a select few comprehend their ideas properly – וְאֵין מֵבִין עִנְיְנֵיהֶם כָּרָאוּי אֶלָּא מְעַט בְּמִסְפָּר: For the source of his halakhot, the Rambam cites the relevant verse that is most easily understood, even if it is not the one mentioned in the Talmuds. Since the purpose of quoting these verses is to make the fulfillment of the mitzvot a more vivid experience, the citations must be made suitable to the students of his age, whose diminished capacity led to the composition of the book in the first place (*Torat Menaḥem, Hitvaaduyot, Parashat Aḥarei [Mot] – Kedoshim* 5745).

**Moses, son of Rabbi Maimon the Sephardi – מֹשֶׁה בְּרַבִּי מַיְמוֹן הַסְּפָרַדִּי: This appellation is important for the Rambam's halakhic rulings throughout the book. For these practical rulings sometimes differ from those of the Sages of Ashkenaz, and they are addressed mainly to Sephardim (*Torat Menaḥem, Hitvaaduyot, Parashat Beshalah* and *Parashat Vaera* 5748).

***Such that everyone would be fluent in the entire Oral Law – עַד שֶׁתְּהֵא תּוֹרָה שֶׁבְּעַל פֶּה כֻּלָּהּ סְדוּרָה בְּפִי הַכֹּל: The Rambam's presentation of the halakhic conclusions alone, without the background discussions, is one of the laudable features of the *Mishne Torah*. For the dialectic of Torah is the wisdom of God, while the halakhot themselves represent His will, which is loftier than wisdom. By studying these halakhot, one "grasps hold of" the Torah itself, which is tied to one's very soul. Accordingly, the book is suitable for the "small and great" alike, since the soul itself is equally present in all (*Torat Menaḥem, Hitvaaduyot, Parashat Shemot* and *Parashat Vaera* 5748).

עַד שֶׁיִּהְיוּ כָּל הַדִּינִים גְּלוּיִים לַקָּטָן וְלַגָּדוֹל בְּדִין כָּל מִצְוָה וּמִצְוָה וּבְדִין כָּל הַדְּבָרִים שֶׁתִּקְּנוּ חֲכָמִים וּנְבִיאִים. כְּלָלוֹ שֶׁל דָּבָר: כְּדֵי שֶׁלֹּא יְהֵא אָדָם צָרִיךְ לְחִבּוּר אַחֵר בָּעוֹלָם בְּדִין מִדִּינֵי יִשְׂרָאֵל, אֶלָּא יִהְיֶה חִבּוּר זֶה מְקַבֵּץ לַתּוֹרָה שֶׁבְּעַל פֶּה כֻּלָּהּ עִם הַתַּקָּנוֹת וְהַמִּנְהָגוֹת וְהַגְּזֵרוֹת שֶׁנַּעֲשׂוּ מִימוֹת מֹשֶׁה רַבֵּנוּ וְעַד חִבּוּר הַתַּלְמוּד, וּכְמוֹ שֶׁפֵּרְשׁוּ לָנוּ הַגְּאוֹנִים בְּכָל חִבּוּרֵיהֶן שֶׁחִבְּרוּ אַחַר הַתַּלְמוּד. לְפִיכָךְ קָרָאתִי שֵׁם חִבּוּר זֶה מִשְׁנֵה תּוֹרָה, לְפִי שֶׁאָדָם קוֹרֵא תּוֹרָה שֶׁבִּכְתָב תְּחִלָּה, וְאַחַר כָּךְ קוֹרֵא בָּזֶה וְיוֹדֵעַ מִמֶּנּוּ תּוֹרָה שֶׁבְּעַל פֶּה כֻּלָּהּ, וְאֵינוֹ צָרִיךְ לִקְרוֹת סֵפֶר אַחֵר בֵּינֵיהֶם.

This will make the Torah so accessible **that all the laws will be revealed to small and great** alike, **regarding the law of each and every mitzva, and the law of all matters that were instituted by the Sages and the prophets. In sum,** I wrote this book **in order that a person will not need any other text for any Jewish law. Instead, this work will collect together the entire Oral Law, with the enactments, customs, and decrees that were imposed from the days of Moses, our teacher, until the completion of the Talmud, as the geonim explained** them **to us in all their works they composed after the Talmud. Therefore, I have called this work *Mishne Torah*** ["second to the Torah"] **for a person** should **first read** the **Written Law, and then read this** text, **and know from it the entire Oral Law, without having to read another book in between.** The Raavad, in his gloss here, takes exception to the Rambam's practice of omitting the sources for his rulings, since it precludes informed discussions of his conclusions. He maintains that writing a book that does not refer to any other work and which does not mention the sources on which it relies, is a sign of pride. Others have further argued that the Rambam implies here that one merely has to read the Written Torah and his *Mishne Torah,* without having to study the Talmud at all. The Rambam addressed these claims in a letter he composed to Rabbi Pineḥas the judge,[a] in which he states, among other things, that he never intended for people to stop studying the Talmud, but rather he wrote his book "due to lack of patience, for one who is unable to plumb the depths of the Talmud, and who will not understand from it what is prohibited and permitted…"

NOTES

a. *Iggerot HaRambam*, Sheilat edition, p. 438 and onward.

GLOSSES OF THE RAAVAD

וְיוֹדֵעַ מִמֶּנּוּ וְכוּ'. אָמַר אַבְרָהָם: סָבַר לְתַקֵּן וְלֹא תִקֵּן, כִּי הוּא עָזַב דֶּרֶךְ כָּל הַמְחַבְּרִים אֲשֶׁר הָיוּ לְפָנָיו. כִּי הֵם הֵבִיאוּ רְאָיָה לְדִבְרֵיהֶם וְכָתְבוּ הַדְּבָרִים בְּשֵׁם אוֹמְרָם, וְהָיָה לוֹ בָּזֶה תּוֹעֶלֶת גְּדוֹלָה. כִּי פְּעָמִים רַבּוֹת יַעֲלֶה עַל לֵב הַדַּיָּן לֶאֱסֹר אוֹ לְהַתִּיר וּרְאָיָתוֹ מִמָּקוֹם אֶחָד, וְאִלּוּ יָדַע כִּי יֵשׁ גָּדוֹל מִמֶּנּוּ הִפְלִיג שְׁמוּעָתוֹ לְדַעַת אַחֶרֶת הָיָה חוֹזֵר בּוֹ. וְעַתָּה לֹא אֵדַע לָמָּה אֶחֱזֹר מִקַּבָּלָתִי וּמֵרְאָיָתִי בִּשְׁבִיל חִבּוּרוֹ שֶׁל זֶה הַמְחַבֵּר. אִם הַחוֹלֵק עָלַי גָּדוֹל מִמֶּנִּי, הֲרֵי טוֹב; וְאִם אֲנִי גָּדוֹל מִמֶּנּוּ, לָמָּה אֲבַטֵּל דַּעְתִּי מִפְּנֵי דַּעְתּוֹ. וְעוֹד, כִּי יֵשׁ דְּבָרִים שֶׁהַגְּאוֹנִים חוֹלְקִים זֶה עַל זֶה, וְזֶה הַמְחַבֵּר בֵּרֵר דִּבְרֵי הָאֶחָד וּכְתָבָם בְּחִבּוּרוֹ; וְלָמָּה אֶסְמֹךְ אֲנִי עַל בֵּרְרָתוֹ וְהִיא לֹא נִרְאֵית בְּעֵינַי, וְלֹא אֵדַע הַחוֹלֵק עִמּוֹ אִם הוּא רָאוּי לַחְלֹק אִם לֹא. אֵין זֶה אֶלָּא כָּל קֳבֵל דִּי רוּחַ יַתִּירָא בֵּהּ.

"And know from it…" **Avraham says:** The Rambam **thought he was fixing** the problem **but he did not** actually **fix it, for he abandoned the approach of all the authors who came before him. For they brought proof for their claims, and wrote** their **statements in the name of those who said them. This is greatly beneficial, since a judge will often think that he should prohibit or permit** something, **and his proof** for such a ruling **is from one place, but had he known that there is** a Sage **wiser than he whose teaching followed a different opinion he would have retracted. Now,** however, **I do not know why I should retract from my tradition and from my proofs** merely **on account of the work of this author: If the one who disagrees with me is greater than me** in wisdom, **then** all is well and **good,** and I should indeed change my mind, **but if I am greater than him, why should I discount my opinion because of his opinion? Furthermore, there are cases where the geonim dispute one another, and this author clarified the statement of one** of them **and wrote it in his work. But why should I rely on his clarification** if **it does not appear correct to me, and I will not know whether** the other gaon **who took issue with** the first one **should have disagreed or not. This is nothing other than** the claim that we should simply accept the Rambam's opinion **"since an extraordinary spirit was in him"** (Daniel 6:4).

וְרָאִיתִי לְחַלֵּק חִבּוּר זֶה הֲלָכוֹת הֲלָכוֹת בְּכָל עִנְיָן וְעִנְיָן, וַאֲחַלֵּק הַהֲלָכוֹת לִפְרָקִים שֶׁבְּאוֹתוֹ עִנְיָן, וְכָל פֶּרֶק וּפֶרֶק אֲחַלֵּק אוֹתוֹ לַהֲלָכוֹת קְטַנּוֹת, כְּדֵי שֶׁיִּהְיוּ סְדוּרִין עַל פֶּה.

I saw fit **to divide this work into separate halakhot** pertaining **to each and every topic, and I** chose to **divide the halakhot into chapters that** deal **with that** same **topic.** Finally, I decided that **I would divide each and every chapter into smaller halakhot, so that they can be remembered by heart.**

אֵלּוּ הַהֲלָכוֹת שֶׁבְּכָל עִנְיָן וְעִנְיָן, יֵשׁ מֵהֶם הֲלָכוֹת שֶׁהֵן מִשְׁפְּטֵי מִצְוָה אַחַת בִּלְבַד, וְהִיא הַמִּצְוָה שֶׁיֵּשׁ בָּהּ דִּבְרֵי קַבָּלָה הַרְבֵּה וְהִיא עִנְיָן בִּפְנֵי עַצְמוֹ, וְיֵשׁ מֵהֶם הֲלָכוֹת שֶׁהֵן כּוֹלְלִין מִשְׁפְּטֵי מִצְוֹת הַרְבֵּה, אִם יִהְיוּ אוֹתָן הַמִּצְוֹת כֻּלָּם בְּעִנְיָן אֶחָד. מִפְּנֵי שֶׁחִלּוּק חִבּוּר זֶה הוּא לְפִי הָעִנְיָנִים, לֹא לְפִי מִנְיַן הַמִּצְוֹת, כְּמוֹ שֶׁיִּתְבָּאֵר לַקּוֹרֵא בּוֹ.

With regard to **these halakhot that** pertain **to different topics, some halakhot contain the laws of only one mitzva, which is** invariably **a mitzva that includes many statements of** the **tradition and is** thus **a distinct topic** in its own right. **Other halakhot incorporate the laws of many mitzvot, if those mitzvot deal with the same topic. For the division of this work is by topic, not by the order of the mitzvot, as will become clear to the reader.**

וּמִנְיַן מִצְוֹת שֶׁל תּוֹרָה הַנּוֹהֲגוֹת לְדוֹרוֹת: שֵׁשׁ מֵאוֹת וּשְׁלֹשׁ עֶשְׂרֵה מִצְוֹת, מֵהֶן מִצְוֹת עֲשֵׂה מָאתַיִם שְׁמוֹנֶה וְאַרְבָּעִים, סִימָן לָהֶם מִנְיַן אֵבָרָיו שֶׁל אָדָם, וּמֵהֶן מִצְוֹת לֹא תַעֲשֶׂה שְׁלֹשׁ מֵאוֹת חָמֵשׁ וְשִׁשִּׁים, סִימָן לָהֶן מִנְיַן יְמוֹת הַחַמָּה.

The number of mitzvot that must be practiced over the generations is 613 mitzvot. Of these, 248 are positive mitzvot, a mnemonic for which is the number of limbs in the human body; while 365 of them are negative mitzvot, a mnemonic for which is the number of days in a solar year. The list of mitzvot that appears below ("the short list of mitzvot") is almost identical to the list in *Sefer HaMitzvot* (except for Positive Mitzvot 17–18, and 310–311, which are in the reverse order in *Sefer HaMitzvot*). Here the mitzvot are presented in concise form, with only their source from the Torah. The purpose of this list, as the Rambam states in his introduction to *Sefer HaMitzvot*, is to ensure that the book is comprehensive and complete, and that no mitzva is left out.

The source for the claim that there are 613 total mitzvot is the Gemara in *Makkot* (23b). Several geonim also provided detailed accounts of how the mitzvot add up to this precise number,[a] despite the fact that some Sages cast doubts on the absolute necessity to reach this exact number.[b] The Rambam has his own method of counting of the mitzvot, which he formulated in fourteen principles (*shorashim*) laid out in his introduction to *Sefer HaMitzvot*, where he explains his differences with those who counted the mitzvot before him. The Ramban wrote glosses on those principles, as well as on some of the details of the mitzvot themselves, although he made clear that he accepted the Rambam's principles in their basic form. In this context, it may be noted that the third of the Rambam's principles is that the 613 mitzvot do not include those commands that were issued to the Jewish people in the wilderness for that time alone, but only the mitzvot that apply down the generations, and thus the list can serve as the foundation for this book of practical halakha.

NOTES

a. See for example, the list of mitzvot in *Halakhot Gedolot*, and Rav Se'adya Gaon and Rabbi Shlomo ibn Gabirol's *Azharot* [didactic liturgical poems].

b. Ralbag; see also the Ramban's gloss on the Rambam's First Principle in his counting of the mitzvot.

מִנְיַן הַמִּצְוֹת

List of the Mitzvot

מִצְוֹת עֲשֵׂה

Positive Mitzvot

Mitzva 1

מִצְוָה רִאשׁוֹנָה מִמִּצְוֹת עֲשֵׂה – לֵידַע שֶׁיֵּשׁ שָׁם אֱלוֹהַּ, שֶׁנֶּאֱמַר: "אָנֹכִי יי" (שמות כ, ב; דברים ה, ו).

The first mitzva of the positive mitzvot* **is to know that there is a God, as it is stated: "I am the Lord"** (Exodus 20:2; Deuteronomy 5:6).

Mitzva 2

לְיַחֲדוֹ, שֶׁנֶּאֱמַר: "יי אֱלֹהֵינוּ יי אֶחָד" (דברים ו, ד).

To acknowledge His unity, as it is stated: "The Lord is our God, the Lord is one" (Deuteronomy 6:4).

Mitzva 3

לְאַהֲבוֹ, שֶׁנֶּאֱמַר: "וְאָהַבְתָּ אֵת יי" (דברים ו, ה; יא, א).

To love Him, as it is stated: "You shall love the Lord your God" (Deuteronomy 6:5, 11:1).

Mitzva 4

לְיִרְאָה מִמֶּנּוּ, שֶׁנֶּאֱמַר: "אֶת יי אֱלֹהֶיךָ תִּירָא" (דברים ו, יג; י, כ).

To fear Him, as it is stated: "You shall fear the Lord your God" (Deuteronomy 6:13, 10:20).

Mitzva 5

לְהִתְפַּלֵּל לוֹ, שֶׁנֶּאֱמַר: "וַעֲבַדְתֶּם אֵת יי אֱלֹהֵיכֶם" (שמות כג, כה), עֲבוֹדָה זוֹ הִיא תְּפִלָּה.

To pray to Him, as it is stated: "You shall serve the Lord your God" (Exodus 23:25).

Mitzva 6

לְדָבְקָה בוֹ, שֶׁנֶּאֱמַר: "וּבוֹ תִדְבָּק" (דברים י, כ).

To cleave to Him, as it is stated: "And to Him you shall cleave" (Deuteronomy 10:20).

Mitzva 7

לְהִשָּׁבַע בִּשְׁמוֹ, שֶׁנֶּאֱמַר: "וּבִשְׁמוֹ תִּשָּׁבֵעַ" (דברים ו, יג; י, כ).

To swear in His name, as it is stated: "And by His name you shall swear" (Deuteronomy 6:13, 10:20).

GLOSSES OF THE RAAVAD

לְהִשָּׁבַע בִּשְׁמוֹ וְכוּ׳. אָמַר אַבְרָהָם: אֵינָהּ מִן הַמִּנְיָן, אֶלָּא בָא לְהַזְהִיר שֶׁלֹּא יִשָּׁבַע בְּאֵל אַחֵר. וְאוּלַי אָמַר זֶה דְּלָאו הַבָּא מִכְּלַל עֲשֵׂה – עֲשֵׂה.

"To swear in His name." Avraham says: **This is not** included **in the list** of positive mitzvot. **Rather, the verse is coming to warn one not to swear in the name of another god. Perhaps** the Rambam said that **this** is a positive mitzva in accordance with the rule that a **prohibition that comes by inference from a positive mitzva** is classified as **a positive mitzva.**

FROM THE LUBAVITCHER REBBE

*The first mitzva of the positive mitzvot – מִצְוָה רִאשׁוֹנָה מִמִּצְוֹת עֲשֵׂה: The Rambam emphasizes that this mitzva is the first, since calling something the "first" (rather than number one) highlights its link with those that come after it. One's knowledge of God affects all the mitzvot he fulfills, as a consequence of this awareness and belief, and it also leads to the observance of the other mitzvot. In practice, this means that one should not consider the closeness to God that results from this knowledge as a sufficient achievement by itself, but rather he must realize that he needs to express this relationship through the actual fulfillment of all the mitzvot (*Torat Menaḥem, Hitvaaduyot, Yud Gimmel Nisan and Aharon shel Pesaḥ* 5745).

Mitzva 8

לְהִדַּמּוֹת בִּדְרָכָיו הַטּוֹבִים הַיְשָׁרִים, שֶׁנֶּאֱמַר: "וְהָלַכְתָּ בִּדְרָכָיו" (דברים כח, ט).

To resemble God in His good and upright ways, as it is stated: "And walk in His ways" (Deuteronomy 28:9).

Mitzva 9

לְקַדֵּשׁ שְׁמוֹ, שֶׁנֶּאֱמַר: "וְנִקְדַּשְׁתִּי בְּתוֹךְ בְּנֵי יִשְׂרָאֵל" (ויקרא כב, לב).

To sanctify His name, as it is stated: "And I shall be sanctified among the children of Israel" (Leviticus 22:32).

Mitzva 10

לִקְרֹא קְרִיַּת שְׁמַע פַּעֲמַיִם בְּכָל יוֹם, שֶׁנֶּאֱמַר: "וְדִבַּרְתָּ בָּם בְּשִׁבְתְּךָ בְּבֵיתֶךָ וּבְלֶכְתְּךָ בַדֶּרֶךְ וּבְשָׁכְבְּךָ וּבְקוּמֶךָ" (דברים ו, ז).

To recite *Shema* twice daily, as it is stated: "And you shall speak of them while you are sitting in your house, and while you are walking on the way, and while you are lying down, and while you are rising" (Deuteronomy 6:7).

Mitzva 11

לִלְמֹד תּוֹרָה וּלְלַמְּדָהּ, שֶׁנֶּאֱמַר: "וְשִׁנַּנְתָּם לְבָנֶיךָ" (שם).

To study and teach Torah, as it is stated: "You shall inculcate them in your children" (Deuteronomy 6:7).

Mitzva 12

לִקְשֹׁר תְּפִלִּין בָּרֹאשׁ, שֶׁנֶּאֱמַר: "וְהָיוּ לְטֹטָפֹת בֵּין עֵינֶיךָ" (דברים ו, ח).

To bind a phylactery on one's head, as it is stated: "And they shall be for ornaments between your eyes" (Deuteronomy 6:8).

Mitzva 13

לִקְשֹׁר תְּפִלִּין בַּיָּד, שֶׁנֶּאֱמַר: "וּקְשַׁרְתָּם לְאוֹת עַל יָדֶךָ" (שם).

To bind a phylactery on one's arm, as it is stated: "You shall bind them as a sign on your arm" (Deuteronomy 6:8).

Mitzva 14

לַעֲשׂוֹת צִיצִית, שֶׁנֶּאֱמַר: "וְעָשׂוּ לָהֶם צִיצִת" (במדבר טו, לח).

To make ritual fringes, as it is stated: "They shall make for themselves a fringe" (Numbers 15:38).

Mitzva 15

לִקְבֹּעַ מְזוּזָה, שֶׁנֶּאֱמַר: "וּכְתַבְתָּם עַל מְזֻזוֹת" (דברים ו, ט; יא, כ).

To affix a mezuza, as it is stated: "You shall write them on the doorposts" (Deuteronomy 6:9, 11:20).

Mitzva 16

לְהַקְהִיל אֶת הָעָם לִשְׁמֹעַ תּוֹרָה בְּמוֹצָאֵי שְׁבִיעִית, שֶׁנֶּאֱמַר: "הַקְהֵל אֶת הָעָם" וגו' (דברים לא, יב).

To assemble the people to hear Torah upon the conclusion of the Sabbatical Year, as it is stated: "Assemble the people..." (Deuteronomy 31:12).

Mitzva 17

לִכְתֹּב כָּל אִישׁ סֵפֶר תּוֹרָה לְעַצְמוֹ, שֶׁנֶּאֱמַר: "כִּתְבוּ לָכֶם אֶת הַשִּׁירָה הַזֹּאת" (דברים לא, יט).

That each man should write a Torah scroll for himself, as it is stated: "Write this poem for you" (Deuteronomy 31:19).

Mitzva 18

לִכְתֹּב הַמֶּלֶךְ סֵפֶר תּוֹרָה לְעַצְמוֹ יָתֵר עַל הָאֶחָד שֶׁל כָּל אָדָם, עַד שֶׁיִּהְיֶה לוֹ שְׁתֵּי תּוֹרוֹת, שֶׁנֶּאֱמַר: "וְכָתַב לוֹ אֶת מִשְׁנֵה הַתּוֹרָה" (דברים יז, יח).

That the king should write a Torah scroll for himself, in addition to the one that must be written by every person, as it is stated: "He shall write for himself a copy of this Torah" (Deuteronomy 17:18).

Mitzva 19

לְבָרֵךְ אַחַר הַמָּזוֹן, שֶׁנֶּאֱמַר: "וְאָכַלְתָּ וְשָׂבָעְתָּ וּבֵרַכְתָּ" (דברים ח, י).

To bless God after a meal, as it is stated: "You will eat and be satisfied, and you shall bless the Lord your God" (Deuteronomy 8:10).

Mitzva 20

לִבְנוֹת בֵּית הַבְּחִירָה, שֶׁנֶּאֱמַר: "וְעָשׂוּ לִי מִקְדָּשׁ" (שמות כה, ח).

To build the Temple, as it is stated: "They shall make for Me a sanctuary" (Exodus 25:8).

GLOSSES OF THE RAAVAD

לִבְנוֹת בֵּית הַבְּחִירָה וְכוּ'. אָמַר אַבְרָהָם: וְלָמָּה הִנִּיחַ לִבְנוֹת מִזְבַּח אֲבָנִים שְׁלֵמוֹת.

"To build the Temple..." Avraham says: Why did the Rambam leave out the positive mitzva to build an altar from whole stones?

Mitzva 21

לִירָאָה מִבַּיִת זֶה, שֶׁנֶּאֱמַר: "וּמִקְדָּשִׁי תִּירָאוּ" (ויקרא יט, ל; כו, ב).

To revere this house of God, as it is stated: "And you shall revere My Sanctuary" (Leviticus 19:30, 26:2).

Mitzva 22

לִשְׁמֹר בַּיִת זֶה תָּמִיד, שֶׁנֶּאֱמַר: "וְאַתָּה וּבָנֶיךָ אִתָּךְ לִפְנֵי אֹהֶל הָעֵדֻת" (במדבר יח, ב).

To keep a watch over this house of God always, as it is stated: "And you and your sons with you, before the Tent of the Testimony" (Numbers 18:2).

Mitzva 23

לִהְיוֹת הַלֵּוִי עוֹבֵד בַּמִּקְדָּשׁ, שֶׁנֶּאֱמַר: "וְעָבַד הַלֵּוִי הוּא" (במדבר יח, כג).

That a Levite should serve in the Temple, as it is stated: "The Levite himself shall perform the service" (Numbers 18:23).

Mitzva 24

לְקַדֵּשׁ הַכֹּהֵן יָדָיו וְרַגְלָיו בִּשְׁעַת הָעֲבוֹדָה, שֶׁנֶּאֱמַר: "וְרָחֲצוּ אַהֲרֹן וּבָנָיו" וכו' (שמות ל, יט).

That a priest shall first **sanctify his hands and his feet at the time of the** Temple **service, as it is stated: "Aaron and his sons shall wash…"** (Exodus 30:19).

Mitzva 25

לַעֲרֹךְ נֵרוֹת בַּמִּקְדָּשׁ, שֶׁנֶּאֱמַר: "יַעֲרֹךְ אֹתוֹ אַהֲרֹן וּבָנָיו" (שמות כז, כא).

To arrange lamps in the Temple, as it is stated: "Aaron and his sons shall arrange it" (Exodus 27:21).

Mitzva 26

לְבָרֵךְ הַכֹּהֲנִים אֶת יִשְׂרָאֵל, שֶׁנֶּאֱמַר: "כֹּה תְבָרְכוּ אֶת בְּנֵי יִשְׂרָאֵל" (במדבר ו, כג).

For the priests to bless Israel, as it is stated: "So shall you bless the children of Israel" (Numbers 6:23).

Mitzva 27

לְהַסְדִּיר לֶחֶם וּלְבֹנָה לִפְנֵי יי בְּכָל שַׁבָּת, שֶׁנֶּאֱמַר: "וְנָתַתָּ עַל הַשֻּׁלְחָן לֶחֶם פָּנִים" (שמות כה, ל).

To arrange bread and frankincense before God every week, as it is stated: "You shall place shewbread upon the table" (Exodus 25:30).

GLOSSES OF THE RAAVAD

לְהַסְדִּיר לֶחֶם וּלְבוֹנָה וְכוּ'. אָמַר אַבְרָהָם: וְלָמָּה לֹא חָשַׁב הַקְטָרַת הַבָּזִיכִין דִּכְתִיב "אִשֶּׁה לַיי" (ויקרא כד, ז), וַאֲכִילַת לֶחֶם דִּכְתִיב "וַאֲכָלוּהוּ בְּמָקוֹם קָדוֹשׁ" (שם כד, ט).

"To arrange bread and frankincense…" Avraham says: Why doesn't the Rambam **include the burning of the bowls** of frankincense, **as it is written:** "You shall place pure frankincense on the arrangement… **a fire offering to the Lord"** (Leviticus 24:7), **and the eating** of the bread, **as it is written: "And they shall eat it in a holy place"** (Leviticus 24:9)?

Mitzva 28

לְהַקְטִיר קְטֹרֶת פַּעֲמַיִם בַּיּוֹם, שֶׁנֶּאֱמַר: "וְהִקְטִיר עָלָיו אַהֲרֹן קְטֹרֶת סַמִּים" (שמות ל, ז).

To burn incense twice daily, as it is stated: "Aaron shall burn on it incense of spices" (Exodus 30:7).

Mitzva 29

לַעֲרֹךְ אֵשׁ בְּמִזְבַּח הָעוֹלָה תָּמִיד, שֶׁנֶּאֱמַר: "אֵשׁ תָּמִיד תּוּקַד עַל הַמִּזְבֵּחַ" (ויקרא ו, ו).

To arrange a perpetual fire on the altar of burnt offering, as it is stated: "A perpetual fire shall be kept burning upon the altar" (Leviticus 6:6).

Mitzva 30

לְהָרִים הַדֶּשֶׁן מֵעַל הַמִּזְבֵּחַ בְּכָל יוֹם, שֶׁנֶּאֱמַר: "וְהֵרִים אֶת הַדֶּשֶׁן" (ויקרא ו, ג).

To remove ashes from upon the altar every day, as it is stated: "And he shall set aside the ashes" (Leviticus 6:3).

Mitzva 31

לְשַׁלַּח טְמֵאִים מִמַּחֲנֵה שְׁכִינָה, שֶׁהוּא הַמִּקְדָּשׁ, שֶׁנֶּאֱמַר: "וִישַׁלְּחוּ מִן הַמַּחֲנֶה כָּל צָרוּעַ" וכו' (במדבר ה, ב).

To send impure individuals **from the camp of the Divine Presence, which is the Temple, as it is stated: "They shall send out from the camp every leper…"** (Numbers 5:2).

Mitzva 32

לַחֲלֹק כָּבוֹד לְזַרְעוֹ שֶׁל אַהֲרֹן וּלְהַקְדִּימוֹ לְכָל דָּבָר שֶׁבִּקְדֻשָּׁה, שֶׁנֶּאֱמַר: "וְקִדַּשְׁתּוֹ" (ויקרא כא, ח).

To honor the descendants of Aaron and to give a priest **precedence in every matter of sanctity, as it is stated: "You shall sanctify him"** (Leviticus 21:8).

Mitzva 33

לִהְיוֹת הַכֹּהֲנִים לוֹבְשִׁים לַעֲבוֹדָה בִּגְדֵי כְּהֻנָּה, שֶׁנֶּאֱמַר: "וְעָשִׂיתָ בִגְדֵי קֹדֶשׁ" וכו' (שמות כח, ב).

That priests shall don the **priestly vestments for the** Temple **service, as it is stated: "You shall make holy vestments…"** (Exodus 28:2).

Mitzva 34

לָשֵׂאת הָאָרוֹן עַל הַכָּתֵף כְּשֶׁנּוֹשְׂאִין אוֹתוֹ, שֶׁנֶּאֱמַר: "בַּכָּתֵף יִשָּׂאוּ" (במדבר ז, ט).

To carry the sacred **ark on the shoulder when it is carried, as it is stated: "They shall bear on the shoulder"** (Numbers 7:9).

Mitzva 35

לִמְשֹׁחַ כֹּהֲנִים גְּדוֹלִים וּמְלָכִים בְּשֶׁמֶן הַמִּשְׁחָה, שֶׁנֶּאֱמַר: "שֶׁמֶן מִשְׁחַת קֹדֶשׁ יִהְיֶה זֶה" (שמות ל, לא).

To anoint High Priests and kings with the anointing oil, as it is stated: "This shall be oil of sacred anointment" (Exodus 30:31).

Mitzva 36

לִהְיוֹת הַכֹּהֲנִים עוֹבְדִין בַּמִּקְדָּשׁ מִשְׁמָרוֹת מִשְׁמָרוֹת, וּבַמּוֹעֲדִים עוֹבְדִין כְּאֶחָד, שֶׁנֶּאֱמַר: "וְכִי יָבֹא הַלֵּוִי וכו' לְבַד מִמְכָּרָיו עַל הָאָבוֹת" (דברים יח, ו-ח).

That the priests shall perform the service **in the Temple in groups of watches, and on festivals they shall** all **perform** the **service together, as it is stated: "And if a Levite shall come… except for that which was sold by the ancestors"** (Deuteronomy 18:6–8).

Mitzva 37

לִהְיוֹת הַכֹּהֲנִים מִטַּמְּאִין לִקְרוֹבֵיהֶם וּמִתְאַבְּלִין עֲלֵיהֶן כִּשְׁאָר יִשְׂרָאֵל שֶׁהֵן מְצֻוִּין לְהִתְאַבֵּל עַל מֵתֵיהֶן, שֶׁנֶּאֱמַר: "לָהּ יִטַּמָּא" (ויקרא כא, ג).

That the priests shall become ritually impure for their relatives and mourn over them, like other Jews who are commanded to mourn for their dead, as it is stated: "For her, he may become impure" (Leviticus 21:3).

Mitzva 38

לִהְיוֹת כֹּהֵן גָּדוֹל נוֹשֵׂא בְּתוּלָה, שֶׁנֶּאֱמַר: "וְהוּא אִשָּׁה בִבְתוּלֶיהָ יִקָּח" (ויקרא כא, יג).

That a High Priest shall marry a virgin, as it is stated: "And he shall marry a woman with her virginity" (Leviticus 21:13).

Mitzva 39

לְהַקְרִיב תְּמִידִין בְּכָל יוֹם, שֶׁנֶּאֱמַר: "שְׁנַיִם לַיּוֹם עֹלָה תָמִיד" (במדבר כח, ג).

To sacrifice the daily offerings every day, as it is stated: "Two each day, a continual burnt offering" (Numbers 28:3).

Mitzva 40

לְהַקְרִיב כֹּהֵן גָּדוֹל מִנְחָה בְּכָל יוֹם, שֶׁנֶּאֱמַר: "זֶה קָרְבַּן אַהֲרֹן וּבָנָיו" (ויקרא ו, יג).

That a High Priest shall sacrifice a meal offering every day, as it is stated: "This is the offering of Aaron and of his sons" (Leviticus 6:13).

Mitzva 41

לְהוֹסִיף קָרְבָּן אַחֵר בְּכָל שַׁבָּת, שֶׁנֶּאֱמַר: "וּבְיוֹם הַשַּׁבָּת שְׁנֵי כְבָשִׂים" (במדבר כח, ט).

To add another offering on every Shabbat, as it is stated: "On the Sabbath day, two unblemished **lambs"** (Numbers 28:9).

Mitzva 42

לְהוֹסִיף קָרְבָּן בְּכָל רֹאשׁ חֹדֶשׁ וָחֹדֶשׁ, שֶׁנֶּאֱמַר: "וּבְרָאשֵׁי חָדְשֵׁיכֶם תַּקְרִיבוּ" וכו' (במדבר כח, יא).

To add an offering on each *Rosh Ḥodesh*, as it is stated: "On your New Moons you shall present…" (Numbers 28:11).

Mitzva 43

לְהוֹסִיף קָרְבָּן בְּחַג הַפֶּסַח, שֶׁנֶּאֱמַר: "שִׁבְעַת יָמִים תַּקְרִיבוּ אִשֶּׁה לַיי" (ויקרא כג, לו).

To add an offering on the festival of Passover, as it is stated: "Seven days you shall present a fire offering to the Lord" (Leviticus 23:36).

Mitzva 44

לְהַקְרִיב מִנְחַת הָעֹמֶר מִמָּחֳרַת רִאשׁוֹן שֶׁל פֶּסַח עִם כֶּבֶשׂ אֶחָד, שֶׁנֶּאֱמַר: "וַהֲבֵאתֶם אֶת עֹמֶר רֵאשִׁית קְצִירְכֶם" (ויקרא כג, י).

To sacrifice the offering of the *omer* on the day after the first **festival day of Passover, as it is stated: "Then you shall bring a sheaf of the first of your harvest"** (Leviticus 23:10).

Mitzva 45

לְהוֹסִיף קָרְבָּן בְּיוֹם עֲצֶרֶת, שֶׁנֶּאֱמַר: "וּבְיוֹם הַבִּכּוּרִים וכו' וְהִקְרַבְתֶּם עוֹלָה לְרֵיחַ" וכו' (במדבר כח, כו-כז).

To add an offering on the day of Shavuot, as it is stated: "On the day of the first fruits…You shall present a burnt offering for a pleasing **aroma…"** (Numbers 28:26–27).

Mitzva 46

לְהָבִיא שְׁתֵּי הַלֶּחֶם עִם הַקָּרְבָּנוֹת הַקְּרֵבִין בִּגְלַל הַלֶּחֶם בְּיוֹם עֲצֶרֶת, שֶׁנֶּאֱמַר: "מִמּוֹשְׁבֹתֵיכֶם תָּבִיאוּ לֶחֶם תְּנוּפָה... וְהִקְרַבְתֶּם עַל הַלֶּחֶם" (ויקרא כג, יז-יח).

To bring the two loaves with the offerings that are sacrificed on account of the loaves on the day of Shavuot, as it is stated: "From your dwellings you shall bring two loaves of **waving…You shall offer with the bread"** (Leviticus 23:17–18).

Mitzva 47

לְהוֹסִיף קָרְבָּן בְּרֹאשׁ הַשָּׁנָה, שֶׁנֶּאֱמַר: "וּבַחֹדֶשׁ הַשְּׁבִיעִי בְּאֶחָד לַחֹדֶשׁ... וַעֲשִׂיתֶם" וכו' (במדבר כט, א-ב).

To add an offering on Rosh HaShana, as it is stated: "In the seventh month, on the first of the month…You shall perform" (Numbers 29:1–2).

Mitzva 48

לְהוֹסִיף קָרְבָּן בְּיוֹם הַצּוֹם, שֶׁנֶּאֱמַר: "וּבֶעָשׂוֹר לַחֹדֶשׁ הַשְּׁבִיעִי" וכו' (במדבר כט, ז).

To add an offering on the Yom Kippur **fast day, as it is stated: "On the tenth of this seventh month…"** (Numbers 29:7).

Mitzva 49

לַעֲשׂוֹת עֲבוֹדַת הַיּוֹם בְּיוֹם הַצּוֹם, שֶׁנֶּאֱמַר: "בְּזֹאת יָבֹא אַהֲרֹן וכו' וּמֵאֵת עֲדַת" וגו' (ויקרא טז, ג-ה), וְכָל הָעֲבוֹדָה הַכְּתוּבָה בְּפָרָשַׁת 'אַחֲרֵי מוֹת'.

To perform the Temple **service of the day on the** Yom Kippur **fast day, as it is stated: "With this shall Aaron come…And from the congregation of…"** (Leviticus 16:3–5). **And this includes the entire service that is written in *Parashat Aharei Mot*.**

Mitzva 50

לְהוֹסִיף קָרְבָּן בְּחַג הַסֻּכּוֹת, שֶׁנֶּאֱמַר: "וְהִקְרַבְתֶּם עֹלָה אִשֵּׁה" (במדבר כט, יג).

To add an offering on the festival of Sukkot, as it is stated: "You shall present a burnt offering, a fire offering" (Numbers 29:13).

Mitzva 51

לְהוֹסִיף קָרְבָּן בְּיוֹם שְׁמִינִי עֲצֶרֶת, שֶׁיּוֹם זֶה רֶגֶל בִּפְנֵי עַצְמוֹ הוּא, שֶׁנֶּאֱמַר: "בַּיּוֹם הַשְּׁמִינִי עֲצֶרֶת" (במדבר כט, לה).

To add an offering on the day of Shemini Atzeret, which is a pilgrimage festival day of its own, as it is stated: "On the eighth day it shall be **an assembly"** (Numbers 29:35).

Mitzva 52

לָחֹג בָּרְגָלִים, שֶׁנֶּאֱמַר: "שָׁלֹשׁ רְגָלִים תָּחֹג לִי בַּשָּׁנָה" (שמות כג, יד).

To celebrate the pilgrimage festivals, as it is stated: "Three times in the year you shall hold a festival to Me" (Exodus 23:14).

Mitzva 53

לְהֵרָאוֹת בָּרְגָלִים, שֶׁנֶּאֱמַר: "שָׁלֹשׁ פְּעָמִים בַּשָּׁנָה" (שמות כג, יז; לד, כג; דברים טז, טז).

To appear before God **on the pilgrimage festivals, as it is stated: "Three times in the year"** (Exodus 23:17, 34:23, Deuteronomy 16:16).

Mitzva 54

לִשְׂמֹחַ בָּרְגָלִים, שֶׁנֶּאֱמַר: "וְשָׂמַחְתָּ בְּחַגֶּךָ אַתָּה וּבִנְךָ וּבִתֶּךָ" (דברים טז, יד).

To rejoice on the pilgrimage festivals, as it is stated: "You shall rejoice on your festival, you, and your son, and your daughter" (Deuteronomy 16:14).

Mitzva 55

לִשְׁחֹט כֶּבֶשׂ הַפֶּסַח, שֶׁנֶּאֱמַר: "וְשָׁחֲטוּ אֹתוֹ כֹּל קְהַל עֲדַת יִשְׂרָאֵל" (שמות יב, ו).

To slaughter the paschal lamb, as it is stated: "And the entire assembly of the congregation of Israel shall slaughter it" (Exodus 12:6).

Mitzva 56

לֶאֱכֹל בְּשַׂר הַפֶּסַח בְּלֵילֵי חֲמִשָּׁה עָשָׂר, שֶׁנֶּאֱמַר: "וְאָכְלוּ אֶת הַבָּשָׂר בַּלַּיְלָה הַזֶּה" (שמות יב, ח).

To eat the meat of the paschal offering on the night of the fifteenth of Nisan, **as it is stated: "They shall eat the meat on that night"** (Exodus 12:8).

Mitzva 57

לַעֲשׂוֹת פֶּסַח שֵׁנִי, שֶׁנֶּאֱמַר: "בַּחֹדֶשׁ הַשֵּׁנִי בְּאַרְבָּעָה עָשָׂר" וכו׳ (במדבר ט, יא).

To perform the rite **of the second paschal offering, as it is stated: "During the second month, on the fourteenth..."** (Numbers 9:11).

Mitzva 58

לֶאֱכֹל פֶּסַח בּוֹ, שֶׁנֶּאֱמַר: "עַל מַצּוֹת וּמְרֹרִים יֹאכְלֻהוּ" (שם).

To eat the paschal offering on that night, **as it is stated: "With unleavened bread and bitter herbs they shall eat it"** (Numbers 9:11).

Mitzva 59

לִתְקֹעַ בַּחֲצוֹצְרוֹת עַל הַקָּרְבָּנוֹת וּבִשְׁעַת הַצָּרוֹת, שֶׁנֶּאֱמַר: "וּתְקַעְתֶּם בַּחֲצֹצְרֹת" (במדבר י, י).

To sound the trumpets over the offerings and at times of trouble, as it is stated: "You shall sound the trumpets" (Numbers 10:10).

Mitzva 60

לִהְיוֹת כָּל קָרְבְּנוֹת בְּהֵמָה מִיּוֹם הַשְּׁמִינִי וָהָלְאָה, שֶׁנֶּאֱמַר: "וּמִיּוֹם הַשְּׁמִינִי וָהָלְאָה" (ויקרא כב, כז).

That all animal offerings shall be offered only **from the eighth day** after their birth **and onward, as it is stated: "And from the eighth day on"** (Leviticus 22:27).

GLOSSES OF THE RAAVAD

לִהְיוֹת כָּל קָרְבְּנוֹת וְכוּ׳. אָמַר אַבְרָהָם: אֵין לָזֶה טַעַם, וְאוּלַי לָאו הַבָּא מִכְּלַל עֲשֵׂה - עֲשֵׂה.

"That all offerings..." Avraham says: There is no reason for this. Perhaps the Rambam maintains that it is a positive mitzva in accordance with the rule that **a prohibition that comes by inference from a positive mitzva** is classified as a **positive mitzva.**

Mitzva 61

לִהְיוֹת כָּל קָרְבַּן בְּהֵמָה תָּמִים, שֶׁנֶּאֱמַר: "תָּמִים יִהְיֶה לְרָצוֹן" וכו׳ (ויקרא כב, כא).

That every animal offering shall be unblemished, as it is stated: "It shall be unblemished to be accepted..." (Leviticus 22:21).

Mitzva 62

לִמְלֹחַ כָּל קָרְבָּן, שֶׁנֶּאֱמַר: "עַל כָּל קָרְבָּנְךָ תַּקְרִיב מֶלַח" (ויקרא ב, יג).

To salt every offering, as it is stated: "On all your offerings you shall bring salt" (Leviticus 2:13).

Mitzva 63

מַעֲשֵׂה הָעוֹלָה, שֶׁנֶּאֱמַר: "אִם עֹלָה קָרְבָּנוֹ" וכו׳ (ויקרא א, ג).

The rite of the burnt offering, as it is stated: "If his offering is a burnt offering..." (Leviticus 1:3).

Mitzva 64

מַעֲשֵׂה הַחַטָּאת, שֶׁנֶּאֱמַר: "זֹאת תּוֹרַת הַחַטָּאת" וכו׳ (ויקרא ו, יח).

The rite of the sin offering, as it is stated: "This is the law of the sin offering..." (Leviticus 6:18).

Mitzva 65

מַעֲשֵׂה הָאָשָׁם, שֶׁנֶּאֱמַר: "וְזֹאת תּוֹרַת הָאָשָׁם" וכו' (ויקרא ז, א).

The rite of the guilt offering, as it is stated: "And this is the law of the guilt offering…" (Leviticus 7:1).

Mitzva 66

מַעֲשֵׂה זֶבַח הַשְּׁלָמִים, שֶׁנֶּאֱמַר: "וְזֹאת תּוֹרַת זֶבַח הַשְּׁלָמִים" (ויקרא ז, יא).

The rite of the peace offering, as it is stated: "And this is the law of the peace offering" (Leviticus 7:11).

Mitzva 67

מַעֲשֵׂה הַמִּנְחָה, שֶׁנֶּאֱמַר: "וְנֶפֶשׁ כִּי תַקְרִיב קָרְבַּן מִנְחָה" (ויקרא ב, א).

The rite of the meal offering, as it is stated: "When a person brings a meal offering" (Leviticus 2:1).

Mitzva 68

לְהַקְרִיב בֵּית דִּין קָרְבָּן אִם טָעוּ בְּהוֹרָאָה, שֶׁנֶּאֱמַר: "וְאִם כָּל עֲדַת יִשְׂרָאֵל" וכו' (ויקרא ד, יג).

That a court must sacrifice an offering if they erred in a ruling, as it is stated: "If the entire congregation of Israel…" (Leviticus 4:13).

Mitzva 69

לְהַקְרִיב הַיָּחִיד קָרְבַּן חַטָּאת אִם שָׁגַג בְּמִצְוַת לֹא תַעֲשֶׂה שֶׁחַיָּבִין עָלֶיהָ כָּרֵת, שֶׁנֶּאֱמַר: "נֶפֶשׁ כִּי תֶחֱטָא בִשְׁגָגָה" (ויקרא ד, ב).

That an individual shall sacrifice a sin offering if he unwittingly sinned **with regard to a prohibition for which one is liable to excision, as it is stated: "When a person sins unwittingly"** (Leviticus 4:2).

Mitzva 70

לְהַקְרִיב הַיָּחִיד קָרְבָּן אִם נִסְתַּפֵּק לוֹ אִם חָטָא בְּחֵטְא שֶׁחַיָּבִין עָלָיו חַטָּאת אוֹ לֹא חָטָא, שֶׁנֶּאֱמַר: "וְלֹא יָדַע וְאָשֵׁם וכו' וְהֵבִיא אֶת אֲשָׁמוֹ" (ויקרא ה, יז-יח, ושם: וְהֵבִיא אַיִל תָּמִים… לְאָשָׁם), וְזֶה הוּא הַנִּקְרָא אָשָׁם תָּלוּי.

That an individual shall sacrifice a sin offering if he is uncertain whether he committed a sin for which one is liable to bring **a sin offering, or** whether he did **not sin, as it is stated: "And he did not know and he is guilty… and he shall bring his guilt offering"** (Leviticus 5:17–18).[a] **This is called a provisional guilt offering.**

Mitzva 71

לְהַקְרִיב הַשּׁוֹגֵג בִּמְעִילָה אוֹ הַחוֹטֵא בְּגֵזֶלָה אוֹ בְּשִׁפְחָה חֲרוּפָה אוֹ שֶׁכָּפַר בְּפִקָּדוֹן וְנִשְׁבַּע, קָרְבַּן אָשָׁם, וְזֶה הוּא הַנִּקְרָא אָשָׁם וַדַּאי.

That an unwitting sinner involving **mis**use of consecrated items, **or one who sinned involving a robbed item, or** who sinned **with an espoused maidservant, or if one** falsely **denied a claim concerning a deposit and swore** to that effect, **shall sacrifice a guilt offering. This is called a definite guilt offering.**

Mitzva 72

לְהַקְרִיב קָרְבָּן עוֹלֶה וְיוֹרֵד, שֶׁנֶּאֱמַר: "וְאִם לֹא תַגִּיעַ יָדוֹ" (ויקרא ה, ז), "וְאִם לֹא תַשִּׂיג" (שם ה, יא).

To sacrifice a sliding-scale offering, as it is stated: "If his means do not suffice" (Leviticus 5:7); **"if** his means **do not suffice"** (Leviticus 5:11).

Mitzva 73

לְהִתְוַדּוֹת לִפְנֵי יי מִכָּל חֵטְא שֶׁיַּעֲשֶׂה הָאָדָם, בִּשְׁעַת הַקָּרְבָּן וְשֶׁלֹּא בִּשְׁעַת הַקָּרְבָּן, שֶׁנֶּאֱמַר: "וְהִתְוַדּוּ אֶת חַטָּאתָם אֲשֶׁר עָשׂוּ" (במדבר ה, ז).

To confess before God for every sin that a person commits, both at the time when he brings **the offering and not at the time** when he brings **the offering, as it is stated: "They shall confess their sin that they had committed"** (Numbers 5:7).

Mitzva 74

לְהַקְרִיב הַזָּב קָרְבָּן אַחַר שֶׁיִּטְהַר, שֶׁנֶּאֱמַר: "וְכִי יִטְהַר הַזָּב" וכו' (ויקרא טו, יג).

That a *zav* shall sacrifice an offering after he is purified, as it is stated: "And when the one who has a discharge shall be cleansed…" (Leviticus 15:13).

Mitzva 75

לְהַקְרִיב הַזָּבָה קָרְבָּן אַחַר שֶׁתִּטְהַר, שֶׁנֶּאֱמַר: "וְאִם טָהֲרָה מִזּוֹבָהּ" (ויקרא טו, כח).

That a *zava* shall sacrifice an offering after she is purified, as it is stated: "But if she was cleansed from her discharge" (Leviticus 15:28).

Mitzva 76

לְהַקְרִיב הַיּוֹלֶדֶת קָרְבָּן אַחַר שֶׁתִּטְהַר, שֶׁנֶּאֱמַר: "וּבִמְלֹאת יְמֵי טָהֳרָהּ" וכו' (ויקרא יב, ו).

That a woman after childbirth shall sacrifice an offering after she is purified, as it is stated: "And with the completion of the days of her purity…" (Leviticus 12:6).

Mitzva 77

לְהַקְרִיב הַמְּצֹרָע קָרְבָּן אַחַר שֶׁיִּטְהַר, שֶׁנֶּאֱמַר: "וּבַיּוֹם הַשְּׁמִינִי" וכו' (ויקרא יד, י).

That a leper shall sacrifice an offering after he is purified, as it is stated: "And on the eighth day…" (Leviticus 14:10).

NOTES

a. Leviticus 5:18 actually reads: "He shall bring an unblemished ram…as a guilt offering." The phrase "and he shall bring his guilt offering" is in fact from Leviticus 5:15, which is dealing with a definite guilt offering, and this quote was possibly inserted here instead of its rightful place, the next mitzva, as it appears in *Sefer HaMitzvot* (*Yad Peshuta*).

Mitzva 78

לְעַשֵּׂר הַבְּהֵמָה, שֶׁנֶּאֱמַר: "וְכָל מַעְשַׂר בָּקָר וָצֹאן כֹּל אֲשֶׁר יַעֲבֹר" וכו' (ויקרא כז, לב).

To tithe animals, as it is stated: "And all the tithe of cattle or the flock, any that passes…" (Leviticus 27:32).

Mitzva 79

לְקַדֵּשׁ בְּכוֹר הַבְּהֵמָה הַטְּהוֹרָה וּלְהַקְרִיבוֹ, שֶׁנֶּאֱמַר: "כָּל הַבְּכוֹר אֲשֶׁר" וכו' (דברים טו, יט).

To consecrate kosher firstborn animals and to sacrifice them, as it is stated: "Any firstborn that…" (Deuteronomy 15:19).

Mitzva 80

לִפְדּוֹת בְּכוֹר אָדָם, שֶׁנֶּאֱמַר: "פָּדֹה תִפְדֶּה אֵת בְּכוֹר הָאָדָם" וכו' (במדבר יח, טו).

To redeem the firstborn of man, as it is stated: "The firstborn of man you shall redeem…" (Numbers 18:15).

Mitzva 81

לִפְדּוֹת פֶּטֶר חֲמוֹר, שֶׁנֶּאֱמַר: "וּפֶטֶר חֲמוֹר תִּפְדֶּה בְשֶׂה" (שמות לד, כ).

To redeem a firstborn donkey, as it is stated: "The first issue of a donkey you shall redeem with a lamb" (Exodus 34:20).

Mitzva 82

לַעֲרֹף פֶּטֶר חֲמוֹר, שֶׁנֶּאֱמַר: "וְאִם לֹא תִפְדֶּה וַעֲרַפְתּוֹ" (שמות יג, יג; לד, כ).

To break the neck of a firstborn donkey, as it is stated: "And if you do not redeem it, then you shall behead it" (Exodus 13:13, 34:20).

Mitzva 83

לְהָבִיא כָּל הַקָּרְבָּנוֹת שֶׁיֵּשׁ עַל הָאָדָם בְּחוֹבָה אוֹ בִנְדָבָה בְּרֶגֶל רִאשׁוֹן שֶׁפָּגַע בּוֹ, שֶׁנֶּאֱמַר: "וּבָאתָ שָׁמָּה...וַהֲבֵאתֶם שָׁמָּה" וכו' (דברים יב, ה-ו).

To bring all of the offerings that are either incumbent upon a person or which are voluntary offerings, on the first pilgrimage festival after his obligation or pledge, as it is stated: "And you shall come there… and you shall bring there" (Deuteronomy 12:5–6).

Mitzva 84

לְהַקְרִיב כָּל הַקָּרְבָּנוֹת בְּבֵית הַבְּחִירָה, שֶׁנֶּאֱמַר: "וְשָׁם תַּעֲשֶׂה כֹּל אֲשֶׁר אָנֹכִי מְצַוֶּךָּ" (דברים יב, יד).

To sacrifice all offerings in the Temple, as it is stated: "And there you shall do everything that I command you" (Deuteronomy 12:14).

Mitzva 85

לְהִטַּפֵּל בַּהֲבָאַת הַקָּרְבָּנוֹת מִחוּצָה לָאָרֶץ לְבֵית הַבְּחִירָה, שֶׁנֶּאֱמַר: "רַק קָדָשֶׁיךָ אֲשֶׁר יִהְיוּ לְךָ וּנְדָרֶיךָ תִּשָּׂא וּבָאתָ" (דברים יב, כו). מִפִּי הַשְּׁמוּעָה לָמְדוּ שֶׁאֵינוֹ מְדַבֵּר אֶלָּא בְּקָדְשֵׁי חוּצָה לָאָרֶץ.

To handle the bringing of offerings from outside of the Land of Israel to the Temple, as it is stated: "Only your sacraments that you will have, and your vows, you shall carry, and come" (Deuteronomy 12:26). The Sages learned, on the basis of the Oral tradition, that this verse is speaking only of sacraments from outside of the Land of Israel.[a]

Mitzva 86

לִפְדּוֹת קָדָשִׁים בַּעֲלֵי מוּמִין וְיִהְיוּ מֻתָּרִין בַּאֲכִילָה, שֶׁנֶּאֱמַר: "רַק בְּכָל אַוַּת נַפְשְׁךָ תִּזְבַּח וְאָכַלְתָּ בָשָׂר" (דברים יב, טו). מִפִּי הַשְּׁמוּעָה לָמְדוּ שֶׁאֵינוֹ מְדַבֵּר אֶלָּא בִּפְסוּלֵי הַמֻּקְדָּשִׁין שֶׁיִּפָּדוּ.

To redeem blemished sacrificial animals, and thus they will be permitted in consumption, as it is stated: "Only, with all of your heart's desire, you may slaughter and eat meat" (Deuteronomy 12:15). The Sages learned, on the basis of the Oral tradition, that this verse is speaking only of disqualified consecrated animals.[b]

Mitzva 87

לִהְיוֹת הַתְּמוּרָה קֹדֶשׁ, שֶׁנֶּאֱמַר: "וְהָיָה הוּא וּתְמוּרָתוֹ יִהְיֶה קֹּדֶשׁ" (ויקרא כז, י; כז, לג).

That a substitute shall be sacred, as it is stated: "It and its substitute shall be sacred" (Leviticus 27:10, 33).

Mitzva 88

לֶאֱכֹל שְׁיָרֵי מְנָחוֹת, שֶׁנֶּאֱמַר: "וְהַנּוֹתֶרֶת מִמֶּנָּה יֹאכְלוּ אַהֲרֹן וּבָנָיו" (ויקרא ו, ט).

To eat the remainders of meal offerings, as it is stated: "And the remnant of it Aaron and his sons shall eat" (Leviticus 6:9).

Mitzva 89

לֶאֱכֹל בְּשַׂר חַטָּאת וְאָשָׁם, שֶׁנֶּאֱמַר: "וְאָכְלוּ אֹתָם אֲשֶׁר כֻּפַּר בָּהֶם" וכו' (שמות כט, לג).

To eat the meat of sin offerings and guilt offerings, as it is stated: "They who have received atonement through them shall eat them…." (Exodus 29:33).

NOTES

a. See *Sifrei* on Deuteronomy 12:26 (*Yad Peshuta*).

b. See *Sifrei* on Deuteronomy 12:26 (*Yad Peshuta*).

Mitzva 90

To burn sacrificial meat that has become ritually impure, as it is stated: "And the flesh that shall touch any impure item shall not be eaten; it shall be burned in fire" (Leviticus 7:19).

לִשְׂרֹף בְּשַׂר קֹדֶשׁ שֶׁנִּטְמָא, שֶׁנֶּאֱמַר: "וְהַבָּשָׂר אֲשֶׁר יִגַּע בְּכָל טָמֵא לֹא יֵאָכֵל בָּאֵשׁ יִשָּׂרֵף" (ויקרא ז, יט).

Mitzva 91

To burn *notar*, as it is stated: "And that which remains of the flesh of the offering on the third day..." (Leviticus 7:17).

לִשְׂרֹף נוֹתָר, שֶׁנֶּאֱמַר: "וְהַנּוֹתָר מִבְּשַׂר הַזָּבַח בַּיּוֹם הַשְּׁלִישִׁי" וכו' (ויקרא ז, יז).

Mitzva 92

That a nazirite shall grow his hair, as it is stated: "The hair of his head shall be grown out" (Numbers 6:5).

לְגַדֵּל הַנָּזִיר שְׂעָרוֹ, שֶׁנֶּאֱמַר: "גַּדֵּל פֶּרַע שְׂעַר רֹאשׁוֹ" (במדבר ו, ה).

Mitzva 93

That a nazirite shall shave his hair based upon the offerings at the completion of the days of his naziriteship, or during the days of his naziriteship if he became impure, as it is stated: "If a corpse dies near him..." (Numbers 6:9).

לְגַלֵּחַ הַנָּזִיר שְׂעָרוֹ עַל קָרְבְּנוֹתָיו בִּמְלֹאת יְמֵי נִזְרוֹ, אוֹ בְּתוֹךְ יְמֵי נִזְרוֹ אִם נִטְמָא, שֶׁנֶּאֱמַר: "וְכִי יָמוּת מֵת עָלָיו" וגו' (במדבר ו, ט).

Mitzva 94

That a person must fulfill all that he articulates with his lips, whether this involves **an offering or charity, as it is stated: "That which emerges from your lips you shall observe and you shall perform..."** (Deuteronomy 23:24).

לְקַיֵּם אָדָם כָּל שֶׁהוֹצִיא בִּשְׂפָתָיו מִקָּרְבָּן אוֹ צְדָקָה וְכַיּוֹצֵא בָּהֶן, שֶׁנֶּאֱמַר: "מוֹצָא שְׂפָתֶיךָ תִּשְׁמֹר וְעָשִׂיתָ" וכו' (דברים כג, כד).

Mitzva 95

To treat the nullification of vows in accordance with **all the laws that are stated in the** relevant **chapter** (Numbers 30:2–17).

לָדוּן בְּהָפֵר נְדָרִים בְּכָל הַדִּינִין הָאֲמוּרִין בַּפָּרָשָׁה (במדבר ל, ב-יז).

Mitzva 96

That every person **who touches an animal carcass shall be ritually impure, as it is stated: "And if any animal** that is for your consumption **shall die..."** (Leviticus 11:39).

לִהְיוֹת כָּל נוֹגֵעַ בִּנְבֵלָה טָמֵא, שֶׁנֶּאֱמַר: "וְכִי יָמוּת מִן הַבְּהֵמָה" וכו' (ויקרא יא, לט).

Mitzva 97

That the eight creeping animals transmit ritual impurity, as it is stated: "And this is impure to you..." (Leviticus 11:29).

לִהְיוֹת שְׁמוֹנָה שְׁרָצִים מְטַמְּאִין, שֶׁנֶּאֱמַר: "וְזֶה לָכֶם הַטָּמֵא" וכו' (ויקרא יא, כט).

Mitzva 98

That food can become ritually impure, as it is stated: "Any food that may be eaten..." (Leviticus 11:34).

לִהְיוֹת הָאֳכָלִין מִתְטַמְּאִין, שֶׁנֶּאֱמַר: "מִכָּל הָאֹכֶל אֲשֶׁר יֵאָכֵל" וכו' (ויקרא יא, לד).

Mitzva 99

That a menstruating woman is ritually impure and transmits impurity to others.

לִהְיוֹת הַנִּדָּה טְמֵאָה וּמְטַמְּאָה לַאֲחֵרִים.

Mitzva 100

That a woman after childbirth is ritually impure like a menstruating woman.

לִהְיוֹת הַיּוֹלֶדֶת טְמֵאָה כַּנִּדָּה.

Mitzva 101

That a leper is ritually impure and transmits impurity.

לִהְיוֹת הַמְּצֹרָע טָמֵא וּמְטַמֵּא.

Mitzva 102

That a garment afflicted with leprosy is ritually impure and transmits impurity.

לִהְיוֹת בֶּגֶד מְנֻגָּע טָמֵא וּמְטַמֵּא.

Mitzva 103

That a house afflicted with leprosy transmits impurity.

לִהְיוֹת בַּיִת מְנֻגָּע מְטַמֵּא.

Mitzva 104

That a *zav* transmits impurity.

לִהְיוֹת הַזָּב מְטַמֵּא.

Mitzva 105

That semen transmits impurity.

לִהְיוֹת שִׁכְבַת זֶרַע מְטַמְּאָה.

Mitzva 106

That a *zava* transmits impurity.

לִהְיוֹת זָבָה מְטַמְּאָה.

Mitzva 107

That a corpse transmits impurity.

לִהְיוֹת הַמֵּת מְטַמֵּא.

Mitzva 108

That the water of sprinkling renders a ritually pure person impure, and purify only from impurity imparted by a **corpse.** Regarding **all of these laws of** those types of **impurity, the majority of the regulations of each one of these impurities is clarified in the Written Torah.**

לִהְיוֹת מֵי נִדָּה מְטַמְּאִין לְאָדָם טָהוֹר וּמְטַהֲרִין מִטֻּמְאַת מֵת בִּלְבַד. וְכָל אֵלּוּ הַדִּינִין שֶׁל טֻמְאוֹת אֵלּוּ – רֹב מִשְׁפַּט כָּל טֻמְאָה וְטֻמְאָה מֵהֶן מְבֹאָר בַּתּוֹרָה שֶׁבִּכְתָב.

GLOSSES OF THE RAAVAD

לִהְיוֹת מֵי נִדָּה וְכוּ׳. אָמַר אַבְרָהָם: וְלָמָּה לֹא יֶחָשְׁבוּ לִשְׁתַּיִם, הַטֻּמְאָה וְהַטָּהֳרָה.

"That the water of sprinkling…" Avraham says: Why doesn't the Rambam **count this as two** mitzvot: **the impurity** the water imparts, **and the purity** it effects?

Mitzva 109

לִהְיוֹת הַטָּהֳרָה מִכָּל הַטֻּמְאוֹת בִּטְבִילָה בְּמֵי מִקְוֶה, שֶׁנֶּאֱמַר: ״וְרָחַץ בַּמַּיִם אֶת כָּל בְּשָׂרוֹ״ (ויקרא טו, טז). כָּךְ לָמְדוּ מִפִּי הַשְּׁמוּעָה, שֶׁרְחִיצָה זוֹ בְּמַיִם שֶׁכָּל גּוּפוֹ עוֹלֶה בָּהֶן בְּבַת אַחַת.

That the purification from all the impurities shall be through immersion in a ritual bath, as it is stated: "Shall bathe all his flesh in water" (Leviticus 15:16). The Sages **learned as follows, on the basis of the** Oral **tradition, that this bathing is** performed **in water into which all of one's body can enter at the same time** (see *Eiruvin* 4b).

Mitzva 110

לִהְיוֹת הַטָּהֳרָה מִן הַצָּרַעַת, בֵּין צָרַעַת אָדָם בֵּין צָרַעַת בַּיִת, בְּעֵץ אֶרֶז וְאֵזוֹב וּשְׁנִי תוֹלַעַת וּשְׁתֵּי צִפֳּרִים וּמַיִם חַיִּים, שֶׁנֶּאֱמַר: ״זֹאת תִּהְיֶה תּוֹרַת הַמְּצֹרָע״ (ויקרא יד, ב).

That the purification from leprosy, whether the leprosy of a person or the leprosy of a house, shall be performed **with cedar wood, hyssop, scarlet** wool, **two birds, and spring water, as it is stated: "This shall be the law of the leper"** (Leviticus 14:2).

Mitzva 111

לִהְיוֹת הַמְּצֹרָע מְגַלֵּחַ כָּל שְׂעָרוֹ, שֶׁנֶּאֱמַר: ״וְהָיָה בַיּוֹם הַשְּׁבִיעִי יְגַלַּח אֶת כָּל שְׂעָרוֹ״ וכו׳ (ויקרא יד, ט).

That the leper shall shave off all of his hair when he is purified, **as it is stated: "It shall be on the seventh day; he shall shave all his hair…"** (Leviticus 14:9).

Mitzva 112

לִהְיוֹת הַמְּצֹרָע יָדוּעַ לַכֹּל בַּדְּבָרִים הָאֲמוּרִים בּוֹ: ״בְּגָדָיו יִהְיוּ פְרֻמִים וְרֹאשׁוֹ יִהְיֶה פָרוּעַ וְעַל שָׂפָם יַעְטֶה וְטָמֵא טָמֵא יִקְרָא״ (ויקרא יג, מה). וְכֵן שְׁאָר הַטְּמֵאִים צְרִיכִין לְהוֹדִיעַ אֶת עַצְמָן.

That the leper shall be recognized to all through the indications mentioned regarding him, as it is stated: "His garments shall be rent, and the hair of his head shall be grown out, and he shall cover his upper lip and shall cry: Impure, impure" (Leviticus 13:45). **Other impure** people **must likewise announce their** status.

Mitzva 113

לַעֲשׂוֹת פָּרָה אֲדֻמָּה לִהְיוֹת אֶפְרָהּ מוּכָן, שֶׁנֶּאֱמַר: ״וְהָיְתָה לַעֲדַת״ וכו׳ (במדבר יט, ט).

To perform the rite of **the red heifer, so that its ashes are ready, as it is stated: "And it shall be for the congregation…"** (Numbers 19:9).

Mitzva 114

לִהְיוֹת מַעֲרִיךְ אָדָם נוֹתֵן דָּמִים הַקְּצוּבִין בַּפָּרָשָׁה, שֶׁנֶּאֱמַר: ״אִישׁ כִּי יַפְלִא נֶדֶר״ (ויקרא כז, ב).

That one who evaluates a person shall give the sum that is **fixed in the** relevant **chapter, as it is stated: "If a man articulates a vow"** (Leviticus 27:2).

Mitzva 115

לִהְיוֹת מַעֲרִיךְ בְּהֵמָה טְמֵאָה נוֹתֵן דָּמֶיהָ, שֶׁנֶּאֱמַר: ״וְהֶעֱמִיד אֶת הַבְּהֵמָה״ וכו׳ (ויקרא כז, יא).

That one who evaluates an impure animal shall give its value, as it is stated: "He shall set the animal…" (Leviticus 27:11).

Mitzva 116

לִהְיוֹת מַעֲרִיךְ בֵּיתוֹ נוֹתֵן כְּעֶרֶךְ הַכֹּהֵן, שֶׁנֶּאֱמַר: ״וְאִישׁ כִּי יַקְדִּשׁ״ וכו׳ (ויקרא כז, יד).

That one who evaluates his house shall give the value **of the assessment of a priest, as it is stated: "And when a man consecrates…"** (Leviticus 27:14).

Mitzva 117

לִתֵּן מַקְדִּישׁ שָׂדֵהוּ עֶרְכָּהּ הָאָמוּר בַּתּוֹרָה, שֶׁנֶּאֱמַר: ״וְאִם מִשְּׂדֵה אֲחֻזָּתוֹ״ וכו׳ (ויקרא כז, טז).

That one who consecrates his field shall give its valuation that is specified in the Torah, as it is stated: "And if from the field of his ancestral portion…." (Leviticus 27:16).

Mitzva 118

לְהוֹסִיף הַמּוֹעֵל אוֹ אוֹכֵל תְּרוּמָה חֹמֶשׁ עַל הַקֶּרֶן וּלְהַחֲזִירוֹ, שֶׁנֶּאֱמַר: ״וְאֵת אֲשֶׁר חָטָא מִן הַקֹּדֶשׁ יְשַׁלֵּם״ וכו׳ (ויקרא ה, טז).

That one who misuses consecrated items **or eats *teruma* shall add one-fifth to the principal and return it, as it is stated: "And that which he sinned from the sacred he shall pay…."** (Leviticus 5:16).

Mitzva 119

לִהְיוֹת נֶטַע רְבָעִי קֹדֶשׁ, שֶׁנֶּאֱמַר: ״יִהְיֶה כָּל פִּרְיוֹ קֹדֶשׁ הִלּוּלִים״ (ויקרא יט, כד).

That a fourth-year sapling shall be holy, as it is stated: "All its fruit shall be sacred for praise" (Leviticus 19:24).

Mitzva 120

לְהַנִּיחַ פֵּאָה.

To leave *pe'a*.

Mitzva 121

לְהַנִּיחַ לֶקֶט.

To leave gleanings.

Mitzva 122

לְהַנִּיחַ עֹמֶר הַשִּׁכְחָה.

To leave a forgotten sheaf.

Mitzva 123

לְהַנִּיחַ עוֹלֵלוֹת בַּכֶּרֶם.

To leave *olelot* in a vineyard.

Mitzva 124

לְהַנִּיחַ פֶּרֶט הַכֶּרֶם. לְפִי שֶׁבְּכָל אֵלּוּ נֶאֱמַר: "לֶעָנִי וְלַגֵּר תַּעֲזֹב אֹתָם" (ויקרא יט, י; כג, כב), וְזוֹ הִיא מִצְוַת עֲשֵׂה שֶׁלָּהֶם.

To leave the *peret* of a vineyard. For regarding all of these it is stated: "For the poor and for the stranger you shall leave them" (Leviticus 19:10, 23:22). **This is the source of their positive mitzva.**

Mitzva 125

לְהָבִיא בִּכּוּרִים לְבֵית הַבְּחִירָה, שֶׁנֶּאֱמַר: "רֵאשִׁית בִּכּוּרֵי אַדְמָתְךָ" וכו' (שמות כג, יט; לד, כו).

To bring the first fruits to the Temple, as it is stated: "The choicest of the first fruits of your land…" (Exodus 23:19, 34:26).

Mitzva 126

לְהַפְרִישׁ תְּרוּמָה גְּדוֹלָה לַכֹּהֵן, שֶׁנֶּאֱמַר: "רֵאשִׁית דְּגָנְךָ תִּירֹשְׁךָ" וכו' (דברים יח, ד).

To separate *teruma gedola*, as it is stated: "The first fruits of your grain, of your wine…" (Deuteronomy 18:4).

Mitzva 127

לְהַפְרִישׁ מַעֲשַׂר דָּגָן לַלְוִיִּם, שֶׁנֶּאֱמַר: "וְכָל מַעְשַׂר הָאָרֶץ מִזֶּרַע הָאָרֶץ" וכו' (ויקרא כז, ל).

To separate the tithe of grain for the Levites, as it is stated: "All the tithe of the land, from the seed of the land…" (Leviticus 27:30).

Mitzva 128

לְהַפְרִישׁ מַעֲשֵׂר שֵׁנִי לְהֵאָכֵל לִבְעָלָיו בִּירוּשָׁלַיִם, שֶׁנֶּאֱמַר: "עַשֵּׂר תְּעַשֵּׂר אֵת כָּל תְּבוּאַת זַרְעֶךָ" וכו' (דברים יד, כב). מִפִּי הַשְּׁמוּעָה לָמְדוּ שֶׁזֶּה הוּא מַעֲשֵׂר שֵׁנִי.

To separate the second tithe for it to be eaten by its owner in Jerusalem, as it is stated: "You shall tithe the entire crop of your sowing…" (Deuteronomy 14:22). The Sages **learned, on the basis of the Oral tradition, that this is** the **second tithe.**[a]

Mitzva 129

לִהְיוֹת הַלְוִיִּם מַפְרִישִׁין מַעֲשֵׂר מִן הַמַּעֲשֵׂר שֶׁלָּקְחוּ מִיִּשְׂרָאֵל וְנוֹתְנִין אוֹתוֹ לַכֹּהֲנִים, שֶׁנֶּאֱמַר: "וְאֶל הַלְוִיִּם תְּדַבֵּר" וכו' (במדבר יח, כו).

That the Levites shall separate a tithe from the tithe they took from an Israelite and give it to priests, as it is stated: "To the Levites you shall speak…" (Numbers 18:26).

Mitzva 130

לְהַפְרִישׁ מַעֲשַׂר עָנִי תַּחַת מַעֲשֵׂר שֵׁנִי בַּשְּׁלִישִׁית וּבַשִּׁשִּׁית בַּשָּׁבוּעַ, שֶׁנֶּאֱמַר: "מִקְצֵה שָׁלֹשׁ שָׁנִים תּוֹצִיא אֶת כָּל מַעְשַׂר" וכו' (דברים יד, כח).

To separate the poor man's tithe instead of second tithe in the third and sixth years **of the seven-year cycle** of the Sabbatical Year, **as it is stated: "At the end of three years, you shall take out all the tithe…"** (Deuteronomy 14:28).

Mitzva 131

לְהִתְוַדּוֹת וִדּוּי מַעֲשֵׂר, שֶׁנֶּאֱמַר: "וְאָמַרְתָּ לִפְנֵי יי אֱלֹהֶיךָ בִּעַרְתִּי" וכו' (דברים כו, יג).

To recite the declaration of tithes, as it is stated: "You shall say before the Lord your God: I have disposed…" (Deuteronomy 26:13).

Mitzva 132

לִקְרוֹת עַל הַבִּכּוּרִים, שֶׁנֶּאֱמַר: "וְעָנִיתָ וְאָמַרְתָּ לִפְנֵי יי אֱלֹהֶיךָ" וכו' (דברים כו, ה).

To read the passage **of the first fruits, as it is stated: "You shall proclaim and you shall say before the Lord your God…"** (Deuteronomy 26:5).

Mitzva 133

לְהַפְרִישׁ חַלָּה לַכֹּהֵן, שֶׁנֶּאֱמַר: "רֵאשִׁית עֲרִסֹתֵכֶם חַלָּה תָּרִימוּ" וכו' (במדבר טו, כ).

To separate *ḥalla* for a priest, as it is stated: "The first of your kneading basket you shall set aside a loaf…" (Numbers 15:20).

Mitzva 134

לְהַשְׁמִיט קַרְקַע, שֶׁנֶּאֱמַר: "וְהַשְּׁבִיעִת תִּשְׁמְטֶנָּה וּנְטַשְׁתָּהּ" (שמות כג, יא).

To leave the product of **the land fallow, as it is stated: "But the seventh year you shall leave it fallow and relinquish it"** (Exodus 23:11).

Mitzva 135

לִשְׁבֹּת מֵעֲבוֹדַת הָאָרֶץ, שֶׁנֶּאֱמַר: "בֶּחָרִישׁ וּבַקָּצִיר תִּשְׁבֹּת" (שמות לד, כא).

To rest from the labor of the land in the seventh year, **as it is stated: "From plowing and from harvest you shall rest"** (Exodus 34:21).

NOTES

a. See *Sifrei* on Deuteronomy 14:22 (*Yad Peshuta*).

Mitzva 136

לְקַדֵּשׁ שְׁנַת יוֹבֵל בִּשְׁבִיתָה כִּשְׁמִטָּה, שֶׁנֶּאֱמַר: "וְקִדַּשְׁתֶּם אֵת שְׁנַת הַחֲמִשִּׁים" (ויקרא כה, י).

To sanctify the Jubilee Year through rest, like the Sabbatical Year, **as it is stated: "You shall sanctify the fiftieth year"** (Leviticus 25:10).

Mitzva 137

לִתְקֹעַ בַּשּׁוֹפָר בִּשְׁנַת יוֹבֵל, שֶׁנֶּאֱמַר: "וְהַעֲבַרְתָּ שׁוֹפַר תְּרוּעָה" (ויקרא כה, ט).

To sound the shofar in the Jubilee Year, as it is stated: "You shall sound an alarm blast of the shofar" (Leviticus 25:9).

Mitzva 138

לִתֵּן גְּאֻלָּה לָאָרֶץ בִּשְׁנַת יוֹבֵל, שֶׁנֶּאֱמַר: "וּבְכֹל אֶרֶץ אֲחֻזַּתְכֶם גְּאֻלָּה תִּתְּנוּ לָאָרֶץ" (ויקרא כה, כד).

To provide redemption for the land in the Jubilee Year, as it is stated: "In all the land of your ancestral portion you shall provide redemption for the land" (Leviticus 25:24).

Mitzva 139

לִהְיוֹת גְּאֻלַּת בָּתֵּי עָרֵי חוֹמָה עַד שָׁנָה, שֶׁנֶּאֱמַר: "וְאִישׁ כִּי יִמְכֹּר בֵּית" וכו׳ (ויקרא כה, כט).

That the redemption of houses of walled cities shall last **for a year, as it is stated: "And if a man sells a house..."** (Leviticus 25:29).

Mitzva 140

לִמְנוֹת שְׁנֵי יוֹבֵל שָׁנִים וּשְׁמִטִּים, שֶׁנֶּאֱמַר: "וְסָפַרְתָּ לְךָ שֶׁבַע שַׁבְּתֹת שָׁנִים" וכו׳ (ויקרא כה, ח).

To count the years toward the **Jubilee** Year, both individual **years and Sabbati**cal Years, **as it is stated: "You shall count for yourselves seven Sabbatical Years..."** (Leviticus 25:8).

Mitzva 141

לְהַשְׁמִיט כְּסָפִים בַּשְּׁבִיעִית, שֶׁנֶּאֱמַר: "שָׁמוֹט כָּל בַּעַל מַשֵּׁה יָדוֹ" (דברים טו, ב).

To release money in the Sabbatical Year, **as it is stated: "Every creditor** that has extended credit to his neighbor **shall remit"** (Deuteronomy 15:2).

Mitzva 142

לִנְגֹּשׂ לַנָּכְרִי, שֶׁנֶּאֱמַר: "אֶת הַנָּכְרִי תִּגֹּשׂ וַאֲשֶׁר יִהְיֶה לְךָ אֶת אָחִיךָ" וכו׳ (דברים טו, ג).

To demand payment of a loan **from a gentile, as it is stated: "From the foreigner you may demand it, but that which you will have with your brother..."** (Deuteronomy 15:3).

Mitzva 143

לִתֵּן מִן הַבְּהֵמָה לַכֹּהֵן הַזְּרוֹעַ וְהַלְּחָיַיִם וְהַקֵּבָה, שֶׁנֶּאֱמַר: "וְנָתַן לַכֹּהֵן" וכו׳ (דברים יח, ג).

To give the foreleg, the jaw, and the maw of an animal to a priest, as it is stated: "He shall give the priest..." (Deuteronomy 18:3).

Mitzva 144

לִתֵּן רֵאשִׁית הַגֵּז לַכֹּהֵן, שֶׁנֶּאֱמַר: "וְרֵאשִׁית גֵּז צֹאנְךָ תִּתֶּן לוֹ" (דברים יח, ד).

To give the first of the sheared wool **to a priest, as it is stated: "You shall give him... the first of the fleece of your flock"** (Deuteronomy 18:4).

Mitzva 145

לָדוּן בְּדִינֵי חֲרָמִים, מֵהֶם לַיי וּמֵהֶם לַכֹּהֵן, שֶׁנֶּאֱמַר: "אַךְ כָּל חֵרֶם" וכו׳ (ויקרא כז, כח).

To adjudicate the laws of one who dedicates his property, which of them must be given **to God and which to a priest, as it is stated: "However, anything proscribed..."** (Leviticus 27:28).

Mitzva 146

לִשְׁחֹט בְּהֵמָה חַיָּה וָעוֹף וְאַחַר כָּךְ יֵאָכֵל בְּשָׂרָן, שֶׁנֶּאֱמַר: "וְזָבַחְתָּ מִבְּקָרְךָ" וכו׳ (דברים יב, כא).

To slaughter a domesticated animal, an undomesticated animal, or a bird, and only **then to eat their flesh, as it is stated: "You shall slaughter from your herd..."** (Deuteronomy 12:21).

GLOSSES OF THE RAAVAD

לִשְׁחֹט בְּהֵמָה וְכוּ׳. אָמַר אַבְרָהָם: זוֹ אֵין לוֹ טַעַם. וְאוּלַי לָאו הַבָּא מִכְּלַל עֲשֵׂה – עֲשֵׂה.

"To slaughter a domesticated animal..." **Avraham says: This** inclusion **has no** justifying **reason. Perhaps** the Rambam meant that **this** is a positive mitzva in accordance with the rule that **a prohibition that comes by inference from a positive mitzva** is classified as **a positive mitzva.**

Mitzva 147

לְכַסּוֹת דַּם חַיָּה וָעוֹף, שֶׁנֶּאֱמַר: "וְשָׁפַךְ אֶת דָּמוֹ וְכִסָּהוּ בֶּעָפָר" (ויקרא יז, יג).

To cover the blood of a slaughtered **undomesticated animal or bird, as it is stated: "He shall pour out its blood and cover it with dirt"** (Leviticus 17:13).

Mitzva 148

לְשַׁלֵּחַ הַקֵּן, שֶׁנֶּאֱמַר: "שַׁלֵּחַ תְּשַׁלַּח אֶת הָאֵם וְאֶת הַבָּנִים תִּקַּח לָךְ" וכו׳ (דברים כב, ז).

To send away the mother bird from **the nest, as it is stated: "You shall send forth the mother, and the offspring take for yourself..."** (Deuteronomy 22:7).

Mitzva 149

לִבְדֹּק בְּסִימָנֵי בְּהֵמָה, שֶׁנֶּאֱמַר: "זֹאת הַחַיָּה אֲשֶׁר תֹּאכְלוּ מִכָּל" וכו' (ויקרא יא, ב).

To examine the signs of a domesticated animal, as it is stated: "These are the living beings that you may eat, from all..." (Leviticus 11:2).

GLOSSES OF THE RAAVAD

לִבְדֹּק בְּסִימָנֵי בְּהֵמָה וְכוּ'. אָמַר אַבְרָהָם: כָּל 'לִבְדֹּק' אֵין לָהֶם טַעַם; אֶלָּא מִשּׁוּם לָאו הַבָּא מִכְּלַל עֲשֵׂה – עֲשֵׂה.

"To examine the signs of a domesticated animal..." Avraham says: All of these descriptions of the positive mitzvot that begin with **"to examine" have no reason** behind them. **Rather,** these are positive mitzvot **due to the rule that a prohibition that comes by inference from a positive mitzva** is classified as a **positive mitzva.**

Mitzva 150

לִבְדֹּק בְּסִימָנֵי הָעוֹף עַד שֶׁיַּבְדִּיל בֵּין טָמֵא שֶׁבּוֹ לְטָהוֹר שֶׁבּוֹ, שֶׁנֶּאֱמַר: "כָּל צִפּוֹר טְהֹרָה תֹּאכֵלוּ" (דברים יד, יא).

To examine the signs of birds until one can distinguish between its non-kosher species **and its kosher** species, **as it is stated: "All pure birds you may eat"** (Deuteronomy 14:11).

Mitzva 151

לִבְדֹּק בְּסִימָנֵי חֲגָבִים לֵידַע טָהוֹר מִן הַטָּמֵא, שֶׁנֶּאֱמַר: "אֲשֶׁר לוֹ כְרָעַיִם" וכו' (ויקרא יא, כא).

To examine the signs of grasshoppers, to know the kosher species **from the non-kosher** species, **as it is stated: "Those that have jointed legs..."** (Leviticus 11:21).

Mitzva 152

לִבְדֹּק בְּסִימָנֵי דָּגִים, שֶׁנֶּאֱמַר: "אֶת זֶה תֹּאכְלוּ מִכֹּל אֲשֶׁר בַּמָּיִם" וכו' (ויקרא יא, ט; דברים יא, ט).

To examine the signs of fish, as it is stated: "This you may eat from everything that is in the water..." (Leviticus 11:9, Deuteronomy 11:9).

Mitzva 153

לְקַדֵּשׁ חֳדָשִׁים וּלְחַשֵּׁב שָׁנִים וָחֳדָשִׁים בְּבֵית דִּין בִּלְבַד, שֶׁנֶּאֱמַר: "הַחֹדֶשׁ הַזֶּה לָכֶם רֹאשׁ חֳדָשִׁים" (שמות יב, ב).

To sanctify the months and to calculate the years and months in a court alone, as it is stated: "This month is for you the beginning of months" (Exodus 12:2).

Mitzva 154

לִשְׁבֹּת בְּשַׁבָּת, שֶׁנֶּאֱמַר: "וּבַיּוֹם הַשְּׁבִיעִי תִּשְׁבֹּת" (שמות כג, יב; לד, כא).

To rest on Shabbat, as it is stated: "And on the seventh day you shall rest" (Exodus 23:12, 34:21).

Mitzva 155

לְקַדֵּשׁ שַׁבָּת, שֶׁנֶּאֱמַר: "זָכוֹר אֶת יוֹם הַשַּׁבָּת לְקַדְּשׁוֹ" (שמות כ, ז).

To sanctify Shabbat, as it is stated: "Remember the Sabbath day, to keep it holy" (Exodus 20:8).

Mitzva 156

לְבַעֵר חָמֵץ, שֶׁנֶּאֱמַר: "בַּיּוֹם הָרִאשׁוֹן תַּשְׁבִּיתוּ שְּׂאֹר" (שמות יב, טו).

To remove leaven, as it is stated: "On the first day you shall eliminate leaven" (Exodus 12:15).

Mitzva 157

לְסַפֵּר בִּיצִיאַת מִצְרַיִם בְּלֵילָה הָרִאשׁוֹן שֶׁל חַג הַמַּצּוֹת, שֶׁנֶּאֱמַר: "וְהִגַּדְתָּ לְבִנְךָ בַּיּוֹם הַהוּא לֵאמֹר" וכו' (שמות יג, ח).

To relate the exodus from Egypt on the first night of the festival of *matzot*, as it is stated: "You shall tell your son on that day, saying..." (Exodus 13:8).

Mitzva 158

לֶאֱכֹל מַצָּה בְּלֵיל זֶה, שֶׁנֶּאֱמַר: "בָּעֶרֶב תֹּאכְלוּ מַצֹּת" (שמות יב, יח).

To eat matza on that night, as it is stated: "In the evening, you shall eat unleavened bread" (Exodus 12:18).

Mitzva 159

לִשְׁבֹּת בָּרִאשׁוֹן שֶׁל פֶּסַח, שֶׁנֶּאֱמַר: "בַּיּוֹם הָרִאשׁוֹן מִקְרָא קֹדֶשׁ" (ויקרא כג, ז; במדבר כח, יח).

To rest on the first day **of Passover, as it is stated: "On the first day a holy convocation"** (Leviticus 23:7, Numbers 28:18).

Mitzva 160

לִשְׁבֹּת בַּשְּׁבִיעִי בּוֹ, שֶׁנֶּאֱמַר: "וּבַיּוֹם הַשְּׁבִיעִי מִקְרָא קֹדֶשׁ" (שמות יב, טז; במדבר כח, כה).

To rest on the seventh day of **Passover, as it is stated: "And a holy convocation on the seventh day"** (Exodus 12:16, Numbers 28:25).

Mitzva 161

לִסְפֹּר מִקְּצִירַת הָעֹמֶר תִּשְׁעָה וְאַרְבָּעִים יוֹם, שֶׁנֶּאֱמַר: "וּסְפַרְתֶּם לָכֶם" וגו' (ויקרא כג, טו).

To count forty-nine days from the reaping of the *omer*, as it is stated: "And you shall count for yourselves..." (Leviticus 23:15).

Mitzva 162

לִשְׁבֹּת בְּיוֹם חֲמִשִּׁים, שֶׁנֶּאֱמַר: "וּקְרָאתֶם בְּעֶצֶם הַיּוֹם הַזֶּה מִקְרָא קֹדֶשׁ" (ויקרא כג, כא).

To rest on the fiftieth day, as it is stated: "You shall proclaim on that very day, a holy convocation" (Leviticus 23:21).

Mitzva 163

לִשְׁבֹּת בְּרִאשׁוֹן שֶׁל חֹדֶשׁ הַשְּׁבִיעִי, שֶׁנֶּאֱמַר: "בְּאֶחָד לַחֹדֶשׁ יִהְיֶה לָכֶם שַׁבָּתוֹן" (ויקרא כג, כד).

To rest on the first day of the seventh month, as it is stated: "In the seventh month, on the first day of the month, shall be a rest for you" (Leviticus 23:24).

Mitzva 164

לְהִתְעַנּוֹת בָּעֲשִׂירִי בּוֹ, שֶׁנֶּאֱמַר: "בֶּעָשׂוֹר לַחֹדֶשׁ תְּעַנּוּ אֶת נַפְשֹׁתֵיכֶם" (ויקרא טז, כט).

To afflict oneself on the tenth day of the seventh month, as it is stated: "On the tenth of the month, you shall afflict yourselves" (Leviticus 16:29).

Mitzva 165

לִשְׁבֹּת בְּיוֹם הַצּוֹם, שֶׁנֶּאֱמַר: "שַׁבַּת שַׁבָּתוֹן הוּא לָכֶם" (ויקרא כג, לב).

To rest on the Yom Kippur fast day, as it is stated: "It is a sabbatical rest for you" (Leviticus 23:32).

Mitzva 166

לִשְׁבֹּת בְּרִאשׁוֹן שֶׁל חַג הַסֻּכּוֹת, שֶׁנֶּאֱמַר: "בַּיּוֹם הָרִאשׁוֹן מִקְרָא קֹדֶשׁ" (ויקרא כג, לה).

To rest on the first day of the festival of Sukkot, as it is stated: "On the first day is a holy convocation" (Leviticus 23:35).

Mitzva 167 ◂

לִשְׁבֹּת בִּשְׁמִינִי שֶׁל חַג, שֶׁנֶּאֱמַר: "וּבַיּוֹם הַשְּׁמִינִי מִקְרָא קֹדֶשׁ" (ויקרא כג, לו, ושם: בַּיּוֹם).

To rest on the eighth day of the festival of Sukkot, as it is stated: "On the eighth day shall be a holy convocation" (Leviticus 23:36).

Mitzva 168

לֵישֵׁב בַּסֻּכָּה שִׁבְעַת יָמִים, שֶׁנֶּאֱמַר: "בַּסֻּכֹּת תֵּשְׁבוּ שִׁבְעַת יָמִים" (ויקרא כג, מב).

To reside in a *sukka* during the seven days of the festival of Sukkot, as it is stated: "You shall live in booths seven days" (Leviticus 23:42).

Mitzva 169

לִטֹּל לוּלָב, שֶׁנֶּאֱמַר: "וּלְקַחְתֶּם לָכֶם בַּיּוֹם הָרִאשׁוֹן פְּרִי עֵץ הָדָר" וכו' (ויקרא כג, מ).

To take a *lulav*, as it is stated: "You shall take for you on the first day: the fruit of a pleasant tree…" (Leviticus 23:40).

Mitzva 170

לִשְׁמֹעַ קוֹל שׁוֹפָר בְּרֹאשׁ הַשָּׁנָה, שֶׁנֶּאֱמַר: "יוֹם תְּרוּעָה יִהְיֶה לָכֶם" (במדבר כט, א).

To hear the sound of a shofar on Rosh HaShana, as it is stated: "A day of sounding the alarm it shall be for you" (Numbers 29:1).

Mitzva 171

לִתֵּן מַחֲצִית הַשֶּׁקֶל בְּכָל שָׁנָה, שֶׁנֶּאֱמַר: "זֶה יִתְּנוּ כָּל הָעֹבֵר" וכו' (שמות ל, יג).

To give a half-shekel every year, as it is stated: "This is what everyone who passes among the counted shall give…" (Exodus 30:13).

Mitzva 172

לִשְׁמֹעַ מִכָּל נָבִיא שֶׁיִּהְיֶה בְּכָל דּוֹר וָדוֹר אִם לֹא יוֹסִיף וְלֹא יִגְרַע, שֶׁנֶּאֱמַר: "אֵלָיו תִּשְׁמָעוּן" (דברים יח, טו).

To listen to every prophet who will arise in each and every generation, if he does not add or subtract from the mitzvot, as it is stated: "A prophet from your midst… him you shall heed" (Deuteronomy 18:15).

Mitzva 173

לְמַנּוֹת מֶלֶךְ, שֶׁנֶּאֱמַר: "שׂוֹם תָּשִׂים עָלֶיךָ מֶלֶךְ" (דברים יז, טו).

To appoint a king, as it is stated: "You shall place a king over you" (Deuteronomy 17:15).

Mitzva 174

לִשְׁמֹעַ מִכָּל בֵּית דִּין הַגָּדוֹל שֶׁיַּעַמְדוּ לָהֶם לְיִשְׂרָאֵל, שֶׁנֶּאֱמַר: "וְעַל הַמִּשְׁפָּט אֲשֶׁר יֹאמְרוּ לְךָ תַּעֲשֶׂה" (דברים יז, יא).

To listen to every High Court [Sanhedrin] that has authority over Israel, as it is stated: "And the judgment that they will say to you, you shall act" (Deuteronomy 17:11).

Mitzva 175

לִנְטוֹת אַחֲרֵי רַבִּים אִם תִּהְיֶה מַחְלֹקֶת בֵּין הַסַּנְהֶדְרִין בְּדִינִין, שֶׁנֶּאֱמַר: "אַחֲרֵי רַבִּים לְהַטֹּת" (שמות כג, ב).

To incline after a majority, if there is a dispute between the members of the Sanhedrin in laws, as it is stated: "Inclining after the majority" (Exodus 23:2).

Mitzva 176

לְמַנּוֹת שׁוֹפְטִים וְשׁוֹטְרִים בְּכָל קָהָל וְקָהָל מִיִּשְׂרָאֵל, שֶׁנֶּאֱמַר: "שֹׁפְטִים וְשֹׁטְרִים תִּתֶּן לְךָ" (דברים טז, יח).

To appoint judges and officers in each and every congregation of Israel, as it is stated: "Judges and officers you shall place for you" (Deuteronomy 16:18).

Mitzva 177

לְהַשְׁווֹת בֵּין בַּעֲלֵי דִּינִין בְּשָׁעָה שֶׁעוֹמְדִין בַּדִּין, שֶׁנֶּאֱמַר: ״בְּצֶדֶק תִּשְׁפֹּט עֲמִיתֶךָ״ (ויקרא יט, טו).

To equate litigants in your treatment of them **when they stand in judgment, as it is stated: "With righteousness you shall judge your counterpart"** (Leviticus 19:15).

Mitzva 178

לְהָעִיד בְּבֵית דִּין לְמִי שֶׁיֵּשׁ לוֹ עֵדוּת, שֶׁנֶּאֱמַר: ״וְהוּא עֵד אוֹ רָאָה אוֹ יָדָע״ (ויקרא ה, א).

That one who has testimony to submit **should testify in court, as it is stated: "And he is a witness who either saw or knew"** (Leviticus 5:1).

Mitzva 179

לַחֲקֹר הָעֵדִים הַרְבֵּה, שֶׁנֶּאֱמַר: ״וְדָרַשְׁתָּ וְחָקַרְתָּ וְשָׁאַלְתָּ הֵיטֵב״ וכו׳ (דברים יג, טו).

To interrogate witnesses thoroughly, as it is stated: "You shall inquire, and interrogate, and ask diligently…" (Deuteronomy 13:15).

Mitzva 180

לַעֲשׂוֹת לְעֵדִים זוֹמְמִים כְּמוֹ שֶׁדִּמּוּ לַעֲשׂוֹת, שֶׁנֶּאֱמַר: ״וַעֲשִׂיתֶם לוֹ כַּאֲשֶׁר״ וכו׳ (דברים יט, יט).

To do to conspiring witnesses as they planned to do to their victim, **as it is stated: "You shall do to him as** he had conspired to do to his brother" (Deuteronomy 19:19).

Mitzva 181

לַעֲרֹף אֶת הָעֶגְלָה כְּמִצְוָתָהּ, שֶׁנֶּאֱמַר: ״וְעָרְפוּ שָׁם אֶת הָעֶגְלָה בַּנָּחַל״ (דברים כא, ד).

To behead the calf in accordance with its mitzva, as it is stated: "And they shall behead the calf there in the ravine" (Deuteronomy 21:4).

Mitzva 182

לְהָכִין שֵׁשׁ עָרֵי מִקְלָט, שֶׁנֶּאֱמַר: ״תָּכִין לְךָ הַדֶּרֶךְ וְשִׁלַּשְׁתָּ אֶת גְּבוּל אַרְצְךָ״ וכו׳ (דברים יט, ג).

To prepare six cities of refuge, as it is stated: "You shall prepare for yourselves the path, and you shall divide the boundaries of your land…" (Deuteronomy 19:3).

Mitzva 183

לָתֵת לַלְוִיִּם עָרִים לָשֶׁבֶת, וְגַם הֵם קוֹלְטוֹת, שֶׁנֶּאֱמַר: ״וְנָתְנוּ לַלְוִיִּם... עָרִים״ (במדבר לה, ב).

To give to the Levites cities for them to **reside** there, **and they too admit** unintentional murderers, like cities of refuge, **as it is stated: "And they shall give to the Levites… cities"** (Numbers 35:2).

Mitzva 184

לַעֲשׂוֹת מַעֲקֶה, שֶׁנֶּאֱמַר: ״וְעָשִׂיתָ מַעֲקֶה לְגַגֶּךָ״ (דברים כב, ח).

To make a parapet, as it is stated: "You shall make a parapet for your roof" (Deuteronomy 22:8).

Mitzva 185

לְאַבֵּד עֲבוֹדָה זָרָה וְכָל מְשַׁמְּשֶׁיהָ, שֶׁנֶּאֱמַר: ״אַבֵּד תְּאַבְּדוּן אֶת כָּל הַמְּקֹמוֹת״ (דברים יב, ב).

To eradicate objects of idolatry and all of its accessories, as it is stated: "You shall eradicate all the places" (Deuteronomy 12:2).

Mitzva 186

לַהֲרֹג אַנְשֵׁי עִיר הַנִּדַּחַת וְלִשְׂרֹף אֶת הָעִיר, שֶׁנֶּאֱמַר: ״וְשָׂרַפְתָּ בָאֵשׁ״ וכו׳ (דברים יג, יז).

To kill the people of a subverted city and to burn down the city, as it is stated: "And you shall burn in fire the city" (Deuteronomy 13:17).

Mitzva 187

לְאַבֵּד שִׁבְעָה עֲמָמִים מֵאֶרֶץ יִשְׂרָאֵל, שֶׁנֶּאֱמַר: ״הַחֲרֵם תַּחֲרִימֵם״ (דברים כ, יז).

To eradicate the seven Canaanite **nations from the Land of Israel, as it is stated: "You shall destroy them"** (Deuteronomy 20:17).

Mitzva 188

לְהַכְרִית זַרְעוֹ שֶׁל עֲמָלֵק, שֶׁנֶּאֱמַר: ״תִּמְחֶה אֶת זֵכֶר עֲמָלֵק״ (דברים כה, יט).

To cut off the seed of Amalek, as it is stated: "You shall expunge the memory of Amalek" (Deuteronomy 25:19).

Mitzva 189

לִזְכֹּר מַה שֶּׁעָשָׂה עֲמָלֵק תָּמִיד, שֶׁנֶּאֱמַר: ״זָכוֹר אֵת אֲשֶׁר עָשָׂה״ וכו׳ (דברים כה, יז).

To remember always what Amalek did, as it is stated: "Remember that which Amalek **did to you…"** (Deuteronomy 25:17).

Mitzva 190

לַעֲשׂוֹת בְּמִלְחֶמֶת הָרְשׁוּת כְּמִשְׁפָּט הַכָּתוּב בַּתּוֹרָה, שֶׁנֶּאֱמַר: ״כִּי תִקְרַב אֶל עִיר״ (דברים כ, י).

To conduct an optional war in the manner written in the Torah, as it is stated: "When you approach a city" (Deuteronomy 20:10).

Mitzva 191

לִמְשֹׁחַ כֹּהֵן לַמִּלְחָמָה, שֶׁנֶּאֱמַר: ״וְהָיָה כְּקָרָבְכֶם אֶל הַמִּלְחָמָה וְנִגַּשׁ הַכֹּהֵן״ (דברים כ, ב).

To anoint a priest for war, as it is stated: "It will be when you advance to the war, the priest shall approach" (Deuteronomy 20:2).

Mitzva 192

לְהַתְקִין יָד בַּמַּחֲנֶה, שֶׁנֶּאֱמַר: "וְיָד תִּהְיֶה לְךָ מִחוּץ לַמַּחֲנֶה" וכו' (דברים כג, יג).

To establish a place in the army camp, **as it is stated: "A place shall be for you outside the camp..."** (Deuteronomy 23:13).

Mitzva 193

לְהַתְקִין יָתֵד, שֶׁנֶּאֱמַר: "וְיָתֵד תִּהְיֶה לְךָ עַל אֲזֵנֶךָ" (דברים כג, יד).

To prepare a spade in that place, **as it is stated: "You shall have a spade for yourselves with your weapons"** (Deuteronomy 23:14).

Mitzva 194

לְהָשִׁיב אֶת הַגָּזֵל, שֶׁנֶּאֱמַר: "וְהֵשִׁיב אֶת הַגְּזֵלָה אֲשֶׁר גָּזָל" (ויקרא ה, כג).

To restore stolen items, as it is stated: "He shall restore the stolen item that he stole" (Leviticus 5:23).

Mitzva 195

לִתֵּן צְדָקָה, שֶׁנֶּאֱמַר: "פָּתֹחַ תִּפְתַּח אֶת יָדְךָ לְאָחִיךָ לַעֲנִיֶּךָ" וכו' (דברים טו, יא).

To give charity, as it is stated: "You shall open your hand to your brother, to your poor..." (Deuteronomy 15:11).

Mitzva 196

לְהַעֲנִיק לְעֶבֶד עִבְרִי, שֶׁנֶּאֱמַר: "הַעֲנֵיק תַּעֲנִיק לוֹ" וכו' (דברים טו, יד), וְכֵן לְאָמָה עִבְרִיָּה.

To give a Hebrew slave a severance gift upon his release, **as it is stated: "You shall grant him..."** (Deuteronomy 15:14), **and the same applies to a Hebrew maidservant.**

Mitzva 197

לְהַלְווֹת לְעָנִי, שֶׁנֶּאֱמַר: "אִם כֶּסֶף תַּלְוֶה אֶת עַמִּי אֶת הֶעָנִי" וכו' (שמות כב, כד). "אִם" זֶה אֵינוֹ רְשׁוּת אֶלָּא מִצְוָה, שֶׁנֶּאֱמַר: "וְהַעֲבֵט תַּעֲבִיטֶנּוּ" (דברים טו, ח).

To lend to the poor, as it is stated: "If you shall lend silver to My people, to the poor..." (Exodus 22:24). **This term "if" does not** indicate that this is merely **an option; rather** it is an **obligatory** positive **mitzva, as it is stated: "And you shall lend him"** (Deuteronomy 15:8).

Mitzva 198

לְהַלְווֹת לְנָכְרִי בְּרִבִּית, שֶׁנֶּאֱמַר: "לַנָּכְרִי תַשִּׁיךְ" (דברים כג, כא). מִפִּי הַשְּׁמוּעָה לָמְדוּ שֶׁזּוֹ מִצְוַת עֲשֵׂה.

To lend to a gentile at interest, as it is stated: "To the foreigner you shall lend" (Deuteronomy 23:21). **The Sages learned, on the basis of the Oral tradition, that this is a positive mitzva.**[a]

NOTES

a. See *Sifrei* on Deuteronomy 23:21 (*Yad Peshuta*).

GLOSSES OF THE RAAVAD

לְהַלְווֹת וְכוּ'. אָמַר אַבְרָהָם: זֶה לֹא נִמְצָא בְּסִפְרִי "לַנָּכְרִי תַשִּׁיךְ זוֹ מִצְוַת עֲשֵׂה" (ספרי כי תצא רסג), אֶלָּא מִשּׁוּם לָאו הַבָּא מִכְּלַל עֲשֵׂה – לְנָכְרִי וְלֹא לְיִשְׂרָאֵל.

"To lend..." Avraham says: This is not found in the *Sifrei*, even though it states: **"to the foreigner you shall lend – this is a positive mitzva"** (*Sifrei, Ki Tetze* 263). **Rather,** it is **due to** the rule that **a prohibition that comes by inference from a positive mitzva** is classified as **a positive mitzva:** You may lend at interest **to a foreigner but not to a Jew.**

Mitzva 199

לְהָשִׁיב הַמַּשְׁכּוֹן לִבְעָלָיו, שֶׁנֶּאֱמַר: "הָשֵׁב תָּשִׁיב לוֹ אֶת הַעֲבוֹט" (דברים כד, יג).

To return a collateral to its owner, as it is stated: "Return him the collateral" (Deuteronomy 24:13).

Mitzva 200

לִתֵּן שְׂכַר שָׂכִיר בִּזְמַנּוֹ, שֶׁנֶּאֱמַר: "בְּיוֹמוֹ תִתֵּן שְׂכָרוֹ" (דברים כד, טו).

To give the wages of a hired laborer at its due time, as it is stated: "On his day you shall give his wage" (Deuteronomy 24:15).

Mitzva 201

לִהְיוֹת הַשָּׂכִיר אוֹכֵל בִּזְמַן שְׂכִירוּתוֹ, שֶׁנֶּאֱמַר: "כִּי תָבֹא בְּכֶרֶם רֵעֶךָ...כִּי תָבֹא בְּקָמַת רֵעֶךָ" (דברים כג, כה-כו).

That a hired laborer may eat during the period of his hire, as it is stated: "When you come into your neighbor's vineyard...When you come into your neighbor's standing grain" (Deuteronomy 23:25–26).

Mitzva 202

לַעֲזֹב מֵעַל חֲבֵרוֹ אוֹ מֵעַל בְּהֶמְתּוֹ, שֶׁנֶּאֱמַר: "עָזֹב תַּעֲזֹב עִמּוֹ" (שמות כג, ה).

To assist with the load **that is upon another** person, **or which is upon his animal, as it is stated: "You shall assist with him"** (Exodus 23:5).

Mitzva 203

לְהָקִים הַמַּשָּׂא עַל הַבְּהֵמָה, שֶׁנֶּאֱמַר: "הָקֵם תָּקִים עִמּוֹ" (דברים כב, ד).

To raise up a burden on his **animal, as it is stated: "You shall raise it up with him"** (Deuteronomy 22:4).

Mitzva 204

לְהָשִׁיב הָאֲבֵדָה, שֶׁנֶּאֱמַר: "הָשֵׁב תְּשִׁיבֵם לְאָחִיךָ" (דברים כב, א).

To return a lost item, as it is stated: "You shall return them to your brother" (Deuteronomy 22:1).

Mitzva 205

לְהוֹכִיחַ הַחוֹטֵא, שֶׁנֶּאֱמַר: "הוֹכֵחַ תּוֹכִיחַ אֶת עֲמִיתֶךָ" (ויקרא יט, יז).

To reprove the sinner, as it is stated: "You shall rebuke your neighbor" (Leviticus 19:17).

Mitzva 206

לֶאֱהֹב כָּל אָדָם מִבְּנֵי בְּרִית, שֶׁנֶּאֱמַר: "וְאָהַבְתָּ לְרֵעֲךָ כָּמוֹךָ" (ויקרא יט, יח).

To love every person who is one of the members of the covenant, i.e., Jews, **as it is stated: "You shall love your neighbor as yourself"** (Leviticus 19:18).

Mitzva 207

לֶאֱהֹב אֶת הַגֵּר, שֶׁנֶּאֱמַר: "וַאֲהַבְתֶּם אֶת הַגֵּר" (דברים י, יט).

To love the convert, as it is stated: "You shall love the stranger" (Deuteronomy 10:19).

Mitzva 208

לְצַדֵּק מֹאזְנַיִם עִם הַמִּשְׁקָלוֹת, שֶׁנֶּאֱמַר: "מֹאזְנֵי צֶדֶק אַבְנֵי צֶדֶק" וכו' (ויקרא יט, לו).

To have accurate scales with their **weights, as it is stated: "Accurate scales, accurate weights..."** (Leviticus 19:36).

Mitzva 209

לְכַבֵּד הַחֲכָמִים, שֶׁנֶּאֱמַר: "מִפְּנֵי שֵׂיבָה תָּקוּם" (ויקרא יט, לב).

To honor the Sages, as it is stated: "You shall rise before the graybeard" (Leviticus 19:32).

Mitzva 210

לְכַבֵּד אָב וָאֵם, שֶׁנֶּאֱמַר: "כַּבֵּד אֶת אָבִיךָ וְאֶת אִמֶּךָ" (שמות כ, יא; דברים ה, טו).

To honor one's father and mother, as it is stated: "Honor your father and your mother" (Exodus 20:12, Deuteronomy 5:15).

Mitzva 211

לְיִרְאָה מֵאָב וָאֵם, שֶׁנֶּאֱמַר: "אִישׁ אִמּוֹ וְאָבִיו תִּירָאוּ" (ויקרא יט, ג).

To revere one's father and mother, as it is stated: "Each of you shall revere his mother and his father" (Leviticus 19:3).

Mitzva 212

לִפְרוֹת וְלִרְבּוֹת, שֶׁנֶּאֱמַר: "פְּרוּ וּרְבוּ" (בראשית ט, ז).

To be fruitful and multiply, as it is stated: "Be fruitful and multiply" (Genesis 9:7).

Mitzva 213

לִבְעֹל בְּקִדּוּשִׁים, שֶׁנֶּאֱמַר: "כִּי יִקַּח אִישׁ אִשָּׁה וּבָא אֵלֶיהָ" (דברים כב, יג).

To have sexual relations through betrothal, as it is stated: "If a man takes a wife, and consorts with her" (Deuteronomy 22:13).

Mitzva 214

לְשַׂמֵּחַ חָתָן אֶת אִשְׁתּוֹ שָׁנָה, שֶׁנֶּאֱמַר: "נָקִי יִהְיֶה לְבֵיתוֹ שָׁנָה אֶחָת" (דברים כד, ה).

That a groom shall rejoice with his wife for a year, as it is stated: "He shall be free for his house one year, and shall gladden his wife, whom he took" (Deuteronomy 24:5).

Mitzva 215

לָמוּל אֶת הַבֵּן, שֶׁנֶּאֱמַר: "וּבַיּוֹם הַשְּׁמִינִי יִמּוֹל בְּשַׂר עָרְלָתוֹ" (ויקרא יב, ג).

To circumcise one's **son, as it is stated: "On the eighth day, the flesh of his foreskin shall be circumcised"*** (Leviticus 12:3).

Mitzva 216

לְיַבֵּם אֵשֶׁת אָח, שֶׁנֶּאֱמַר: "יְבָמָהּ יָבֹא עָלֶיהָ" (דברים כה, ה).

To consummate levirate marriage with one's late, childless **brother's wife, as it is stated: "Her husband's brother shall consort with her"** (Deuteronomy 25:5).

Mitzva 217

לַחֲלֹץ לַיָּבָם, שֶׁנֶּאֱמַר: "וְחָלְצָה נַעֲלוֹ מֵעַל רַגְלוֹ" (דברים כה, ט).

To perform *ḥalitza* with a *yavam*, as it is stated: "And she shall remove his shoe from his foot" (Deuteronomy 25:9).

Mitzva 218

לִשָּׂא אוֹנֵס אֶת אֲנוּסָתוֹ, שֶׁנֶּאֱמַר: "וְלוֹ תִהְיֶה לְאִשָּׁה" (דברים כב, כט).

That a rapist shall marry the woman he raped, as it is stated: "And she shall be a wife to him" (Deuteronomy 22:29).

Mitzva 219

לֵישֵׁב מוֹצִיא שֵׁם רַע עִם אִשְׁתּוֹ כָּל יָמָיו, שֶׁנֶּאֱמַר: "וְלוֹ תִהְיֶה לְאִשָּׁה" (דברים כב, יט).

That a defamer shall stay with his wife all his days, as it is stated: "And she shall be a wife to him" (Deuteronomy 22:19).

FROM THE LUBAVITCHER REBBE

***As it is stated, on the eighth day the flesh of his foreskin shall be circumcised – שֶׁנֶּאֱמַר וּבַיּוֹם הַשְּׁמִינִי יִמּוֹל בְּשַׂר עָרְלָתוֹ:** The Rambam cites this verse, from *Parashat Tazria*, as the source of the mitzva of circumcision, rather than the verse from *Parashat Lekh Lekha* that he quotes in *Sefer HaMitzvot*. The reason is that after the giving of the Torah our obligation in the mitzvot applies only to what was said to Moses, our teacher, not to anything stated beforehand. Nevertheless, *Sefer HaMitzvot* presents God's words to Abraham, because the essential definition of the mitzva is that it is "the covenant of our forefather Abraham," which is a direct continuation of the original covenant that God enacted with Abraham, and in *Sefer HaMitzvot* the Rambam is dealing with the meaning and essence of the mitzva, not the source of the obligation (*Torat Menaḥem*, *Hitvaaduyot*, *Purim* and *Tet-Zayin Adar* 5747; *Likkutei Siḥot* 30, p. 53).

Mitzva 220

To sentence a seducer to the fifty-shekel fine, together with the rest of his laws, as it is stated: "If a man seduces…" (Exodus 22:15).

לָדוּן בִּמְפַתֶּה בַּחֲמִשִּׁים שֶׁקֶל עִם שְׁאָר דִּינָיו, שֶׁנֶּאֱמַר: "כִּי יְפַתֶּה אִישׁ" וכו' (שמות כב, טו, ושם: וְכִי).

Mitzva 221

To treat a beautiful woman captured in war in the manner **that is written** in the Torah, **as it is stated: "And you see in captivity a beautiful woman"** (Deuteronomy 21:11).

לַעֲשׂוֹת לִיפַת תֹּאַר כַּכָּתוּב, שֶׁנֶּאֱמַר: "וְרָאִיתָ בַּשִּׁבְיָה אֵשֶׁת יְפַת תֹּאַר" (דברים כא, יא).

Mitzva 222

To divorce one's wife by means of **a bill** of divorce, **as it is stated: "And he wrote her a bill of divorce, and he placed it in her hand"** (Deuteronomy 24:1, 3).

לְגָרֵשׁ בִּשְׁטָר, שֶׁנֶּאֱמַר: "וְכָתַב לָהּ סֵפֶר כְּרִיתֻת וְנָתַן בְּיָדָהּ" (דברים כד, א; כד, ג).

Mitzva 223

To treat a *sota* in accordance with her ritual, as it is stated: "The priest shall perform for her this entire ritual" (Numbers 5:30).

לַעֲשׂוֹת לַשּׂוֹטָה בְּתוֹרָתָהּ, שֶׁנֶּאֱמַר: "וְעָשָׂה לָהּ הַכֹּהֵן אֵת כָּל הַתּוֹרָה הַזֹּאת" (במדבר ה, ל).

Mitzva 224

To flog the wicked, as it is stated: "The judge shall cast him down, and he shall flog him" (Deuteronomy 25:2).

לְהַלְקוֹת הָרְשָׁעִים, שֶׁנֶּאֱמַר: "וְהִפִּילוֹ הַשֹּׁפֵט וְהִכָּהוּ" (דברים כה, ב).

Mitzva 225

To exile an unwitting murderer, as it is stated: "And he shall live in it until the death of the High **Priest"** (Numbers 35:25).

לְהַגְלוֹת רוֹצֵחַ בִּשְׁגָגָה, שֶׁנֶּאֱמַר: "וְיָשַׁב שָׁם עַד מוֹת הַכֹּהֵן" וכו' (במדבר לה, כה, ושם: וְיָשַׁב בָּהּ).

Mitzva 226

That a court shall execute certain guilty individuals **by the sword, as it is stated: "He shall be avenged"** (Exodus 21:20).

לִהְיוֹת בֵּית דִּין הוֹרְגִין בְּסַיִף, שֶׁנֶּאֱמַר: "נָקֹם יִנָּקֵם" (שמות כא, כ).

Mitzva 227

That a court shall execute certain guilty individuals **by strangulation, as it is stated: "The adulterer and the adulteress shall be put to death"** (Leviticus 20:10).

לִהְיוֹת בֵּית דִּין הוֹרְגִין בְּחֶנֶק, שֶׁנֶּאֱמַר: "מוֹת יוּמַת הַנֹּאֵף וְהַנֹּאָפֶת" (ויקרא כ, י).

Mitzva 228

That a court shall burn certain guilty individuals **in fire, as it is stated: "He and they shall be burned in fire"** (Leviticus 20:14).

לִהְיוֹת בֵּית דִּין שׂוֹרְפִין בָּאֵשׁ, שֶׁנֶּאֱמַר: "בָּאֵשׁ יִשְׂרְפוּ אֹתוֹ וְאֶתְהֶן" (ויקרא כ, יד).

Mitzva 229

That a court shall stone certain guilty individuals **with stones, as it is stated: "And you shall stone them"** (Deuteronomy 22:24).

לִהְיוֹת בֵּית דִּין סוֹקְלִין בַּאֲבָנִים, שֶׁנֶּאֱמַר: "וּסְקַלְתֶּם אֹתָם" (דברים כב, כד).

Mitzva 230

To hang one who is found **liable to hanging, as it is stated: "You shall hang him on a tree"** (Deuteronomy 21:22).

לִתְלוֹת מִי שֶׁנִּתְחַיֵּב תְּלִיָּה, שֶׁנֶּאֱמַר: "וְתָלִיתָ אֹתוֹ עַל עֵץ" (דברים כא, כב).

Mitzva 231

To bury the executed on the **day** of his execution, **as it is stated: "Rather, you shall bury him on that day"** (Deuteronomy 21:23).

לִקְבֹּר הַנֶּהֱרָג בְּיוֹמוֹ, שֶׁנֶּאֱמַר: "כִּי קָבוֹר תִּקְבְּרֶנּוּ בַּיּוֹם הַהוּא" (דברים כא, כג).

Mitzva 232

To treat a Hebrew slave in accordance with his laws, as it is stated: "If you acquire a Hebrew slave…" (Exodus 21:2).

לָדוּן בְּעֶבֶד עִבְרִי כְּהִלְכוֹתָיו, שֶׁנֶּאֱמַר: "כִּי תִקְנֶה עֶבֶד עִבְרִי" וכו' (שמות כא, ב).

Mitzva 233

To designate a Hebrew maidservant as a wife for oneself or one's son, **as it is stated: "To whom she was designated… If he designates her for his son"** (Exodus 21:8–9).

לְיַעֵד אָמָה עִבְרִיָּה, שֶׁנֶּאֱמַר: "אֲשֶׁר לֹא יְעָדָהּ... וְאִם לִבְנוֹ יִיעָדֶנָּה" (שמות כא, ח-ט כנוסח הכתיב, ונוסח הקרי: אֲשֶׁר לוֹ).

Mitzva 234

To redeem a Hebrew maidservant, as it is stated: "He shall facilitate her redemption" (Exodus 21:8).

לִפְדּוֹת אָמָה עִבְרִיָּה, שֶׁנֶּאֱמַר: "וְהֶפְדָּהּ" (שמות כא, ח).

Mitzva 235

To enslave a Canaanite slave forever, as it is stated: "You shall enslave them forever" (Leviticus 25:46).

לַעֲבֹד בְּעֶבֶד כְּנַעֲנִי לְעוֹלָם, שֶׁנֶּאֱמַר: "לְעֹלָם בָּהֶם תַּעֲבֹדוּ" (ויקרא כה, מו).

Mitzva 236

לִהְיוֹת הַחוֹבֵל מְשַׁלֵּם מָמוֹן, שֶׁנֶּאֱמַר: "וְכִי יְרִיבֻן אֲנָשִׁים וְהִכָּה" (שמות כא, יח).

That one who injures another **shall pay money, as it is stated: "If men quarrel** and one **strikes** the other" (Exodus 21:18).

Mitzva 237

לָדוּן בְּנִזְקֵי בְהֵמָה, שֶׁנֶּאֱמַר: "כִּי יִגֹּף שׁוֹר אִישׁ אֶת שׁוֹר רֵעֵהוּ" (שמות כא, לה, ושם: וְכִי).

To adjudicate the damages caused **by an animal, as it is stated: "If the ox of a man shall strike the ox of his neighbor"** (Exodus 21:35).

Mitzva 238

לָדוּן בְּנִזְקֵי הַבּוֹר, שֶׁנֶּאֱמַר: "כִּי יִפְתַּח אִישׁ בּוֹר" (שמות כא, לג, ושם: וְכִי).

To adjudicate the damages caused **by a pit, as it is stated: "If a man shall uncover a pit"** (Exodus 21:33).

Mitzva 239

לָדוּן בְּגַנָּב בְּתַשְׁלוּמִין אוֹ בְּמִיתָה, שֶׁנֶּאֱמַר: "וְכִי יִגְנֹב" וכו' (שמות כא, לז, ושם: כִּי), "אִם בַּמַּחְתֶּרֶת" וכו' (שמות כב, א), "וְגֹנֵב אִישׁ" וגו' (שמות כא, טז).

To adjudicate the cases of **a thief,** who steals property or kidnaps a person, by sentencing him **to payment or death,** respectively, **as it is stated: "If** a man **steals** an ox" (Exodus 21:37); **"if** the thief is found **while excavating…"** (Exodus 22:1); **"one who abducts a man…"** (Exodus 21:16).

GLOSSES OF THE RAAVAD

לָדוּן בְּגַנָּב וְכוּ'. אָמַר אַבְרָהָם: וְלָמָּה לֹא יֵחָשְׁבוּ לִשְׁתַּיִם וְשָׁלֹשׁ.

"To adjudicate the cases of a thief…" Avraham says: Why doesn't the Rambam **count this as two or three** mitzvot?

Mitzva 240

לָדוּן בְּנִזְקֵי הֶבְעֵר, שֶׁנֶּאֱמַר: "כִּי יַבְעֶר אִישׁ שָׂדֶה אוֹ כֶרֶם" (שמות כב, ד).

To adjudicate the damages caused **by grazing,** i.e., the primary categories of Eating and Trampling, **as it is stated: "If a man grazes an animal in a field or a vineyard"** (Exodus 22:4).

Mitzva 241

לָדוּן בְּנִזְקֵי הָאֵשׁ, שֶׁנֶּאֱמַר: "כִּי תֵצֵא אֵשׁ וּמָצְאָה קֹצִים וְנֶאֱכַל" (שמות כב, ה).

To adjudicate the damages caused **by fire,** as it is stated: **"If a fire spreads and encounters thorns, and** a grain pile or standing grain or a field **is consumed"** (Exodus 22:5).

Mitzva 242

לָדוּן בְּדִין שׁוֹמֵר חִנָּם, שֶׁנֶּאֱמַר: "כִּי יִתֵּן אִישׁ אֶל רֵעֵהוּ כֶּסֶף אוֹ כֵלִים" (שמות כב, ו).

To adjudicate cases of an unpaid bailee, as it is stated: "If a man gives silver or vessels to his neighbor to safeguard" (Exodus 22:6).

Mitzva 243

לָדוּן בְּדִין נוֹשֵׂא שָׂכָר וְשׂוֹכֵר, שֶׁנֶּאֱמַר: "כִּי יִתֵּן אִישׁ אֶל רֵעֵהוּ חֲמוֹר אוֹ שׁוֹר" וכו' (שמות כב, ט).

To adjudicate cases of a paid bailee and of **one who hires** a laborer, **as it is stated: "If a man shall give his neighbor a donkey, or an ox…"** (Exodus 22:9).

Mitzva 244

לָדוּן בְּדִין הַשּׁוֹאֵל, שֶׁנֶּאֱמַר: "וְכִי יִשְׁאַל אִישׁ מֵעִם רֵעֵהוּ" (שמות כב, יג).

To adjudicate cases of a borrower, as it is stated: "If a man borrows from his neighbor" (Exodus 22:13).

Mitzva 245

לָדוּן בְּדִין מֶקַח וּמִמְכָּר, שֶׁנֶּאֱמַר: "וְכִי תִמְכְּרוּ מִמְכָּר לַעֲמִיתֶךָ" (ויקרא כה, יד).

To adjudicate cases of buying and selling, as it is stated: "And if you sell a sale item to your counterpart" (Leviticus 25:14).

Mitzva 246

לָדוּן בְּדִין טוֹעֵן וְכוֹפֵר, שֶׁנֶּאֱמַר: "עַל כָּל דְּבַר פֶּשַׁע עַל שׁוֹר" וכו' (שמות כב, ח).

To adjudicate cases of one who issues a claim against another, **and** that person **denies it, as it is stated: "For every matter of transgression, whether for an ox…"** (Exodus 22:8).

Mitzva 247

לְהַצִּיל הַנִּרְדָּף וַאֲפִלּוּ בְּנֶפֶשׁ הָרוֹדֵף, שֶׁנֶּאֱמַר: "וְקַצֹּתָה אֶת כַּפָּהּ" (דברים כה, יב).

To save the pursued even **at** the expense **of the life of the pursuer, as it is stated: "You shall sever her hand"** (Deuteronomy 25:12).

Mitzva 248

לָדוּן בְּדִינֵי נְחָלוֹת, שֶׁנֶּאֱמַר: "אִישׁ כִּי יָמוּת וּבֵן אֵין לוֹ וכו' וְהָיְתָה לִבְנֵי יִשְׂרָאֵל" (במדבר כז, ח-יא).

To adjudicate cases of inheritances,* **as it is stated: "If a man will die, and he has no son… It shall be for the children of Israel** a statute of justice" (Numbers 27:8–11).

FROM THE LUBAVITCHER REBBE

*To adjudicate cases of inheritances – לָדוּן בְּדִינֵי נְחָלוֹת: On a deeper level, the term "inheritances" alludes to the future reward, which is described in similar terms: "The Holy One, Blessed be He, will bequeath to every righteous individual…" (*Uktzin* 3:12). This reward is called an "inheritance" and a "heritage," for it reflects the absolute unification of the Jew with the selfhood of God, just as an heir takes the place of the one who bequeaths to him. It is thus fitting that this is the last mitzva in the list of positive mitzvot, for this is the reward one receives for the full observance of all the mitzvot (*Torat Menaḥem*, *Hitvaaduyot*, *Purim* and *Tet-Zayin Adar* 5747; *Likkutei Siḥot* 30, p. 53).

מִצְוֹת לֹא תַעֲשֶׂה
Negative Mitzvot

Mitzva 1

מִצְוָה רִאשׁוֹנָה מִמִּצְווֹת לֹא תַעֲשֶׂה, שֶׁלֹּא לַעֲלוֹת בְּמַחֲשָׁבָה שֶׁיֵּשׁ שָׁם אֱלוֹהַּ זוּלָתִי יי, שֶׁנֶּאֱמַר: ״לֹא יִהְיֶה לְךָ אֱלֹהִים אֲחֵרִים עַל פָּנָי״ (שמות כ, ב; דברים ה, ו).

The first mitzva of the negative mitzvot is not to contemplate that there is another god apart from the Lord, as it is stated: "You shall have no other gods before Me" (Exodus 20:3, Deuteronomy 5:6).

Mitzva 2

שֶׁלֹּא לַעֲשׂוֹת פֶּסֶל, לֹא יַעֲשֶׂה בְּיָדוֹ וְלֹא יַעֲשׂוּ לוֹ אֲחֵרִים, שֶׁנֶּאֱמַר: ״לֹא תַעֲשֶׂה לְךָ פֶסֶל וְכָל תְּמוּנָה״ (שמות כ, ג).

Not to make an idol. One may not make an idol **with his own hand, and others may not make** one **for him, as it is stated: "You shall not make for you an idol, nor any image"** (Exodus 20:3).

Mitzva 3

שֶׁלֹּא לַעֲשׂוֹת עֲבוֹדָה זָרָה וַאֲפִלּוּ לַאֲחֵרִים, שֶׁנֶּאֱמַר: ״וֵאלֹהֵי מַסֵּכָה לֹא תַעֲשׂוּ לָכֶם״ (ויקרא יט, ד).

Not to make objects of idol worship even for others, as it is stated: "And do not fashion for yourselves cast gods" (Leviticus 19:4).

Mitzva 4

שֶׁלֹּא לַעֲשׂוֹת צוּרוֹת לְנוֹי וְאַף עַל פִּי שֶׁאֵין עוֹבְדִין אוֹתָן, שֶׁנֶּאֱמַר: ״לֹא תַעֲשׂוּן אִתִּי״ וכו׳ (שמות כ, יט).

Not to make images as ornaments, even if they are not worshipped, as it is stated: "You shall not make with Me gods of silver or gods of gold" (Exodus 20:19).

Mitzva 5

שֶׁלֹּא לְהִשְׁתַּחֲווֹת לַעֲבוֹדָה זָרָה אַף עַל פִּי שֶׁאֵין דֶּרֶךְ עֲבוֹדָתָהּ בְּהִשְׁתַּחֲוָיָה, שֶׁנֶּאֱמַר: ״לֹא תִשְׁתַּחֲוֶה לָהֶם״ (שמות כ, ד; דברים ה, ח).

Not to prostrate oneself to an object of idol worship, even if its manner of worship is not through prostration, as it is stated: "You shall not prostrate yourselves to them" (Exodus 20:4, Deuteronomy 5:9).

Mitzva 6

שֶׁלֹּא לַעֲבֹד עֲבוֹדָה זָרָה בִּדְבָרִים שֶׁדַּרְכָּהּ לְהֵעָבֵד בָּהֶן, שֶׁנֶּאֱמַר: ״וְלֹא תָעָבְדֵם״ (שמות כ, ד; כג, כד; דברים ה, ח).

Not to worship idolatry by one of the **manners in which it is worshipped, as it is stated: "You shall not serve them"** (Exodus 20:4, 23:24, Deuteronomy 5:9).

Mitzva 7

שֶׁלֹּא לְהַעֲבִיר לַמֹּלֶךְ, שֶׁנֶּאֱמַר: ״וּמִזַּרְעֲךָ לֹא תִתֵּן לְהַעֲבִיר לַמֹּלֶךְ״ (ויקרא יח, כא).

Not to pass one's child through the fire **to Molekh, as it is stated: "And you shall not give from your offspring to pass to Molekh"** (Leviticus 18:21).

Mitzva 8

שֶׁלֹּא לַעֲשׂוֹת מַעֲשֵׂה אוֹב, שֶׁנֶּאֱמַר: ״אַל תִּפְנוּ אֶל הָאֹבֹת״ (ויקרא יט, לא).

Not to perform the acts of a necromancer, as it is stated: "Do not turn to necromancers" (Leviticus 19:31).

Mitzva 9

שֶׁלֹּא לַעֲשׂוֹת מַעֲשֵׂה יִדְּעוֹנִי, שֶׁנֶּאֱמַר: "וְאֶל הַיִּדְּעֹנִים" וכו' (שם).

Not to perform the acts of a sorcerer, as it is stated: "Or to sorcerers..." (Leviticus 19:31).

Mitzva 10

שֶׁלֹּא לִפְנוֹת אַחַר עֲבוֹדָה זָרָה, שֶׁנֶּאֱמַר: "אַל תִּפְנוּ אֶל הָאֱלִילִם" (ויקרא יט, ד).

Not to go astray after idolatry, as it is stated: "Do not turn to the false gods" (Leviticus 19:4).

Mitzva 11

שֶׁלֹּא לְהָקִים מַצֵּבָה, שֶׁנֶּאֱמַר: "וְלֹא תָקִים לְךָ מַצֵּבָה" (דברים טז, כב).

Not to establish a monument, as it is stated: "You shall not establish for you a monument" (Deuteronomy 16:22).

Mitzva 12

שֶׁלֹּא לִתֵּן אֶבֶן מַשְׂכִּית, שֶׁנֶּאֱמַר: "וְאֶבֶן מַשְׂכִּית לֹא תִתְּנוּ בְּאַרְצְכֶם" (ויקרא כו, א).

Not to place an ornamented stone, as it is stated: "And an ornamented stone you shall not place in your land" (Leviticus 26:1).

Mitzva 13

שֶׁלֹּא לִטַּע אִילָן בַּמִּקְדָּשׁ, שֶׁנֶּאֱמַר: "לֹא תִטַּע לְךָ אֲשֵׁרָה כָּל עֵץ" וכו' (דברים טז, כא).

Not to plant a tree in the Temple, as it is stated: "You shall not plant for you any kind of sacred tree..." (Deuteronomy 16:21).

Mitzva 14

שֶׁלֹּא לִשָּׁבַע בַּעֲבוֹדָה זָרָה לְעוֹבְדֶיהָ וְלֹא מַשְׁבִּיעִין אוֹתָן בָּהּ, שֶׁנֶּאֱמַר: "וְשֵׁם אֱלֹהִים אֲחֵרִים לֹא תַזְכִּירוּ" (שמות כג, יג).

Not to swear by idolatry to its worshippers, nor to have them swear by it, as it is stated: "You shall not mention the name of other gods" (Exodus 23:13).

Mitzva 15

שֶׁלֹּא לְהַדִּיחַ בְּנֵי יִשְׂרָאֵל אַחַר עֲבוֹדָה זָרָה, שֶׁנֶּאֱמַר: "לֹא יִשָּׁמַע עַל פִּיךָ" (שם) – זוֹ אַזְהָרָה לַמַּדִּיחַ.

Not to subvert the children of Israel after idolatry, as it is stated: "They shall not be heard from your mouth" (Exodus 23:13).

Mitzva 16

שֶׁלֹּא לְהָסִית אָדָם מִיִּשְׂרָאֵל אַחַר עֲבוֹדָה זָרָה, שֶׁנֶּאֱמַר בַּמֵּסִית: "וְלֹא יוֹסִפוּ לַעֲשׂוֹת כַּדָּבָר הָרָע" וגו' (דברים יג, יב).

Not to incite a Jewish person after idolatry, as it is stated with regard to the inciter: "And they will not continue to perform like this evil matter..." (Deuteronomy 13:12).

Mitzva 17

שֶׁלֹּא לֶאֱהֹב הַמֵּסִית, שֶׁנֶּאֱמַר: "לֹא תֹאבֶה לוֹ" (דברים יג, ט).

Not to love an inciter, as it is stated: "You shall not accede to him" (Deuteronomy 13:9).

Mitzva 18

שֶׁלֹּא לַעֲזֹב הַשִּׂנְאָה לַמֵּסִית, שֶׁנֶּאֱמַר: "וְלֹא תִשְׁמַע אֵלָיו" (שם).

Not to renounce one's **hatred of an inciter, as it is stated: "And you shall not heed him"** (Deuteronomy 13:9).

Mitzva 19

שֶׁלֹּא לְהַצִּיל הַמֵּסִית, אֶלָּא עוֹמֵד עַל דָּמוֹ, שֶׁנֶּאֱמַר: "וְלֹא תָחוֹס עֵינְךָ עָלָיו" (שם).

Not to rescue an inciter, but rather one should **stand by his blood,**[a] **as it is stated: "And your eye shall not pity him"** (Deuteronomy 13:9).

Mitzva 20

שֶׁלֹּא יְלַמֵּד הַמּוּסָת זְכוּת עַל הַמֵּסִית, שֶׁנֶּאֱמַר: "וְלֹא תַחְמֹל" (שם).

That the incited should not teach a reason **to acquit the inciter, as it is stated: "And you shall not be compassionate"** (Deuteronomy 13:9).

Mitzva 21

שֶׁלֹּא יִשְׁתֹּק הַמּוּסָת מִלְּלַמֵּד חוֹבָה עַל הַמֵּסִית אִם יָדַע לוֹ חוֹבָה, שֶׁנֶּאֱמַר: "וְלֹא תְכַסֶּה עָלָיו" (שם).

That the enticed should not remain silent from teaching a reason to find **the inciter liable, if he knows** a reason why **he is liable, as it is stated: "And you shall not cover up for him"** (Deuteronomy 13:9).

NOTES

a. See Negative Mitzva 297.

Mitzva 22

Not to derive benefit from the coating of a worshipped object, as it is stated: "You shall not covet the silver or gold that is on them" (Deuteronomy 7:25).

שֶׁלֹּא לֵהָנוֹת בְּצִפּוּיֵי נֶעֱבָד, שֶׁנֶּאֱמַר: "לֹא תַחְמֹד כֶּסֶף וְזָהָב עֲלֵיהֶם" (דברים ז, כה).

Mitzva 23

Not to rebuild an idolatrous city to its former condition, as it is stated: "It shall not be rebuilt" (Deuteronomy 13:17).

שֶׁלֹּא לִבְנוֹת עִיר הַנִּדַּחַת לִכְמוֹת שֶׁהָיְתָה, שֶׁנֶּאֱמַר: "לֹא תִבָּנֶה עוֹד" (דברים יג, יז).

Mitzva 24

Not to derive benefit from the property of an idolatrous city, as it is stated: "Nothing of the proscribed **property shall cleave to your hand..."** (Deuteronomy 13:18).

שֶׁלֹּא לֵהָנוֹת בְּמָמוֹן עִיר הַנִּדַּחַת, שֶׁנֶּאֱמַר: "וְלֹא יִדְבַּק בְּיָדְךָ מְאוּמָה" וכו' (דברים יג, יח).

Mitzva 25

Not to derive benefit from idolatry, or from any of its accessories, or from its offering, or from the wine that was poured as a libation to it, as it is stated: "You shall not bring an abomination into your house" (Deuteronomy 7:26).

שֶׁלֹּא לֵהָנוֹת בַּעֲבוֹדָה זָרָה וּבְכָל מְשַׁמְּשֶׁיהָ וּבְתִקְרֹבֶת שֶׁלָּהּ וּבְיַיִן שֶׁנִּתְנַסֵּךְ לָהּ, שֶׁנֶּאֱמַר: "וְלֹא תָבִיא תוֹעֵבָה אֶל בֵּיתֶךָ" (דברים ז, כו).

Mitzva 26

Not to prophesy in the name of idolatry, **as it is stated: "Or who will speak in the name of other gods..."** (Deuteronomy 18:20).

שֶׁלֹּא לְהִתְנַבֵּא בִּשְׁמָהּ, שֶׁנֶּאֱמַר: "וַאֲשֶׁר יְדַבֵּר בְּשֵׁם אֱלֹהִים אֲחֵרִים" וגו' (דברים יח, כ).

Mitzva 27

Not to prophesy falsely, as it is stated: "Who will speak with intent a matter in My name that I did not command him to speak" (Deuteronomy 18:20).

שֶׁלֹּא לְהִתְנַבֵּא בְּשֶׁקֶר, שֶׁנֶּאֱמַר: "אֲשֶׁר יָזִיד לְדַבֵּר דָּבָר בִּשְׁמִי אֵת אֲשֶׁר לֹא צִוִּיתִיו" (שם).

Mitzva 28

Not to listen to one who prophesies in the name of idolatry, as it is stated: "You shall not heed the words of that **prophet"** (Deuteronomy 13:4).

שֶׁלֹּא לִשְׁמֹעַ לַמִּתְנַבֵּא בְּשֵׁם עֲבוֹדָה זָרָה, שֶׁנֶּאֱמַר: "לֹא תִשְׁמַע אֶל דִּבְרֵי הַנָּבִיא" (דברים יג, ד).

Mitzva 29

Not to refrain from executing a false prophet, and that we should not fear him, as it is stated: "You shall not be daunted by him" (Deuteronomy 18:22).

שֶׁלֹּא נִמָּנַע מֵהֲרִיגַת נְבִיא הַשֶּׁקֶר וְלֹא נִירָא מִמֶּנּוּ, שֶׁנֶּאֱמַר: "לֹא תָגוּר מִמֶּנּוּ" (דברים יח, כב).

Mitzva 30

Not to follow the practices of idol worshippers or their customs, as it is stated: "And you shall not follow the practices of the nation" (Leviticus 20:23).

שֶׁלֹּא לָלֶכֶת בְּחֻקּוֹת עוֹבְדֵי עֲבוֹדָה זָרָה וְלֹא בְּמִנְהֲגוֹתָם, שֶׁנֶּאֱמַר: "וְלֹא תֵלְכוּ בְּחֻקֹּת הַגּוֹי" (ויקרא כ, כג).

Mitzva 31

Not to divine, as it is stated: "There shall not be found among you... a diviner" (Deuteronomy 18:10).

שֶׁלֹּא לִקְסֹם, שֶׁנֶּאֱמַר: "לֹא יִמָּצֵא בְךָ וגו' קֹסֵם קְסָמִים" (דברים יח, י).

Mitzva 32

Not to soothsay, as it is stated: "And you shall not practice soothsaying" (Leviticus 19:26).

שֶׁלֹּא לְעוֹנֵן, שֶׁנֶּאֱמַר: "וְלֹא תְעוֹנֵנוּ" (ויקרא יט, כו).

Mitzva 33

Not to practice enchantment, as it is stated: "You shall not practice enchantment" (Leviticus 19:26).

שֶׁלֹּא לְנַחֵשׁ, שֶׁנֶּאֱמַר: "לֹא תְנַחֲשׁוּ" (שם).

Mitzva 34

Not to practice witchcraft, as it is stated: "There shall not be found among you... a warlock" (Deuteronomy 18:10).

שֶׁלֹּא לְכַשֵּׁף, שֶׁנֶּאֱמַר: "לֹא יִמָּצֵא בְךָ" וגו' עַד "וּמְכַשֵּׁף" (דברים יח, י).

Mitzva 35

שֶׁלֹּא לַחֲבֹר חֶבֶר, שֶׁנֶּאֱמַר: "וְחֹבֵר חָבֶר" (דברים יח, יא).

Not to enchant, as it is stated: "Or an enchanter" (Deuteronomy 18:11).

Mitzva 36

שֶׁלֹּא לִשְׁאֹל בְּאוֹב, שֶׁנֶּאֱמַר: "וְשֹׁאֵל אוֹב" (שם).

Not to inquire of a medium, as it is stated: "Or one who inquires of a medium" (Deuteronomy 18:11).

Mitzva 37

שֶׁלֹּא לִשְׁאֹל בְּיִדְּעוֹנִי, שֶׁנֶּאֱמַר: "וְשֹׁאֵל אוֹב וְיִדְּעֹנִי" (שם).

Not to inquire of an oracle, as it is stated: "Or one who inquires of an oracle or a necromancer" (Deuteronomy 18:11).

Mitzva 38

שֶׁלֹּא לִשְׁאֹל בַּחֲלוֹם מִן הַמֵּתִים, שֶׁנֶּאֱמַר: "וְדֹרֵשׁ אֶל הַמֵּתִים" (שם).

Not to direct inquiries to the dead in a dream, as it is stated: "Or one who inquires of the dead" (Deuteronomy 18:11).

Mitzva 39

שֶׁלֹּא תַּעְדֶּה אִשָּׁה עֲדִי אִישׁ, שֶׁנֶּאֱמַר: "לֹא יִהְיֶה כְלִי גֶבֶר עַל אִשָּׁה" (דברים כב, ה).

That a woman may not adorn himself with the adornments of a man, as it is stated: "A man's garment shall not be on a woman" (Deuteronomy 22:5).

Mitzva 40

שֶׁלֹּא יַעְדֶּה הָאִישׁ עֲדִי אִשָּׁה, שֶׁנֶּאֱמַר: "וְלֹא יִלְבַּשׁ גֶּבֶר שִׂמְלַת אִשָּׁה" (שם). מִפְּנֵי שֶׁזֶּה הָיָה מִנְהַג עוֹבְדֵי עֲבוֹדָה זָרָה, וְכֵן מְפֹרָשׁ בְּסִפְרֵי עֲבוֹדָתָהּ.

That a man may not adorn himself with the adornments of a woman, as it is stated: "And a man shall not wear a woman's garment" (Deuteronomy 22:5). The reason is **because this was a custom of idol worshippers, and it is explicitly** stated **as much in the books of its worship.**

Mitzva 41

שֶׁלֹּא לִכְתֹּב בַּגּוּף כְּעוֹבְדֵי עֲבוֹדָה זָרָה, שֶׁנֶּאֱמַר: "וּכְתֹבֶת קַעֲקַע לֹא תִתְּנוּ בָּכֶם" (ויקרא יט, כח).

Not to write on one's **body like idol worshippers** would do, **as it is stated: "And the imprint of a tattoo you shall not place upon you"** (Leviticus 19:28).

Mitzva 42

שֶׁלֹּא לִלְבֹּשׁ שַׁעַטְנֵז כְּמוֹ שֶׁלּוֹבְשִׁין כָּמְרֵי עֲבוֹדָה זָרָה, שֶׁנֶּאֱמַר: "לֹא תִלְבַּשׁ שַׁעַטְנֵז" (דברים כב, יא).

Not to wear diverse kinds of wool and linen, **as priests of idol worship wear, as it is stated: "You shall not wear a mixture of fibers"** (Deuteronomy 22:11).

Mitzva 43

שֶׁלֹּא לְהַקִּיף פְּאַת רֹאשׁ כְּכָמְרֵי עֲבוֹדָה זָרָה, שֶׁנֶּאֱמַר: "לֹא תַקִּפוּ פְּאַת רֹאשְׁכֶם" (ויקרא יט, כז).

Not to round the corners of the hair on the **head like priests of idol worship, as it is stated: "You shall not round the edge of your head"** (Leviticus 19:27).

GLOSSES OF THE RAAVAD

שֶׁלֹּא לְהַקִּיף וְכוּ'. אָמַר אַבְרָהָם: לָאו לַמַּקִּיף וְלָאו לַנִּקָּף, לָאו לַמַּשְׁחִית וְלָאו לַנִּשְׁחָת.

"Not to round..." Avraham says: One **prohibition** applies **to the one who rounds** the head of another, **and** another **prohibition** applies **to the one whose** head **is rounded,** and likewise for the next mitzva, one **prohibition** applies **to the one who mars** the beard of another, **and** one other **prohibition** applies **to the one whose** beard **is marred.**

Mitzva 44

שֶׁלֹּא לְהַשְׁחִית כָּל הַזָּקָן כְּעוֹבְדֵי עֲבוֹדָה זָרָה, שֶׁנֶּאֱמַר: "וְלֹא תַשְׁחִית אֵת פְּאַת זְקָנֶךָ" (שם).

Not to mar the entire beard like priests of idol worship, as it is stated: "And you shall not mar the edge of your beard" (Leviticus 19:27).

Mitzva 45

שֶׁלֹּא לְהִתְגּוֹדֵד כְּעוֹבְדֵי עֲבוֹדָה זָרָה, שֶׁנֶּאֱמַר: "לֹא תִתְגֹּדְדוּ" (דברים יד, א). וּגְדִידָה וּשְׂרִיטָה אַחַת הִיא.

Not to cut oneself like priests of idol worship, as it is stated: "You shall not cut yourselves" (Deuteronomy 14:1). **Cutting and** making **a laceration** (Leviticus 19:28) are **one** and the same.

Mitzva 46

שֶׁלֹּא לִשְׁכֹּן בְּאֶרֶץ מִצְרַיִם לְעוֹלָם, שֶׁנֶּאֱמַר: "לֹא תֹסִפוּן לָשׁוּב" וכו' (דברים יז, טז).

Never to reside in the land of Egypt, as it is stated: "You shall not return again..." (Deuteronomy 17:16).

Mitzva 47

שֶׁלֹּא לָתוּר אַחַר מַחֲשָׁבוֹת הַלֵּב וּרְאִיַּת הָעֵינַיִם, שֶׁנֶּאֱמַר: "וְלֹא תָתוּרוּ אַחֲרֵי לְבַבְכֶם" (במדבר טו, לט).

Not to stray after the thoughts of the heart and the sight of the eyes, as it is stated: "And you shall not rove after your heart and after your eyes" (Numbers 15:39).

Mitzva 48

שֶׁלֹּא לִכְרֹת בְּרִית לְשִׁבְעָה עֲמָמִין, שֶׁנֶּאֱמַר: "לֹא תִכְרֹת לָהֶם בְּרִית" (דברים ז, ב).

Not to enact a covenant with the **seven** Canaanite **nations, as it is stated: "You shall not establish a covenant with them"** (Deuteronomy 7:2).

Mitzva 49

שֶׁלֹּא לְהַחֲיוֹת אָדָם מִשִּׁבְעָה עֲמָמִים, שֶׁנֶּאֱמַר: "לֹא תְחַיֶּה כָּל נְשָׁמָה" (דברים כ, טז).

Not to keep any person from the **seven** Canaanite **nations alive, as it is stated: "You shall not keep any person alive"** (Deuteronomy 20:16).

Mitzva 50

שֶׁלֹּא לָחֹן עַל עוֹבְדֵי עֲבוֹדָה זָרָה, שֶׁנֶּאֱמַר: "וְלֹא תְחָנֵּם" (דברים ז, ב).

Not to show favor to idol worshippers, as it is stated: "And you shall not show them favor" (Deuteronomy 7:2).

Mitzva 51

שֶׁלֹּא לְהוֹשִׁיב עוֹבְדֵי עֲבוֹדָה זָרָה בְּאַרְצֵנוּ, שֶׁנֶּאֱמַר: "לֹא יֵשְׁבוּ בְּאַרְצְךָ" (שמות כג, לג).

Not to settle idol worshippers in our land, as it is stated: "They shall not live in your land" (Exodus 23:33).

Mitzva 52

שֶׁלֹּא לְהִתְחַתֵּן בְּעוֹבְדֵי עֲבוֹדָה זָרָה, שֶׁנֶּאֱמַר: "וְלֹא תִתְחַתֵּן בָּם" (דברים ז, ג).

Not to marry idol worshippers, as it is stated: "You shall not marry them" (Deuteronomy 7:3).

Mitzva 53

שֶׁלֹּא יִשָּׂא עַמּוֹנִי וּמוֹאָבִי בַּת יִשְׂרָאֵל לְעוֹלָם, שֶׁנֶּאֱמַר: "לֹא יָבֹא עַמּוֹנִי וּמוֹאָבִי" וכו' (דברים כג, ד).

That an Amonite and a Moavite may never marry a Jewish woman, as it is stated: "An Amonite or a Moavite shall not enter into the assembly of the Lord" (Deuteronomy 23:4).

Mitzva 54

שֶׁלֹּא לְהַרְחִיק זֶרַע עֵשָׂו מִן הַקָּהָל אֶלָּא עַד שְׁלֹשָׁה דּוֹרוֹת, שֶׁנֶּאֱמַר: "לֹא תְתַעֵב אֲדֹמִי" (דברים כג, ח).

Not to prevent the descendants of Esau from entering the congregation, except for three generations after conversion, **as it is stated: "You shall not despise an Edomite"** (Deuteronomy 23:8).

Mitzva 55

שֶׁלֹּא לְהַרְחִיק מִצְרִי מִלָּבוֹא בַּקָּהָל אֶלָּא עַד שְׁלֹשָׁה דּוֹרוֹת, שֶׁנֶּאֱמַר: "לֹא תְתַעֵב מִצְרִי" (שם).

Not to prevent an Egyptian from entering the congregation, except for three generations after conversion, **as it is stated: "You shall not despise an Egyptian"** (Deuteronomy 23:8).

Mitzva 56

שֶׁלֹּא לִקְרֹא שָׁלוֹם לְעַמּוֹן וּמוֹאָב בַּתְּחִלָּה בִּשְׁעַת הַמִּלְחָמָה כִּשְׁאָר הַגּוֹיִם, שֶׁנֶּאֱמַר: "לֹא תִדְרֹשׁ שְׁלֹמָם וְטֹבָתָם" (דברים כג, ז).

Not to seek peace with Ammon and Moab at a time of war before engaging in warfare with them, as is required when fighting **other nations, as it is stated: "You shall not seek their peace or their welfare"** (Deuteronomy 23:7).

Mitzva 57

שֶׁלֹּא לְהַשְׁחִית אִילָנֵי מַאֲכָל, וְכֵן כָּל שֶׁיֵּשׁ בּוֹ הַשְׁחָתָה אָסוּר, שֶׁנֶּאֱמַר: "לֹא תַשְׁחִית אֶת עֵצָהּ" (דברים כ, יט).

Not to destroy fruit-bearing trees, and any similar act **of destruction** is likewise **prohibited, as it is stated: "You shall not destroy its trees"** (Deuteronomy 20:19).

Mitzva 58

שֶׁלֹּא יִירְאוּ אַנְשֵׁי הַמִּלְחָמָה וְלֹא יִפְחֲדוּ מִן אוֹיְבֵיהֶם בִּשְׁעַת מִלְחָמָה, שֶׁנֶּאֱמַר: "לֹא תַעֲרֹץ מִפְּנֵיהֶם" (דברים ז, כא), "לֹא תִּירָאוּם" (שם ג, כב).

That the men of war shall not fear or be afraid of their enemies during a time of war, as it is stated: "Do not be broken before them" (Deuteronomy 7:21); **"you shall not fear them"** (Deuteronomy 3:22).

GLOSSES OF THE RAAVAD

שֶׁלֹּא יִירְאוּ וְכוּ'. אָמַר אַבְרָהָם: הַבְטָחָה הִיא וְאֵינָהּ אַזְהָרָה.

"Shall not fear..." Avraham says: This is a promise, not an admonition.

Mitzva 59

שֶׁלֹּא יָסוּר מִלִּבֵּנוּ מַעֲשֶׂה עֲמָלֵק הָרַע שֶׁעָשָׂה לָנוּ, שֶׁנֶּאֱמַר: "לֹא תִּשְׁכָּח" (דברים כה, יט).

That the evil deed which Amalek did to us shall not be removed from our hearts, as it is stated: "You shall not forget" (Deuteronomy 25:19).

Mitzva 60

שֶׁאָנוּ מֻזְהָרִין עַל בִּרְכַּת הַשֵּׁם, שֶׁנֶּאֱמַר: "אֱלֹהִים לֹא תְקַלֵּל" (שמות כב, כז), וְנֶאֱמַר בָּעֹנֶשׁ: "וְנֹקֵב שֵׁם יי מוֹת יוּמָת" (ויקרא כד, טז), וְזֶה הַכְּלָל: כָּל שֶׁעָנַשׁ עָלָיו הַכָּתוּב כָּרֵת אוֹ מִיתַת בֵּית דִּין – הֲרֵי זוֹ מִצְוַת לֹא תַעֲשֶׂה, חוּץ מִמִּילָה וּפֶסַח, שֶׁהֵן בְּכָרֵת וְהֵן מִצְוַת עֲשֵׂה.

That we are warned against blessing, a euphemism for cursing, **God, as it is stated: "You shall not curse God"** (Exodus 22:27), **and it is stated as the punishment** for this offense: **"And one who blasphemes the name of the Lord shall be put to death"** (Leviticus 24:16). **This is the** general **rule: Any** offense **which the verse punished** with **excision** [*karet*] **or** the **court-imposed death penalty is a negative mitzva, except for circumcision and the Paschal offering, which are** punishable **by excision and** yet **are positive mitzvot.**

Mitzva 61

שֶׁלֹּא לַעֲבֹר עַל שְׁבוּעַת בִּטּוּי, שֶׁנֶּאֱמַר: "וְלֹא תִשָּׁבְעוּ בִשְׁמִי לַשָּׁקֶר" (ויקרא יט, יב).

Not to violate "an oath on a statement," i.e., a case where one swore to prohibit himself in something or to obligate himself to perform an action, **as it is stated: "You shall not take an oath in My name falsely"** (Leviticus 19:12).

Mitzva 62

שֶׁלֹּא לִשָּׁבַע לַשָּׁוְא, שֶׁנֶּאֱמַר: "לֹא תִשָּׂא אֶת שֵׁם יי אֱלֹהֶיךָ לַשָּׁוְא" (שמות כ, ו; דברים ה, י).

Not to swear in vain, as it is stated: "You shall not take the name of the Lord your God in vain" (Exodus 20:7, Deuteronomy 5:11).

Mitzva 63

שֶׁלֹּא לְחַלֵּל אֶת הַשֵּׁם הַקָּדוֹשׁ בָּרוּךְ הוּא, שֶׁנֶּאֱמַר: "וְלֹא תְחַלְּלוּ אֶת שֵׁם קָדְשִׁי" (ויקרא כב, לב).

Not to desecrate the holy name, which is blessed, as it is stated: "And you shall not profane My holy name" (Leviticus 22:32).

Mitzva 64

שֶׁלֹּא לְנַסּוֹת אֶת דְּבַר יי, שֶׁנֶּאֱמַר: "לֹא תְנַסּוּ אֶת יי אֱלֹהֵיכֶם" (דברים ו, טז).

Not to test the word of God, as it is stated: "You shall not test the Lord your God" (Deuteronomy 6:16).

Mitzva 65

שֶׁלֹּא לְאַבֵּד בֵּית הַמִּקְדָּשׁ אוֹ בָּתֵּי כְנֵסִיּוֹת וּבָתֵּי מִדְרָשׁוֹת, וְכֵן אֵין מוֹחֲקִין הַשֵּׁמוֹת הַמְקֻדָּשִׁין וְאֵין מְאַבְּדִין אֶת כִּתְבֵי הַקֹּדֶשׁ, שֶׁנֶּאֱמַר: "אַבֵּד תְּאַבְּדוּן וכו' וַאֲשֵׁרֵיהֶם תִּשְׂרְפוּן... לֹא תַעֲשׂוּן כֵּן לַיי אֱלֹהֵיכֶם" (דברים יב, ב-ד).

Not to destroy the Temple or synagogues or houses of study, and likewise one may not erase the holy names of God **or destroy the holy writings, as it is stated: "You shall eradicate... and their sacred trees you shall burn... You shall not do so to the Lord your God"** (Deuteronomy 12:2–4).

Mitzva 66

שֶׁלֹּא יָלִין הַצָּלוּב עַל הָעֵץ, שֶׁנֶּאֱמַר: "לֹא תָלִין נִבְלָתוֹ עַל הָעֵץ" (דברים כא, כג).

That the body **of the crucified shall not remain overnight on the tree, as it is stated: "His carcass shall not remain overnight upon the tree"** (Deuteronomy 21:23).

Mitzva 67

שֶׁלֹּא לְהַשְׁבִּית שְׁמִירָה סָבִיב לַמִּקְדָּשׁ, שֶׁנֶּאֱמַר: "וּשְׁמַרְתֶּם אֵת מִשְׁמֶרֶת הַקֹּדֶשׁ" (במדבר יח, ה).

Not to remove the watch around the Temple, as it is stated: "You shall keep the commission of the sacred" (Numbers 18:5).

Mitzva 68

שֶׁלֹּא יִכָּנֵס כֹּהֵן לַהֵיכָל בְּכָל עֵת, שֶׁנֶּאֱמַר: "וְאַל יָבֹא בְכָל עֵת אֶל הַקֹּדֶשׁ" (ויקרא טז, ב).

That a priest may not enter the Sanctuary at all times, as it is stated: "That he shall not come at all times into the Sanctum" (Leviticus 16:2).

Mitzva 69

שֶׁלֹּא יִכָּנֵס בַּעַל מוּם מִן הַמִּזְבֵּחַ וְלִפְנִים לַהֵיכָל, שֶׁנֶּאֱמַר: "אַךְ אֶל הַפָּרֹכֶת לֹא יָבֹא" (ויקרא כא, כג).

That a blemished person may not enter from the altar and inward, in the direction **of the Sanctuary, as it is stated: "However, he shall not come to the curtain"** (Leviticus 21:23).

Mitzva 70

שֶׁלֹּא יַעֲבֹד בַּעַל מוּם, שֶׁנֶּאֱמַר: "אֲשֶׁר יִהְיֶה בוֹ מוּם לֹא יִקְרַב" (ויקרא כא, יז).

That a blemished person may not perform the Temple **service, as it is stated: "In whom there shall be a blemish shall not approach"** (Leviticus 21:17).

Mitzva 71

שֶׁלֹּא יַעֲבֹד בַּעַל מוּם עוֹבֵר, שֶׁנֶּאֱמַר: "כָּל אִישׁ אֲשֶׁר בּוֹ מוּם לֹא יִקְרָב" (ויקרא כא, יח).

That a person **with a temporary blemish may not perform the** Temple **service, as it is stated: "Any man in whom there is a blemish shall not approach"** (Leviticus 21:18).

Mitzva 72

שֶׁלֹּא יִתְעַסְּקוּ הַלְוִיִּם בַּעֲבוֹדַת הַכֹּהֲנִים וְלֹא כֹּהֲנִים בַּעֲבוֹדַת הַלְוִיִּם, שֶׁנֶּאֱמַר: "אַךְ אֶל כְּלֵי הַקֹּדֶשׁ וְאֶל הַמִּזְבֵּחַ לֹא יִקְרָבוּ וְלֹא יָמֻתוּ גַם הֵם גַּם אַתֶּם" (במדבר יח, ג).

That the Levites shall not engage in the Temple **service of the priests, nor the priests in the service of the Levites, as it is stated: "However, they shall not come close to the sacred vessels and to the altar, and neither they nor you will die"** (Numbers 18:3).

Mitzva 73

שֶׁלֹּא יִכָּנֵס לַמִּקְדָּשׁ וְלֹא יוֹרֶה בַּתּוֹרָה שְׁתוּי יַיִן, שֶׁנֶּאֱמַר: "יַיִן וְשֵׁכָר אַל תֵּשְׁתְּ...בְּבֹאֲכֶם וכו' וּלְהוֹרֹת אֶת בְּנֵי יִשְׂרָאֵל" (ויקרא י, ט-יא).

That those who are drunk with wine may not enter the Temple or issue Torah rulings, as it is stated: "You shall not drink wine or intoxicating drink…upon your entry…and to teach the children of Israel" (Leviticus 10:9–11).

Mitzva 74

שֶׁלֹּא יַעֲבֹד הַזָּר בַּמִּקְדָּשׁ, שֶׁנֶּאֱמַר: "וְזָר לֹא יִקְרַב אֲלֵיכֶם" (במדבר יח, ד).

That a non-priest may not serve in the Temple, as it is stated: "A non-priest shall not approach you" (Numbers 18:4).

Mitzva 75

שֶׁלֹּא יַעֲבֹד כֹּהֵן טָמֵא, שֶׁנֶּאֱמַר: "וְיִנָּזְרוּ מִקָּדְשֵׁי בְנֵי יִשְׂרָאֵל" וכו' (ויקרא כב, ב).

That a ritually impure priest may not serve in the Temple, as it is stated: "That they shall refrain from the sacred items of the children of Israel" (Leviticus 22:2).

Mitzva 76

שֶׁלֹּא יַעֲבֹד כֹּהֵן טְבוּל יוֹם עַד שֶׁיַּעֲרִיב שִׁמְשׁוֹ, שֶׁנֶּאֱמַר: "וְלֹא יְחַלְּלוּ שֵׁם אֱלֹהֵיהֶם" (ויקרא כא, ו).

That a priest who immersed that day may not perform the Temple **service until the sun has set upon him, as it is stated: "And they shall not profane the name of their God"** (Leviticus 21:6).

Mitzva 77

שֶׁלֹּא יִכָּנֵס טָמֵא לָעֲזָרָה, שֶׁנֶּאֱמַר: "וְלֹא יְטַמְּאוּ אֶת מַחֲנֵיהֶם" (במדבר ה, ג) – זֶה מַחֲנֵה שְׁכִינָה.

That a ritually impure person may not enter the Temple **courtyard, as it is stated: "And they shall not render impure their camp"** (Numbers 5:3) – **this is** referring to **the camp of the Divine Presence.**

Mitzva 78

שֶׁלֹּא יִכָּנֵס טָמֵא לְמַחֲנֵה לְוִיָּה שֶׁכְּנֶגְדּוֹ לְדוֹרוֹת הַר הַבַּיִת, שֶׁנֶּאֱמַר: "לֹא יָבֹא אֶל תּוֹךְ הַמַּחֲנֶה" (דברים כג, יא) – זֶה מַחֲנֵה לְוִיָּה.

That a ritually impure person may not enter the Levite camp, whose corresponding place throughout **the generations is the Temple mount, as it is stated: "He shall not come into the camp"** (Deuteronomy 23:11) – **this is** referring to **the Levite camp.**

Mitzva 79

שֶׁלֹּא לִבְנוֹת אַבְנֵי מִזְבֵּחַ גָּזִית, שֶׁנֶּאֱמַר: "לֹא תִבְנֶה אֶתְהֶן גָּזִית" (שמות כ, כא).

Not to build an altar of hewn stones, as it is stated: "You shall not build it of hewn stones" (Exodus 20:22).

Mitzva 80

שֶׁלֹּא לִפְסֹעַ עַל הַמִּזְבֵּחַ, שֶׁנֶּאֱמַר: "וְלֹא תַעֲלֶה בְמַעֲלֹת עַל מִזְבְּחִי" (שמות כ, כב).

Not to take large **steps** by ascending on stairs **to the altar, as it is stated: "You shall not ascend on stairs to My altar"** (Exodus 20:23).

Mitzva 81

שֶׁלֹּא לְכַבּוֹת אֵשׁ הַמִּזְבֵּחַ, שֶׁנֶּאֱמַר: "אֵשׁ תָּמִיד תּוּקַד עַל הַמִּזְבֵּחַ לֹא תִכְבֶּה" (ויקרא ו, ו).

Not to extinguish the fire of the altar, as it is stated: "A perpetual fire shall be kept burning upon the altar; it shall not be extinguished" (Leviticus 6:6).

Mitzva 82

שֶׁלֹּא לְהַקְטִיר וּלְהַקְרִיב בְּמִזְבַּח הַזָּהָב, שֶׁנֶּאֱמַר: "לֹא תַעֲלוּ עָלָיו קְטֹרֶת זָרָה" וכו' (שמות ל, ט).

Not to burn or sacrifice offerings **upon the golden altar, as it is stated: "You shall not offer up on it strange incense…"** (Exodus 30:9).

Mitzva 83

שֶׁלֹּא לַעֲשׂוֹת בְּמַתְכֹּנֶת שֶׁמֶן הַמִּשְׁחָה, שֶׁנֶּאֱמַר: "וּבְמַתְכֻּנְתּוֹ לֹא תַעֲשׂוּ כָּמֹהוּ" (שמות ל, לב).

Not to make oil for personal use **according to the formula of the anointing oil, as it is stated: "And you shall not make like it according to its formula"** (Exodus 30:32).

Mitzva 84

שֶׁלֹּא לָסוּךְ בְּשֶׁמֶן הַמִּשְׁחָה זָר, שֶׁנֶּאֱמַר: "עַל בְּשַׂר אָדָם לֹא יִיסָךְ" (שם).

Not to anoint a non-priest with the anointing oil, as it is stated: "It shall not be poured on a person's flesh" (Exodus 30:32).

Mitzva 85

שֶׁלֹּא לַעֲשׂוֹת בְּמַתְכֹּנֶת הַקְּטֹרֶת, שֶׁנֶּאֱמַר: "וּבְמַתְכֻּנְתָּהּ לֹא תַעֲשׂוּ לָכֶם" (שמות ל, לז).

Not to make incense for personal use **according to the formula of the incense, as it is stated: "You shall not make for yourselves according to its formula"** (Exodus 30:37).

Mitzva 86

שֶׁלֹּא לְהוֹצִיא בַּדֵּי הָאָרוֹן, שֶׁנֶּאֱמַר: "לֹא יָסֻרוּ מִמֶּנּוּ" (שמות כה, טו).

Not to remove the staves from the ark, as it is stated: "They shall not be removed from it" (Exodus 25:15).

Mitzva 87

שֶׁלֹּא יִזַּח הַחֹשֶׁן מֵעַל הָאֵפוֹד, שֶׁנֶּאֱמַר: "וְלֹא יִזַּח הַחֹשֶׁן" וכו' (שמות כח, כח; לט, כא).

That the breastplate shall not be detached from upon the ephod, as it is stated: "And the breast piece shall not be detached…" (Exodus 28:28, 39:21).

Mitzva 88

שֶׁלֹּא יִקָּרַע הַמְּעִיל, שֶׁנֶּאֱמַר: "כְּפִי תַחְרָא יִהְיֶה לּוֹ לֹא יִקָּרֵעַ" (שמות כח, לב).

That the robe shall not be rent, as it is stated: "Like the opening of a coat of mail it shall be for it; it shall not be rent" (Exodus 28:32).

Mitzva 89

שֶׁלֹּא לְהַעֲלוֹת קָדָשִׁים בַּחוּץ, שֶׁנֶּאֱמַר: "הִשָּׁמֶר לְךָ פֶּן תַּעֲלֶה עֹלֹתֶיךָ" וכו' (דברים יב, יג).

Not to offer sacrificial animals **outside** the Temple courtyard, **as it is stated: "Beware, lest you offer up your burnt offerings…"** (Deuteronomy 12:13).

Mitzva 90

שֶׁלֹּא לִשְׁחֹט קָדָשִׁים בַּחוּץ, שֶׁנֶּאֱמַר: "אֲשֶׁר יִשְׁחַט שׁוֹר אוֹ כֶשֶׂב וכו' וְאֶל פֶּתַח אֹהֶל מוֹעֵד וכו' וְנִכְרַת" (ויקרא יז, ג-ד).

Not to slaughter sacrificial animals **outside** the Temple courtyard, **as it is stated: "Who shall slaughter a bull or a sheep… and** he did not bring it **to the entrance of the Tent of Meeting… and** that man **shall be excised"** (Leviticus 17:3–4).

Mitzva 91

שֶׁלֹּא לְהַקְדִּישׁ בַּעֲלֵי מוּמִין לַמִּזְבֵּחַ, שֶׁנֶּאֱמַר: "כֹּל אֲשֶׁר בּוֹ מוּם לֹא תַקְרִיבוּ" (ויקרא כב, כ) – זֶה הוּא אִסּוּר הֶקְדֵּשׁוֹ.

Not to consecrate blemished animals **to the altar, as it is stated: "Any in which there is a blemish you shall not offer"** (Leviticus 22:20) – **this is** the **prohibition** against **consecrating** such an animal.

Mitzva 92

שֶׁלֹּא לִשְׁחֹט בַּעֲלֵי מוּמִין לְשֵׁם קָרְבָּן, שֶׁנֶּאֱמַר: "לֹא תַקְרִיבוּ אֵלֶּה לַיי" (ויקרא כב, כב).

Not to slaughter blemished animals **blemished for the purpose of an offering, as it is stated: "You shall not offer these to the Lord"** (Leviticus 22:22).

Mitzva 93

שֶׁלֹּא לִזְרֹק דַּם בַּעֲלֵי מוּמִין לְגַבֵּי הַמִּזְבֵּחַ, שֶׁנֶּאֱמַר בְּבַעֲלֵי מוּמִין: "לֹא תַקְרִיבוּ לַיי" (ויקרא כב, כד), וְזֶה הוּא אִסּוּר זְרִיקַת דָּמוֹ.

Not to sprinkle the blood of blemished animals **upon the altar, as it is stated, with regard to blemished** animals: **"You shall not present to the Lord"** (Leviticus 22:24), **and this is** referring to **the prohibition** against **sprinkling its blood.**

Mitzva 94

שֶׁלֹּא לְהַקְטִיר אֵמוּרֵי בַּעֲלֵי מוּמִין, שֶׁנֶּאֱמַר: "וְאִשֶּׁה לֹא תִתְּנוּ מֵהֶם עַל הַמִּזְבֵּחַ" (ויקרא כב, כב).

Not to burn the fats of blemished animals, **as it is stated: "And you shall not place them as a fire offering upon the altar"** (Leviticus 22:22).

Mitzva 95

שֶׁלֹּא לְהַקְרִיב בַּעַל מוּם עוֹבֵר, שֶׁנֶּאֱמַר: "לֹא תִזְבַּח לַיי אֱלֹהֶיךָ שׁוֹר וָשֶׂה אֲשֶׁר יִהְיֶה בוֹ מוּם" (דברים יז, א) – זֶה מוּם עוֹבֵר.

Not to sacrifice an animal **with a temporary blemish, as it is stated: "You shall not slaughter to the Lord your God an ox, or a lamb, in which there is a blemish"** (Deuteronomy 17:1) – **this is a temporary blemish.**

Mitzva 96

שֶׁלֹּא לְהַקְרִיב בַּעַל מוּם מִיַּד הַגּוֹיִם, שֶׁנֶּאֱמַר: "וּמִיַּד בֶּן נֵכָר לֹא תַקְרִיבוּ" (ויקרא כב, כה).

Not to sacrifice a blemished animal even when received **from gentiles, as it is stated: "And from the hand of a foreigner you shall not present"** (Leviticus 22:25).

Mitzva 97

שֶׁלֹּא לִתֵּן מוּם בְּקָדָשִׁים, שֶׁנֶּאֱמַר: "כָּל מוּם לֹא יִהְיֶה בּוֹ" (ויקרא כב, כא), כְּלוֹמַר: וְאַל תִּתֵּן בּוֹ מוּם.

Not to inflict a blemish upon sacrificial animals, **as it is stated: "No blemish shall be in it"** (Leviticus 22:21). **In other words, do not inflict a blemish upon it.**

Mitzva 98

שֶׁלֹּא לְהַקְרִיב שְׂאֹר אוֹ דְּבַשׁ, שֶׁנֶּאֱמַר: "כִּי כָל שְׂאֹר וְכָל דְּבַשׁ לֹא תַקְטִירוּ" וכו' (ויקרא ב, יא).

Not to sacrifice leaven or honey upon the altar, **as it is stated: "For all leaven and all honey, you shall not burn…"** (Leviticus 2:11).

Mitzva 99

שֶׁלֹּא לְהַקְרִיב תָּפֵל, שֶׁנֶּאֱמַר: "וְלֹא תַשְׁבִּית מֶלַח בְּרִית אֱלֹהֶיךָ" (ויקרא ב, יג).

Not to sacrifice an offering **that has not been salted, as it is stated: "You shall not withhold the salt of the covenant of your God"** (Leviticus 2:13).

Mitzva 100

שֶׁלֹּא לְהַקְרִיב אֶתְנָן וּמְחִיר, שֶׁנֶּאֱמַר: "לֹא תָבִיא אֶתְנַן זוֹנָה וּמְחִיר כֶּלֶב" (דברים כג, יט).

Not to sacrifice the fee of a harlot **or the price** of a dog, **as it is stated: "You shall not bring the fee of a harlot or the price of a dog"** (Deuteronomy 23:19).

Mitzva 101

שֶׁלֹּא לִשְׁחֹט אוֹתוֹ וְאֶת בְּנוֹ, שֶׁנֶּאֱמַר: "אֹתוֹ וְאֶת בְּנוֹ לֹא תִשְׁחֲטוּ" (ויקרא כב, כח).

Not to slaughter an animal **and its offspring** on the same day, **as it is stated: "It and its offspring you shall not slaughter** on one day" (Leviticus 22:28).

Mitzva 102

שֶׁלֹּא לִתֵּן זַיִת בְּמִנְחַת חוֹטֵא, שֶׁנֶּאֱמַר: "לֹא יָשִׂים עָלֶיהָ שֶׁמֶן" (ויקרא ה, יא).

Not to place olive oil on the meal offering of a sinner, as it is stated: "He shall not place oil on it" (Leviticus 5:11).

Mitzva 103

שֶׁלֹּא לִתֵּן עָלֶיהָ לְבֹנָה, שֶׁנֶּאֱמַר: "וְלֹא יִתֵּן עָלֶיהָ לְבֹנָה" (שם).

Not to place frankincense on the meal offering of a sinner, **as it is stated: "Nor shall he place frankincense on it"** (Leviticus 5:11).

Mitzva 104

שֶׁלֹּא לִתֵּן זַיִת בְּקָרְבַּן שׁוֹטָה, שֶׁנֶּאֱמַר: "לֹא יִצֹק עָלָיו שֶׁמֶן" (במדבר ה, טו).

Not to place olive oil on the offering of a *sota*, as it is stated: "He shall not pour oil upon it" (Numbers 5:15).

Mitzva 105

שֶׁלֹּא לִתֵּן עָלָיו לְבֹנָה, שֶׁנֶּאֱמַר: "וְלֹא יִתֵּן עָלָיו לְבֹנָה" (שם).

Not to place frankincense on the offering of a *sota*, **as it is stated: "And he shall not place frankincense upon it"** (Numbers 5:15).

Mitzva 106

שֶׁלֹּא לְהָמִיר, שֶׁנֶּאֱמַר: "לֹא יַחֲלִיפֶנּוּ וְלֹא יָמִיר אֹתוֹ" (ויקרא כז, י).

Not to substitute a consecrated animal for another animal, **as it is stated: "One shall not exchange it and not substitute it"** (Leviticus 27:10).

Mitzva 107

שֶׁלֹּא לְשַׁנּוֹת הַקֳּדָשִׁים מִקָּרְבָּן לְקָרְבָּן, שֶׁנֶּאֱמַר בִּבְכוֹר: "לֹא יַקְדִּישׁ אִישׁ אֹתוֹ" (ויקרא כז, כו), כְּלוֹמַר לֹא יַקְדִּישֶׁנּוּ לְקָרְבָּן אַחֵר.

Not to change sacrificial animals **from one type of offering for another offering, as it is stated with regard to a firstborn** animal: **"No man shall consecrate it"** (Leviticus 27:26). **In other words,** one **shall not consecrate it to be a different offering.**

Mitzva 108

שֶׁלֹּא לִפְדּוֹת בְּכוֹר בְּהֵמָה טְהוֹרָה, שֶׁנֶּאֱמַר: "אַךְ בְּכוֹר שׁוֹר וכו' לֹא תִפְדֶּה" (במדבר יח, יז).

Not to redeem the male firstborn of a kosher animal, as it is stated: "However, the firstborn of an ox…you shall not redeem" (Numbers 18:17).

Mitzva 109

שֶׁלֹּא לִמְכֹּר מַעְשַׂר בְּהֵמָה, שֶׁנֶּאֱמַר: "לֹא יִגָּאֵל" (ויקרא כז, לג).

Not to sell an animal tithe, as it is stated: "It shall not be redeemed" (Leviticus 27:33).

Mitzva 110

שֶׁלֹּא לִמְכֹּר שְׂדֵה הַחֵרֶם, שֶׁנֶּאֱמַר: "כָּל חֵרֶם...לֹא יִמָּכֵר" (ויקרא כז, כח).

Not to sell a proscribed field, as it is stated: "Anything proscribed ... shall not be sold" (Leviticus 27:28).

Mitzva 111

שֶׁלֹּא לִפְדּוֹת שְׂדֵה הַחֵרֶם, שֶׁנֶּאֱמַר: "וְלֹא יִגָּאֵל" (שם).

Not to redeem a proscribed field, as it is stated: "And shall not be redeemed" (Leviticus 27:28).

Mitzva 112

שֶׁלֹּא יַבְדִּיל בְּחַטַּאת הָעוֹף, שֶׁנֶּאֱמַר: "וּמָלַק אֶת רֹאשׁוֹ מִמּוּל עָרְפּוֹ וְלֹא יַבְדִּיל" (ויקרא ה, ח).

Not to separate the head of **a bird sin offering** from its body, **as it is stated: "He shall pinch its head adjacent to its nape, but shall not separate"** (Leviticus 5:8).

Mitzva 113

שֶׁלֹּא לַעֲבֹד בַּקֳּדָשִׁים, שֶׁנֶּאֱמַר: "לֹא תַעֲבֹד בִּבְכֹר שׁוֹרֶךָ" (דברים טו, יט).

Not to perform labor with sacrificial animals, **as it is stated: "You shall not work with the firstborn of your ox"** (Deuteronomy 15:19).

Mitzva 114

שֶׁלֹּא לִגְזֹז אֶת הַקֳּדָשִׁים, שֶׁנֶּאֱמַר: "וְלֹא תָגֹז בְּכוֹר צֹאנֶךָ" (שם).

Not to shear sacrificial animals, **as it is stated: "And you shall not shear the firstborn of your flock"** (Deuteronomy 15:19).

Mitzva 115

שֶׁלֹּא יִשְׁחַט הַפֶּסַח וְהֶחָמֵץ קַיָּם, שֶׁנֶּאֱמַר: "לֹא תִשְׁחַט עַל חָמֵץ דַּם זִבְחִי" (שמות לד, כה).

Not to sacrifice the Paschal offering while one's **leaven is still in existence, as it is stated: "You shall not slaughter with leavened bread the blood of My offering"** (Exodus 34:25).

Mitzva 116

שֶׁלֹּא לְהַנִּיחַ אֵמוּרֵי הַפֶּסַח עַד שֶׁיִּפָּסְלוּ בְּלִינָה, שֶׁנֶּאֱמַר: "וְלֹא יָלִין חֵלֶב חַגִּי עַד בֹּקֶר" (שמות כג, יח).

Not to leave the sacrificial parts of the Paschal offering until they are disqualified by being left overnight, as it is stated: "And the fat of My offering shall not remain overnight until morning" (Exodus 23:18).

Mitzva 117

שֶׁלֹּא לְהוֹתִיר מִבְּשַׂר הַפֶּסַח, שֶׁנֶּאֱמַר: "לֹא תוֹתִירוּ מִמֶּנּוּ עַד בֹּקֶר" (ויקרא כב, ל).

Not to leave over any of the flesh of the Paschal offering, as it is stated: "You shall not leave from it until morning" (Leviticus 22:30).

Mitzva 118

שֶׁלֹּא לְהוֹתִיר מֵחֲגִיגַת אַרְבָּעָה עָשָׂר לַיּוֹם הַשְּׁלִישִׁי, שֶׁנֶּאֱמַר: "וְלֹא יָלִין מִן הַבָּשָׂר" (דברים טז, ד). מִפִּי הַשְּׁמוּעָה לָמְדוּ שֶׁבִּבְשַׂר חֲגִיגַת אַרְבָּעָה עָשָׂר הַכָּתוּב מְדַבֵּר, וְזֶה שֶׁנֶּאֱמַר "לַבֹּקֶר" (שם) – לְבָקְרוֹ שֶׁל יוֹם שֵׁנִי שֶׁל פֶּסַח, שֶׁהוּא שְׁלִישִׁי לִשְׁחִיטָה.

Not to leave over any **of the festival** peace **offering to the third day, as it is stated: "And the meat ... shall not remain overnight** until morning" (Deuteronomy 16:4). The Sages **learned, on the basis of the** Oral **tradition, that the verse is speaking of the flesh of the festival** peace **offering of the fourteenth** of Nisan, **and when it states "until morning"** it means **until the morning of the second day of Passover, which** is the **third** day **to the slaughter** of the offering (see *Pesaḥim* 71a).

Mitzva 119

שֶׁלֹּא לְהוֹתִיר מִבְּשַׂר פֶּסַח שֵׁנִי עַד בֹּקֶר, שֶׁנֶּאֱמַר: "לֹא יַשְׁאִירוּ מִמֶּנּוּ עַד בֹּקֶר" (במדבר ט, יב).

Not to leave over any **of the flesh of the second Paschal offering until** the **morning, as it is stated: "They shall not leave from it until the morning"** (Numbers 9:12).

Mitzva 120

שֶׁלֹּא לְהוֹתִיר מִבְּשַׂר הַתּוֹדָה עַד בֹּקֶר, שֶׁנֶּאֱמַר: "לֹא תוֹתִירוּ מִמֶּנּוּ עַד בֹּקֶר" (ויקרא כב, ל), וְהוּא הַדִּין לִשְׁאָר הַקֳּדָשִׁים שֶׁאֵין מַנִּיחִין אוֹתָן לְאַחַר זְמַן אֲכִילָתָן.

Not to leave over any **of the flesh of a thanks offering, as it is stated: "You shall not leave from it until morning"** (Leviticus 22:30). **The same is true of the other sacrificial** animals, **that one may not leave them** until **after the** fixed **time for their consumption.**

Mitzva 121

שֶׁלֹּא לִשְׁבֹּר עֶצֶם בַּפֶּסַח, שֶׁנֶּאֱמַר: "וְעֶצֶם לֹא תִשְׁבְּרוּ בוֹ" (שמות יב, מו).

Not to break a bone from the Paschal offering, as it is stated: "And you shall not break a bone of it" (Exodus 12:46).

Mitzva 122

שֶׁלֹּא לִשְׁבֹּר עֶצֶם בְּפֶסַח שֵׁנִי, שֶׁנֶּאֱמַר: "וְעֶצֶם לֹא יִשְׁבְּרוּ בוֹ" (במדבר ט, יב).

Not to break a bone from the second Paschal offering, as it is stated: "And they shall not break a bone in it" (Numbers 9:12).

Mitzva 123 ◂

שֶׁלֹּא לְהוֹצִיא מִבְּשַׂר הַפֶּסַח מִן הַחֲבוּרָה, שֶׁנֶּאֱמַר: "לֹא תוֹצִיא מִן הַבַּיִת" וכו' (שמות יב, מו).

Not to take out any of the flesh of the Paschal offering from the group, as it is stated: "You shall not remove any of the meat **from the house…"** (Exodus 12:46).

Mitzva 124

שֶׁלֹּא לַעֲשׂוֹת שִׁירֵי מְנָחוֹת חָמֵץ, שֶׁנֶּאֱמַר: "לֹא תֵאָפֶה חָמֵץ חֶלְקָם" (ויקרא ו, י).

Not to leaven the remainders of meal offerings, as it is stated: "It shall not be baked leavened… their portion" (Leviticus 6:10).

Mitzva 125

שֶׁלֹּא לֶאֱכֹל בְּשַׂר הַפֶּסַח נָא וּמְבֻשָּׁל, שֶׁנֶּאֱמַר: "אַל תֹּאכְלוּ מִמֶּנּוּ נָא וּבָשֵׁל מְבֻשָּׁל" (שמות יב, ט).

Not to eat the flesh of the Paschal offering half cooked or cooked, as it is stated: "You shall not eat from it half cooked, nor cooked" (Exodus 12:9).

Mitzva 126

שֶׁלֹּא לְהַאֲכִיל בְּשַׂר הַפֶּסַח לְגֵר תּוֹשָׁב, שֶׁנֶּאֱמַר: "תּוֹשָׁב וְשָׂכִיר לֹא יֹאכַל בּוֹ" (שמות יב, מה).

Not to feed any **flesh from the Paschal offering to a *ger toshav*, as it is stated: "A resident alien and a hired laborer shall not eat from it"** (Exodus 12:45).

Mitzva 127

שֶׁלֹּא יֹאכַל הֶעָרֵל בְּשַׂר הַפֶּסַח, שֶׁנֶּאֱמַר: "כָּל עָרֵל לֹא יֹאכַל בּוֹ" (שמות יב, מח, ושם: וְכָל).

That an uncircumcised man may not eat from the flesh of the Paschal offering, as it is stated: "All uncircumcised persons shall not eat from it" (Exodus 12:48).

Mitzva 128

שֶׁלֹּא לְהַאֲכִיל בְּשַׂר הַפֶּסַח לְיִשְׂרָאֵל שֶׁנִּשְׁתַּמֵּד, שֶׁנֶּאֱמַר: "כָּל בֶּן נֵכָר לֹא יֹאכַל בּוֹ" (שמות יב, מג), כְּלוֹמַר: יִשְׂרָאֵל שֶׁנִּלְוָה לִבְנֵי נֵכָר וְעָבַד עֲבוֹדָה זָרָה כְּמוֹתָם לֹא יֹאכַל בּוֹ.

Not to feed any **flesh from the Paschal offering to an apostate Jew, as it is stated: "No foreigner shall eat from it"** (Exodus 12:43). **In other words, a Jew who has joined foreigners and worships idols like them may not eat from it.**

Mitzva 129

שֶׁלֹּא יֹאכַל אָדָם שֶׁנִּטְמָא קָדָשִׁים, שֶׁנֶּאֱמַר: "וְהַנֶּפֶשׁ אֲשֶׁר תֹּאכַל בָּשָׂר מִזֶּבַח הַשְּׁלָמִים" וכו' (ויקרא ז, כ).

That a person who was rendered ritually impure may not eat sacrificial food, **as it is stated: "And the person who eats flesh of the peace offering…"** (Leviticus 7:20).

Mitzva 130

שֶׁלֹּא לֶאֱכֹל מִן הַקֳּדָשִׁים שֶׁנִּטְמְאוּ, שֶׁנֶּאֱמַר: "וְהַבָּשָׂר אֲשֶׁר יִגַּע בְּכָל טָמֵא לֹא יֵאָכֵל" (ויקרא ז, יט).

Not to eat sacrificial food **that was rendered ritually impure, as it is stated: "And the flesh that shall touch any impure item shall not be eaten"** (Leviticus 7:19).

Mitzva 131

שֶׁלֹּא לֶאֱכֹל נוֹתָר, שֶׁנֶּאֱמַר: "וְאֹכְלָיו עֲוֹנוֹ יִשָּׂא וכו' וְנִכְרְתָה הַנֶּפֶשׁ" (ויקרא יט, ח).

Not to eat *notar*, as it is stated: "And he who eats it shall bear his iniquity… and that person shall be excised" (Leviticus 19:8).

Mitzva 132

שֶׁלֹּא לֶאֱכֹל פִּגּוּל, שֶׁנֶּאֱמַר: "הַמַּקְרִיב אֹתוֹ לֹא יֵחָשֵׁב לוֹ פִּגּוּל יִהְיֶה וְהַנֶּפֶשׁ הָאֹכֶלֶת מִמֶּנּוּ עֲוֹנָהּ תִּשָּׂא" (ויקרא ז, יח), וְהוּא בְּכָרֵת.

Not to eat *piggul* [detestable], **as it is stated: "Nor shall it be credited to him that presents it; it shall be a detestable thing; the person who eats from it shall bear his iniquity"** (Leviticus 7:18), **which is** the punishment **of excision** [*karet*].

Mitzva 133

שֶׁלֹּא יֹאכַל זָר תְּרוּמוֹת, שֶׁנֶּאֱמַר: "וְכָל זָר לֹא יֹאכַל קֹדֶשׁ" (ויקרא כב, י).

That a non-priest may not eat *terumot*, as it is stated: "And no non-priest shall partake of sacred items" (Leviticus 22:10).

Mitzva 134

שֶׁלֹּא יֹאכַל אֲפִלּוּ תּוֹשַׁב כֹּהֵן וּשְׂכִירוֹ תְּרוּמָה, שֶׁנֶּאֱמַר: "תּוֹשַׁב כֹּהֵן וְשָׂכִיר" וכו' (ויקרא כב, י).

That not even a resident with a priest or his hired laborer may eat *teruma*, as it is stated: "One who resides with a priest, or a hired laborer, shall not partake of sacred items" (Leviticus 22:10).

Mitzva 135

שֶׁלֹּא יֹאכַל עָרֵל תְּרוּמָה, וְהוּא הַדִּין לִשְׁאָר קָדָשִׁים. וְדָבָר זֶה לְמָדוֹ הַכָּתוּב מִן הַפֶּסַח בִּגְזֵרָה שָׁוָה, וְאֵינוֹ בְּפֵרוּשׁ מִן הַתּוֹרָה. וּמִפִּי הַשְּׁמוּעָה לָמְדוּ שֶׁאִסּוּר עָרֵל בְּקָדָשִׁים מִגּוּפֵי תּוֹרָה וְאֵינוֹ מִדִּבְרֵי סוֹפְרִים.

That an uncircumcised man may not eat *teruma*, and the same is true of other sacrificial foods. **The verse taught this** law **by verbal analogy from the Paschal offering, and it is not explicit in the Torah.** The Sages **learned, on the basis of the** Oral **tradition, that the prohibition** against **an uncircumcised man** partaking **of sacrificial** foods is **an essential part of the Torah, and it is not** prohibited merely **by rabbinic law** (see *Yevamot* 70a). The phrase "an essential part of the Torah" means laws that are expressly stated in the Torah.[a] The Rambam includes in his list of the 613 mitzvot only those that are formulated in the Written Law, or regarding which there is a tradition from Moses that they are "an essential part of the Torah."[b] Accordingly, the prohibition that an uncircumcised man may not eat sacrificial foods is counted as one of the 613 mitzvot, despite the fact that it is not explicitly stated in the Torah.[c]

Mitzva 136

שֶׁלֹּא יֹאכַל כֹּהֵן טָמֵא תְּרוּמָה, שֶׁנֶּאֱמַר: "אִישׁ מִזַּרְעֲךָ וכו' בַּקֳּדָשִׁים לֹא יֹאכַל" (ויקרא כב, ד, ושם: מִזֶּרַע אַהֲרֹן).

That a ritually impure priest may not eat *teruma*, as it is stated: "Any man from your descendants[d] **... shall not partake of the sacred items"** (see Leviticus 22:4).

NOTES

a. See *Hilkhot Shegagot* 14:1–2.

b. See the second rule of *Sefer HaMitzvot*.

c. See also Negative Mitzva 336.

d. The precise wording of Leviticus 22:4 is: "Any man from the descendants of Aaron."

Mitzva 137

שֶׁלֹּא תֹּאכַל חֲלָלָה קֹדֶשׁ, לֹא תְּרוּמוֹת וְלֹא חָזֶה וָשׁוֹק, שֶׁנֶּאֱמַר: "וּבַת כֹּהֵן כִּי תִהְיֶה לְאִישׁ זָר וגו' בִּתְרוּמַת הַקֳּדָשִׁים לֹא תֹאכֵל" (ויקרא כב, יב).

That a *halala* may not eat sacrificial food, **nor *terumot*, nor the breast and thigh,** which are designated for the priests from peace offerings, **as it is stated: "And if the daughter of a priest is married to a non-priest,** she **shall not partake from gifts of the sacred items"** (Leviticus 22:12).

Mitzva 138

שֶׁלֹּא תֵּאָכֵל מִנְחַת כֹּהֵן, שֶׁנֶּאֱמַר: "וְכָל מִנְחַת כֹּהֵן כָּלִיל תִּהְיֶה לֹא תֵאָכֵל" (ויקרא ו, טז).

That the meal offering of a priest shall not be eaten, as it is stated: "And every meal offering of the priest shall be offered in its entirety; it shall not be eaten" (Leviticus 6:16).

Mitzva 139

שֶׁלֹּא לֶאֱכֹל בְּשַׂר חַטָּאוֹת הַנַּעֲשׂוֹת בִּפְנִים, שֶׁנֶּאֱמַר: "וְכָל חַטָּאת אֲשֶׁר יוּבָא" (ויקרא ו, כג).

Not to eat the flesh of a sin offering whose rites **are performed within** the Sanctuary, **as it is stated: "And every sin offering** from which blood **shall be brought** to the Tent of Meeting" (Leviticus 6:23).

Mitzva 140

שֶׁלֹּא לֶאֱכֹל פְּסוּלֵי הַמֻּקְדָּשִׁין שֶׁהֻטַּל בָּהֶם מוּם בְּכַוָּנָה, שֶׁנֶּאֱמַר: "לֹא תֹאכַל כָּל תּוֹעֵבָה" (דברים יד, ג). לָמַדְנוּ מִפִּי הַשְּׁמוּעָה שֶׁבִּפְסוּלֵי הַמֻּקְדָּשִׁין שֶׁהֻטַּל בָּהֶם מוּם הַכָּתוּב מְדַבֵּר.

Not to eat disqualified sacrificial animals whose **blemish was intentionally inflicted upon them, as it is stated: "You shall not eat any abomination"** (Deuteronomy 14:3). **The Sages learned, on the basis of the** Oral **tradition, that** this **verse is speaking of disqualified sacrificial** animals **which had been inflicted by a blemish.**[d]

Mitzva 141

שֶׁלֹּא לֶאֱכֹל מַעֲשֵׂר שֵׁנִי שֶׁל דָּגָן חוּץ לִירוּשָׁלַיִם, שֶׁנֶּאֱמַר: "לֹא תוּכַל לֶאֱכֹל בִּשְׁעָרֶיךָ" וכו' (דברים יב, יז).

Not to eat second tithe of grain outside Jerusalem, as it is stated: "You may not eat within your gates..." (Deuteronomy 12:17).

NOTES

d. See *Sifrei* on Deuteronomy 14:3 (*Yad Peshuta*).

Mitzva 142

שֶׁלֹּא לֶאֱכֹל מַעֲשֵׂר שֵׁנִי שֶׁל תִּירוֹשׁ חוּץ לִירוּשָׁלַיִם, שֶׁנֶּאֱמַר: "תִּירֹשְׁךָ" (שם, ושם: וְתִירֹשְׁךָ).

Not to eat second tithe of wine outside Jerusalem, as it is stated: "Your wine" (Deuteronomy 12:17).

Mitzva 143

שֶׁלֹּא לֶאֱכֹל מַעֲשֵׂר שֵׁנִי שֶׁל יִצְהָר חוּץ לִירוּשָׁלַיִם, שֶׁנֶּאֱמַר: "וְיִצְהָרֶךָ" (שם).

Not to eat second tithe of oil outside Jerusalem, as it is stated: "And your oil" (Deuteronomy 12:17).

Mitzva 144

שֶׁלֹּא לֶאֱכֹל בְּכוֹר תָּמִים חוּץ לִירוּשָׁלַיִם, שֶׁנֶּאֱמַר: "לֹא תוּכַל וכו' וּבְכֹרֹת" (שם).

Not to eat an unblemished firstborn animal **outside Jerusalem, as it is stated: "You may not…or the firstborn"** (Deuteronomy 12:17).

Mitzva 145

שֶׁלֹּא יֹאכְלוּ הַכֹּהֲנִים חַטָּאת וְאָשָׁם חוּץ לָעֲזָרָה, שֶׁנֶּאֱמַר: "לֹא תוּכַל וכו' בְּקָרְךָ וְצֹאנֶךָ" (שם). מִפִּי הַשְּׁמוּעָה לָמְדוּ שֶׁלֹּא בָּא הַכָּתוּב אֶלָּא לֶאֱסֹר בְּשַׂר חַטָּאוֹת וַאֲשָׁמוֹת חוּץ לָעֲזָרָה, לְפִי שֶׁכָּל דָּבָר שֶׁיֵּאָכֵל חוּץ לִמְקוֹם אֲכִילָתוֹ – "לֹא תוּכַל לֶאֱכֹל בִּשְׁעָרֶיךָ" אֶקְרָא בּוֹ.

That the priests may not eat a sin offering or a guilt offering outside the Temple **courtyard, as it is stated: "You may not…your cattle and of your flocks"** (Deuteronomy 12:17). The Sages **learned, on the basis of the** Oral **tradition, that** this **verse is coming only to prohibit** partaking of **the flesh of sin offerings and guilt offerings outside the** Temple **courtyard.** This **because** one **reads** the phrase **"you may not eat within your gates"** as referring to **anything that is eaten outside the** proper **place for its consumption** (see *Makkot* 17a – b).

Mitzva 146

שֶׁלֹּא לֶאֱכֹל בְּשַׂר הָעוֹלָה, שֶׁנֶּאֱמַר: "לֹא תוּכַל וכו' וְכָל נְדָרֶיךָ אֲשֶׁר תִּדֹּר" (שם), כְּלוֹמַר: לֹא תוּכַל לֶאֱכֹל נְדָרֶיךָ אֲשֶׁר תִּדּוֹר. וְזוֹ הִיא אַזְהָרָה שֶׁל כָּל מוֹעֵל, שֶׁלֹּא יֵהָנֶה מִן הַקֳּדָשִׁים הָאֲסוּרִין לֵהָנוֹת מֵהֶם, וְאִם נֶהֱנָה – מָעַל.

Not to eat the flesh of a burnt offering, as it is stated: "You may not…or any of your vows that you will vow" (Deuteronomy 12:17). **In other words, you may not eat** from **your vows that you will vow. This is** the **prohibition** that applies **to every** person **who misuses** consecrated food, **that one may not derive benefit from consecrated** items **from which it is prohibited to derive benefit, and if one did derive benefit** from them **he has misused** consecrated property.

Mitzva 147

שֶׁלֹּא לֶאֱכֹל בְּשַׂר קָדָשִׁים קַלִּים קֹדֶם זְרִיקַת דָּמִים, שֶׁנֶּאֱמַר: "לֹא תוּכַל וכו' וְנִדְבֹתֶיךָ" (שם), כְּלוֹמַר: לֹא תוּכַל לֶאֱכֹל נִדְבוֹתֶיךָ עַד שֶׁיִּזָּרֵק דָּמָם.

Not to eat the flesh of offerings of lesser sanctity before the sprinkling of the blood, as it is stated: "You may not…or your pledges" (Deuteronomy 12:17). **In other words, you may not eat** from **your pledges until their blood has been sprinkled.**

Mitzva 148

שֶׁלֹּא יֹאכַל זָר בְּשַׂר קָדְשֵׁי קָדָשִׁים, שֶׁנֶּאֱמַר: "וְזָר לֹא יֹאכַל כִּי קֹדֶשׁ הֵם" (שמות כט, לג).

That a non-priest may not partake of the flesh of offerings of the most sacred order, as it is stated: "But a stranger shall not eat, because they are sacred" (Exodus 29:33).

Mitzva 149

שֶׁלֹּא יֹאכַל כֹּהֵן בִּכּוּרִים קֹדֶם הַנָּחָה בָּעֲזָרָה, שֶׁנֶּאֱמַר: "לֹא תוּכַל וכו' וּתְרוּמַת יָדֶךָ" (דברים יב, יז) – אֵלּוּ הַבִּכּוּרִים.

That a priest may not eat the **first fruits before** their **placement in the** Temple **courtyard, as it is stated: "You may not…or the gift of your hand"** (Deuteronomy 12:17).

Mitzva 150

שֶׁלֹּא לֶאֱכֹל מַעֲשֵׂר שֵׁנִי בְּטֻמְאָה וַאֲפִלּוּ בִּירוּשָׁלַיִם עַד שֶׁיִּפָּדֶה, שֶׁנֶּאֱמַר: "וְלֹא בִעַרְתִּי מִמֶּנּוּ בְּטָמֵא" (דברים כו, יד).

Not to eat second tithe in a state of **ritual impurity, even in Jerusalem, until it has been redeemed, as it is stated: "And I did not dispose of it in a state of impurity"** (Deuteronomy 26:14).

Mitzva 151

שֶׁלֹּא לֶאֱכֹל מַעֲשֵׂר שֵׁנִי בַּאֲנִינוּת, שֶׁנֶּאֱמַר: "לֹא אָכַלְתִּי בְאֹנִי מִמֶּנּוּ" (שם).

Not to eat second tithe in a state of **acute mourning, as it is stated: "I did not eat from it during my mourning"** (Deuteronomy 26:14).

Mitzva 152

שֶׁלֹּא לְהוֹצִיא דְּמֵי מַעֲשֵׂר שֵׁנִי בִּשְׁאָר דְּבָרִים שֶׁאֵין בָּהֶם אֲכִילָה וּשְׁתִיָּה, שֶׁנֶּאֱמַר: "וְלֹא נָתַתִּי מִמֶּנּוּ לְמֵת" (שם), וְכָל שֶׁהוּא חוּץ לְצָרְכֵי הַגּוּף הַחַי – "נָתַתִּי מִמֶּנּוּ לְמֵת" אֶקְרָא בּוֹ.

Not to spend second tithe money on other things that do not involve eating and drinking, as it is stated: "And I did not give from it for the dead" (Deuteronomy 26:14). One **reads** the phrase **"give from it for the dead"** as referring to **anything other than the requirements of a living body.**

Mitzva 153

שֶׁלֹּא לֶאֱכֹל טֶבֶל, וְהַטֶּבֶל הוּא הַדָּבָר שֶׁגִּדּוּלָיו מִן הָאָרֶץ הַחַיָּב בִּתְרוּמוֹת וּמַעַשְׂרוֹת שֶׁלֹּא הוֹצִיאוּ מִמֶּנּוּ תְּרוּמוֹת יי, שֶׁנֶּאֱמַר: "וְלֹא יְחַלְּלוּ אֶת קָדְשֵׁי בְּנֵי יִשְׂרָאֵל אֵת אֲשֶׁר יָרִימוּ לַיי" (ויקרא כב, טו), כְּלוֹמַר: דְּבָרִים שֶׁהֵן עֲתִידִין לְהָרִים אוֹתָם לַיי לֹא יַעֲשׂוּ אוֹתָם חֹל וְיֹאכְלוּ אוֹתָם בְּטִבְלָם.

Not to eat ***tevel*** [untithed produce]. ***Tevel*** **is something that grows from the ground,** from **which** one **is obligated to** separate ***terumot*** **and tithes, but from which the** ***terumot*** **of the Lord were not removed, as it is stated: "And they shall not profane the sacraments of the children of Israel that they set aside for the Lord"** (Leviticus 22:15). **In other words, they shall should not render profane** those **items that they will in the future set aside for the Lord,** by **eating them in their untithed state.**

Mitzva 154

שֶׁלֹּא לְהַקְדִּים תְּרוּמָה לַבִּכּוּרִים, וְלֹא מַעֲשֵׂר רִאשׁוֹן לַתְּרוּמָה, וְלֹא מַעֲשֵׂר שֵׁנִי לָרִאשׁוֹן, אֶלָּא מוֹצִיאִין עַל הַסֵּדֶר: בִּכּוּרִים תְּחִלָּה, וְאַחַר כָּךְ תְּרוּמָה גְּדוֹלָה, וְאַחַר כָּךְ מַעֲשֵׂר רִאשׁוֹן, וְאַחַר כָּךְ מַעֲשֵׂר שֵׁנִי, שֶׁנֶּאֱמַר: "מְלֵאָתְךָ וְדִמְעֲךָ לֹא תְאַחֵר" (שמות כב, כח), כְּלוֹמַר: לֹא תְּאַחֵר דָּבָר הָרָאוּי לְהַקְדִּימוֹ.

Not to separate ***teruma*** **before the first fruits, nor the first tithe before** ***teruma,*** **nor the second tithe before the first. Rather, one should remove them in the** correct **order, starting** with **the first fruits, then** ***teruma gedola,*** **then the first tithe, and then the second tithe, as it is stated: "The surfeit of your crops and the outpouring of your juices you shall not delay"** (Exodus 22:28). **In other words, do not delay something that is fit to** be separated **before** another gift, by separating it later.

Mitzva 155

שֶׁלֹּא לְאַחֵר הַנְּדָרִים וְהַנְּדָבוֹת שֶׁנָּדַר וְשֶׁנָּדַב, שֶׁנֶּאֱמַר: "לֹא תְאַחֵר לְשַׁלְּמוֹ" וכו' (דברים כג, כב).

Not to delay bringing **the vows and voluntary** offerings **that** one **vowed and volunteered** to bring, **as it is stated: "You shall not delay to pay it..."** (Deuteronomy 23:22).

Mitzva 156

שֶׁלֹּא לַעֲלוֹת לֶחָג בְּלֹא קָרְבָּן, שֶׁנֶּאֱמַר: "וְלֹא יֵרָאוּ פָנַי רֵיקָם" (שמות כג, טו).

Not to ascend to Jerusalem **to celebrate** a pilgrimage festival **without** bringing **an offering, as it is stated: "They shall not appear before Me empty-handed"** (Exodus 23:15).

Mitzva 157

שֶׁלֹּא לַעֲבֹר עַל דְּבָרִים שֶׁאָסַר אָדָם עַל נַפְשׁוֹ, שֶׁנֶּאֱמַר: "לֹא יַחֵל דְּבָרוֹ" (במדבר ל, ג).

Not to violate those **injunctions that a person has prohibited upon himself, as it is stated: "He shall not profane his word"** (Numbers 30:3).

Mitzva 158

שֶׁלֹּא יִקַּח כֹּהֵן זוֹנָה, שֶׁנֶּאֱמַר: "אִשָּׁה זֹנָה...לֹא יִקָּחוּ" (ויקרא כא, ז).

That a priest should not take for his wife **a** ***zona,*** i.e., a woman who has engaged in sexual relations with a man forbidden to her by the Torah, **as it is stated: "A licentious woman...they shall not marry"** (Leviticus 21:7).

Mitzva 159

שֶׁלֹּא יִקַּח כֹּהֵן חֲלָלָה, שֶׁנֶּאֱמַר: "וַחֲלָלָה לֹא יִקָּחוּ" (שם).

That a priest should not take a ***ḥalala,*** **as it is stated: "Or a profaned woman they shall not marry"** (Leviticus 21:7).

Mitzva 160

שֶׁלֹּא יִקַּח כֹּהֵן גְּרוּשָׁה, שֶׁנֶּאֱמַר: "וְאִשָּׁה גְּרוּשָׁה מֵאִישָׁהּ לֹא יִקָּחוּ" (שם).

That a priest should not take a divorced woman, as it is stated: "And a woman divorced from her husband they shall not marry" (Leviticus 21:7).

Mitzva 161

שֶׁלֹּא יִקַּח כֹּהֵן גָּדוֹל אַלְמָנָה, שֶׁנֶּאֱמַר: "אַלְמָנָה וּגְרוּשָׁה וַחֲלָלָה זֹנָה" וגו' (ויקרא כא, יד).

That a High Priest may not take a widow, as it is stated: "A widow or a divorcée, or a profaned woman, or a licentious woman..." (Leviticus 21:14).

Mitzva 162

שֶׁלֹּא יִבְעֹל כֹּהֵן גָּדוֹל אַלְמָנָה וַאֲפִלּוּ בְּלֹא קִדּוּשִׁים, מִפְּנֵי שֶׁמְּחַלְּלָהּ, וְנֶאֱמַר: "וְלֹא יְחַלֵּל זַרְעוֹ בְּעַמָּיו" (ויקרא כא, טו) – הֲרֵי הוּא מֻזְהָר שֶׁלֹּא לְחַלֵּל כְּשֵׁרָה.

That a High Priest may not have intercourse with a widow, even without marriage, because he thereby renders her a ***ḥalala,*** **as it is stated: "And he shall not profane his offspring among his people"** (Leviticus 21:15). **He is thus warned not to profane a fit woman.**

Mitzva 163

שֶׁלֹּא יִכָּנֵס כֹּהֵן לַמִּקְדָּשׁ פְּרוּעַ רֹאשׁ, שֶׁנֶּאֱמַר: "רָאשֵׁיכֶם אַל תִּפְרָעוּ" (ויקרא י, ו).

That a priest may not enter the Temple with long hair, as it is stated: "You shall not grow out the hair of your heads" (Leviticus 10:6).

Mitzva 164

That a priest may not enter the Temple with torn vestments, as it is stated: "And you shall not rend your garments" (Leviticus 10:6).

שֶׁלֹּא יִכָּנֵס כֹּהֵן לַמִּקְדָּשׁ קְרוּעַ בְּגָדִים, שֶׁנֶּאֱמַר: "וּבִגְדֵיכֶם לֹא תִפְרֹמוּ" (שם).

Mitzva 165

That a priest may not leave the Temple during the service, as it is stated: "And from the entrance of the Tent of Meeting you shall not emerge, that you not die" (Leviticus 10:7).

שֶׁלֹּא יֵצֵא הַכֹּהֵן מִן הָעֲזָרָה בִּשְׁעַת הָעֲבוֹדָה, שֶׁנֶּאֱמַר: "וּמִפֶּתַח אֹהֶל מוֹעֵד לֹא תֵצְאוּ פֶּן תָּמֻתוּ" (ויקרא י, ז).

Mitzva 166

That an ordinary priest may not become impure for other dead people, apart from his close relatives, **as it is stated: "He shall not become impure from a dead person among his people"** (Leviticus 21:1).

שֶׁלֹּא יִטַּמֵּא כֹּהֵן הֶדְיוֹט לִשְׁאָר מֵתִים, שֶׁנֶּאֱמַר: "לְנֶפֶשׁ לֹא יִטַּמָּא בְּעַמָּיו" (ויקרא כא, א).

Mitzva 167

That a High Priest may not become impure even for his **relatives, as it is stated: "He shall not become impure for his father and for his mother"** (Leviticus 21:11).

שֶׁלֹּא יִטַּמֵּא כֹּהֵן גָּדוֹל וַאֲפִלּוּ לַקְּרוֹבִין, שֶׁנֶּאֱמַר: "לְאָבִיו וּלְאִמּוֹ לֹא יִטַּמָּא" (ויקרא כא, יא).

Mitzva 168

That a High Priest may not enter a tent and be there together **with a corpse, as it is stated: "And he shall not go near any dead people"** (Leviticus 21:11). The Sages **learned the following, on the basis of the** Oral **tradition, that he is liable for** violating the command **"he shall not go near" and he is** also **liable for** violating the command **"he shall not become impure."**[a]

שֶׁלֹּא יִכָּנֵס כֹּהֵן גָּדוֹל עִם מֵת, שֶׁנֶּאֱמַר: "וְעַל כָּל נַפְשֹׁת מֵת לֹא יָבֹא" (שם). **כָּךְ לָמְדוּ מִפִּי הַשְּׁמוּעָה, שֶׁהוּא חַיָּב בְּבַל יָבֹא וְחַיָּב בְּבַל יִטַּמֵּא.**

NOTES

a. See *Safra* on Leviticus 21:11 (*Yad Peshuta*).

Mitzva 169

That the entire tribe of Levi shall not take a portion in the Land of Israel, **as it is stated: "He shall not have an inheritance"** (Deuteronomy 18:2).

שֶׁלֹּא יִקַּח כָּל שֵׁבֶט לֵוִי חֵלֶק בָּאָרֶץ, שֶׁנֶּאֱמַר: "וְנַחֲלָה לֹא יִהְיֶה לּוֹ" (דברים יח, ב).

Mitzva 170

That the entire tribe of Levi shall not take a share in the plunder at the time of the conquest of the Land of Israel, **as it is stated: "There shall not be for the priests..."** (Deuteronomy 18:1).

שֶׁלֹּא יִקַּח כָּל שֵׁבֶט לֵוִי חֵלֶק בַּבִּזָּה בִּשְׁעַת כִּבּוּשׁ הָאָרֶץ, שֶׁנֶּאֱמַר: "לֹא יִהְיֶה לַכֹּהֲנִים" וגו' (דברים יח, א).

Mitzva 171

Not to make a bald spot in mourning **for the dead, as it is stated: "And you shall not place a bald spot between your eyes for the dead"** (Deuteronomy 14:1).

שֶׁלֹּא לַעֲשׂוֹת קָרְחָה עַל מֵת, שֶׁנֶּאֱמַר: "וְלֹא תָשִׂימוּ קָרְחָה בֵּין עֵינֵיכֶם לָמֵת" (דברים יד, א).

Mitzva 172

Not to eat a non-kosher domesticated animal, as it is stated: "However, these you shall not eat from those that bring up the cud" (Leviticus 11:4, Deuteronomy 14:7).

שֶׁלֹּא לֶאֱכֹל בְּהֵמָה טְמֵאָה, שֶׁנֶּאֱמַר: "אַךְ אֶת זֶה לֹא תֹאכְלוּ מִמַּעֲלֵי הַגֵּרָה" (ויקרא יא, ד; יד, ז).

Mitzva 173

Not to eat a non-kosher fish, as it is stated: "They shall be a detestable thing to you; you shall not eat from their flesh" (Leviticus 11:11).

שֶׁלֹּא לֶאֱכֹל דָּג טָמֵא, שֶׁנֶּאֱמַר: "וְשֶׁקֶץ יִהְיוּ לָכֶם מִבְּשָׂרָם לֹא תֹאכֵלוּ" (ויקרא יא, יא).

Mitzva 174

Not to eat a non-kosher bird, as it is stated: "And these you shall detest among the fowls; they shall not be eaten" (Leviticus 11:13).

שֶׁלֹּא לֶאֱכֹל עוֹף טָמֵא, שֶׁנֶּאֱמַר: "וְאֶת אֵלֶּה תְּשַׁקְּצוּ מִן הָעוֹף לֹא יֵאָכְלוּ" (ויקרא יא, יג).

Mitzva 175

Not to eat winged swarming things, as it is stated: "Every flying swarming creature is impure for you" (Deuteronomy 14:19).

שֶׁלֹּא לֶאֱכֹל שֶׁרֶץ הָעוֹף, שֶׁנֶּאֱמַר: "כֹּל שֶׁרֶץ הָעוֹף טָמֵא הוּא לָכֶם" (דברים יד, יט, ושם: וְכָל).

Mitzva 176

שֶׁלֹּא לֶאֱכֹל שֶׁרֶץ הָאָרֶץ, שֶׁנֶּאֱמַר: "וְכָל הַשֶּׁרֶץ הַשֹּׁרֵץ עַל הָאָרֶץ שֶׁקֶץ הוּא" (ויקרא יא, מא).

Not to eat swarming animals of the earth, as it is stated: "And any swarming creature that swarms upon the earth is a detestable thing" (Leviticus 11:41).

Mitzva 177

שֶׁלֹּא לֶאֱכֹל רֶמֶשׂ הָאָרֶץ, שֶׁנֶּאֱמַר: "וְלֹא תְטַמְּאוּ אֶת נַפְשֹׁתֵיכֶם" (ויקרא יא, מד).

Not to eat creeping creatures of the earth, as it is stated: "And you shall not render yourselves impure" (Leviticus 11:44).

Mitzva 178

שֶׁלֹּא לֶאֱכֹל תּוֹלַעַת הַפֵּרוֹת כְּשֶׁתֵּצֵא לָאֲוִיר, שֶׁנֶּאֱמַר: "לְכָל הַשֶּׁרֶץ הַשֹּׁרֵץ עַל הָאָרֶץ" וגו' (ויקרא יא, מב).

Not to eat worms of fruits when they emerge into the air, as it is stated: "Among all swarming creatures that swarm on the earth..." (Leviticus 11:42).

Mitzva 179

שֶׁלֹּא לֶאֱכֹל שֶׁרֶץ הַמַּיִם, שֶׁנֶּאֱמַר: "אַל תְּשַׁקְּצוּ אֶת נַפְשֹׁתֵיכֶם בְּכָל הַשֶּׁרֶץ" וגו' (ויקרא יא, מג).

Not to eat creeping animals of the water, as it is stated: "You shall not render yourselves detestable with any swarming creature..." (Leviticus 11:43).

Mitzva 180

שֶׁלֹּא לֶאֱכֹל מֵתָה, שֶׁנֶּאֱמַר: "לֹא תֹאכְלוּ כָל נְבֵלָה" (דברים יד, כא).

Not to eat a dead animal, **as it is stated: "You shall not eat any unslaughtered carcass"** (Deuteronomy 14:21).

Mitzva 181

שֶׁלֹּא לֶאֱכֹל טְרֵפָה, שֶׁנֶּאֱמַר: "וּבָשָׂר בַּשָּׂדֶה טְרֵפָה לֹא תֹאכֵלוּ" וכו' (שמות כב, ל).

Not to eat a *tereifa* [mauled animal], **as it is stated: "You shall not eat meat of a mauled animal in the field..."** (Exodus 22:30).

Mitzva 182

שֶׁלֹּא לֶאֱכֹל אֵבֶר מִן הַחַי, שֶׁנֶּאֱמַר: "לֹא תֹאכַל הַנֶּפֶשׁ עִם הַבָּשָׂר" (דברים יב, כג, ושם: וְלֹא).

Not to eat a limb from a living animal, as it is stated: "You shall not eat the life with the flesh" (Deuteronomy 12:23).

Mitzva 183

שֶׁלֹּא לֶאֱכֹל גִּיד הַנָּשֶׁה, שֶׁנֶּאֱמַר: "לֹא יֹאכְלוּ בְנֵי יִשְׂרָאֵל אֶת גִּיד הַנָּשֶׁה" (בראשית לב, לג).

Not to eat the sciatic nerve, as it is stated: "The children of Israel do not eat the sciatic nerve" (Genesis 32:32).

Mitzva 184

שֶׁלֹּא לֶאֱכֹל דָּם, שֶׁנֶּאֱמַר: "וְכָל דָּם לֹא תֹאכְלוּ בְּכֹל מוֹשְׁבֹתֵיכֶם" (ויקרא ז, כו).

Not to eat blood, as it is stated: "And all blood you shall not eat in any of your dwellings" (Leviticus 7:26).

Mitzva 185

שֶׁלֹּא לֶאֱכֹל חֵלֶב, שֶׁנֶּאֱמַר: "כָּל חֵלֶב שׁוֹר וְכֶשֶׂב וָעֵז לֹא תֹאכֵלוּ" (ויקרא ז, כג).

Not to eat forbidden **fat, as it is stated: "Any fat of a bull, or a sheep, or a goat you shall not eat"** (Leviticus 7:23).

Mitzva 186

שֶׁלֹּא לְבַשֵּׁל בָּשָׂר בְּחָלָב, שֶׁנֶּאֱמַר: "לֹא תְבַשֵּׁל גְּדִי בַּחֲלֵב אִמּוֹ" (שמות כג, יט).

Not to cook meat in milk, as it is stated: "You shall not cook a kid in its mother's milk" (Exodus 23:19).

Mitzva 187

שֶׁלֹּא לֶאֱכֹל בָּשָׂר בְּחָלָב, שֶׁנֶּאֱמַר: "לֹא תְבַשֵּׁל גְּדִי בַּחֲלֵב אִמּוֹ" (שמות לד, כו) **פַּעַם שְׁנִיָּה. כָּךְ לָמְדוּ מִפִּי הַשְּׁמוּעָה, שֶׁאֶחָד לְאִסּוּר בִּשּׁוּל וְאֶחָד לְאִסּוּר אֲכִילָה.**

Not to eat meat cooked **in milk, as it is stated, a second time: "You shall not cook a kid in its mother's milk"** (Exodus 34:26). The Sages **learned the following, on the basis of the** Oral **tradition, that one** verse is speaking **of the prohibition of cooking** meat and milk together, **and one** verse is speaking **of the prohibition of eating** that cooked dish (see *Ḥullin* 114a).

Mitzva 188

שֶׁלֹּא לֶאֱכֹל בְּשַׂר שׁוֹר הַנִּסְקָל, שֶׁנֶּאֱמַר: "וְלֹא יֵאָכֵל אֶת בְּשָׂרוֹ" (שמות כא, כח).

Not to eat the flesh of an ox that is stoned, as it is stated: "And its meat shall not be eaten" (Exodus 21:28).

Mitzva 189

שֶׁלֹּא לֶאֱכֹל פַּת תְּבוּאָה חֲדָשָׁה קֹדֶם הַפֶּסַח, שֶׁנֶּאֱמַר: "וְלֶחֶם וְקָלִי וְכַרְמֶל לֹא תֹאכְלוּ עַד עֶצֶם הַיּוֹם הַזֶּה" (ויקרא כג, יד).

Not to eat bread from **the new crop before Passover, as it is stated: "Bread, roasted grain, or fresh kernels you shall not eat until that very day"** (Leviticus 23:14).

Mitzva 190

שֶׁלֹּא לֶאֱכֹל קָלִי מִן הֶחָדָשׁ, שֶׁנֶּאֱמַר: "וְקָלִי...לֹא תֹאכְלוּ עַד עֶצֶם" וגו' (שם).

Not to eat roasted kernels from the new crop, as it is stated: "Roasted grain...you shall not eat until that very day" (Leviticus 23:14).

Mitzva 191

שֶׁלֹּא לֶאֱכֹל כַּרְמֶל מִתְּבוּאָה חֲדָשָׁה, שֶׁנֶּאֱמַר: "וְכַרְמֶל לֹא תֹאכְלוּ" (שם).

Not to eat fresh kernels from the new crop, as it is stated: "Or fresh kernels you shall not eat" (Leviticus 23:14).

Mitzva 192

שֶׁלֹּא לֶאֱכֹל עָרְלָה, שֶׁנֶּאֱמַר: "שָׁלֹשׁ שָׁנִים יִהְיֶה לָכֶם עֲרֵלִים לֹא יֵאָכֵל" (ויקרא יט, כג).

Not to eat *orla*, as it is stated: "Three years it shall be sealed for you; it shall not be eaten" (Leviticus 19:23).

Mitzva 193

שֶׁלֹּא לֶאֱכֹל כִּלְאֵי הַכֶּרֶם, שֶׁנֶּאֱמַר: "פֶּן תִּקְדַּשׁ הַמְלֵאָה הַזֶּרַע אֲשֶׁר תִּזְרָע וּתְבוּאַת הַכָּרֶם" (דברים כב, ט) – זֶה הוּא אִסּוּר אֲכִילָה.

Not to eat diverse kinds in a vineyard, as it is stated: "Lest the growth be forbidden: The seed that you will sow, and the produce of the vineyard" (Deuteronomy 22:9) – this is a prohibition of eating.

Mitzva 194

שֶׁלֹּא לִשְׁתּוֹת יֵין נֶסֶךְ, שֶׁנֶּאֱמַר: "אֲשֶׁר חֵלֶב זְבָחֵימוֹ יֹאכֵלוּ יִשְׁתּוּ יֵין נְסִיכָם" (דברים לב, לח).

Not to drink wine used for a libation, as it is stated: "The fat of whose offerings they would eat, the wine of whose libations they would drink" (Deuteronomy 32:38).

Mitzva 195

שֶׁלֹּא לֶאֱכֹל וְלִשְׁתּוֹת דֶּרֶךְ זוֹלֵל וְסוֹבֵא, שֶׁנֶּאֱמַר: "בְּנֵנוּ זֶה וכו' זוֹלֵל וְסֹבֵא" (דברים כא, כ).

Not to eat and drink in the manner of a glutton and a drunkard, as it is stated: "This son of ours is...a glutton and a drunkard" (Deuteronomy 21:20).

Mitzva 196

שֶׁלֹּא לֶאֱכֹל בְּיוֹם הַצּוֹם, שֶׁנֶּאֱמַר: "כִּי כָל הַנֶּפֶשׁ אֲשֶׁר לֹא תְעֻנֶּה...וְהַאֲבַדְתִּי וְנִכְרְתָה" (ויקרא כג, כט, ושם בלי 'והאבדתי').

Not to eat on the day of the Yom Kippur fast, as it is stated: "For any person who is not afflicted...I shall destroy[a] and he shall be excised" (see Leviticus 23:29).

Mitzva 197

שֶׁלֹּא לֶאֱכֹל חָמֵץ בְּפֶסַח, שֶׁנֶּאֱמַר: "וְלֹא יֵאָכֵל חָמֵץ" (שמות יג, ג).

Not to eat leaven on Passover, as it is stated: "And leavened bread may not be eaten" (Exodus 13:3).

Mitzva 198

שֶׁלֹּא לֶאֱכֹל תַּעֲרֹבֶת חָמֵץ, שֶׁנֶּאֱמַר: "כָּל מַחְמֶצֶת לֹא תֹאכֵלוּ" (שמות יב, כ).

Not to eat a mixture of leavened bread on Passover, as it is stated: "You shall not anything leavened" (Exodus 12:20).

Mitzva 199

שֶׁלֹּא לֶאֱכֹל חָמֵץ אַחַר חֲצוֹת יוֹם אַרְבָּעָה עָשָׂר, שֶׁנֶּאֱמַר: "לֹא תֹאכַל עָלָיו חָמֵץ" (דברים טז, ג).

Not to eat leavened bread after midday of the day of the fourteenth of Nisan until the conclusion of Passover, as it is stated: "You shall not eat with it leavened bread" (Deuteronomy 16:3).

Mitzva 200

שֶׁלֹּא יֵרָאֶה חָמֵץ, שֶׁנֶּאֱמַר: "וְלֹא יֵרָאֶה לְךָ חָמֵץ" (שמות יג, ז).

That leavened bread should not be seen in one's possession throughout Passover, as it is stated: "Nor shall leaven be seen with you" (Exodus 13:7).

Mitzva 201

שֶׁלֹּא יִמָּצֵא חָמֵץ, שֶׁנֶּאֱמַר: "שְׂאֹר לֹא יִמָּצֵא בְּבָתֵּיכֶם" (שמות יב, יט).

That leavened bread should not be found in one's possession throughout Passover, as it is stated: "Leaven shall not be found in your houses" (Exodus 12:19).

Mitzva 202

שֶׁלֹּא יִשְׁתֶּה הַנָּזִיר יַיִן וְלֹא דָּבָר שֶׁנִּתְעָרֵב בּוֹ יַיִן וְטַעְמוֹ כְּטַעַם יַיִן, שֶׁנֶּאֱמַר: "וְכָל מִשְׁרַת עֲנָבִים" (במדבר ו, ג). וַאֲפִלּוּ הֶחֱמִיץ הַיַּיִן אוֹ דָּבָר שֶׁנִּתְעָרֵב בּוֹ הַיַּיִן – הֲרֵי זֶה אָסוּר עָלָיו, שֶׁנֶּאֱמַר: "חֹמֶץ יַיִן וְחֹמֶץ שֵׁכָר לֹא יִשְׁתֶּה" (שם).

That a nazirite may not drink wine or anything in which wine has been mixed and which has the taste of wine, as it is stated: "All grapes that were soaked" (Numbers 6:3). Even if the wine or that substance in which the wine was mixed turned to vinegar, it is still prohibited to a nazirite, as it is stated: "Vinegar of wine and vinegar of intoxicating drink he shall not drink" (Numbers 6:3).

NOTES

a. The phrase "I shall destroy" does not appear in the verse.

Mitzva 203

שֶׁלֹּא יֹאכַל עֲנָבִים לַחִים, שֶׁנֶּאֱמַר: "וַעֲנָבִים לַחִים... לֹא יֹאכֵל" (שם).

That a nazirite **may not eat fresh grapes, as it is stated: "And grapes, fresh... he shall not eat"** (Numbers 6:3).

Mitzva 204

שֶׁלֹּא יֹאכַל עֲנָבִים יְבֵשִׁים, שֶׁנֶּאֱמַר: "וִיבֵשִׁים לֹא יֹאכֵל" (שם).

That a nazirite **may not eat dried grapes, as it is stated:** "And grapes, fresh **or dried, he shall not eat"** (Numbers 6:3).

Mitzva 205

שֶׁלֹּא יֹאכַל חַרְצַנִּים, שֶׁנֶּאֱמַר: "מֵחַרְצַנִּים וכו' לֹא יֹאכֵל" (במדבר ו, ד).

That a nazirite **may not eat pits** of grapes, **as it is stated: "From pits... he shall not eat"** (Numbers 6:4).

Mitzva 206

שֶׁלֹּא יֹאכַל זַגִּים, שֶׁנֶּאֱמַר: "וְעַד זָג לֹא יֹאכֵל" (שם).

That a nazirite **may not eat skins** of grapes, **as it is stated:** "From pits **to skin, he shall not eat"** (Numbers 6:4).

Mitzva 207

שֶׁלֹּא יִטַּמֵּא הַנָּזִיר לְמֵת, שֶׁנֶּאֱמַר: "לְאָבִיו וּלְאִמּוֹ וכו' לֹא יִטַּמָּא לָהֶם בְּמֹתָם" (במדבר ו, ז).

That a nazirite may not become impure through contact with **the dead, as it is stated: "To his father and to his mother... he shall not become impure for them upon their death"** (Numbers 6:7).

Mitzva 208

שֶׁלֹּא יִכָּנֵס בְּאֹהֶל הַמֵּת, שֶׁנֶּאֱמַר: "עַל נֶפֶשׁ מֵת לֹא יָבֹא" (במדבר ו, ו).

That a nazirite **may not enter a tent** that is spread over **a corpse, as it is stated: "He shall not approach a corpse"** (Numbers 6:6).

Mitzva 209

שֶׁלֹּא יְגַלֵּחַ הַנָּזִיר, שֶׁנֶּאֱמַר: "תַּעַר לֹא יַעֲבֹר עַל רֹאשׁוֹ" (במדבר ו, ה).

That a nazirite may not shave, as it is stated: "A razor shall not pass on his head" (Numbers 6:5).

Mitzva 210

שֶׁלֹּא לִקְצֹר כָּל הַשָּׂדֶה, שֶׁנֶּאֱמַר: "לֹא תְכַלֶּה פְּאַת שָׂדְךָ בְּקֻצְרֶךָ" (ויקרא כג, כב).

Not to reap all of one's **field, as it is stated: "You shall not finish the corner of your field in your reaping"** (Leviticus 23:22).

Mitzva 211

שֶׁלֹּא לְלַקֵּט הַשִּׁבֳּלִים הַנּוֹפְלוֹת בִּשְׁעַת קְצִירָה, שֶׁנֶּאֱמַר: "וְלֶקֶט קְצִירְךָ לֹא תְלַקֵּט" (ויקרא יט, ט; כג, כב).

Not to gather the stalks that fall during the harvest, as it is stated: "And the gleanings of your harvest you shall not gather" (Leviticus 19:9, 23:22).

Mitzva 212

שֶׁלֹּא לִבְצֹר עוֹלְלוֹת הַכֶּרֶם, שֶׁנֶּאֱמַר: "וְכַרְמְךָ לֹא תְעוֹלֵל" (ויקרא יט, י).

Not to harvest the *olelot* of a vineyard, as it is stated: "And your vineyard you shall not harvest completely" (Leviticus 19:10).

Mitzva 213

שֶׁלֹּא לְלַקֵּט פֶּרֶט הַכֶּרֶם, שֶׁנֶּאֱמַר: "וּפֶרֶט כַּרְמְךָ לֹא תְלַקֵּט" (שם).

Not to gather the *peret* of a vineyard, as it is stated: "And the fallen fruit of your vineyard you shall not gather" (Leviticus 19:10).

Mitzva 214

שֶׁלֹּא לִקַּח עֹמֶר הַשִּׁכְחָה, שֶׁנֶּאֱמַר: "לֹא תָשׁוּב לְקַחְתּוֹ" (דברים כד, יט). וְכֵן לְכָל הָאִילָנוֹת יֵשׁ שִׁכְחָה, שֶׁנֶּאֱמַר: "לֹא תְפַאֵר אַחֲרֶיךָ" (שם כד, כ).

Not to return **to take a forgotten sheaf, as it is stated: "You shall not return to take it"** (Deuteronomy 24:19). **Similarly,** the law of **forgotten** produce applies **to all trees, as it is stated: "You shall not search the boughs again"** (Deuteronomy 24:20).

Mitzva 215

שֶׁלֹּא לִזְרֹעַ כִּלְאֵי זְרָעִים, שֶׁנֶּאֱמַר: "שָׂדְךָ לֹא תִזְרַע כִּלְאָיִם" (ויקרא יט, יט).

Not to sow diverse kinds of seeds, as it is stated: "You shall not sow your field with diverse kinds" (Leviticus 19:19).

Mitzva 216

שֶׁלֹּא לִזְרֹעַ תְּבוּאָה אוֹ יָרָק בַּכֶּרֶם, שֶׁנֶּאֱמַר: "לֹא תִזְרַע כַּרְמְךָ כִּלְאָיִם" (דברים כב, ט).

Not to sow grain or vegetables in a vineyard, as it is stated: "You shall not sow your vineyard with diverse kinds" (Deuteronomy 22:9).

Mitzva 217

שֶׁלֹּא לְהַרְבִּיעַ בְּהֵמָה מִין עִם שֶׁאֵינוֹ מִינוֹ, שֶׁנֶּאֱמַר: "בְּהֶמְתְּךָ לֹא תַרְבִּיעַ כִּלְאַיִם" (ויקרא יט, יט).

Not to mate one **animal species with** an animal **that is not of its** same **species, as it is stated: "You shall not breed your animal with diverse kinds"** (Leviticus 19:19).

Mitzva 218

שֶׁלֹּא יַעֲשֶׂה מְלָאכָה בִּשְׁנֵי מִינֵי בְהֵמָה כְּאֶחָד, שֶׁנֶּאֱמַר: "לֹא תַחֲרֹשׁ בְּשׁוֹר וּבַחֲמֹר יַחְדָּו" (דברים כב, י).

Not to perform labor with two species of animals together, as it is stated: "You shall not plow with an ox and a donkey together" (Deuteronomy 22:10).

Mitzva 219

שֶׁלֹּא לַחְסֹם בְּהֵמָה בִּשְׁעַת מְלָאכָה בְּדָבָר שֶׁאוֹכֶלֶת מִמֶּנּוּ וְנֶהֱנֵית, שֶׁנֶּאֱמַר: "לֹא תַחְסֹם שׁוֹר בְּדִישׁוֹ" (דברים כה, ד).

Not to muzzle an animal during its labor, when it is working **with something from which it eats and derives benefit, as it is stated: "You shall not muzzle an ox while it is threshing"** (Deuteronomy 25:4).

Mitzva 220

שֶׁלֹּא לַעֲבֹד אֲדָמָה בַּשְּׁבִיעִית, שֶׁנֶּאֱמַר: "שָׂדְךָ לֹא תִזְרָע" (ויקרא כה, ד).

Not to work the earth in the seventh year, **as it is stated: "Your field you shall not sow"** (Leviticus 25:4).

Mitzva 221

שֶׁלֹּא לַעֲבֹד אִילָן בַּשְּׁבִיעִית, שֶׁנֶּאֱמַר: "וְכַרְמְךָ לֹא תִזְמֹר" (שם).

Not to perform the labor of trees in the seventh year, **as it is stated: "And your vineyard you shall not prune"** (Leviticus 25:4).

Mitzva 222

שֶׁלֹּא לִקְצֹר סְפִיחֵי שְׁבִיעִית כְּדֶרֶךְ שֶׁקּוֹצְרִין בִּשְׁאָר הַשָּׁנִים, שֶׁנֶּאֱמַר: "אֵת סְפִיחַ קְצִירְךָ לֹא תִקְצוֹר" (ויקרא כה, ה).

Not to reap the aftergrowths of the seventh year **in the manner that they are reaped in the other years, as it is stated: "The aftergrowth of your reaping you shall not reap"** (Leviticus 25:5).

Mitzva 223

שֶׁלֹּא לֶאֱסֹף פֵּרוֹת הָאִילָן בַּשְּׁבִיעִית כְּדֶרֶךְ שֶׁאוֹסְפִין בְּכָל שָׁנָה, שֶׁנֶּאֱמַר: "וְאֶת עִנְּבֵי נְזִירֶךָ לֹא תִבְצֹר" (שם).

Not to gather the fruit of trees in the seventh year **in the manner that they are gathered in every** other **year, as it is stated: "And the uncultivated grapes of your vine you shall not gather"** (Leviticus 25:5).

Mitzva 224

שֶׁלֹּא לַעֲבֹד בִּשְׁנַת יוֹבֵל בֵּין אֲדָמָה בֵּין אִילָן, שֶׁנֶּאֱמַר בָּהּ: "לֹא תִזְרָעוּ" (ויקרא כה, יא).

Not to perform labor in the Jubilee Year, whether on the **earth or** on **trees,** as it is stated: "It is a Jubilee... **you shall not sow"** (Leviticus 25:11).

Mitzva 225

שֶׁלֹּא לִקְצֹר סְפִיחֵי יוֹבֵל כִּשְׁאָר הַשָּׁנִים, שֶׁנֶּאֱמַר בּוֹ: "לֹא תִקְצְרוּ אֶת סְפִיחֶיהָ" (שם, ושם: וְלֹא).

Not to reap the aftergrowths of the Jubilee Year **like in the other years, as it is stated: "You shall not reap its aftergrowth"** (Leviticus 25:11).

Mitzva 226

שֶׁלֹּא לֶאֱסֹף פֵּרוֹת יוֹבֵל כַּאֲסִיפַת שְׁאָר הַשָּׁנִים, שֶׁנֶּאֱמַר בּוֹ: "וְלֹא תִבְצְרוּ אֶת נְזִרֶיהָ" (שם).

Not to gather the produce of the Jubilee Year **in** the manner **of the gathering of the other years, as it is stated: "And you shall not gather its uncultivated grapes"** (Leviticus 25:11).

Mitzva 227

שֶׁלֹּא לִמְכֹּר שָׂדֶה בְּאֶרֶץ יִשְׂרָאֵל לִצְמִיתוּת, שֶׁנֶּאֱמַר: "וְהָאָרֶץ לֹא תִמָּכֵר לִצְמִתֻת" (ויקרא כה, כג).

Not to sell a field in the Land of Israel in perpetuity, as it is stated: "And the land shall not be sold in perpetuity" (Leviticus 25:23).

Mitzva 228

שֶׁלֹּא לְשַׁנּוֹת מִגְרְשֵׁי הַלְוִיִּם וּשְׂדוֹתֵיהֶם, שֶׁנֶּאֱמַר: "וּשְׂדֵה מִגְרַשׁ עָרֵיהֶם לֹא יִמָּכֵר" (ויקרא כה, לד). מִפִּי הַשְּׁמוּעָה לָמְדוּ שֶׁזּוֹ אַזְהָרָה שֶׁלֹּא יִשְׁתַּנֶּה.

Not to change the perimeter areas **and fields of** the cities **of the Levites, as it is stated: "But the fields of the perimeter of their cities shall not be sold"** (Leviticus 25:34). The Sages **learned, on the basis of the** Oral **tradition, that this is a prohibition that** these areas **may not be changed** (see *Arakhin* 33b).

Mitzva 229

שֶׁלֹּא לַעֲזֹב הַלְוִיִּם, שֶׁנֶּאֱמַר: "הִשָּׁמֶר לְךָ פֶּן תַּעֲזֹב אֶת הַלֵּוִי" (דברים יב, יט), אֶלָּא נוֹתְנִין לָהֶם מַתְּנוֹתֵיהֶם וּמְשַׂמְּחִין אוֹתָן בָּהֶן בְּכָל רֶגֶל וָרֶגֶל.

Not to forsake the Levites, as it is stated: "Beware, lest you forsake the Levite" (Deuteronomy 12:19). **Rather, one gives them their gifts and enables them to rejoice on each and every pilgrimage festival.**

Mitzva 230

שֶׁלֹּא יִתְבַּע הַלְוָאָה שֶׁעָבְרָה עָלֶיהָ שְׁבִיעִית, שֶׁנֶּאֱמַר: "לֹא יִגֹּשׂ אֶת רֵעֵהוּ וְאֶת אָחִיו" (דברים טו, ב).

Not to demand payment of **a loan after the seventh** year **has passed, as it is stated: "He shall not demand it from his neighbor or his brother"** (Deuteronomy 15:2).

Mitzva 231

שֶׁלֹּא יִמָּנַע מִלְּהַלְווֹת לֶעָנִי מִפְּנֵי הַשְּׁמִטָּה, שֶׁנֶּאֱמַר: "הִשָּׁמֶר לְךָ פֶּן יִהְיֶה דָבָר" וכו' (דברים טו, ט). זֶה הַכְּלָל: כָּל מָקוֹם שֶׁנֶּאֱמַר "הִשָּׁמֶר" אוֹ "פֶּן" אוֹ "אַל" – אֵינוֹ אֶלָּא מִצְוַת לֹא תַעֲשֶׂה.

Not to refrain from lending to a poor person on account of the Sabbatical Year, **as it is stated: "Beware, lest there be** a wicked **thought…"** (Deuteronomy 15:9). **This is the** general **rule: Any place where it is stated "beware" or "lest" or "do not," it is nothing other than a negative mitzva.**

Mitzva 232

שֶׁלֹּא לְהִמָּנַע מִלְּהַחֲיוֹת לֶעָנִי וּמִלִּתֵּן לוֹ מַה שֶּׁהוּא צָרִיךְ, שֶׁנֶּאֱמַר: "לֹא תְאַמֵּץ אֶת לְבָבְךָ" וכו' (דברים טו, ז). נִמְצָא הַנּוֹתֵן צְדָקָה עוֹשֶׂה מִצְוַת עֲשֵׂה, וְהַמַּעְלִים עֵינָיו מִן הַצְּדָקָה – יָתֵר עַל שֶׁבִּטֵּל עֲשֵׂה, עָבַר עַל לֹא תַעֲשֶׂה.

Not to refrain from providing sustenance to a poor person or from giving him what he needs, as it is stated: "You shall not harden your heart…" (Deuteronomy 15:7). **Thus, one who gives charity has performed a positive mitzva, while one who averts his eyes from** the obligation to give **charity, in addition to negating a positive mitzva, has** also **violated a negative mitzva.**

Mitzva 233

שֶׁלֹּא לְשַׁלֵּחַ עֶבֶד עִבְרִי רֵיקָם כְּשֶׁיֵּצֵא חָפְשִׁי, שֶׁנֶּאֱמַר: "לֹא תְשַׁלְּחֶנּוּ רֵיקָם" (דברים טו, יג).

Not to send away a Hebrew slave empty-handed when he goes free, as it is stated: "You shall not release him empty-handed" (Deuteronomy 15:13).

Mitzva 234

שֶׁלֹּא יִתְבַּע הֶעָנִי בְּחוֹבוֹ כְּשֶׁיֵּדַע שֶׁהוּא עָנִי וְלֹא יָצֵר לוֹ, שֶׁנֶּאֱמַר: "לֹא תִהְיֶה לוֹ כְּנֹשֶׁה" (שמות כב, כד).

Not to sue a poor person for his debt, knowing that he is poor, and one may not oppress him, as it is stated: "You shall not be as a creditor to him" (Exodus 22:24).

Mitzva 235

שֶׁלֹּא לְהַלְווֹת בְּרִבִּית לְיִשְׂרָאֵל, שֶׁנֶּאֱמַר: "אֶת כַּסְפְּךָ לֹא תִתֵּן לוֹ בְּנֶשֶׁךְ וּבְמַרְבִּית" (ויקרא כה, לז).

Not to loan to a Jew at interest, as it is stated: "Your silver you shall not give him with interest and with increase" (Leviticus 25:37).

Mitzva 236

שֶׁלֹּא לִלְווֹת בְּרִבִּית, שֶׁנֶּאֱמַר: "לֹא תַשִּׁיךְ לְאָחִיךָ" (דברים כג, כ). כָּךְ לָמְדוּ מִפִּי הַשְּׁמוּעָה, שֶׁזּוֹ אַזְהָרָה לַלֹּוֶה שֶׁלֹּא יַנֵּשֵׁךְ לַמַּלְוֶה.

Not to borrow with interest, as it is stated: "You shall not be lent to with interest" (Deuteronomy 23:20). Although this verse can be read as "you shall not lend with interest," the Sages **learned as follows, on the basis of the** Oral **tradition, that it is a prohibition** applying **to the borrower, that he should not receive a loan with interest from the lender** (see *Bava Metzia* 75b).

Mitzva 237

שֶׁלֹּא לְהָשִׁית יָד בֵּין לֹוֶה וּמַלְוֶה בְּרִבִּית, לֹא לִהְיוֹת עָרֵב וְלֹא עֵד וְלֹא לִכְתֹּב שְׁטָר בֵּינֵיהֶם, שֶׁנֶּאֱמַר: "לֹא תְשִׂימוּן עָלָיו נֶשֶׁךְ" (שמות כב, כד).

Not to extend a hand to assist in the transactions **between a borrower and lender at interest, not be a guarantor** for them, **nor** serve as **a witness, nor write** a promissory **note for them, as it is stated: "You shall not impose upon him interest"** (Exodus 22:24).

Mitzva 238

שֶׁלֹּא לְאַחֵר פְּעֻלַּת שָׂכִיר, שֶׁנֶּאֱמַר: "לֹא תָלִין פְּעֻלַּת שָׂכִיר" וכו' (ויקרא יט, יג).

Not to delay the wages of a hired laborer, as it is stated: "You shall not keep the wages of a hired laborer…" (Leviticus 19:13).

Mitzva 239

שֶׁלֹּא יְמַשְׁכֵּן בַּעַל חוֹב בִּזְרוֹעַ, שֶׁנֶּאֱמַר: "לֹא תָבֹא אֶל בֵּיתוֹ לַעֲבֹט עֲבֹטוֹ" (דברים כד, י).

That a creditor may not take collateral forcibly, as it is stated: "You shall not go into his house to take his collateral" (Deuteronomy 24:10).

Mitzva 240

שֶׁלֹּא לִמְנֹעַ הָעֲבוֹט מִבְּעָלָיו הֶעָנִי בְּעֵת שֶׁהוּא צָרִיךְ לוֹ, שֶׁנֶּאֱמַר: "לֹא תִשְׁכַּב בַּעֲבֹטוֹ" (דברים כד, יב), כְּלוֹמַר: לֹא תִשְׁכַּב וַעֲבוֹטוֹ עִמְּךָ, אֶלָּא תְּשִׁיבֶנּוּ לוֹ בַּלַּיְלָה, הוֹאִיל וְהוּא צָרִיךְ לוֹ בַּלַּיְלָה.

Not to withhold collateral from its owner, if he is **a poor person, when he needs it, as it is stated: "You shall not sleep with his collateral"** (Deuteronomy 24:12). **In other words, do not sleep** while **his collateral is with you; instead, return it to him at night, since he needs it at night.**

Mitzva 241

שֶׁלֹּא לְמַשְׁכֵּן הָאַלְמָנָה, שֶׁנֶּאֱמַר: "וְלֹא תַחֲבֹל בֶּגֶד אַלְמָנָה" (דברים כד, יז).

Not to take an item from **a widow as collateral, as it is stated: "And you shall not take a widow's garment as collateral"** (Deuteronomy 24:17).

Mitzva 242

שֶׁלֹּא לַחֲבֹל כֵּלִים שֶׁעוֹשִׂין בָּהֶן אֹכֶל נֶפֶשׁ, שֶׁנֶּאֱמַר: "לֹא יַחֲבֹל רֵחַיִם וָרָכֶב" (דברים כד, ו).

Not to take as collateral any **implements with which food is prepared, as it is stated: "One shall not take the lower millstone or the upper millstone as collateral"** (Deuteronomy 24:6).

Mitzva 243

שֶׁלֹּא לִגְנֹב נֶפֶשׁ מִיִּשְׂרָאֵל, שֶׁנֶּאֱמַר: "לֹא תִגְנֹב" (שמות כ, יב; דברים ה, טז) – **זֶה גּוֹנֵב נֶפֶשׁ.**

Not to kidnap a Jew, as it is stated: "You shall not steal" (Exodus 20:13, Deuteronomy 5:17) – **this is** one who **steals a person.**

Mitzva 244

שֶׁלֹּא לִגְנֹב מָמוֹן, שֶׁנֶּאֱמַר: "לֹא תִּגְנֹבוּ" (ויקרא יט, יא) – **זוֹ הִיא גְּנֵבַת מָמוֹן.**

Not to steal property, as it is stated: "You shall not steal" (Leviticus 19:11) – **this** verse **is** referring to **stealing property.**

Mitzva 245

שֶׁלֹּא לִגְזֹל, שֶׁנֶּאֱמַר: "וְלֹא תִגְזֹל" (ויקרא יט, יג).

Not to rob, as it is stated: "And you shall not rob" (Leviticus 19:13).

Mitzva 246

שֶׁלֹּא לְהַשִּׂיג גְּבוּלוֹת, שֶׁנֶּאֱמַר: "לֹא תַשִּׂיג גְּבוּל רֵעֲךָ" (דברים יט, יד, ושם: תַסִּיג).

Not to move boundaries, as it is stated: "You shall not move your neighbor's boundary" (Deuteronomy 19:14).

Mitzva 247

שֶׁלֹּא לַעֲשֹׁק, שֶׁנֶּאֱמַר: "לֹא תַעֲשֹׁק אֶת רֵעֲךָ" (ויקרא יט, יג).

Not to exploit, as it is stated: "You shall not exploit your neighbor" (Leviticus 19:13).

Mitzva 248

שֶׁלֹּא לְכַחֵשׁ בְּמָמוֹן חֲבֵרוֹ, שֶׁנֶּאֱמַר: "וְלֹא תְכַחֲשׁוּ" (ויקרא יט, יא).

Not to falsely **deny a claim involving the property of another, as it is stated: "Nor shall you falsely deny a claim"** (Leviticus 19:11).

Mitzva 249

שֶׁלֹּא לִשָּׁבַע עַל כְּפִירַת מָמוֹן חֲבֵרוֹ, שֶׁנֶּאֱמַר: "וְלֹא תְשַׁקְּרוּ" (שם), **כְּלוֹמַר: לֹא תִשָּׁבַע עַל שֶׁקֶר בְּמָמוֹן שֶׁיֵּשׁ לַחֲבֵרְךָ בְּיָדְךָ.**

Not to swear falsely **regarding the denial of a monetary matter** involving **another, as it is stated: "Nor shall you lie"** (Leviticus 19:11). **In other words, do not swear falsely regarding money that another** person owns which is currently **in your possession.**

Mitzva 250

שֶׁלֹּא יוֹנֶה בְּמֶקַח וּמִמְכָּר, שֶׁנֶּאֱמַר: "אַל תּוֹנוּ אִישׁ אֶת אָחִיו" (ויקרא כה, יד).

Not to defraud when buying and selling, as it is stated: "You shall not exploit one another" (Leviticus 25:14).

Mitzva 251

שֶׁלֹּא יוֹנֶה בִּדְבָרִים, שֶׁנֶּאֱמַר: "וְלֹא תוֹנוּ אִישׁ אֶת עֲמִיתוֹ וְיָרֵאתָ מֵאֱלֹהֶיךָ" (ויקרא כה, יז) – **זוֹ אוֹנָאַת דְּבָרִים.**

Not to verbally mistreat another, **as it is stated: "And you shall not wrong one another, and you shall fear your God"** (Leviticus 25:17) – **this** verse **is** referring to **verbal mistreatment.**

Mitzva 252

שֶׁלֹּא לְהוֹנוֹת אֶת הַגֵּר בִּדְבָרִים, שֶׁנֶּאֱמַר: "וְגֵר לֹא תוֹנֶה" (שמות כב, כ).

Not to verbally mistreat a convert, as it is stated: "You shall not mistreat a stranger" (Exodus 22:20).

Mitzva 253

שֶׁלֹּא לְהוֹנוֹת אֶת הַגֵּר בְּמֶקַח וּמִמְכָּר, שֶׁנֶּאֱמַר: "וְלֹא תִלְחָצֶנּוּ" (שם).

Not to mistreat a convert in his transactions of **buying and selling, as it is stated: "And you shall not oppress him"** (Exodus 22:20).

Mitzva 254

שֶׁלֹּא לְהַחֲזִיר עֶבֶד שֶׁבָּרַח לְאֶרֶץ יִשְׂרָאֵל לַאֲדוֹנָיו שֶׁבְּחוּצָה לָאָרֶץ, שֶׁנֶּאֱמַר: "לֹא תַסְגִּיר עֶבֶד אֶל אֲדֹנָיו" (דברים כג, טז).

Not to return a slave who fled to the Land of Israel to his master who is outside of the Land, as it is stated: "You shall not hand over to his master a slave" (Deuteronomy 23:16).

Mitzva 255

שֶׁלֹּא לְהוֹנוֹת עֶבֶד זֶה, שֶׁנֶּאֱמַר: "עִמְּךָ יֵשֵׁב בְּקִרְבְּךָ וכו' לֹא תּוֹנֶנּוּ" (דברים כג, יז).

Not to exploit this slave, as it is stated: "With you he shall reside, in your midst…you shall not mistreat him" (Deuteronomy 23:17).

Mitzva 256

שֶׁלֹּא לְעַנּוֹת יָתוֹם וְאַלְמָנָה, שֶׁנֶּאֱמַר: "כָּל אַלְמָנָה וְיָתוֹם לֹא תְעַנּוּן" (שמות כב, כא).

Not to afflict an orphan or widow, as it is stated: "You shall not afflict any widow or orphan" (Exodus 22:21).

Mitzva 257

שֶׁלֹּא לַעֲבֹד בְּעֶבֶד עִבְרִי עֲבוֹדַת עֶבֶד, שֶׁנֶּאֱמַר: "לֹא תַעֲבֹד בּוֹ עֲבֹדַת עָבֶד" (ויקרא כה, לט).

Not to put a Hebrew slave to work as a slave, as it is stated: "You shall not work him as a slave" (Leviticus 25:39).

Mitzva 258

שֶׁלֹּא לִמְכֹּר אוֹתוֹ מִמְכֶּרֶת עֲבָדִים, שֶׁנֶּאֱמַר: "לֹא יִמָּכְרוּ מִמְכֶּרֶת עָבֶד" (ויקרא כה, מב).

Not to sell a Hebrew slave as a slave, as it is stated: "They shall not be sold as slaves" (Leviticus 25:42).

Mitzva 259

שֶׁלֹּא לַעֲבֹד בְּעֶבֶד עִבְרִי בְּפֶרֶךְ, שֶׁנֶּאֱמַר: "לֹא תִרְדֶּה בוֹ בְּפָרֶךְ" (ויקרא כה, מג; כה, מו).

Not to make a Hebrew slave perform hard labor, as it is stated: "You shall not oppress him with hard labor" (Leviticus 25:43, 46).

Mitzva 260

שֶׁלֹּא לְהַנִּיחַ הַגּוֹי לַעֲבֹד בְּעֶבֶד עִבְרִי הַנִּמְכָּר לוֹ בְּפֶרֶךְ, שֶׁנֶּאֱמַר: "לֹא יִרְדֶּנּוּ בְּפֶרֶךְ לְעֵינֶיךָ" (ויקרא כה, נג).

Not to allow a gentile to make a Hebrew slave, who was sold to him, perform hard labor, as it is stated: "He shall not oppress him with hard labor before your eyes" (Leviticus 25:53).

Mitzva 261

שֶׁלֹּא לִמְכֹּר אָמָה עִבְרִיָּה לְאַחֵר, שֶׁנֶּאֱמַר: "לֹא יִמְשֹׁל לְמָכְרָהּ בְּבִגְדוֹ בָהּ" (שמות כא, ח).

Not to sell a Hebrew maidservant to another, as it is stated: "He shall not presume to sell her to a foreign people **in his betrayal of her"** (Exodus 21:8).

Mitzva 262

שֶׁלֹּא לִמְנֹעַ מֵאָמָה עִבְרִיָּה הַיְעוּדָה שְׁאֵר כְּסוּת וְעוֹנָה, שֶׁנֶּאֱמַר: "שְׁאֵרָהּ כְּסוּתָהּ וְעֹנָתָהּ לֹא יִגְרָע" (שמות כא, י), וְהוּא הַדִּין לִשְׁאָר כָּל הַנָּשִׁים.

Not to withhold from a designated Hebrew maidservant her **food, clothing, and conjugal rights, as it is stated: "He shall not diminish her food, her garments, or her conjugal rights"** (Exodus 21:10). **The same is true of all other** married **women.**

Mitzva 263

שֶׁלֹּא לִמְכֹּר אֵשֶׁת יְפַת תֹּאַר, שֶׁנֶּאֱמַר: "וּמָכֹר לֹא תִמְכְּרֶנָּה בַּכָּסֶף" (דברים כא, יד).

Not to sell a beautiful woman captured in war, **as it is stated: "You shall not sell her for silver"** (Deuteronomy 21:14).

Mitzva 264

שֶׁלֹּא לִכְבֹּשׁ אֵשֶׁת יְפַת תֹּאַר שִׁפְחָה, שֶׁנֶּאֱמַר: "לֹא תִתְעַמֵּר בָּהּ" (שם).

Not to subjugate a beautiful woman captured in war by treating her like a **maidservant, as it is stated: "You shall not enslave her"** (Deuteronomy 21:14).

Mitzva 265

שֶׁלֹּא לַחְמֹד, שֶׁנֶּאֱמַר: "לֹא תַחְמֹד אֵשֶׁת רֵעֶךָ" (שמות כ, יג), "שָׂדֵהוּ" וכו' (דברים ה, יז).

Not to covet, as it is stated: "You shall not covet your neighbor's wife" (Exodus 20:14) **"his field…"** (Deuteronomy 5:18).

Mitzva 266

שֶׁלֹּא לְהִתְאַוּוֹת, שֶׁנֶּאֱמַר: "וְלֹא תִתְאַוֶּה בֵּית רֵעֶךָ" (שם).

Not to desire that which belongs to another, **as it is stated: "And you shall not desire your neighbor's house"** (Deuteronomy 5:18).

Mitzva 267

שֶׁלֹּא יֹאכַל הַשָּׂכִיר שֶׁלֹּא בִּשְׁעַת גְּמַר מְלָאכָה מִן הַמְחֻבָּר שֶׁהוּא עוֹשֶׂה בּוֹ, שֶׁנֶּאֱמַר: "וְחֶרְמֵשׁ לֹא תָנִיף" וכו' (דברים כג, כו).

That a hired laborer may not eat from the attached produce **with which he is working, when it is not at the time of the completion of** its **labor, as it is stated: "But you shall not wield a sickle…"** (Deuteronomy 23:26).

Mitzva 268

שֶׁלֹּא יִקַּח הַשָּׂכִיר יָתֵר עַל אֲכִילָתוֹ, שֶׁנֶּאֱמַר: "וְאָכַלְתָּ עֲנָבִים כְּנַפְשְׁךָ שָׂבְעֶךָ וְאֶל" וכו' (דברים כג, כה).

That a hired laborer may not take more than he has eaten, as it is stated: "You may eat grapes as you desire, to your contentment, but into your vessel you shall not place" (Deuteronomy 23:25).

Mitzva 269

שֶׁלֹּא יִתְעַלֵּם מִן הָאֲבֵדָה, שֶׁנֶּאֱמַר: "לֹא תוּכַל לְהִתְעַלֵּם" (דברים כב, ג).

Not to disregard a lost item, as it is stated: "You shall not disregard" (Deuteronomy 22:3).

Mitzva 270

שֶׁלֹּא לְהַנִּיחַ הַבְּהֵמָה רוֹבֶצֶת תַּחַת מַשָּׂאָהּ בַּדֶּרֶךְ, שֶׁנֶּאֱמַר: "כִּי תִרְאֶה חֲמוֹר שֹׂנַאֲךָ" וכו' (שמות כג, ה).

Not to leave an animal crouching under its burden on the way, as it is stated: "If you see the donkey of your enemy crouching under its burden" (Exodus 23:5).

Mitzva 271

שֶׁלֹּא לַעֲשׂוֹת עָוֶל בַּמִּדָּה, שֶׁנֶּאֱמַר: "לֹא תַעֲשׂוּ עָוֶל בַּמִּשְׁפָּט בַּמִּדָּה" (ויקרא יט, לה). מִפִּי הַשְּׁמוּעָה לָמְדוּ שֶׁהַכָּתוּב מַזְהִיר: לֹא תַעֲשׂוּ עָוֶל בְּמִשְׁפַּט הַמִּדָּה.

Not to do injustice in measures, as it is stated: "You shall do no injustice in judgment, in measure, in weight" (Leviticus 19:35). The Sages learned, on the basis of the Oral tradition, that the verse is warning: Do no injustice in the judgment of your measures.[a]

Mitzva 272

שֶׁלֹּא לִהְיוֹת אֶצְלֵנוּ אֵיפָה וְאֵיפָה, אֶבֶן וָאָבֶן, שֶׁנֶּאֱמַר: "לֹא יִהְיֶה לְךָ בְּבֵיתְךָ אֵיפָה וְאֵיפָה גְּדוֹלָה וּקְטַנָּה" (דברים כה, יד), "לֹא יִהְיֶה לְךָ בְּכִיסְךָ אֶבֶן וָאָבֶן גְּדוֹלָה וּקְטַנָּה" (שם כה, יג).

That one may not keep in his possession different weights and different measures, as it is stated: "You shall not have in your house different measures, great and small" (Deuteronomy 25:14); "you shall not have in your pouch different weights, great and small" (Deuteronomy 25:13).

Mitzva 273

שֶׁלֹּא לְעַוֵּל הַמִּשְׁפָּט, שֶׁנֶּאֱמַר: "לֹא תַעֲשׂוּ עָוֶל בַּמִּשְׁפָּט" (ויקרא יט, טו).

Not to perform injustice in judgment, as it is stated: "You shall not perform injustice in judgment" (Leviticus 19:15).

Mitzva 274

שֶׁלֹּא לִקַּח שֹׁחַד, שֶׁנֶּאֱמַר: "וְשֹׁחַד לֹא תִקָּח" (שמות כג, ח).

Not to take a bribe, as it is stated: "You shall not take a bribe" (Exodus 23:8).

Mitzva 275

שֶׁלֹּא לְכַבֵּד גָּדוֹל בַּדִּין, שֶׁנֶּאֱמַר: "וְלֹא תֶהְדַּר פְּנֵי גָדוֹל" (ויקרא יט, טו).

Not to honor a great person in judgment, as it is stated: "You shall not defer to the great" (Leviticus 19:15).

Mitzva 276

שֶׁלֹּא יִירָא הַדַּיָּן בַּדִּין מֵאָדָם רַע, שֶׁנֶּאֱמַר: "לֹא תָגוּרוּ מִפְּנֵי אִישׁ" (דברים א, יז).

That a judge should not fear a wicked person in judgment, as it is stated: "You shall not fear due to any man" (Deuteronomy 1:17).

Mitzva 277

שֶׁלֹּא לְרַחֵם עַל עָנִי בַּדִּין, שֶׁנֶּאֱמַר: "וְדָל לֹא תֶהְדַּר בְּרִיבוֹ" (שמות כג, ג).

Not to show pity to a poor person in judgment, as it is stated: "You shall not favor a poor man in his dispute" (Exodus 23:3).

Mitzva 278

שֶׁלֹּא לְהַטּוֹת מִשְׁפַּט אָדָם חוֹטֵא, שֶׁנֶּאֱמַר: "לֹא תַטֶּה מִשְׁפַּט אֶבְיֹנְךָ" (שמות כג, ו). לָמְדוּ מִפִּי הַשְּׁמוּעָה שֶׁזֶּה אֶבְיוֹן בְּמִצְוֹת.

Not to distort the judgment of a sinner, as it is stated: "You shall not distort the judgment of your poor in his dispute" (Exodus 23:6). The Sages learned, on the basis of the Oral tradition, that this is referring to one who is poor in mitzvot.[b]

Mitzva 279

שֶׁלֹּא לְרַחֵם עַל הַמַּזִּיק בְּדִינֵי קְנָסוֹת, שֶׁנֶּאֱמַר: "לֹא תָחוֹס עֵינֶךָ" וכו' (דברים יט, כא, ושם: וְלֹא).

Not to show pity to one who causes damage, with respect to the laws of fines, as it is stated: "Your eye shall not pity..." (Deuteronomy 19:21).

Mitzva 280

שֶׁלֹּא לְהַטּוֹת מִשְׁפַּט גֵּרִים וִיתוֹמִים, שֶׁנֶּאֱמַר: "לֹא תַטֶּה מִשְׁפַּט גֵּר יָתוֹם" (דברים כד, יז).

Not to distort the judgment of converts or orphans, as it is stated: "You shall not distort the judgment against a stranger or an orphan" (Deuteronomy 24:17).

NOTES

a. See *Sifra* on Leviticus 19:35 (*Yad Peshuta*).

b. See *Mekhilta DeRabbi Yishmael* on Exodus 23:6 (*Yad Peshuta*).

Mitzva 281

שֶׁלֹּא לִשְׁמֹעַ מֵאֶחָד מִבַּעֲלֵי דִּינִין וְאֵין חֲבֵרוֹ עִמּוֹ, שֶׁנֶּאֱמַר: "לֹא תִשָּׂא שֵׁמַע שָׁוְא" (שמות כג, א).

Not to hear from one of the litigants when his counterpart is not with him, as it is stated: "You shall not accept a false report" (Exodus 23:1).

Mitzva 282

שֶׁלֹּא לִנְטוֹת אַחֲרֵי רַבִּים בְּדִינֵי נְפָשׁוֹת אִם הָיוּ הַמְחַיְּבִין יָתֵר עַל הַמְזַכִּין אֶחָד, שֶׁנֶּאֱמַר: "לֹא תִהְיֶה אַחֲרֵי רַבִּים לְרָעֹת" (שמות כג, ב).

Not to incline after a majority, in cases of capital law, if those condemning him are only **one man more than the acquitters, as it is stated: "You shall not follow the majority for evil"** (Exodus 23:2).

Mitzva 283

שֶׁלֹּא יְלַמֵּד חוֹבָה מִי שֶׁלִּמֵּד זְכוּת תְּחִלָּה בְּדִינֵי נְפָשׁוֹת, שֶׁנֶּאֱמַר: "לֹא תַעֲנֶה עַל רִב לִנְטֹת" (שם, ושם: וְלֹא).

That one who initially taught a reason to **acquit the accused may not** subsequently **teach** a reason to **condemn** him, **in cases of capital law, as it is stated: "You shall not follow the majority for evil"** (Exodus 23:2).

GLOSSES OF THE RAAVAD

שֶׁלֹּא יְלַמֵּד חוֹבָה מִי שֶׁלִּמֵּד זְכוּת תְּחִלָּה בְּדִינֵי נְפָשׁוֹת שֶׁנֶּאֱמַר לֹא תַעֲנֶה עַל רִב לִנְטֹת. אָמַר אַבְרָהָם: אֵין זֶה כְּלוּם שֶׁהֲרֵי בִּגְמַר דִּין חוֹזֵר.

"That one who initially taught a reason to acquit the accused may not teach a reason to condemn him, in cases of capital law, as it is stated, you shall not follow the majority for evil." Avraham says: This is nothing, for he can retract at the verdict.

Mitzva 284

שֶׁלֹּא לְמַנּוֹת בְּדַיָּנִין אָדָם שֶׁאֵינוֹ חָכָם בְּדִינֵי תּוֹרָה אַף עַל פִּי שֶׁהוּא חָכָם בְּחָכְמוֹת אֲחֵרוֹת, שֶׁנֶּאֱמַר: "לֹא תַכִּירוּ פָנִים בַּמִּשְׁפָּט" (דברים א, יז).

Not to appoint a judge who is not versed in the laws of the Torah, even if he is versed in other fields of wisdom, **as it is stated: "You shall not give preference in judgment"** (Deuteronomy 1:17).

Mitzva 285

שֶׁלֹּא לְהָעִיד בְּשֶׁקֶר, שֶׁנֶּאֱמַר: "לֹא תַעֲנֶה בְרֵעֲךָ עֵד שָׁקֶר" (שמות כ, יב).

Not to testify falsely, as it is stated: "You shall not bear false witness against your neighbor" (Exodus 20:13).

Mitzva 286

שֶׁלֹּא יָעִיד בַּעַל עֲבֵרָה, שֶׁנֶּאֱמַר: "אַל תָּשֶׁת יָדְךָ עִם רָשָׁע לִהְיֹת עֵד חָמָס" (שמות כג, א).

That a transgressor may not give testimony, as it is stated: "Do not place your hand with the wicked to be a corrupt witness" (Exodus 23:1).

Mitzva 287

שֶׁלֹּא יָעִיד קָרוֹב, שֶׁנֶּאֱמַר: "לֹא יוּמְתוּ אָבוֹת עַל בָּנִים וּבָנִים לֹא יוּמְתוּ עַל אָבוֹת" (דברים כד, טז). מִפִּי הַשְּׁמוּעָה שֶׁלֹּא יוּמְתוּ אָבוֹת בְּעֵדוּת בָּנִים, וְהוּא הַדִּין לִשְׁאָר הַקְּרוֹבִים.

That a family **relative may not give testimony, as it is stated: "The fathers shall not be put to death for the sons, and the sons shall not be put to death for the fathers"** (Deuteronomy 24:16). The Sages **learned, on the basis of the** Oral **tradition, that this** means **that fathers shall not be put to death through the testimony of** their **sons,**[a] **and the same is true of the other** family **relatives.**

Mitzva 288

שֶׁלֹּא לִכְרֹת הַדִּין עַל פִּי עֵד אֶחָד, שֶׁנֶּאֱמַר: "לֹא יָקוּם עֵד אֶחָד בְּאִישׁ" (דברים יט, טו).

Not to reach a verdict on the testimony **of one witness, as it is stated: "One witness shall not stand against a man"** (Deuteronomy 19:15).

Mitzva 289

שֶׁלֹּא לַהֲרֹג נָקִי, שֶׁנֶּאֱמַר: "לֹא תִרְצָח" (שמות כ, יב; דברים ה, טז).

Not to kill an innocent person, as it is stated: "You shall not murder" (Exodus 20:13, Deuteronomy 5:17).

Mitzva 290

שֶׁלֹּא לַחְתֹּךְ הַדִּין בְּאֹמֶד הַדַּעַת, עַד שֶׁיִּרְאוּ שְׁנֵי עֵדִים גּוּפוֹ שֶׁל דָּבָר, שֶׁנֶּאֱמַר: "וְנָקִי וְצַדִּיק אַל תַּהֲרֹג" (שמות כג, ז).

Not to establish a verdict through speculation, but **only when two witnesses have observed the matter itself, as it is stated: "And you shall not kill the innocent and the righteous"** (Exodus 23:7).

NOTES

a. See *Sifrei* on Deuteronomy 24:16 (*Yad Peshuta*).

Mitzva 291

שֶׁלֹּא יוֹרֶה הָעֵד בְּדִין שֶׁהֵעִיד בּוֹ בְּדִינֵי נְפָשׁוֹת, שֶׁנֶּאֱמַר: "וְעֵד...לֹא יַעֲנֶה בְנֶפֶשׁ" (במדבר לה, ל).

That a witness may not issue a ruling in a case regarding which he has testified, in cases of capital law, as it is stated: "But one **witness shall not testify against a person** to die" (Numbers 35:30).

Mitzva 292

שֶׁלֹּא לַהֲרֹג מְחֻיַּב הֲרִיגָה קֹדֶם שֶׁיַּעֲמֹד בַּדִּין, שֶׁנֶּאֱמַר: "וְלֹא יָמוּת הָרֹצֵחַ עַד עָמְדוֹ לִפְנֵי הָעֵדָה" (במדבר לה, יב).

Not to execute one who is liable to execution before he has been brought for judgment, as it is stated: "That the murderer shall not die, until he stands before the congregation for judgment" (Numbers 35:12).

Mitzva 293

שֶׁלֹּא לָחוּס עַל הָרוֹדֵף, אֶלָּא הוֹרְגִין אוֹתוֹ קֹדֶם שֶׁיַּגִּיעַ לַנִּרְדָּף וְיַהַרְגֶנּוּ אוֹ יְגַלֶּה עֶרְוָתוֹ, שֶׁנֶּאֱמַר: "וְקַצֹּתָה אֶת כַּפָּהּ לֹא תָחוֹס עֵינֶךָ" (דברים כה, יב).

Not to have mercy on a pursuer, as it is stated: "You shall sever her hand; your eye shall not pity" (Deuteronomy 25:12).

Mitzva 294

שֶׁלֹּא לַעֲנֹשׁ הָאָנוּס, שֶׁנֶּאֱמַר: "וְלַנַּעֲרָה לֹא תַעֲשֶׂה דָבָר" (דברים כב, כו, ושם: וְלַנַּעַר).

Not to punish a victim of circumstances beyond his control, as it is stated: "But to the young woman you shall do nothing" (Deuteronomy 22:26).

Mitzva 295

שֶׁלֹּא לִקַּח כֹּפֶר מִן הָרוֹצֵחַ, שֶׁנֶּאֱמַר: "וְלֹא תִקְחוּ כֹפֶר לְנֶפֶשׁ רֹצֵחַ" (במדבר לה, לא).

Not to take ransom from a murderer in exchange for his life, **as it is stated: "You shall not take ransom for the life of a murderer"** (Numbers 35:31).

Mitzva 296

שֶׁלֹּא לִקַּח כֹּפֶר בִּגְלוּת רוֹצֵחַ בִּשְׁגָגָה, שֶׁנֶּאֱמַר: "וְלֹא תִקְחוּ כֹפֶר לָנוּס אֶל עִיר מִקְלָטוֹ" (במדבר לה, לב).

Not to take ransom in exchange **for the exile of an unwitting murderer, as it is stated: "You shall not take ransom from one who fled to the city of his refuge"** (Numbers 35:32).

Mitzva 297

שֶׁלֹּא לַעֲמֹד עַל הַדָּם, שֶׁנֶּאֱמַר: "לֹא תַעֲמֹד עַל דַּם רֵעֶךָ" (ויקרא יט, טז).

Not to stand by the blood of one's neighbor, **as it is stated: "You shall not stand by the blood of your neighbor"** (Leviticus 19:16).

Mitzva 298

שֶׁלֹּא לְהַנִּיחַ מִכְשׁוֹל, שֶׁנֶּאֱמַר: "וְלֹא תָשִׂים דָּמִים בְּבֵיתֶךָ" (דברים כב, ח).

Not to leave a stumbling-block, as it is stated: "And you shall not place blood in your house" (Deuteronomy 22:8).

Mitzva 299

שֶׁלֹּא לְהַכְשִׁיל תָּם בַּדֶּרֶךְ, שֶׁנֶּאֱמַר: "וְלִפְנֵי עִוֵּר לֹא תִתֵּן מִכְשֹׁל" (ויקרא יט, יד).

Not to cause one who is naive about a matter to stumble on the way, as it is stated: "You shall not place an obstacle before the blind" (Leviticus 19:14).

Mitzva 300

שֶׁלֹּא לְהוֹסִיף בְּמַלְקוּת הַמְחֻיָּב מַלְקוּת, שֶׁנֶּאֱמַר: "לֹא יֹסִיף...פֶּן יֹסִיף" (דברים כה, ג).

Not to add to the lashes of one who is liable to a flogging, as it is stated: "He shall not continue, lest he continue" (Deuteronomy 25:3).

Mitzva 301

שֶׁלֹּא לְרַגֵּל, שֶׁנֶּאֱמַר: "לֹא תֵלֵךְ רָכִיל בְּעַמֶּיךָ" (ויקרא יט, טז).

Not to act as a talebearer, as it is stated: "You shall not go as a gossip among your people" (Leviticus 19:16).

Mitzva 302

שֶׁלֹּא לִשְׂנֹא בַּלֵּב, שֶׁנֶּאֱמַר: "לֹא תִשְׂנָא אֶת אָחִיךָ בִּלְבָבֶךָ" (ויקרא יט, יז).

Not to hate in one's **heart, as it is stated: "You shall not hate your brother in your heart"** (Leviticus 19:17).

Mitzva 303

שֶׁלֹּא לְהַלְבִּין פְּנֵי אָדָם מִיִּשְׂרָאֵל, שֶׁנֶּאֱמַר: "הוֹכֵחַ תּוֹכִיחַ אֶת עֲמִיתֶךָ וְלֹא תִשָּׂא עָלָיו חֵטְא" (שם).

Not to humiliate a Jewish person, as it is stated: "You shall rebuke your neighbor, and you shall not bear a sin because of him" (Leviticus 19:17).

Mitzva 304

שֶׁלֹּא לִנְקֹם, שֶׁנֶּאֱמַר: "לֹא תִקֹּם" (ויקרא יט, יח).

Not to take vengeance, as it is stated: "You shall not take vengeance" (Leviticus 19:18).

Mitzva 305

שֶׁלֹּא לִנְטֹר, שֶׁנֶּאֱמַר: "וְלֹא תִטֹּר" (שם).

Not to bear a grudge, as it is stated: "You shall not bear any grudge" (Leviticus 19:18).

Mitzva 306

שֶׁלֹּא לִקַּח אֵם עִם הַבָּנִים, שֶׁנֶּאֱמַר: "לֹא תִקַּח הָאֵם עַל הַבָּנִים" (דברים כב, ו).

Not to take the mother bird **with** its **offspring, as it is stated: "You shall not take the mother with the offspring"** (Deuteronomy 22:6).

Mitzva 307

שֶׁלֹּא לְגַלֵּחַ שְׂעַר הַנֶּתֶק, שֶׁנֶּאֱמַר: "וְאֶת הַנֶּתֶק לֹא יְגַלֵּחַ" (ויקרא יג, לג).

Not to shave off a leprous **scall, as it is stated: "But the scall he shall not shave"** (Leviticus 13:33).

Mitzva 308

שֶׁלֹּא לִתְלֹשׁ סִימָנֵי צָרַעַת, שֶׁנֶּאֱמַר: "הִשָּׁמֶר בְּנֶגַע הַצָּרַעַת" (דברים כד, ח).

Not to cut off the signs of leprosy, as it is stated: "Be careful with the mark of leprosy" (Deuteronomy 24:8).

Mitzva 309

שֶׁלֹּא לַעֲבֹד וְלִזְרֹעַ בְּנַחַל אֵיתָן, שֶׁנֶּאֱמַר: "אֲשֶׁר לֹא יֵעָבֵד בּוֹ וְלֹא יִזָּרֵעַ" (דברים כא, ד).

Not to work or sow in the **harsh ravine, as it is stated:** "The elders of that city shall take the calf down to a harsh ravine, **in which work will not be done and it will not be sown"** (Deuteronomy 21:4).

Mitzva 310

שֶׁלֹּא יִתְחַיֵּב חָתָן בְּדָבָר מִצָּרְכֵי רַבִּים כָּל שְׁנָתוֹ, כְּגוֹן צָבָא וּשְׁמִירַת הַחוֹמָה וְכַיּוֹצֵא בָּהֶן, שֶׁנֶּאֱמַר: "לֹא יֵצֵא בַּצָּבָא וְלֹא יַעֲבֹר עָלָיו לְכָל דָּבָר" (דברים כד, ה).

That a groom is not obligated in any **matter of public requirements** throughout **his whole** first **year** of marriage, **such as army** service, **guarding** the city **wall, and the like, as it is stated: "He shall not go out in the army, and for no matter shall he be obligated"** (Deuteronomy 24:5).

Mitzva 311

שֶׁלֹּא לְהַחְיוֹת מְכַשֵּׁף, שֶׁנֶּאֱמַר: "מְכַשֵּׁפָה לֹא תְחַיֶּה" (שמות כב, יז).

Not to allow a warlock to live, as it is stated: "You shall not keep a witch alive" (Exodus 22:17).

Mitzva 312

שֶׁלֹּא לְהַמְרוֹת עַל פִּי בֵּית דִּין, שֶׁנֶּאֱמַר: "לֹא תָסוּר מִכָּל הַדָּבָר" (דברים יז, יא, ושם: מִן הַדָּבָר).

Not to rebel against a court ruling, as it is stated: "You shall not deviate from the entire[a] matter" (Deuteronomy 17:11).

Mitzva 313

שֶׁלֹּא לְהוֹסִיף עַל מִצְוֹות הַתּוֹרָה, בֵּין תּוֹרָה שֶׁבִּכְתָב בֵּין בְּפֵרוּשָׁהּ שֶׁקִּבְּלוּ עַל פֶּה, שֶׁנֶּאֱמַר: "אֵת כָּל הַדָּבָר אֲשֶׁר אָנֹכִי מְצַוֶּה אֶתְכֶם אֹתוֹ תִשְׁמְרוּ לַעֲשׂוֹת לֹא תֹסֵף עָלָיו" (דברים יג, א).

Not to add to the mitzvot of the Torah, whether the Written Torah or its interpretation which the Sages **received by oral** tradition, **as it is stated: "All this matter that I command you, you shall take care to perform; you shall not add to it"** (Deuteronomy 13:1).

Mitzva 314

שֶׁלֹּא לִגְרֹעַ מִכָּל מִצְוֹות הַתּוֹרָה, שֶׁנֶּאֱמַר: "וְלֹא תִגְרַע מִמֶּנּוּ" (שם).

Not to subtract from any of the mitzvot of the Torah, as it is stated: "And you shall not subtract from it" (Deuteronomy 13:1).

Mitzva 315

שֶׁלֹּא לְקַלֵּל הַדַּיָּן, שֶׁנֶּאֱמַר: "אֱלֹהִים לֹא תְקַלֵּל" (שמות כב, כז).

Not to curse a judge, as it is stated: "You shall not curse judges" (Exodus 22:27).

Mitzva 316

שֶׁלֹּא לְקַלֵּל הַנָּשִׂיא, וְהוּא הַמֶּלֶךְ אוֹ רֹאשׁ יְשִׁיבַת אֶרֶץ יִשְׂרָאֵל, שֶׁנֶּאֱמַר: "וְנָשִׂיא בְעַמְּךָ לֹא תָאֹר" (שם).

Not to curse a *Nasi*, which means a **king of the head of the** leading **academy of the Land of Israel, as it is stated: "And a prince** [*Nasi*] **among your people you shall not imprecate"** (Exodus 22:27).

NOTES

a. The word "entire" does not appear in the verse.

Mitzva 317

שֶׁלֹּא לְקַלֵּל אֶחָד מִשְּׁאָר יִשְׂרָאֵל, שֶׁנֶּאֱמַר: "לֹא תְקַלֵּל חֵרֵשׁ" (ויקרא יט, יד).

Not to curse one of the rest of the Jewish people, as it is stated: "You shall not curse a deaf person" (Leviticus 19:14).

Mitzva 318

שֶׁלֹּא לְקַלֵּל אָב וָאֵם, שֶׁנֶּאֱמַר: "וּמְקַלֵּל אָבִיו וְאִמּוֹ מוֹת יוּמָת" (שמות כא, יז).

Not to curse one's **father or mother, as it is stated: "One who curses his father or his mother shall be put to death"** (Exodus 21:17).

Mitzva 319

שֶׁלֹּא לְהַכּוֹת אָב וָאֵם, שֶׁנֶּאֱמַר: "וּמַכֵּה אָבִיו וְאִמּוֹ מוֹת יוּמָת" (שמות כא, טו).

Not to strike one's **father or mother, as it is stated: "One who strikes his father or his mother shall be put to death"** (Exodus 21:15).

Mitzva 320

שֶׁלֹּא לַעֲשׂוֹת מְלָאכָה בְּשַׁבָּת, שֶׁנֶּאֱמַר: "לֹא תַעֲשֶׂה כָל מְלָאכָה" (שמות כ, ט; דברים ה, יג).

Not to perform labor on Shabbat, as it is stated: "You shall not perform any labor" (Exodus 20:10, Deuteronomy 5:14).

Mitzva 321

שֶׁלֹּא לְהַלֵּךְ חוּץ לִתְחוּם מְדִינָה כְּהוֹלְכֵי דְּרָכִים בְּשַׁבָּת, שֶׁנֶּאֱמַר: "אַל יֵצֵא אִישׁ מִמְּקֹמוֹ" (שמות טז, כט).

Not to walk beyond the city boundary on Shabbat, in the manner of travelers, as it is stated: "No man shall leave his place on the seventh day" (Exodus 16:29).

Mitzva 322

שֶׁלֹּא לַעֲנֹשׁ בְּשַׁבָּת, שֶׁנֶּאֱמַר: "לֹא תְבַעֲרוּ אֵשׁ בְּכֹל מֹשְׁבֹתֵיכֶם" וגו' (שמות לה, ג).

Not to administer judicial **punishments on Shabbat, as it is stated: "You shall not kindle fire in all your dwellings** on the Sabbath day" (Exodus 35:3).

Mitzva 323

שֶׁלֹּא לַעֲשׂוֹת מְלָאכָה בְּרִאשׁוֹן שֶׁל פֶּסַח, שֶׁנֶּאֱמַר: "כָּל מְלָאכָה לֹא יֵעָשֶׂה בָהֶם" (שמות יב, טז).

Not to perform labor on the first day **of Passover, as it is stated: "No labor shall be performed on them"** (Exodus 12:16).

Mitzva 324

שֶׁלֹּא לַעֲשׂוֹת מְלָאכָה בַּשְּׁבִיעִי שֶׁל פֶּסַח, שֶׁנֶּאֱמַר: "כָּל מְלָאכָה לֹא יֵעָשֶׂה בָהֶם" (שם).

Not to perform labor on the seventh day **of Passover, as it is stated: "No labor shall be performed on them"** (Exodus 12:16).

Mitzva 325

שֶׁלֹּא לַעֲשׂוֹת מְלָאכָה בְּחַג הַשָּׁבוּעוֹת, שֶׁנֶּאֱמַר בּוֹ: "כָּל מְלֶאכֶת עֲבֹדָה לֹא תַעֲשׂוּ" (ויקרא כג, כא; במדבר כח, כו).

Not to perform labor on the festival of Shavuot, as it is stated regarding it: "You shall not perform any toilsome labor" (Leviticus 23:21, Numbers 28:26).

Mitzva 326

שֶׁלֹּא לַעֲשׂוֹת מְלָאכָה בְּאֶחָד לַחֹדֶשׁ הַשְּׁבִיעִי, שֶׁנֶּאֱמַר בּוֹ: "כָּל מְלֶאכֶת עֲבֹדָה לֹא תַעֲשׂוּ" (ויקרא כג, כה; במדבר כט, א).

Not to perform labor on the first day **of the seventh month,** Rosh HaShana, **as it is stated regarding it: "You shall not perform any toilsome labor"** (Leviticus 23:25, Numbers 29:1).

Mitzva 327

שֶׁלֹּא לַעֲשׂוֹת מְלָאכָה בְּיוֹם הַכִּפּוּרִים, שֶׁנֶּאֱמַר בּוֹ: "וְכָל מְלָאכָה לֹא תַעֲשׂוּ" (ויקרא טז, כט; כג, כח).

Not to perform labor on Yom Kippur, as it is stated regarding it: "And you shall not perform any labor" (Leviticus 16:29, 23:28).

Mitzva 328

שֶׁלֹּא לַעֲשׂוֹת מְלָאכָה בְּרִאשׁוֹן שֶׁל חַג, שֶׁנֶּאֱמַר בּוֹ: "כָּל מְלֶאכֶת עֲבֹדָה לֹא תַעֲשׂוּ" (ויקרא כג, לה; במדבר כט, יב).

Not to perform labor on the festival of Sukkot, **as it is stated regarding it: "You shall not perform any toilsome labor"** (Leviticus 23:35, Numbers 29:12).

Mitzva 329

שֶׁלֹּא לַעֲשׂוֹת מְלָאכָה בְּיוֹם שְׁמִינִי שֶׁל חַג, שֶׁנֶּאֱמַר בּוֹ: "כָּל מְלֶאכֶת עֲבֹדָה לֹא תַעֲשׂוּ" (ויקרא כג, לו; במדבר כט, לה).

Not to perform labor on the eighth day of the festival of Sukkot, Shemini Atzeret, **as it is stated regarding it: "You shall not perform any toilsome labor"** (Leviticus 23:36, Numbers 29:35).

Mitzva 330

שֶׁלֹּא לְגַלּוֹת עֶרְוַת אֵם, שֶׁנֶּאֱמַר: ״אִמְּךָ הִיא לֹא תְגַלֶּה עֶרְוָתָהּ״ (ויקרא יח, ז).

Not to uncover the nakedness of one's **mother, as it is stated: "She is your mother; you shall not uncover her nakedness"** (Leviticus 18:7).

Mitzva 331

שֶׁלֹּא לְגַלּוֹת עֶרְוַת אֵשֶׁת אָב, שֶׁנֶּאֱמַר: ״עֶרְוַת אֵשֶׁת אָבִיךָ לֹא תְגַלֵּה״ (ויקרא יח, ח).

Not to uncover the nakedness of one's **father's wife, as it is stated: "The nakedness of your father's wife you shall not uncover"** (Leviticus 18:8).

Mitzva 332

שֶׁלֹּא לְגַלּוֹת עֶרְוַת אָחוֹת, שֶׁנֶּאֱמַר: ״עֶרְוַת אֲחוֹתְךָ בַת אָבִיךָ וכו׳ לֹא תְגַלֶּה״ (ויקרא יח, ט).

Not to uncover the nakedness of one's **sister, as it is stated: "The nakedness of your sister, the daughter of your father…you shall not uncover"** (Leviticus 18:9).

Mitzva 333

שֶׁלֹּא לְגַלּוֹת עֶרְוַת אָחוֹת מִן הָאָב וּמִן הָאֵם, שֶׁנֶּאֱמַר: ״עֶרְוַת בַּת אֵשֶׁת אָבִיךָ מוֹלֶדֶת אָבִיךָ אֲחוֹתְךָ הִיא לֹא תְגַלֶּה עֶרְוָתָהּ״ (ויקרא יח, יא).

Not to uncover the nakedness of one's **sister from** one's **father and from** one's **mother, as it is stated: "The nakedness of the daughter of your father's wife, born to your father, she is your sister, you shall not uncover her nakedness"** (Leviticus 18:11).

Mitzva 334

שֶׁלֹּא לְגַלּוֹת עֶרְוַת בַּת הַבֵּן, שֶׁנֶּאֱמַר: ״עֶרְוַת בַּת בִּנְךָ אוֹ בַת בִּתְּךָ לֹא תְגַלֶּה עֶרְוָתָהּ״ (ויקרא יח, י, ושם: עֶרְוָתָן).

Not to uncover the nakedness of one's **son's daughter, as it is stated: "The nakedness of the daughter of your son, or of the daughter of your daughter, you shall not uncover their nakedness"** (Leviticus 18:10).

Mitzva 335

שֶׁלֹּא לְגַלּוֹת עֶרְוַת בַּת הַבַּת, שֶׁנֶּאֱמַר: ״אוֹ בַת בִּתְּךָ לֹא תְגַלֶּה עֶרְוָתָן״ (שם).

Not to uncover the nakedness of one's **daughter's daughter, as it is stated: "Or of the daughter of your daughter, you shall not uncover their nakedness"** (Leviticus 18:10).

Mitzva 336

שֶׁלֹּא לְגַלּוֹת עֶרְוַת הַבַּת. וְלָמָּה לֹא נִתְפָּרְשָׁה בַּתּוֹרָה? מִפְּנֵי שֶׁאָסַר בַּת הַבַּת, שָׁתַק מִן הַבַּת. וּמִפִּי הַשְּׁמוּעָה לָמְדוּ שֶׁאִסּוּר הַבַּת מִגּוּפֵי תוֹרָה כִּשְׁאָר עֲרָיוֹת.

Not to uncover the nakedness of one's **daughter. Why isn't** this case **explicitly** mentioned **in the Torah?** The reason is that **since** the Torah expressly **prohibited** one's **daughter's daughter, it remains silent with regard to the daughter herself.** The Sages **learned, on the basis of the** Oral **tradition, that the prohibition of a daughter is** one of **the "essential parts of the Torah,"** i.e., it has the same status as a law that is explicitly stated in the Torah,[a] **like the rest of those with whom relations are forbidden** (see *Yevamot* 3a).

Mitzva 337

שֶׁלֹּא לְגַלּוֹת עֶרְוַת אִשָּׁה וּבִתָּהּ, שֶׁנֶּאֱמַר: ״עֶרְוַת אִשָּׁה וּבִתָּהּ לֹא תְגַלֵּה״ (ויקרא יח, יז).

Not to uncover the nakedness of a woman and her daughter, as it is stated: "The nakedness of a woman and her daughter you shall not uncover" (Leviticus 18:17).

Mitzva 338

שֶׁלֹּא לְגַלּוֹת עֶרְוַת אִשָּׁה וּבַת בְּנָהּ, שֶׁנֶּאֱמַר: ״אֶת בַּת בְּנָהּ״ וכו׳ (שם).

Not to uncover the nakedness of a woman and her son's daughter, as it is stated: "Her son's daughter…" (Leviticus 18:17).

Mitzva 339

שֶׁלֹּא לְגַלּוֹת עֶרְוַת אִשָּׁה וּבַת בִּתָּהּ, שֶׁנֶּאֱמַר: ״וְאֶת בַּת בִּתָּהּ לֹא תִקַּח״ וכו׳ (שם).

Not to uncover the nakedness of a woman and her daughter's daughter, as it is stated: "Or her daughter's daughter you shall not take…" (Leviticus 18:17).

Mitzva 340

שֶׁלֹּא לְגַלּוֹת עֶרְוַת אֲחוֹת הָאָב, שֶׁנֶּאֱמַר: ״עֶרְוַת אֲחוֹת אָבִיךָ לֹא תְגַלֵּה״ (ויקרא יח, יב).

Not to uncover the nakedness of one's **father's sister, as it is stated: "The nakedness of your father's sister you shall not uncover"** (Leviticus 18:12).

NOTES

a. See commentary to Mitzva 135.

Mitzva 341

שֶׁלֹּא לְגַלּוֹת עֶרְוַת אֲחוֹת הָאֵם, שֶׁנֶּאֱמַר: "עֶרְוַת אֲחוֹת אִמְּךָ לֹא תְגַלֵּה" (ויקרא יח, יג).

Not to uncover the nakedness of one's mother's sister, as it is stated: "The nakedness of your mother's sister you shall not uncover" (Leviticus 18:13).

Mitzva 342

שֶׁלֹּא לְגַלּוֹת עֶרְוַת אֵשֶׁת אֲחִי הָאָב, שֶׁנֶּאֱמַר: "אֶל אִשְׁתּוֹ לֹא תִקְרָב דֹּדָתְךָ הִיא" (ויקרא יח, יד).

Not to uncover the nakedness of the wife of one's father's brother, as it is stated: "You shall not approach his wife; she is your aunt" (Leviticus 18:14).

Mitzva 343

שֶׁלֹּא לְגַלּוֹת עֶרְוַת אֵשֶׁת הַבֵּן, שֶׁנֶּאֱמַר: "עֶרְוַת כַּלָּתְךָ לֹא תְגַלֵּה" (ויקרא יח, טו).

Not to uncover the nakedness of the wife of one's son, as it is stated: "The nakedness of your daughter-in-law you shall not uncover" (Leviticus 18:15).

Mitzva 344

שֶׁלֹּא לְגַלּוֹת עֶרְוַת אֵשֶׁת אָח, שֶׁנֶּאֱמַר: "עֶרְוַת אֵשֶׁת אָחִיךָ לֹא תְגַלֵּה" (ויקרא יח, טז).

Not to uncover the nakedness of the wife of one's brother, as it is stated: "The nakedness of your brother's wife you shall not uncover" (Leviticus 18:16).

Mitzva 345

שֶׁלֹּא לְגַלּוֹת עֶרְוַת אֲחוֹת אִשָּׁה, שֶׁנֶּאֱמַר: "וְאִשָּׁה אֶל אֲחֹתָהּ לֹא תִקָּח" (ויקרא יח, יח).

Not to uncover the nakedness of the sister of one's wife, as it is stated: "And a woman with her sister you shall not take" (Leviticus 18:18).

Mitzva 346

שֶׁלֹּא לְגַלּוֹת עֶרְוַת נִדָּה, שֶׁנֶּאֱמַר: "וְאֶל אִשָּׁה בְּנִדַּת טֻמְאָתָהּ לֹא תִקְרַב" (ויקרא יח, יט).

Not to uncover the nakedness of a menstruating woman, as it is stated: "And to a woman in her state of menstrual impurity you shall not approach" (Leviticus 18:19).

Mitzva 347

שֶׁלֹּא לְגַלּוֹת עֶרְוַת אֵשֶׁת אִישׁ, שֶׁנֶּאֱמַר: "וְאֶל אֵשֶׁת עֲמִיתְךָ" (ויקרא יח, כ).

Not to uncover the nakedness of a married woman, as it is stated: "And with the wife of your counterpart" (Leviticus 18:20).

Mitzva 348

שֶׁלֹּא לִשְׁכַּב עִם בְּהֵמָה, שֶׁנֶּאֱמַר: "וּבְכָל בְּהֵמָה לֹא תִתֵּן שְׁכָבְתְּךָ לְטָמְאָה בָהּ" (ויקרא יח, כג).

Not to lie with an animal, as it is stated: "And with any animal you shall not engage sexually to defile yourself with it" (Leviticus 18:23).

Mitzva 349

שֶׁלֹּא תָּבִיא אִשָּׁה בְּהֵמָה עָלֶיהָ, שֶׁנֶּאֱמַר: "וְאִשָּׁה לֹא תַעֲמֹד לִפְנֵי בְהֵמָה" (שם).

That a woman may not engage in intercourse with an animal, as it is stated: "And a woman shall not stand before an animal" (Leviticus 18:23).

Mitzva 350

שֶׁלֹּא לִשְׁכַּב עִם זָכוּר, שֶׁנֶּאֱמַר: "וְאֶת זָכָר לֹא תִשְׁכַּב" (ויקרא יח, כב).

Not to lie with a male, as it is stated: "And you shall not lie with a male" (Leviticus 18:22).

Mitzva 351

שֶׁלֹּא לְגַלּוֹת עֶרְוַת הָאָב עַצְמוֹ, שֶׁנֶּאֱמַר: "עֶרְוַת אָבִיךָ...לֹא תְגַלֵּה" (ויקרא יח, ז).

Not to uncover the nakedness of one's father himself, as it is stated: "The nakedness of your father…you shall not uncover" (Leviticus 18:7).

Mitzva 352

שֶׁלֹּא לְגַלּוֹת עֶרְוַת אֲחִי הָאָב עַצְמוֹ, שֶׁנֶּאֱמַר: "עֶרְוַת אֲחִי אָבִיךָ לֹא תְגַלֵּה" (ויקרא יח, יד).

Not to uncover the nakedness of one's father's brother himself, as it is stated: "The nakedness of your father's brother you shall not uncover" (Leviticus 18:14).

Mitzva 353

שֶׁלֹּא לִקְרַב לַעֲרָיוֹת בִּדְבָרִים הַמְּבִיאִים לִידֵי גִּלּוּי עֶרְוָה, כְּגוֹן חִבּוּק וְנִשּׁוּק וּרְמִיזָה וּקְפִיצָה, שֶׁנֶּאֱמַר: "אִישׁ אִישׁ אֶל כָּל שְׁאֵר בְּשָׂרוֹ לֹא תִקְרְבוּ לְגַלּוֹת עֶרְוָה" (ויקרא יח, ו). מִפִּי הַשְּׁמוּעָה לָמְדוּ שֶׁזּוֹ אַזְהָרָה לִקְרִיבָה הַמְּבִיאָה לִידֵי גִּלּוּי עֶרְוָה.

Not to approach near one of the forbidden relations through acts that can lead to the uncovering of nakedness, such as embracing, kissing, winking, and flirtatious movements, as it is stated: "Any man of you shall not approach his kin to uncover nakedness" (Leviticus 18:6). The Sages learned, on the basis of the Oral tradition, that this is a prohibition that applies to the type of approaching that can lead to the uncovering of nakedness.[a]

NOTES

a. See *Sifra* on Leviticus 18:19 (*Yad Peshuta*).

Mitzva 354

That a ***mamzer*** **may not marry a Jewish woman, as it is stated: "A child born from incest or adultery shall not enter into the assembly of the Lord"** (Deuteronomy 23:3).

שֶׁלֹּא יִשָּׂא מַמְזֵר בַּת יִשְׂרָאֵל, שֶׁנֶּאֱמַר: "לֹא יָבֹא מַמְזֵר בִּקְהַל יי" (דברים כג, ג).

Mitzva 355

That a woman **may not be a** ***kedesha,*** **which is** a woman **who has intercourse without a marriage contract and betrothal, as it is stated: "There shall not be a prostitute** [*kedesha*]**"** (Deuteronomy 23:18).

שֶׁלֹּא תִּהְיֶה קְדֵשָׁה, וְהִיא הַנִּבְעֶלֶת בְּלֹא כְּתֻבָּה וְקִדּוּשִׁין, שֶׁנֶּאֱמַר: "לֹא תִהְיֶה קְדֵשָׁה" (דברים כג, יח).

Mitzva 356

That one who divorces his wife **may not remarry his divorced wife after she has married another** man, **as it is stated: "Her** former **husband,** who sent her, **may not** take her again to be a wife" (Deuteronomy 24:4).

שֶׁלֹּא יַחֲזִיר הַמְגָרֵשׁ גְּרוּשָׁתוֹ אַחַר שֶׁנִּשֵּׂאת לְאַחֵר, שֶׁנֶּאֱמַר: "לֹא יוּכַל בַּעְלָהּ" וכו' (דברים כד, ד).

Mitzva 357

That a ***yevama*** **may not marry another** man **apart from her** ***yavam,*** **as it is stated: "The wife of the dead shall not be married outside"** (Deuteronomy 25:5).

שֶׁלֹּא תִּנָּשֵׂא הַיְבָמָה לְאַחֵר חוּץ מִיְבָמָהּ, שֶׁנֶּאֱמַר: "לֹא תִהְיֶה אֵשֶׁת הַמֵּת הַחוּצָה" (דברים כה, ה).

Mitzva 358

That the rapist may not divorce his rape victim, as it is stated: "He may not release her all his days" (Deuteronomy 22:29).

שֶׁלֹּא יְגָרֵשׁ הָאוֹנֵס אֲנוּסָתוֹ, שֶׁנֶּאֱמַר: "לֹא יוּכַל שַׁלְּחָהּ כָּל יָמָיו" (דברים כב, כט).

Mitzva 359

That the defamer may not divorce his wife, as it is stated: "He may not release her all his days" (Deuteronomy 22:19).

שֶׁלֹּא יְגָרֵשׁ מוֹצִיא שֵׁם רַע אֶת אִשְׁתּוֹ, שֶׁנֶּאֱמַר בּוֹ: "לֹא יוּכַל לְשַׁלְּחָהּ כָּל יָמָיו" (דברים כב, יט).

Mitzva 360

That a eunuch may not take a Jewish woman for a wife, **as it is stated: "One with crushed testicles** and one with a severed penis **shall not enter…"** (Deuteronomy 23:2).

שֶׁלֹּא יִקַּח סָרִיס בַּת יִשְׂרָאֵל, שֶׁנֶּאֱמַר: "לֹא יָבֹא פְצוּעַ דַּכָּא" וכו' (דברים כג, ב).

Mitzva 361

Not to castrate a male of any species, not a person, nor a domesticated animal, an undomesticated animal, or a bird, as it is stated: "And you shall not do so **in your land"** (Leviticus 22:24).

שֶׁלֹּא לְסָרֵס זָכָר מִכָּל הַמִּינִים, לֹא אָדָם וְלֹא בְּהֵמָה חַיָּה וָעוֹף, שֶׁנֶּאֱמַר: "וּבְאַרְצְכֶם לֹא תַעֲשׂוּ" (ויקרא כב, כד).

Mitzva 362

Not to appoint a man from the congregation of converts over Israel, as it is stated: "You may not place over you a foreign man" (Deuteronomy 17:15).

שֶׁלֹּא לְמַנּוֹת עַל יִשְׂרָאֵל אִישׁ מִקְּהַל גֵּרִים, שֶׁנֶּאֱמַר: "לֹא תוּכַל לָתֵת עָלֶיךָ אִישׁ נָכְרִי" (דברים יז, טו).

Mitzva 363

That a king may not amass horses, as it is stated: "He shall not amass horses for himself" (Deuteronomy 17:16).

שֶׁלֹּא יַרְבֶּה הַמֶּלֶךְ סוּסִים, שֶׁנֶּאֱמַר: "לֹא יַרְבֶּה לּוֹ סוּסִים" (דברים יז, טז).

Mitzva 364

That a king may not amass wives, as it is stated: "He shall not amass wives" (Deuteronomy 17:17).

שֶׁלֹּא יַרְבֶּה הַמֶּלֶךְ נָשִׁים, שֶׁנֶּאֱמַר: "וְלֹא יַרְבֶּה לּוֹ נָשִׁים" (דברים יז, יז).

Mitzva 365

That a king may not amass silver and gold for himself, as it is stated: "And silver and gold he shall not amass greatly" (Deuteronomy 17:17).

שֶׁלֹּא יַרְבֶּה לוֹ כֶּסֶף וְזָהָב, שֶׁנֶּאֱמַר: "וְכֶסֶף וְזָהָב לֹא יַרְבֶּה לּוֹ מְאֹד" (שם).

מִצְווֹת שֶׁאֵינָן מִן הַתּוֹרָה
Mitzvot That Are Not from the Torah

אֵלּוּ הֵם שֵׁשׁ מֵאוֹת וּשְׁלֹשׁ עֶשְׂרֵה מִצְווֹת שֶׁנֶּאֶמְרוּ לוֹ לְמֹשֶׁה בְּסִינַי, הֵן וּכְלָלוֹתֵיהֶן וּפְרָטוֹתֵיהֶן וְדִקְדּוּקֵיהֶן. וְכָל אוֹתָן הַכְּלָלוֹת וְהַפְּרָטוֹת וְהַדִּקְדּוּקִין וְהַבֵּאוּרִין שֶׁל כָּל מִצְוָה וּמִצְוָה – הִיא תּוֹרָה שֶׁבְּעַל פֶּה שֶׁקִּבְּלוּ בֵּית דִּין מִפִּי בֵּית דִּין. וְיֵשׁ מִצְווֹת אֲחֵרוֹת שֶׁנִּתְחַדְּשׁוּ אַחַר מַתַּן תּוֹרָה, וְקָבְעוּ אוֹתָן נְבִיאִים וַחֲכָמִים, וּפָשְׁטוּ בְּכָל יִשְׂרָאֵל, כְּגוֹן: מִקְרָא מְגִלָּה, וְנֵר חֲנֻכָּה, וְתַעֲנִית תִּשְׁעָה בְּאָב, וְיָדַיִם, וְעֵרוּבִין. וְיֵשׁ לְכָל מִצְוָה מֵאֵלּוּ פֵּרוּשִׁין וְדִקְדּוּקִין, וְהַכֹּל יִתְבָּאֵר בְּחִבּוּר זֶה.

These are the 613 mitzvot that were stated to Moses at Sinai, they and their generalizations, details, and particulars. All of those generalizations, details, particulars, and clarifications of each and every mitzva constitute the **Oral Law that** each **court received from** the previous **court. There are** also **other mitzvot that were innovated after the giving of the Torah,* which were established by prophets and Sages and which spread throughout Israel, such as the reading of the Megilla, the Hanukkah lamp, the fast of the Ninth of Av,** washing one's **hands** for food, **and *eiruvin*. Each of these mitzvot** comes with its own **explanations and particulars,** and they will **all be clarified in this work.**

FROM THE LUBAVITCHER REBBE

*There are also other mitzvot that were innovated after the giving of the Torah – **וְיֵשׁ מִצְווֹת אֲחֵרוֹת שֶׁנִּתְחַדְּשׁוּ אַחַר מַתַּן תּוֹרָה**: The Rambam does not count up these mitzvot that apply by rabbinic law, despite the fact that in several places in his work he does count mitzvot, both one by one and in general, following the order of the books, in all the Hilkhot sections. The reason is that the permanent number of the mitzvot of the Torah reflects its eternal nature, for it will not change nor receive additions. By contrast, the mitzvot that apply by rabbinic law are by their very nature innovative ("that were innovated"). Moreover, these mitzvot were instituted to meet the requirements of the hour. Accordingly, their number is not fixed or limited, in theory at least, and many more mitzvot could be added as the needs arise (*Torat Menaḥem, Hitvaaduyot, Aḥaron shel Pesaḥ, Parashat Shemini, and Parashat Aḥarei-Mot Kedoshim 5745; Likkutei Siḥot* 29, p. 104).

NOTES

a. The word "entire" does not appear in the verse.

b. See Mitzva 313.

כָּל אֵלּוּ הַמִּצְווֹת שֶׁנִּתְחַדְּשׁוּ – חַיָּבִין אָנוּ לְקַבְּלָם וּלְשָׁמְרָם, שֶׁנֶּאֱמַר: "לֹא תָסוּר מִכָּל הַדָּבָר" וכו' (דברים יז, יא, ושם: מִן הַדָּבָר), וְאֵינָם תּוֹסֶפֶת עַל מִצְוֹת הַתּוֹרָה. וְעַל מָה הִזְהִירָה תּוֹרָה: "לֹא תֹסֵף" "וְלֹא תִגְרַע" (שם יג, א)? שֶׁלֹּא יְהְיֶה נָבִיא רַשַּׁאי לְחַדֵּשׁ דָּבָר וְלוֹמַר שֶׁהַקָּדוֹשׁ בָּרוּךְ הוּא צִוָּהוּ בְּמִצְוָה זוֹ לְהוֹסִיפָהּ לְמִצְוֹת הַתּוֹרָה, אוֹ לְחַסֵּר אַחַת מֵאֵלּוּ הַשֵּׁשׁ מֵאוֹת וּשְׁלֹשׁ עֶשְׂרֵה מִצְוֹת.

We are obligated to accept and observe all of these innovated mitzvot, as it is stated: "You shall not deviate from the entire[a] **matter** that they will tell you" (see Deuteronomy 17:11), **and they are not** considered a prohibited **addition to the mitzvot of the Torah.**[b] If so, **with regard to what** practice **does the Torah warn** that **"you shall not add** to it **and you shall not subtract** from it" (Deuteronomy 13:1)? This means **that a prophet is not allowed to innovate something and say that the Holy One blessed be He commanded him regarding this mitzva to add it to the mitzvot of the Torah, or to remove one of these 613 mitzvot.**

אֲבָל אִם הוֹסִיפוּ בֵּית דִּין עִם נָבִיא שֶׁיִּהְיֶה בְּאוֹתוֹ הַזְּמַן מִצְוָה דֶּרֶךְ תַּקָּנָה אוֹ דֶּרֶךְ הוֹרָאָה אוֹ דֶּרֶךְ גְּזֵרָה – אֵין זוֹ תּוֹסֶפֶת, שֶׁהֲרֵי לֹא אָמְרוּ שֶׁהַקָּדוֹשׁ בָּרוּךְ הוּא צִוָּה לַעֲשׂוֹת עֵרוּב אוֹ לִקְרוֹת הַמְּגִלָּה בְּעוֹנָתָהּ, וְאִלּוּ אָמְרוּ כֵּן הָיוּ מוֹסִיפִין עַל הַתּוֹרָה.

If, however, a court, together **with a prophet who** is active **at that time, add a mitzva in the form of an enactment, or in the form of an instruction** of theirs, **or in the form of a decree, this is not an addition. For they did not state that the Holy One blessed be He commanded** us **to make an *eiruv* or read the Megilla at its** fixed **time. Had they said that, they would** indeed **be adding to** the mitzvot of **the Torah.**

אֶלָּא כָּךְ אָנוּ אוֹמְרִין: שֶׁהַנְּבִיאִים עִם בֵּית דִּין תִּקְּנוּ וְצִוּוּ לִקְרֹאות הַמְּגִלָּה בְּעוֹנָתָהּ כְּדֵי לְהַזְכִּיר שְׁבָחָיו שֶׁל הַקָּדוֹשׁ בָּרוּךְ הוּא וּתְשׁוּעוֹת שֶׁעָשָׂה לָנוּ, וְהָיָה קָרוֹב לְשַׁוְעֵנוּ, כְּדֵי לְבָרְכוֹ וּלְהַלְּלוֹ, וּכְדֵי לְהוֹדִיעַ לַדּוֹרוֹת הַבָּאִים שֶׁאֱמֶת מַה שֶּׁהִבְטִיחָנוּ בַּתּוֹרָה: "כִּי מִי גוֹי גָּדוֹל אֲשֶׁר לוֹ אֱלֹהִים קְרֹבִים אֵלָיו כַּיי אֱלֹהֵינוּ בְּכָל קָרְאֵנוּ אֵלָיו" (דברים ד, ז). וְעַל דֶּרֶךְ זוֹ הִיא כָּל מִצְוָה וּמִצְוָה שֶׁהִיא מִדִּבְרֵי סוֹפְרִים, בֵּין עֲשֵׂה בֵּין לֹא תַעֲשֶׂה.

Rather, this is what we are saying, that the prophets, with the **court, instituted and commanded** us **to read the Megilla at its** fixed **time, in order to remember the glory of the Holy One blessed be He and the salvations that He performed for us, and** how He **was near to our cry.** Thus, we read the Megilla **in order to bless** God **and praise Him, and in order to inform the ensuing generations that what** God **promised us in the Torah is true: "For who is a great nation that has God near it, as the Lord our God in all of our calling to Him?"** (Deuteronomy 4:7). **Each and every mitzva that is from rabbinic law** can be explained **in this manner, whether** it is **a positive mitzva or a negative mitzva.**

The Books of the *Mishne Torah* and Their Content

וְרָאִיתִי לְחַלֵּק חִבּוּר זֶה לְאַרְבָּעָה עָשָׂר סְפָרִים:

I saw fit to divide this work into fourteen books:

סֵפֶר רִאשׁוֹן – אֶכְלֹל בּוֹ כָּל הַמִּצְווֹת שֶׁהֵן עִקַּר דַּת מֹשֶׁה רַבֵּנוּ, וְצָרִיךְ אָדָם לֵידַע אוֹתָן תְּחִלַּת הַכֹּל, כְּגוֹן יִחוּד שְׁמוֹ בָּרוּךְ הוּא וְאִסּוּר עֲבוֹדָה זָרָה. וְקָרָאתִי שֵׁם סֵפֶר זֶה סֵפֶר הַמַּדָּע.

The first book: In which I will include all the mitzvot that are the foundations of the precepts of Moses, our teacher, which a person must know before anything else, **such as the unity of God's name, blessed be He, and the prohibition against idol worship. I have called this book** ***Sefer Madda*** [The Book of Knowledge].

סֵפֶר שֵׁנִי – אֶכְלֹל בּוֹ הַמִּצְווֹת שֶׁהֵן תְּדִירוֹת, שֶׁנִּצְטַוִּינוּ בָּהֶם כְּדֵי לֶאֱהֹב אֶת הַמָּקוֹם וְלְזָכְרוֹ תָּמִיד, כְּגוֹן קְרִיַּת שְׁמַע וּתְפִלָּה וּתְפִלִּין וּבְרָכוֹת, וּמִילָה בִּכְלָלָן, לְפִי שֶׁהִיא אוֹת בִּבְשָׂרֵנוּ לְהַזְכִּיר תָּמִיד בְּשָׁעָה שֶׁאֵין שָׁם לֹא תְּפִלִּין וְלֹא צִיצִית וְכַיּוֹצֵא בָּהֶן. וְקָרָאתִי שֵׁם סֵפֶר זֶה סֵפֶר אַהֲבָה.

The second book: In which I will include all the mitzvot that are observed **frequently, and in which we were commanded in order that we will love the Omnipresent and remember Him always, such as the recitation of** ***Shema*****; prayer; phylacteries; and blessings. Circumcision is included** in this category **because it is a sign in our flesh** with which **to remember** God **constantly, when there are no phylacteries, ritual fringes, or something similar** upon us. **I have called this book** ***Sefer Ahava*** [The Book of Love (of God)].

סֵפֶר שְׁלִישִׁי – אֶכְלֹל בּוֹ הַמִּצְווֹת שֶׁהֵם בִּזְמַנִּים יְדוּעִים, כְּגוֹן שַׁבָּת וּמוֹעֲדוֹת. וְקָרָאתִי שֵׁם סֵפֶר זֶה סֵפֶר זְמַנִּים.

The third book: In which I will include the mitzvot that are in force **at specific times, such as Shabbat and the festivals. I have called this book** ***Sefer Zemanim*** [The Book of Holidays (literally, "Times")].

סֵפֶר רְבִיעִי – אֶכְלֹל בּוֹ מִצְווֹת שֶׁל בְּעִילָה, כְּגוֹן קִדּוּשִׁין וְגֵרוּשִׁין וְיִבּוּם וַחֲלִיצָה. וְקָרָאתִי שֵׁם סֵפֶר זֶה סֵפֶר נָשִׁים.

The fourth book: In which I will include mitzvot that involve sexual intercourse, such as betrothal, divorce, levirate marriage, and ***ḥalitza*****. I have called this book** ***Sefer Nashim*** [The Book of (Laws Pertaining to) Women].

סֵפֶר חֲמִישִׁי – אֶכְלֹל בּוֹ מִצְווֹת שֶׁל בִּיאוֹת אֲסוּרוֹת וּמִצְווֹת שֶׁל מַאֲכָלוֹת אֲסוּרוֹת, לְפִי שֶׁבִּשְׁנֵי עִנְיָנִים הָאֵלּוּ קִדְּשָׁנוּ הַמָּקוֹם וְהִבְדִּילָנוּ מִן הָאֻמּוֹת, בַּעֲרָיוֹת וּבְמַאֲכָלוֹת אֲסוּרוֹת, וּבִשְׁנֵיהֶם נֶאֱמַר: "וָאַבְדִּל אֶתְכֶם מִן הָעַמִּים" (ויקרא כ, כו), "אֲשֶׁר הִבְדַּלְתִּי אֶתְכֶם מִן הָעַמִּים" (שם כ, כד). וְקָרָאתִי שֵׁם סֵפֶר זֶה סֵפֶר קְדֻשָּׁה.

The fifth book: In which I will include mitzvot that involve forbidden relations and mitzvot involving forbidden foods. For through these two matters, God sanctified us and separated us from the other **nations; through** prohibiting to us **those with whom relations are forbidden, and through** prohibiting to us **forbidden foods. With regard to both,** a similar expression **is stated: "And I have distinguished you from the peoples"** (Leviticus 20:26); **"who has distinguished you from the peoples"** (Leviticus 20:24). **I have called this book** ***Sefer Kedusha*** [The Book of Holiness].

סֵפֶר שִׁשִּׁי – אֶכְלֹל בּוֹ מִצְוֹת שֶׁיִּתְחַיֵּב בָּהֶם מִי שֶׁאָסַר עַצְמוֹ בִּדְבָרִים, כְּגוֹן שְׁבוּעוֹת וּנְדָרִים. וְקָרָאתִי שֵׁם סֵפֶר זֶה סֵפֶר הַפְלָאָה.

The **sixth book: In which I will include mitzvot in which one who prohibits himself through** his **speech is obligated, such as** through **oaths and vows. I have called this book *Sefer Haflaa*** [The Book of Speech Acts (literally, "Articulation")].

סֵפֶר שְׁבִיעִי – אֶכְלֹל בּוֹ מִצְוֹת שֶׁהֵם בְּזֶרַע הָאָרֶץ, כְּגוֹן שְׁמִטִּים וְיוֹבְלוֹת וּמַעַשְׂרוֹת וּתְרוּמוֹת, וּשְׁאָר מִצְוֹת הַנִּגְלָלִים עִמָּהֶן מֵעִנְיָנָם. וְקָרָאתִי שֵׁם סֵפֶר זֶה סֵפֶר זְרָעִים.

The **seventh book: In which I will include mitzvot that** apply **to the seed of the earth, such as** the mitzvot of the **Sabbatical and Jubilee** Years, **tithes, *terumot*, and other mitzvot of the same type that go together with them. I have called this book *Sefer Zera'im*** [The Book of Seeds].

סֵפֶר שְׁמִינִי – אֶכְלֹל בּוֹ מִצְוֹת שֶׁהֵן בְּבִנְיַן מִקְדָּשׁ וְקָרְבְּנוֹת צִבּוּר הַתְּמִידִין. וְקָרָאתִי שֵׁם סֵפֶר זֶה סֵפֶר עֲבוֹדָה.

The **eighth book: In which I will include mitzvot that involve the construction of** the **Temple and the regular communal offerings. I have called this book *Sefer Avoda*** [The Book of the (Temple) Service].

סֵפֶר תְּשִׁיעִי – אֶכְלֹל בּוֹ מִצְוֹת שֶׁהֵם בְּקָרְבְּנוֹת הַיָּחִיד. וְקָרָאתִי שֵׁם סֵפֶר זֶה סֵפֶר קָרְבָּנוֹת.

The **ninth book: In which I will include mitzvot that involve the offerings of an individual. I have called this book *Sefer Korbanot*** [The Book of Offerings].

סֵפֶר עֲשִׂירִי – אֶכְלֹל בּוֹ מִצְוֹת שֶׁהֵן בְּטַהֲרוֹת וְטֻמְאוֹת. וְקָרָאתִי שֵׁם סֵפֶר זֶה סֵפֶר טָהֳרָה.

The **tenth book: In which I will include mitzvot involving ritual purities and impurities. I have called this book *Sefer Tahara*** [The Book of Purity].

סֵפֶר אַחַד עָשָׂר – אֶכְלֹל בּוֹ מִצְוֹת שֶׁבֵּין אָדָם לַחֲבֵרוֹ וְיֵשׁ בָּהֶם הֶזֵּק תְּחִלָּה, בְּמָמוֹן אוֹ בְּגוּף. וְקָרָאתִי שֵׁם סֵפֶר זֶה סֵפֶר נְזָקִים.

The **eleventh book: In which I will include mitzvot that** apply **to interpersonal relations and which are prompted by damage to property, or personal** injury. **I have called this book *Sefer Nezakim*** [The Book of Damages (Torts)].

סֵפֶר שְׁנֵים עָשָׂר – אֶכְלֹל בּוֹ מִצְוֹת מְכִירָה וּקְנִיָּה. וְקָרָאתִי שֵׁם סֵפֶר זֶה סֵפֶר קִנְיָן.

The **twelfth book: In which I will include mitzvot** involving **sales and acquisitions. I have called this book *Sefer Kinyan*** [The Book of Acquisitions].

סֵפֶר שְׁלֹשָׁה עָשָׂר – אֶכְלֹל בּוֹ מִצְוֹת שֶׁבֵּין אָדָם לַחֲבֵרוֹ בִּשְׁאָר הַדִּינִין שֶׁאֵין בִּתְחִלָּתָן הֶזֵּק, כְּגוֹן שׁוֹמְרִים וּבַעֲלֵי חוֹבוֹת וּטְעָנוֹת וּכְפִירוֹת. וְקָרָאתִי סֵפֶר זֶה סֵפֶר מִשְׁפָּטִים.

The **thirteenth book: In which I will include** different **mitzvot that** apply **to interpersonal relations, involving the other laws,** those **which are not prompted by damages, such as** the laws of **bailees, debtors, and** financial **claims and denials. I have called this book *Sefer Mishpatim*** [The Book of Transactions].

סֵפֶר אַרְבָּעָה עָשָׂר – אֶכְלֹל בּוֹ מִצְוֹת שֶׁהֵן מְסוּרִין לְסַנְהֶדְרִין, כְּגוֹן מִיתוֹת בֵּית דִּין וְקַבָּלַת עֵדוּת וְדִין הַמֶּלֶךְ וּמִלְחֲמוֹתָיו. וְקָרָאתִי שֵׁם סֵפֶר זֶה סֵפֶר שׁוֹפְטִים.

The **fourteenth book: In which I will include mitzvot that are delegated to the Sanhedrin, such as court-imposed capital punishment, the acceptance of testimony, and the laws of a king and his wars. I have called this book *Sefer Shofetim*** [The Book of Judges].

וְזֶה הוּא חִלּוּק הֲלָכוֹת שֶׁל חִבּוּר זֶה לְפִי עִנְיְנֵי הַסְּפָרִים, וְחִלּוּק הַמִּצְוֹת לְפִי עִנְיְנֵי הַהֲלָכוֹת:

This is the division of *Hilkhot* sections in this work, in accordance with the subject matter of the books. Below I present **the division of the mitzvot in accordance with the subject matter of the *Hilkhot* sections.** In this list the Rambam once again lists all 613 mitzvot, this time arranged in accordance with the books of the *Mishne Torah* and the *Hilkhot* sections of each book (we have added in parentheses the number of the mitzva from the Rambam's short list of mitzvot). The relevant sections of this list are repeated verbatim at the start of each *Sefer* and each "*Hilkhot*" section. Thus, the list serves as a kind of index, or contents, to the entire *Mishne Torah*.

סֵפֶר הַמַּדָּע

1. Sefer Madda

הִלְכוֹתָיו חָמֵשׁ, וְזֶה הוּא סִדּוּרָן: הִלְכוֹת יְסוֹדֵי הַתּוֹרָה, הִלְכוֹת דֵּעוֹת, הִלְכוֹת תַּלְמוּד תּוֹרָה, הִלְכוֹת עֲבוֹדָה זָרָה וְחֻקּוֹת הַגּוֹיִם, הִלְכוֹת תְּשׁוּבָה.

Sefer Madda contains **five sections, in the following order: *Hilkhot Yesodei HaTorah*** (Laws of the Foundations of the Torah), ***Hilkhot Deot*** (Laws of Character Traits), ***Hilkhot Talmud Torah*** (Laws of Torah Study), ***Hilkhot Avoda Zara VeḤukkot HaGoyim*** (Laws Pertaining to Idolatry and Gentile Practices), and ***Hilkhot Teshuva*** (Laws of Repentance).

הִלְכוֹת יְסוֹדֵי הַתּוֹרָה - יֵשׁ בִּכְלָלָן עֶשֶׂר מִצְוֹת, שֵׁשׁ מִצְוֹת עֲשֵׂה וְאַרְבַּע מִצְוֹת לֹא תַעֲשֶׂה, וְזֶה הוּא פְּרָטָן: א) לֵידַע שֶׁיֵּשׁ שָׁם אֱלוֹהַּ (עשה א). ב) שֶׁלֹּא יַעֲלֶה בְּמַחֲשָׁבָה שֶׁיֵּשׁ שָׁם אֱלוֹהַּ זוּלָתִי יי (לא תעשה א). ג) לְיַחֲדוֹ (עשה ב). ד) לְאָהֲבוֹ (עשה ג). ה) לְיִרְאָה מִמֶּנּוּ (עשה ד). ו) לְקַדֵּשׁ שְׁמוֹ (עשה ט). ז) שֶׁלֹּא לְחַלֵּל אֶת שְׁמוֹ (לא תעשה סג). ח) שֶׁלֹּא לְאַבֵּד דְּבָרִים שֶׁנִּקְרָא שְׁמוֹ עֲלֵיהֶן (לא תעשה סה). ט) לִשְׁמֹעַ מִן הַנָּבִיא הַמְדַבֵּר בִּשְׁמוֹ (עשה קעב). י) שֶׁלֹּא לְנַסּוֹתוֹ (לא תעשה סד).

***Hilkhot Yesodei HaTorah* include ten mitzvot: six positive mitzvot and four negative mitzvot. Their enumeration follows: 1) To know that there is a God** (positive mitzva 1); **2) Not to contemplate that there is another god apart from Him** (negative mitzva 1); **3) To acknowledge His unity** (positive mitzva 2); **4) To love Him** (positive mitzva 3); **5) To fear Him** (positive mitzva 4); **6) To sanctify His name** (positive mitzva 9); **7) Not to desecrate His name** (negative mitzva 63); **8) Not to eradicate items that have His name upon them** (negative mitzva 65); **9) To listen to the prophet who speaks in His name** (positive mitzva 172); **10) Not to test Him** (negative mitzva 64).

הִלְכוֹת דֵּעוֹת - יֵשׁ בִּכְלָלָן אַחַת עֶשְׂרֵה מִצְוֹת, חָמֵשׁ מִצְוֹת עֲשֵׂה וְשֵׁשׁ מִצְוֹת לֹא תַעֲשֶׂה, וְזֶה הוּא פְּרָטָן: א) לְהִדַּמּוֹת בִּדְרָכָיו (עשה ח). ב) לְהִדַּבֵּק בְּיוֹדְעָיו (עשה ו). ג) לֶאֱהֹב אֶת רֵעִים (עשה רו). ד) לֶאֱהֹב אֶת הַגֵּרִים (עשה רז). ה) שֶׁלֹּא לִשְׂנֹא אַחִים (לא תעשה שב). ו) לְהוֹכִיחַ (עשה רה). ז) שֶׁלֹּא לְהַלְבִּין פָּנִים (לא תעשה שג). ח) שֶׁלֹּא לְעַנּוֹת אֲמֵלָלִין (לא תעשה רנו). ט) שֶׁלֹּא לַהֲלֹךְ רָכִיל (לא תעשה שא). י) שֶׁלֹּא לִנְקֹם (לא תעשה שד). יא) שֶׁלֹּא לִנְטֹר (לא תעשה שה).

***Hilkhot Deot* include eleven mitzvot: five positive mitzvot and six negative mitzvot. Their enumeration follows: 1) To resemble God in His ways** (positive mitzva 8); **2) To cleave to those who know Him** (positive mitzva 6); **3) To love one's fellows** (positive mitzva 206); **4) To love converts** (positive mitzva 207); **5) Not to hate one's brothers** (negative mitzva 302); **6) To reprove** (positive mitzva 205); **7) Not to humiliate** others (negative mitzva 303); **8) Not to afflict the downtrodden** (negative mitzva 256); **9) Not to go about as a talebearer** (negative mitzva 301); **10) Not to take vengeance** (negative mitzva 304); **11) Not to bear a grudge** (negative mitzva 305).

הִלְכוֹת תַּלְמוּד תּוֹרָה – יֵשׁ בִּכְלָלָן שְׁתֵּי מִצְווֹת עֲשֵׂה: רִאשׁוֹנָה – לִלְמֹד תּוֹרָה (עשה יא), שְׁנִיָּה – לְכַבֵּד מְלַמְּדֶיהָ וְיוֹדְעֶיהָ (עשה רט).

Hilkhot Talmud Torah **include two positive mitzvot:** The **first is to study Torah** (positive mitzva 11), and the **second is to honor its teachers and its scholars** (positive mitzva 209).

הִלְכוֹת עֲבוֹדָה זָרָה וְחֻקּוֹת הַגּוֹיִם – יֵשׁ בִּכְלָלָן אַחַת וַחֲמִשִּׁים מִצְווֹת, שְׁתֵּי מִצְווֹת עֲשֵׂה וְתֵשַׁע וְאַרְבָּעִים מִצְווֹת לֹא תַעֲשֶׂה, וְזֶה הוּא פְּרָטָן: א) שֶׁלֹּא לִפְנוֹת אַחַר עֲבוֹדָה זָרָה (לא תעשה י). ב) שֶׁלֹּא לָתוּר אַחַר הִרְהוּר הַלֵּב וּרְאִיַּת הָעֵינַיִם (לא תעשה מז). ג) שֶׁלֹּא לְגַדֵּף (לא תעשה ס). ד) שֶׁלֹּא יַעֲבֹד אוֹתָהּ כְּדֶרֶךְ עֲבוֹדָתָהּ (לא תעשה ו). ה) שֶׁלֹּא יִשְׁתַּחֲוֶה לָהּ (לא תעשה ה). ו) שֶׁלֹּא לַעֲשׂוֹת פֶּסֶל לְעַצְמוֹ (לא תעשה ב). ז) שֶׁלֹּא לַעֲשׂוֹת פֶּסֶל אֲפִלּוּ לַאֲחֵרִים (לא תעשה ג). ח) שֶׁלֹּא לַעֲשׂוֹת צוּרוֹת אֲפִלּוּ לְנוֹי (לא תעשה ד). ט) שֶׁלֹּא לְהַדִּיחַ אֲחֵרִים אַחֲרֶיהָ (לא תעשה טו). י) לִשְׂרֹף עִיר הַנִּדַּחַת (עשה קפו). יא) שֶׁלֹּא לִבְנוֹתָהּ (לא תעשה כג). יב) שֶׁלֹּא לֵהָנוֹת מִכָּל מָמוֹנָהּ (לא תעשה כד). יג) שֶׁלֹּא לְהָסִית יָחִיד לְעָבְדָהּ (לא תעשה יו). יד) שֶׁלֹּא לֶאֱהֹב הַמֵּסִית (לא תעשה יז). טו) שֶׁלֹּא לַעֲזֹב שִׂנְאָתוֹ (לא תעשה יח). יו) שֶׁלֹּא לְהַצִּילוֹ (לא תעשה יט). יז) שֶׁלֹּא לְלַמֵּד עָלָיו זְכוּת (לא תעשה כ). יח) שֶׁלֹּא יִמָּנַע מִלְּלַמֵּד עָלָיו חוֹבָה (לא תעשה כא). יט) שֶׁלֹּא לְהִתְנַבֵּא בִּשְׁמָהּ (לא תעשה כו). כ) שֶׁלֹּא לִשְׁמֹעַ מִן הַמִּתְנַבֵּא בִּשְׁמָהּ (לא תעשה כח). כא) שֶׁלֹּא לְהִתְנַבֵּא בְּשֶׁקֶר וַאֲפִלּוּ בְּשֵׁם יי (לא תעשה כז). כב) שֶׁלֹּא לָגוּר מֵהֲרִיגַת נְבִיא שֶׁקֶר (לא תעשה כט). כג) שֶׁלֹּא לִשָּׁבַע בְּשֵׁם עֲבוֹדָה זָרָה (לא תעשה יד). כד) שֶׁלֹּא לַעֲשׂוֹת אוֹב (לא תעשה ח). כה) שֶׁלֹּא לַעֲשׂוֹת יִדְּעוֹנִי (לא תעשה ט).

Hilkhot Avoda Zara VeḤukkot HaGoyim **include fifty-one mitzvot: two positive mitzvot and forty-nine negative mitzvot. Their enumeration follows: 1) Not to go astray after idolatry** (negative mitzva 10); **2) Not to stray after the thoughts of the heart and the sight of the eyes** (negative mitzva 47); **3) Not to blaspheme** (negative mitzva 60); **4) Not to worship** idolatry **in the manner of its worship** (negative mitzva 6); **5) Not to prostrate oneself to** idols (negative mitzva 5); **6) Not to make an idol for oneself** (negative mitzva 2); **7) Not to make an idol even for others** (negative mitzva 3); **8) Not to make images, even as ornaments** (negative mitzva 4); **9) Not to subvert others to follow** idolatry (negative mitzva 15); **10) To burn a subverted city** [*ir hanidaḥat*] (positive mitzva 186); **11) Not to build** such a city again (negative mitzva 23); **12) Not to derive benefit from any of its property** (negative mitzva 24); **13) Not to incite an individual to worship** idols (negative mitzva 16); **14) Not to love an inciter** toward idolatry (negative mitzva 17); **15) Not to renounce one's hatred of him** (negative mitzva 18); **16) Not to rescue him** (negative mitzva 19); **17) Not to teach** a reason **to acquit him** (negative mitzva 20); **18) Not to refrain from teaching** a reason **to find him liable** (negative mitzva 21); **19) Not to prophesy in the name of** idolatry (negative mitzva 26); **20) Not to listen to one who prophesies in its name** (negative mitzva 28); **21) Not to prophesy falsely, even in the name of God** (negative mitzva 27); **22) Not to be afraid of executing a false prophet** (negative mitzva 29); **23) Not to swear in the name of idolatry** (negative mitzva 14); **24) Not to perform** the acts of **a necromancer** (negative mitzva 8); **25) Not to perform** the acts of **a sorcerer** (negative mitzva 9); **26) Not to pass** one's child through the fire **to Molekh** (negative mitzva 7); **27) Not to establish a monument** (negative mitzva 11); **28) Not to bow down on an ornamented stone** (negative mitzva 12); **29) Not to plant an** *ashera* tree (negative mitzva 13); **30) To eradicate idolatry and anything made for it** (positive mitzva 185); **31) Not to derive benefit from idolatry or any of its accessories** (negative mitzva 25); **32) Not to derive benefit from the coating of a worshipped object** (negative mitzva 22); **33) Not to enact a covenant with idol worshippers** (negative mitzva 48); **34) Not to show favor to them** (negative mitzva 50); **35) Not** to let **them reside in**

כו) שֶׁלֹּא לְהַעֲבִיר לַמֹּלֶךְ (לא תעשה ז). כז) שֶׁלֹּא לְהָקִים מַצֵּבָה (לא תעשה יא). כח) שֶׁלֹּא לְהִשְׁתַּחֲווֹת עַל אֶבֶן מַשְׂכִּית (לא תעשה יב). כט) שֶׁלֹּא לִטַּע אֲשֵׁרָה (לא תעשה יג). ל) לְאַבֵּד עֲבוֹדָה זָרָה וְכָל הַנַּעֲשֶׂה בִּשְׁבִילָהּ (עשה קפה). לא) שֶׁלֹּא לֵהָנוֹת בַּעֲבוֹדָה זָרָה וּבְכָל מְשַׁמְּשֶׁיהָ (לא תעשה כה). לב) שֶׁלֹּא לֵהָנוֹת בְּצִפּוּיֵי נֶעֱבָד (לא תעשה כב). לג) שֶׁלֹּא לִכְרוֹת בְּרִית לְעוֹבְדֵי עֲבוֹדָה זָרָה (לא תעשה מח). לד) שֶׁלֹּא לָחֹן עֲלֵיהֶם (לא תעשה נ). לה) שֶׁלֹּא יֵשְׁבוּ בְּאַרְצֵנוּ (לא תעשה נא). לו) שֶׁלֹּא לְהִדַּמּוֹת בְּמִנְהֲגוֹתָם וּבְמַלְבּוּשָׁם (לא תעשה ל). לז) שֶׁלֹּא לְנַחֵשׁ (לא תעשה לג). לח) שֶׁלֹּא לִקְסֹם (לא תעשה לא). לט) שֶׁלֹּא לְעוֹנֵן (לא תעשה לב). מ) שֶׁלֹּא לַחֲבֹר חֶבֶר (לא תעשה לה). מא) שֶׁלֹּא לִדְרֹשׁ אֶל הַמֵּתִים (לא תעשה לח). מב) שֶׁלֹּא לִשְׁאֹל בְּאוֹב (לא תעשה לו). מג) שֶׁלֹּא לִשְׁאֹל בְּיִדְּעוֹנִי (לא תעשה לז). מד) שֶׁלֹּא לְכַשֵּׁף (לא תעשה לד). מה) שֶׁלֹּא לְהַקִּיף פְּאַת רֹאשׁ (לא תעשה מג). מו) שֶׁלֹּא לְהַשְׁחִית פְּאַת הַזָּקָן (לא תעשה מד). מז) שֶׁלֹּא יַעְדֶּה אִישׁ עֲדִי אִשָּׁה (לא תעשה מ). מח) שֶׁלֹּא תַּעְדֶּה אִשָּׁה עֲדִי אִישׁ (לא תעשה לט). מט) שֶׁלֹּא לִכְתֹּב קַעֲקַע (לא תעשה מא). נ) שֶׁלֹּא לְהִתְגּוֹדֵד (לא תעשה מה). נא) שֶׁלֹּא לַעֲשׂוֹת קָרְחָה עַל מֵת (לא תעשה קעא).

our land (negative mitzva 51); **36) Not to resemble** idol worshippers **in their customs and** manner of **dress** (negative mitzva 30); **37) Not to practice enchantment** (negative mitzva 33); **38) Not to divine** (negative mitzva 31); **39) Not to soothsay** (negative mitzva 32); **40) Not to charm** (negative mitzva 35); **41) Not to direct inquiries to the dead** (negative mitzva 38); **42) Not to inquire of a necromancer** (negative mitzva 36); **43) Not to inquire of a sorcerer** (negative mitzva 37); **44) Not to practice witchcraft** (negative mitzva 34); **45) Not to round the corners of the** hair on the **head** (negative mitzva 43); **46) Not to destroy the corners of the beard** (negative mitzva 44); **47) A man may not adorn himself with the adornments of a woman** (negative mitzva 40); **48) A woman may not adorn himself with the adornments of a man** (negative mitzva 39); **49) Not to make a tattoo** (negative mitzva 41); **50) Not to cut oneself** (negative mitzva 45); **51) Not to make a bald spot** in mourning **for the dead** (negative mitzva 171).

הִלְכוֹת תְּשׁוּבָה – מִצְוַת עֲשֵׂה אַחַת, וְהִיא שֶׁיָּשׁוּב הַחוֹטֵא מֵחֶטְאוֹ לִפְנֵי יי וְיִתְוַדֶּה (עשה עג).

Hilkhot Teshuva include **one positive mitzva, which is that the sinner must repent of his sin before God, and confess** (positive mitzva 73).

נִמְצְאוּ כָּל הַמִּצְווֹת הַנִּכְלָלוֹת בְּסֵפֶר זֶה חָמֵשׁ וְשִׁבְעִים, שֵׁשׁ עֶשְׂרֵה מֵהֶן מִצְווֹת עֲשֵׂה וְתֵשַׁע וַחֲמִשִּׁים מִצְווֹת לֹא תַעֲשֶׂה.

Thus, all the mitzvot that are **included in this *Sefer* are seventy-five: Sixteen of them are positive mitzvot and** the other **fifty-nine** are **negative mitzvot.**

סֵפֶר אַהֲבָה

2. Sefer Ahava

הִלְכוֹתָיו שֵׁשׁ, וְזֶה הוּא סִדּוּרָן: הִלְכוֹת קְרִיַּת שְׁמַע, הִלְכוֹת תְּפִלָּה וּבִרְכַּת כֹּהֲנִים, הִלְכוֹת תְּפִלִּין וּמְזוּזָה וְסֵפֶר תּוֹרָה, הִלְכוֹת צִיצִית, הִלְכוֹת בְּרָכוֹת, הִלְכוֹת מִילָה.

Sefer Ahava contains **six sections, in the following order: *Hilkhot Keriat Shema*** (Laws of Reciting *Shema*), ***Hilkhot Tefilla UVirkat Kohanim*** (Laws of Prayer and the Priestly Benediction), ***Hilkhot Tefillin UMezuza VeSefer Torah*** (Laws of Phylacteries, Mezuza, and Torah Scrolls), ***Hilkhot Tzitzit*** (Laws of Ritual Fringes), ***Hilkhot Berakhot*** (Laws of Blessings), and ***Hilkhot Mila*** (Laws of Circumcision).

הִלְכוֹת קְרִיַּת שְׁמַע – מִצְוַת עֲשֵׂה אַחַת, וְהִיא לִקְרֹא קְרִיַּת שְׁמַע פַּעֲמַיִם בַּיּוֹם (עשה י).

Hilkhot Keriat Shema include **one positive mitzva, which is to recite *Shema* twice daily** (positive mitzva 10).

הִלְכוֹת תְּפִלָּה וּבִרְכַּת כֹּהֲנִים – יֵשׁ בִּכְלָלָן שְׁתֵּי מִצְוֹת עֲשֵׂה, אַחַת – לַעֲבֹד אֶת יי בִּתְפִלָּה בְּכָל יוֹם (עשה ה), שְׁנִיָּה – לְבָרֵךְ כֹּהֲנִים אֶת יִשְׂרָאֵל בְּכָל יוֹם (עשה כו).

Hilkhot Tefilla UVirkat Kohanim include two positive mitzvot; one is to serve God through prayer every day (positive mitzva 5), and the second is for the priests to bless Israel every day (positive mitzva 26).

הִלְכוֹת תְּפִלִּין וּמְזוּזָה וְסֵפֶר תּוֹרָה – יֵשׁ בִּכְלָלָן חָמֵשׁ מִצְוֹת עֲשֵׂה, וְזֶה הוּא פְּרָטָן: א) לִהְיוֹת תְּפִלִּין עַל הָרֹאשׁ (עשה יב). ב) לְקָשְׁרָם עַל הַיָּד (עשה יג). ג) לִקְבֹּעַ מְזוּזָה בְּפִתְחֵי הַשְּׁעָרִים (עשה טו). ד) לִכְתֹּב כָּל אִישׁ סֵפֶר תּוֹרָה לְעַצְמוֹ (עשה יז). ה) לִכְתֹּב הַמֶּלֶךְ סֵפֶר שֵׁנִי לְעַצְמוֹ כְּדֵי שֶׁיִּהְיֶה לוֹ שְׁנֵי סִפְרֵי תּוֹרָה (עשה יח).

Hilkhot Tefillin UMezuza VeSefer Torah include five positive mitzvot. Their enumeration follows: 1) That a phylactery should be on one's head (positive mitzva 12); 2) To bind a phylactery to one's arm (positive mitzva 13); 3) To affix a mezuza to the entrances of one's gates (positive mitzva 15); 4) That each man should write a Torah scroll for himself (positive mitzva 17); 5) That the king should write a second Torah scroll for himself so that he will have two Torah scrolls (positive mitzva 18).

הִלְכוֹת צִיצִית – מִצְוַת עֲשֵׂה אַחַת, וְהִיא לַעֲשׂוֹת צִיצִית עַל כַּנְפֵי הַכְּסוּת (עשה יד).

Hilkhot Tzitzit include **one positive mitzva, which is to make ritual fringes on the corners of garments** (positive mitzva 14).

הִלְכוֹת בְּרָכוֹת – מִצְוַת עֲשֵׂה אַחַת, וְהִיא לְבָרֵךְ אֶת שְׁמוֹ אַחַר אֲכִילָה (עשה יט).

Hilkhot Berakhot include **one positive mitzva, which is to bless** God's **name after eating** (positive mitzva 19).

הִלְכוֹת מִילָה – מִצְוַת עֲשֵׂה אַחַת, וְהִיא לָמוּל אֶת הַזְּכָרִים בַּיּוֹם הַשְּׁמִינִי (עשה רטו).

Hilkhot Mila include **one positive mitzva, which is to circumcise males on the eighth day** (positive mitzva 215).

נִמְצְאוּ כָּל הַמִּצְוֹת הַנִּכְלָלוֹת בְּסֵפֶר זֶה אַחַת עֶשְׂרֵה מִצְוֹת עֲשֵׂה.

Thus, all the mitzvot that are **included in this *Sefer*** are **eleven positive mitzvot.**

סֵפֶר זְמַנִּים

3. Sefer Zemanim

הִלְכוֹתָיו עֶשֶׂר, וְזֶה הוּא סִדּוּרָן: הִלְכוֹת שַׁבָּת, הִלְכוֹת עֵרוּבִין, הִלְכוֹת שְׁבִיתַת עָשׂוֹר, הִלְכוֹת שְׁבִיתַת יוֹם טוֹב, הִלְכוֹת חָמֵץ וּמַצָּה, הִלְכוֹת שׁוֹפָר וְסֻכָּה וְלוּלָב, הִלְכוֹת שְׁקָלִים, הִלְכוֹת קִדּוּשׁ הַחֹדֶשׁ, הִלְכוֹת תַּעֲנִיּוֹת, הִלְכוֹת מְגִלָּה וַחֲנֻכָּה.

Sefer Zemanim contains **ten sections, in the following order: *Hilkhot Shabbat*** (Laws of Shabbat), ***Hilkhot Eiruvin*** (Laws of Mergings), ***Hilkhot Shevitat Asor*** (Laws of Resting on the Tenth [of Tishrei]), ***Hilkhot Yom Tov*** (Laws of Festivals), ***Hilkhot Ḥametz UMatza*** (Laws of Leavened and Unleavened Bread), ***Hilkhot Shofar VeSukka VeLulav*** (Laws of the Shofar, *Sukka* and *Lulav*), ***Hilkhot Shekalim*** (Laws of *Shekalim*), ***Hilkhot Kiddush HaḤodesh*** (Laws of the Sanctification of the New Moon), ***Hilkhot Taaniyot*** (Laws of Fast Days), and ***Hilkhot Megilla VaḤanukka*** (Laws of Megilla and Hanukkah).

הִלְכוֹת שַׁבָּת – יֵשׁ בִּכְלָלָן חָמֵשׁ מִצְווֹת, שְׁתֵּי מִצְווֹת עֲשֵׂה וְשָׁלֹשׁ מִצְווֹת לֹא תַעֲשֶׂה, וְזֶה הוּא פְּרָטָן: א) **לִשְׁבֹּת בַּשְּׁבִיעִי** (עשה קנד). ב) **שֶׁלֹּא לַעֲשׂוֹת בּוֹ מְלָאכָה** (לא תעשה שכ). ג) **שֶׁלֹּא לַעֲנֹשׁ בְּשַׁבָּת** (לא תעשה שכב). ד) **שֶׁלֹּא לָצֵאת חוּץ לַגְּבוּל בְּשַׁבָּת** (לא תעשה שכא). ה) **לְקַדֵּשׁ הַיּוֹם בִּזְכִירָה** (עשה קנה).

Hilkhot Shabbat **include five mitzvot: two positive mitzvot and three negative mitzvot. Their enumeration follows: 1) To rest on the seventh** day (positive mitzva 154); **2) Not to perform labor** on that day (negative mitzva 320); **3) Not to administer** judicial **punishments on Shabbat** (negative mitzva 322); **4) Not to go beyond** the established **boundary on Shabbat** (negative mitzva 321); **5) To sanctify the day through** verbal **mention** (positive mitzva 155).

הִלְכוֹת עֵרוּבִין – מִצְוַת עֲשֵׂה אַחַת, וְהִיא מִדִּבְרֵי סוֹפְרִים, וְאֵינָהּ מִן הַמִּנְיָן.

Hilkhot Eiruvin include **one positive mitzva, which** applies **by rabbinic law, and is** therefore **not counted** as one of the six hundred and thirteen mitzvot of the Torah.

הִלְכוֹת שְׁבִיתַת עָשׂוֹר – יֵשׁ בִּכְלָלָן אַרְבַּע מִצְווֹת, שְׁתֵּי מִצְווֹת עֲשֵׂה וּשְׁתֵּי מִצְווֹת לֹא תַעֲשֶׂה, וְזֶה הוּא פְּרָטָן: א) **לִשְׁבֹּת בּוֹ מִמְּלָאכָה** (עשה קסה). ב) **שֶׁלֹּא לַעֲשׂוֹת בּוֹ מְלָאכָה** (לא תעשה שכז). ג) **לְהִתְעַנּוֹת בּוֹ** (עשה קסד). ד) **שֶׁלֹּא לֶאֱכֹל וְלִשְׁתּוֹת בּוֹ** (לא תעשה קצו).

Hilkhot Shevitat Asor **include four mitzvot: two positive mitzvot and two negative mitzvot. Their enumeration follows: 1) To rest on this day from** prohibited **labor** (positive mitzva 165); **2) Not to perform labor on it** (negative mitzva 327); **3) To afflict oneself on it** (positive mitzva 164); **4) Not to eat or drink on it** (negative mitzva 196).

הִלְכוֹת שְׁבִיתַת יוֹם טוֹב – יֵשׁ בִּכְלָלָן שְׁתֵּים עֶשְׂרֵה מִצְווֹת, שֵׁשׁ מִצְווֹת עֲשֵׂה וְשֵׁשׁ מִצְווֹת לֹא תַעֲשֶׂה, וְזֶה הוּא פְּרָטָן: א) **לִשְׁבֹּת בָּרִאשׁוֹן שֶׁל פֶּסַח** (עשה קנט). ב) **שֶׁלֹּא לַעֲשׂוֹת בּוֹ מְלָאכָה** (לא תעשה שכג). ג) **לִשְׁבֹּת בַּשְּׁבִיעִי שֶׁל פֶּסַח** (עשה קס). ד) **שֶׁלֹּא לַעֲשׂוֹת בּוֹ מְלָאכָה** (לא תעשה שכד). ה) **לִשְׁבֹּת בְּיוֹם חַג הַשָּׁבוּעוֹת** (עשה קסב). ו) **שֶׁלֹּא לַעֲשׂוֹת בּוֹ מְלָאכָה** (לא תעשה שכה). ז) **לִשְׁבֹּת בְּרֹאשׁ הַשָּׁנָה** (עשה קסג). ח) **שֶׁלֹּא לַעֲשׂוֹת בּוֹ מְלָאכָה** (לא תעשה שכו). ט) **לִשְׁבֹּת בָּרִאשׁוֹן שֶׁל חַג הַסֻּכּוֹת** (עשה קסו). י) **שֶׁלֹּא לַעֲשׂוֹת בּוֹ מְלָאכָה** (לא תעשה שכח). יא) **לִשְׁבֹּת בַּשְּׁמִינִי שֶׁל חַג** (עשה קסז). יב) **שֶׁלֹּא לַעֲשׂוֹת בּוֹ מְלָאכָה** (לא תעשה שכט).

Hilkhot Yom Tov **include twelve mitzvot: six positive mitzvot and six negative mitzvot. Their enumeration follows: 1) To rest on the first** day **of Passover** (positive mitzva 159); **2) Not to perform labor on it** (negative mitzva 323); **3) To rest on the seventh** day **of Passover** (positive mitzva 160); **4) Not to perform labor on it** (negative mitzva 324); **5) To rest on the day of the festival of Shavuot** (positive mitzva 162); **6) Not to perform labor on it** (negative mitzva 325); **7) To rest on Rosh HaShana** (positive mitzva 163); **8) Not to perform labor on it** (negative mitzva 326); **9) To rest on the first** day **of the festival of Sukkot** (positive mitzva 166); **10) Not to perform labor on it** (negative mitzva 328); **11) To rest on the eighth** day **of** that **festival** (positive mitzva 167); **12) Not to perform labor on it** (negative mitzva 329).

הִלְכוֹת חָמֵץ וּמַצָּה – יֵשׁ בִּכְלָלָן שְׁמוֹנֶה מִצְווֹת, שָׁלֹשׁ מִצְווֹת עֲשֵׂה וְחָמֵשׁ מִצְווֹת לֹא תַעֲשֶׂה, וְזֶה הוּא פְּרָטָן: א) **שֶׁלֹּא לֶאֱכֹל חָמֵץ בְּיוֹם אַרְבָּעָה עָשָׂר מֵחֲצוֹת הַיּוֹם וּלְמַעְלָה** (לא תעשה קצט). ב) **לְהַשְׁבִּית שְׂאֹר מֵאַרְבָּעָה עָשָׂר** (עשה קנו). ג) **שֶׁלֹּא לֶאֱכֹל חָמֵץ כָּל שִׁבְעָה** (לא תעשה קצז). ד) **שֶׁלֹּא לֶאֱכֹל תַּעֲרֹבֶת חָמֵץ כָּל שִׁבְעָה** (לא תעשה קצח). ה) **שֶׁלֹּא יֵרָאֶה חָמֵץ כָּל שִׁבְעָה** (לא תעשה ר). ו) **שֶׁלֹּא יִמָּצֵא חָמֵץ כָּל שִׁבְעָה** (לא תעשה רא). ז) **לֶאֱכֹל**

Hilkhot Ḥametz UMatza **include eight mitzvot: three positive mitzvot and five negative mitzvot. Their enumeration follows: 1) Not to eat leavened bread on the day of the fourteenth** of Nisan **from midday onward** (negative mitzva 199); **2) To remove leaven** starting **from the fourteenth** of Nisan (positive mitzva 156); **3) Not to eat leavened bread all seven** days of Passover (negative mitzva 197); **4) Not to eat a mixture of leavened bread all seven** days of Passover (negative mitzva 198); **5) Leavened bread should not be seen** in one's possession **all seven** days of Passover (negative mitzva 200); **6) Leavened bread should not be found** in one's possession **all seven** days of Passover (negative mitzva 201); **7) To eat**

מַצָּה בְּלֵילֵי הַפֶּסַח (עשה קנח). ח) לְסַפֵּר בִּיצִיאַת מִצְרַיִם בְּאוֹתוֹ הַלַּיְלָה (עשה קנז).

matza (unleavened bread) **on the night of Passover** (positive mitzva 158); 8) **To relate the exodus from Egypt on that night** (positive mitzva 157).

הִלְכוֹת שׁוֹפָר וְסֻכָּה וְלוּלָב – יֵשׁ בִּכְלָלָן שָׁלֹשׁ מִצְווֹת עֲשֵׂה, וְזֶה הוּא פְּרָטָן: א) לִשְׁמֹעַ קוֹל שׁוֹפָר בְּאֶחָד בְּתִשְׁרֵי (עשה קע). ב) לֵישֵׁב בַּסֻּכָּה שִׁבְעַת יְמֵי הֶחָג (עשה קסח). ג) לִנְטֹל לוּלָב בַּמִּקְדָּשׁ כָּל שִׁבְעַת יְמֵי הֶחָג (עשה קסט).

Hilkhot Shofar VeSukka VeLulav **include three positive mitzvot. Their enumeration follows: 1) To hear the sound of a shofar on the first of Tishrei** (positive mitzva 170); **2) To reside in a *sukka*** during the **seven days of the festival** of Sukkot (positive mitzva 168); **3) To take a *lulav* in the Temple all seven days** of Sukkot (positive mitzva 169).

הִלְכוֹת שְׁקָלִים – מִצְוַת עֲשֵׂה אַחַת, וְהִיא לִתֵּן כָּל אִישׁ מַחֲצִית הַשֶּׁקֶל בְּכָל שָׁנָה (עשה קעא).

Hilkhot Shekalim include **one positive mitzva, which is that every man must give a half-shekel every year** (positive mitzva 171).

הִלְכוֹת קִדּוּשׁ הַחֹדֶשׁ – מִצְוַת עֲשֵׂה אַחַת, וְהִיא לַחֲשֹׁב וְלֵידַע וְלִקְבֹּעַ בְּאֵיזֶה יוֹם הוּא תְּחִלַּת כָּל חֹדֶשׁ וְחֹדֶשׁ מֵחָדְשֵׁי הַשָּׁנָה (עשה קנג).

Hilkhot Kiddush HaḤodesh include **one positive mitzva, which is to calculate, know, and establish which day is the beginning of each and every month of the year** (positive mitzva 153).

הִלְכוֹת תַּעֲנִיּוֹת – מִצְוַת עֲשֵׂה אַחַת, וְהִיא לְהִתְעַנּוֹת וְלִזְעֹק לִפְנֵי יי בְּעֵת כָּל צָרָה גְּדוֹלָה שֶׁתָּבֹא עַל הַצִּבּוּר (עשה נט).

Hilkhot Taaniyot include **one positive mitzva, which is to fast and cry out before God at any time of great trouble that befalls the community** (positive mitzva 59).

הִלְכוֹת מְגִלָּה וַחֲנֻכָּה – יֵשׁ בִּכְלָלָן שְׁתֵּי מִצְווֹת עֲשֵׂה מִדִּבְרֵי סוֹפְרִים, וְאֵינָם מִן הַמִּנְיָן.

***Hilkhot Megilla VaḤanukka* include two mitzvot** that apply **by rabbinic law, and are** therefore **not counted** among the six hundred and thirteen mitzvot of the Torah.

נִמְצְאוּ כָּל הַמִּצְווֹת שֶׁל תּוֹרָה הַנִּכְלָלוֹת בְּסֵפֶר זֶה חָמֵשׁ וּשְׁלֹשִׁים, תְּשַׁע עֶשְׂרֵה מֵהֶן מִצְווֹת עֲשֵׂה וְשֵׁשׁ עֶשְׂרֵה מִצְווֹת לֹא תַּעֲשֶׂה, וְיֵשׁ בּוֹ שָׁלֹשׁ מִצְווֹת מִדִּבְרֵי סוֹפְרִים.

Thus, all the mitzvot of the Torah that are included in this *Sefer* are thirty-five: Nineteen of them are **positive mitzvot and** the other **sixteen** are **negative mitzvot.** The *Sefer* also **includes three mitzvot** that apply **by rabbinic law.**

סֵפֶר נָשִׁים

4. Sefer Nashim

הִלְכוֹתָיו חָמֵשׁ, וְזֶה הוּא סִדּוּרָן: הִלְכוֹת אִישׁוּת, הִלְכוֹת גֵּרוּשִׁין, הִלְכוֹת יִבּוּם וַחֲלִיצָה, הִלְכוֹת נַעֲרָה בְּתוּלָה, הִלְכוֹת שׁוֹטָה.

Sefer Nashim contains **five *Hilkhot*, in the following order: *Hilkhot Ishut*** (Laws of Marriage), ***Hilkhot Geirushin*** (Laws of Divorce), ***Hilkhot Yibbum VaḤalitza*** (Laws of Levirate Marriage and Release), ***Hilkhot Naara Betula*** (Laws of a Young Virgin Woman), and ***Hilkhot Sota*** (Laws of *Sota*).

הִלְכוֹת אִישׁוּת – יֵשׁ בִּכְלָלָן אַרְבַּע מִצְווֹת, שְׁתֵּי מִצְווֹת עֲשֵׂה וּשְׁתֵּי מִצְווֹת לֹא תַּעֲשֶׂה, וְזֶה הוּא פְּרָטָן: א) לִשָּׂא אִשָּׁה בִּכְתֻבָּה וְקִדּוּשִׁין (עשה ריג). ב) שֶׁלֹּא תִּבָּעֵל אִשָּׁה בְּלֹא כְּתֻבָּה וְקִדּוּשִׁין (לא תעשה שנה). ג) שֶׁלֹּא יִמְנַע שְׁאֵר כְּסוּת וְעוֹנָה (לא תעשה רסב). ד) לִפְרוֹת וְלִרְבּוֹת מִמֶּנָּה (עשה ריב).

Hilkhot Ishut include four mitzvot: two positive mitzvot and two negative mitzvot. Their enumeration follows: 1) To marry a woman with a marriage contract and betrothal (positive mitzva 213); 2) Not to have intercourse without a marriage contract and betrothal (negative mitzva 355); 3) Not to withhold food, clothing, and conjugal rights from one's wife (negative mitzva 262); 4) To be fruitful and multiply with her (positive mitzva 212).

***Hilkhot Geirushin* include two mitzvot: one positive mitzva, which is that one who divorces must do so with a document** (positive mitzva 222), **and a second** mitzva, a negative mitzva, which is **that one may not remarry his divorced wife after she has married another man** (negative mitzva 356).

הִלְכוֹת גֵּרוּשִׁין – שְׁתֵּי מִצְוֹת, אַחַת מִצְוַת עֲשֵׂה, וְהִיא שֶׁיְּגָרֵשׁ הַמְגָרֵשׁ בְּסֵפֶר (עשה רכב), **שְׁנִיָּה – שֶׁלֹּא יַחֲזִיר גְּרוּשָׁתוֹ מִשֶּׁנִּשֵּׂאת** (לא תעשה שנו).

Hilkhot Yibbum VaḤalitza* include three mitzvot: two positive mitzvot and one negative mitzva. Their enumeration follows: 1) To consummate levirate marriage** (positive mitzva 216); **2) To perform *ḥalitza [release] (positive mitzva 217); **3) That a *yevama* may not marry "a strange man" until the authority of the *yavam* is removed from over her** (negative mitzva 357).

הִלְכוֹת יִבּוּם וַחֲלִיצָה – יֵשׁ בִּכְלָלָן שָׁלֹשׁ מִצְוֹת, שְׁתֵּי מִצְוֹת עֲשֵׂה וְאַחַת מִצְוַת לֹא תַעֲשֶׂה, וְזֶה הוּא פְּרָטָן: א) לְיַבֵּם (עשה ריו). **ב) לַחֲלֹץ** (עשה ריז). **ג) שֶׁלֹּא תִּנָּשֵׂא יְבָמָה לְאִישׁ זָר עַד שֶׁתָּסוּר רְשׁוּת הַיָּבָם מֵעָלֶיהָ** (לא תעשה שנז).

Hilkhot Naara Betula include five mitzvot: three positive mitzvot and two negative mitzvot. Their enumeration follows: 1) To penalize the seducer (positive mitzva 220); 2) That the rapist must marry the woman he raped (positive mitzva 218); 3) That the rapist may not divorce his victim (negative mitzva 358); 4) That the wife of the defamer remain under the jurisdiction of her husband forever (positive mitzva 219); 5) That the defamer may not divorce his wife (negative mitzva 359).

הִלְכוֹת נַעֲרָה בְּתוּלָה – יֵשׁ בִּכְלָלָן חָמֵשׁ מִצְוֹת, שָׁלֹשׁ מִצְוֹת עֲשֵׂה וּשְׁתֵּי מִצְוֹת לֹא תַעֲשֶׂה, וְזֶה הוּא פְּרָטָן: א) לִקְנֹס הַמְפַתֶּה (עשה רכ). **ב) שֶׁיִּשָּׂא הָאוֹנֵס אֲנוּסָתוֹ** (עשה ריח). **ג) שֶׁלֹּא יְגָרֵשׁ הָאוֹנֵס** (לא תעשה שנח). **ד) שֶׁתֵּשֵׁב אֵשֶׁת מוֹצִיא שֵׁם רַע תַּחַת בַּעְלָהּ לְעוֹלָם** (עשה ריט). **ה) שֶׁלֹּא יְגָרֵשׁ מוֹצִיא שֵׁם רַע אֶת אִשְׁתּוֹ** (לא תעשה שנט).

Hilkhot Sota include three mitzvot: one positive mitzva and two negative mitzvot. Their enumeration follows: 1) To treat a *sota* in accordance with the law of jealousy that is set forth in the Torah (positive mitzva 223); 2) Not to place oil on her offering (negative mitzva 104); 3) Not to place frankincense on her offering (negative mitzva 105).

הִלְכוֹת שׂוֹטָה – יֵשׁ בִּכְלָלָן שָׁלֹשׁ מִצְוֹת, אַחַת מִצְוַת עֲשֵׂה וּשְׁתַּיִם מִצְוֹת לֹא תַעֲשֶׂה, וְזֶה הוּא פְּרָטָן: א) לַעֲשׂוֹת לַשּׂוֹטָה כְּתוֹרַת הַקְּנָאוֹת הַסְּדוּרָה בַּתּוֹרָה (עשה רכג). **ב) שֶׁלֹּא לִתֵּן שֶׁמֶן עַל קָרְבָּנָהּ** (לא תעשה קד). **ג) שֶׁלֹּא לִתֵּן עָלָיו לְבֹנָה** (לא תעשה קה).

Thus, all the mitzvot that are included in this *Sefer* are **seventeen: Nine of them** are **positive mitzvot and** the other **eight** are **negative mitzvot.**

נִמְצְאוּ כָּל הַמִּצְוֹת הַנִּכְלָלוֹת בְּסֵפֶר זֶה שְׁבַע עֶשְׂרֵה, מֵהֶן תֵּשַׁע מִצְוֹת עֲשֵׂה וּשְׁמוֹנֶה מִצְוֹת לֹא תַעֲשֶׂה.

סֵפֶר קְדֻשָּׁה
5. Sefer Kedusha

Sefer Kedusha contains **three *Hilkhot*, in the following order: *Hilkhot Issurei Bia*** (Laws of Prohibited Relations), ***Hilkhot Maakhalot Asurot*** (Laws of Forbidden Foods), and ***Hilkhot Sheḥita*** (Laws of Ritual Slaughter).

הִלְכוֹתָיו שָׁלֹשׁ, וְזֶה הוּא סִדּוּרָן: הִלְכוֹת אִסּוּרֵי בִּיאָה, הִלְכוֹת מַאֲכָלוֹת אֲסוּרוֹת, הִלְכוֹת שְׁחִיטָה.

הִלְכוֹת אִסּוּרֵי בִּיאָה – יֵשׁ בִּכְלָלָן שֶׁבַע וּשְׁלֹשִׁים מִצְווֹת, אַחַת מִצְוַת עֲשֵׂה וְשֵׁשׁ וּשְׁלֹשִׁים מִצְווֹת לֹא תַעֲשֶׂה, וְזֶה הוּא פְּרָטָן: **א) שֶׁלֹּא לָבֹא עַל הָאֵם** (לא תעשה של). **ב) שֶׁלֹּא לָבֹא עַל אֵשֶׁת אָב** (לא תעשה שלא). **ג) שֶׁלֹּא לִבְעֹל אָחוֹת** (לא תעשה שלב). **ד) שֶׁלֹּא לִבְעֹל בַּת אֵשֶׁת אָב** (לא תעשה שלג). **ה) שֶׁלֹּא לִבְעֹל בַּת הַבֵּן** (לא תעשה שלד). **ו) שֶׁלֹּא לִבְעֹל בַּת** (לא תעשה שלו). **ז) שֶׁלֹּא לִבְעֹל בַּת הַבַּת** (לא תעשה שלה). **ח) שֶׁלֹּא לִשָּׂא אִשָּׁה וּבִתָּהּ** (לא תעשה שלז). **ט) שֶׁלֹּא לִשָּׂא אִשָּׁה וּבַת בְּנָהּ** (לא תעשה שלח). **י) שֶׁלֹּא לִשָּׂא אִשָּׁה וּבַת בִּתָּהּ** (לא תעשה שלט). **יא) שֶׁלֹּא לִבְעֹל אֲחוֹת אָב** (לא תעשה שמ). **יב) שֶׁלֹּא לִבְעֹל אֲחוֹת אֵם** (לא תעשה שמא). **יג) שֶׁלֹּא לִבְעֹל אֵשֶׁת אֲחִי הָאָב** (לא תעשה שמב). **יד) שֶׁלֹּא לִבְעֹל אֵשֶׁת הַבֵּן** (לא תעשה שמג). **טו) שֶׁלֹּא לִבְעֹל אֵשֶׁת אָח** (לא תעשה שמד). **יו) שֶׁלֹּא לִבְעֹל אֲחוֹת אִשְׁתּוֹ** (לא תעשה שמה). **יז) שֶׁלֹּא לִשְׁכַּב עִם בְּהֵמָה** (לא תעשה שמח). **יח) שֶׁלֹּא תָּבִיא אִשָּׁה בְּהֵמָה עָלֶיהָ** (לא תעשה שמט). **יט) שֶׁלֹּא לִשְׁכַּב עִם זָכָר** (לא תעשה שנ). **כ) שֶׁלֹּא לְגַלּוֹת עֶרְוַת אָב** (לא תעשה שנא). **כא) שֶׁלֹּא לְגַלּוֹת עֶרְוַת אֲחִי אָב** (לא תעשה שנב). **כב) שֶׁלֹּא לִבְעֹל אֵשֶׁת אִישׁ** (לא תעשה שמז). **כג) שֶׁלֹּא לִבְעֹל נִדָּה** (לא תעשה שמו). **כד) שֶׁלֹּא לְהִתְחַתֵּן בַּגּוֹיִם** (לא תעשה נב). **כה) שֶׁלֹּא יָבֹא עַמּוֹנִי וּמוֹאָבִי בַּקָּהָל** (לא תעשה נג). **כו) שֶׁלֹּא לְהַרְחִיק דּוֹר שְׁלִישִׁי מִצְרִי מִלָּבֹא בַּקָּהָל** (לא תעשה נה). **כז) שֶׁלֹּא לְהַרְחִיק דּוֹר שְׁלִישִׁי אֲדוֹמִי מִלָּבֹא בַּקָּהָל** (לא תעשה נד). **כח) שֶׁלֹּא יָבֹא מַמְזֵר בַּקָּהָל** (לא תעשה שנד). **כט) שֶׁלֹּא יָבֹא סָרִיס בַּקָּהָל** (לא תעשה שס). **ל) שֶׁלֹּא לְסָרֵס זָכָר, אֲפִלּוּ בְּהֵמָה חַיָּה וָעוֹף** (לא תעשה שסא). **לא) שֶׁלֹּא יִשָּׂא כֹּהֵן גָּדוֹל אַלְמָנָה** (לא תעשה קסא). **לב) שֶׁלֹּא יִבְעֹל כֹּהֵן גָּדוֹל**

Hilkhot Issurei Bia* include thirty-seven mitzvot: one positive mitzva and thirty-six negative mitzvot. Their enumeration follows: 1) Not to have intercourse with one's mother** (negative mitzva 330); **2) Not to have intercourse with one's father's wife** (negative mitzva 331); **3) Not to have intercourse with one's sister** (negative mitzva 332); **4) Not to have intercourse with the daughter of one's father's wife** (negative mitzva 333); **5) Not to have intercourse with the daughter of one's son** (negative mitzva 334); **6) Not to have intercourse with one's daughter** (negative mitzva 336); **7) Not to have intercourse with the daughter of one's daughter** (negative mitzva 335); **8) Not to marry a woman and her daughter** (negative mitzva 337); **9) Not to marry a woman and her son's daughter** (negative mitzva 338); **10) Not to marry a woman and her daughter's daughter** (negative mitzva 339); **11) Not to have intercourse with one's father's sister** (negative mitzva 340); **12) Not to have intercourse with one's mother's sister** (negative mitzva 341); **13) Not to have intercourse with the wife of one's father's brother** (negative mitzva 342); **14) Not to have intercourse with the wife of one's son** (negative mitzva 343); **15) Not to have intercourse with the wife of one's brother** (negative mitzva 344); **16) Not to have intercourse with the sister of one's wife** (negative mitzva 345); **17) Not to lie with an animal** (negative mitzva 348); **18) That a woman may not engage in intercourse with an animal** (negative mitzva 349); **19) Not to lie with a male** (negative mitzva 350); **20) Not to uncover the nakedness of one's father** (negative mitzva 351); **21) Not to uncover the nakedness of the brother of one's father** (negative mitzva 352); **22) Not to have intercourse with a married woman** (negative mitzva 347); **23) Not to have intercourse with a menstruating woman** (negative mitzva 346); **24) Not to marry a gentile** (negative mitzva 52); **25) That an Amonite and a Moavite may not enter into the congregation of the Lord** (negative mitzva 53); **26) Not to prevent a third-generation Egyptian from entering the congregation** (negative mitzva 55); **27) Not to prevent a third-generation Edomite from entering the congregation** (negative mitzva 54); **28) That a *mamzer* may not enter into the assembly of the Lord** (negative mitzva 354); **29) That a eunuch may not enter into the assembly of the Lord** (negative mitzva 360); **30) Not to castrate a male, even of a domesticated animal, an undomesticated animal, or a bird** (negative mitzva 361); **31) That a High Priest may not marry a widow** (negative mitzva 161); **32) That a High Priest may not have intercourse with a widow, even without marriage** (negative mitzva 162); 33) **That a High Priest should marry a virgin in her youth** (positive mitzva 38); 34) **That a priest should not marry a divorced woman** (negative mitzva 160); 35) **That a priest should not marry a *zona*,** i.e., a woman who has engaged in sexual relations with a man forbidden to her by the Torah (negative mitzva 158); 36) **That a priest should not marry a *ḥalala (negative mitzva 159); 37) **That a person should not approach near one of the forbidden relatives, even if he does not have intercourse** with them (negative mitzva 353).

אַלְמָנָה אֲפִלּוּ בְּלֹא נִשּׂוּאִין (לא תעשה קסב). לג) שֶׁיִּשָּׂא כֹּהֵן גָּדוֹל בְּתוּלָה בִּנְעוּרוֹתֶיהָ (עשה לח). לד) שֶׁלֹּא יִשָּׂא כֹּהֵן גְּרוּשָׁה (לא תעשה קס). לה) שֶׁלֹּא יִשָּׂא זוֹנָה (לא תעשה קנח). לו) שֶׁלֹּא יִשָּׂא חֲלָלָה (לא תעשה קנט). לז) שֶׁלֹּא יִקְרַב אָדָם לְאַחַת מִכָּל הָעֲרָיוֹת, וְאַף עַל פִּי שֶׁלֹּא בָּעַל (לא תעשה שנג).

Hilkhot Maakhalot Asurot include twenty-eight mitzvot: four positive mitzvot and twenty-four negative mitzvot. Their enumeration follows: 1) To examine the signs of domesticated and undomesticated animals, to distinguish between the kosher and the non-kosher (positive mitzva 149); 2) To examine the signs of birds, to distinguish between the kosher and the non-kosher (positive mitzva 150); 3) To examine the signs of grasshoppers, to distinguish between the kosher and the non-kosher (positive mitzva 151); 4) To examine the signs of fish, to distinguish between the kosher and the non-kosher (positive mitzva 152); 5) Not to eat non-kosher domesticated or undomesticated animals (negative mitzva 172); 6) Not to eat non-kosher birds (negative mitzva 174); 7) Not to eat non-kosher fish (negative mitzva 173); 8) Not to eat winged swarming things (negative mitzva 175); 9) Not to eat creeping animals of the earth (negative mitzva 176); 10) Not to eat swarming creatures of the earth (negative mitzva 177); 11) Not to eat worms of fruits when they emerge upon the earth (negative mitzva 178); 12) Not to eat creeping animals of the water (negative mitzva 179); 13) Not to eat an animal carcass (negative mitzva 180); 14) Not to derive benefit from an ox that is stoned (negative mitzva 188); 15) Not to eat a *tereifa* (negative mitzva 181); 16) Not to eat a limb from a living animal (negative mitzva 182); 17) Not to eat blood (negative mitzva 184); 18) Not to eat the forbidden fat of a kosher domesticated animal (negative mitzva 185); 19) Not to eat the sciatic nerve (negative mitzva 183); 20) Not to eat meat cooked in milk (negative mitzva 187); 21) Not to cook meat in milk (negative mitzva 186); 22) Not to eat bread from the new crop (negative mitzva 189); 23) Not to eat roasted kernels from the new crop (negative mitzva 190); 24) Not to eat fresh kernels from the new crop (negative mitzva 191); 25) Not to eat *orla* (negative mitzva 192); 26) Not to eat diverse kinds in a vineyard (negative mitzva 193); 27) Not to eat untithed produce (negative mitzva 153); 28) Not to drink wine used for a libation (negative mitzva 194).

הִלְכוֹת מַאֲכָלוֹת אֲסוּרוֹת – יֵשׁ בִּכְלָלָן שְׁמוֹנֶה וְעֶשְׂרִים מִצְוֹת, אַרְבַּע מִצְוֹת עֲשֵׂה וְאַרְבַּע וְעֶשְׂרִים מִצְוֹת לֹא תַעֲשֶׂה, וְזֶה הוּא פְּרָטָן: א) לִבְדֹּק בְּסִימָנֵי בְּהֵמָה וְחַיָּה לְהַבְדִּיל בֵּין טְמֵאָה לִטְהוֹרָה (עשה קמט). ב) לִבְדֹּק בְּסִימָנֵי הָעוֹף לְהַבְדִּיל בֵּין טָמֵא לְטָהוֹר (עשה קנ). ג) לִבְדֹּק בְּסִימָנֵי חֲגָבִים לְהַבְדִּיל בֵּין טָמֵא לְטָהוֹר (עשה קנא). ד) לִבְדֹּק בְּסִימָנֵי דָגִים לְהַבְדִּיל בֵּין טָמֵא לְטָהוֹר (עשה קנב). ה) שֶׁלֹּא לֶאֱכֹל בְּהֵמָה וְחַיָּה טְמֵאָה (לא תעשה קעב). ו) שֶׁלֹּא לֶאֱכֹל עוֹף טָמֵא (לא תעשה קעד). ז) שֶׁלֹּא לֶאֱכֹל דָּגִים טְמֵאִים (לא תעשה קעג). ח) שֶׁלֹּא לֶאֱכֹל שֶׁרֶץ הָעוֹף (לא תעשה קעה). ט) שֶׁלֹּא לֶאֱכֹל שֶׁרֶץ הָאָרֶץ (לא תעשה קעו). י) שֶׁלֹּא לֶאֱכֹל רֶמֶשׂ הָאָרֶץ (לא תעשה קעז). יא) שֶׁלֹּא לֶאֱכֹל תּוֹלַעַת הַפֵּירוֹת כְּשֶׁתֵּצֵא לָאָרֶץ (לא תעשה קעח). יב) שֶׁלֹּא לֶאֱכֹל שֶׁרֶץ הַמַּיִם (לא תעשה קעט). יג) שֶׁלֹּא לֶאֱכֹל נְבֵלָה (לא תעשה קפ). יד) שֶׁלֹּא לֵהָנוֹת בְּשׁוֹר הַנִּסְקָל (לא תעשה קפח). טו) שֶׁלֹּא לֶאֱכֹל טְרֵפָה (לא תעשה קפא). טז) שֶׁלֹּא לֶאֱכֹל אֵבֶר מִן הַחַי (לא תעשה קפב). יז) שֶׁלֹּא לֶאֱכֹל דָּם (לא תעשה קפד). יח) שֶׁלֹּא לֶאֱכֹל חֵלֶב בְּהֵמָה טְהוֹרָה (לא תעשה קפה). יט) שֶׁלֹּא לֶאֱכֹל גִּיד הַנָּשֶׁה (לא תעשה קפג). כ) שֶׁלֹּא לֶאֱכֹל בָּשָׂר בְּחָלָב (לא תעשה קפז). כא) שֶׁלֹּא לְבַשְּׁלוֹ (לא תעשה קפו). כב) שֶׁלֹּא לֶאֱכֹל לֶחֶם תְּבוּאָה חֲדָשָׁה (לא תעשה קפט). כג) שֶׁלֹּא לֶאֱכֹל קָלִי מִן הֶחָדָשׁ (לא תעשה קצ). כד) שֶׁלֹּא לֶאֱכֹל כַּרְמֶל מִן הֶחָדָשׁ (לא תעשה קצא). כה) שֶׁלֹּא לֶאֱכֹל עָרְלָה (לא תעשה קצב). כו) שֶׁלֹּא לֶאֱכֹל כִּלְאֵי הַכֶּרֶם (לא תעשה קצג). כז) שֶׁלֹּא לֶאֱכֹל טֶבֶל (לא תעשה קנג). כח) שֶׁלֹּא לִשְׁתּוֹת יֵין נֶסֶךְ (לא תעשה קצד).

הִלְכוֹת שְׁחִיטָה – יֵשׁ בִּכְלָלָן חָמֵשׁ מִצְוֹת, שָׁלֹשׁ מִצְוֹת עֲשֵׂה וּשְׁתַּיִם מִצְוֹת לֹא תַעֲשֶׂה, וְזֶה הוּא פְּרָטָן: א) לִשְׁחֹט וְאַחַר כָּךְ יֹאכַל (עשה קמו). ב) שֶׁלֹּא לִשְׁחֹט אוֹתוֹ וְאֶת בְּנוֹ בְּיוֹם אֶחָד (לא תעשה קא). ג) לְכַסּוֹת דַּם חַיָּה וָעוֹף (עשה קמז). ד) שֶׁלֹּא לִקַּח הָאֵם עַל הַבָּנִים (לא תעשה שו). ה) לְשַׁלֵּחַ הָאֵם אִם לְקָחָהּ עַל הַבָּנִים (עשה קמח).

Hilkhot Sheḥita include five mitzvot: three positive mitzvot and two negative mitzvot. Their enumeration follows: 1) To perform ritual slaughter and only then to eat the meat of an animal (positive mitzva 146); 2) Not to slaughter an animal and its offspring on the same day (negative mitzva 101); 3) To cover the blood of an undomesticated animal or a bird (positive mitzva 147); 4) Not to take the mother bird with its offspring (negative mitzva 306); 5) To send away the mother bird if one took it with its offspring (positive mitzva 148).

נִמְצְאוּ כָּל הַמִּצְוֹת הַנִּכְלָלוֹת בְּסֵפֶר זֶה שִׁבְעִים, מֵהֶם שְׁמוֹנֶה מִצְוֹת עֲשֵׂה וּשְׁתַּיִם וְשִׁשִּׁים מִצְוֹת לֹא תַעֲשֶׂה.

Thus, all the mitzvot that are included in this *Sefer* are seventy: Eight of them are **positive mitzvot and sixty-two** are **negative mitzvot.**

סֵפֶר הַפְלָאָה

6. Sefer Haflaa

הִלְכוֹתָיו אַרְבַּע, וְזֶה הוּא סִדּוּרָן: הִלְכוֹת שְׁבוּעוֹת, הִלְכוֹת נְדָרִים, הִלְכוֹת נְזִירוּת, הִלְכוֹת עֲרָכִין וַחֲרָמִין.

Sefer Haflaa contains **four *Hilkhot*, in the following order:** ***Hilkhot Shevuot*** (Laws of Oaths), ***Hilkhot Nedarim*** (Laws of Vows), ***Hilkhot Nezirut*** (Laws of Naziriteship), and ***Hilkhot Arakhin VaḤaramim*** (Laws of Appraisals [for the Temple] and Consecrated Property).

הִלְכוֹת שְׁבוּעוֹת – יֵשׁ בִּכְלָלָן חָמֵשׁ מִצְוֹת, אַחַת מִצְוַת עֲשֵׂה וְאַרְבַּע מִצְוֹת לֹא תַעֲשֶׂה, וְזֶה הוּא פְּרָטָן: א) שֶׁלֹּא לִשָּׁבַע בִּשְׁמוֹ לַשֶּׁקֶר (לא תעשה סא). ב) שֶׁלֹּא לִשָּׂא שְׁמוֹ לַשָּׁוְא (לא תעשה סב). ג) שֶׁלֹּא לְכַפֵּר בְּפִקָּדוֹן (לא תעשה רמח). ד) שֶׁלֹּא לִשָּׁבַע עַל כְּפִירַת מָמוֹן (לא תעשה רמט). ה) לִשָּׁבַע בִּשְׁמוֹ בֶּאֱמֶת (עשה ז).

Hilkhot Shevuot include five mitzvot: one positive mitzva and four negative mitzvot. Their enumeration follows: 1) Not to swear falsely in God's name (negative mitzva 61); 2) Not to take God's name in vain (negative mitzva 62); 3) Not to falsely deny a claim concerning a deposit (negative mitzva 248); 4) Not to swear falsely regarding the denial of a monetary matter (negative mitzva 249); 5) To swear truthfully in God's name (positive mitzva 7).

הִלְכוֹת נְדָרִים – יֵשׁ בִּכְלָלָן שָׁלֹשׁ מִצְוֹת, שְׁתֵּי מִצְוֹת עֲשֵׂה וְאַחַת מִצְוַת לֹא תַעֲשֶׂה, וְזֶה הוּא פְּרָטָן: א) שֶׁיִּשְׁמֹר מוֹצָא שְׂפָתָיו וְיַעֲשֶׂה כְּמוֹ שֶׁנָּדַר (עשה צד). ב) שֶׁלֹּא יַחֵל דְּבָרוֹ (לא תעשה קנז). ג) שֶׁיּוּפַר הַנֶּדֶר אוֹ הַשְּׁבוּעָה, וְזֶה הוּא דִּין הָפֵר נְדָרִים הַמְפֹרָשׁ בַּתּוֹרָה שֶׁבִּכְתָב (עשה צה).

Hilkhot Nedarim include three mitzvot: two positive mitzvot and one negative mitzva. Their enumeration follows: 1) That one must observe that which emerges from his lips and act as one vowed (positive mitzva 94); 2) Not to break one's word (negative mitzva 157); 3) That a vow or oath shall be nullified under the appropriate conditions, and this is the law of the nullification of vows that is explicitly stated in the Written Torah (positive mitzva 95).

הִלְכוֹת נְזִירוּת – יֵשׁ בִּכְלָלָן עֶשֶׂר מִצְוֹת, שְׁתֵּי מִצְוֹת עֲשֵׂה וּשְׁמוֹנֶה מִצְוֹת לֹא תַעֲשֶׂה, וְזֶה הוּא פְּרָטָן: א) שֶׁיְּגַדֵּל הַנָּזִיר פֶּרַע (עשה צב). ב) שֶׁלֹּא יְגַלֵּחַ שְׂעָרוֹ כָּל יְמֵי נִזְרוֹ (לא תעשה רט). ג) שֶׁלֹּא יִשְׁתֶּה הַנָּזִיר יַיִן וְלֹא תַעֲרֹבֶת

***Hilkhot Nezirut* include ten mitzvot: two positive mitzvot and eight negative mitzvot. Their enumeration follows: 1) That a nazirite must grow long hair** (positive mitzva 92); **2) That he may not shave his hair all the days of his naziriteship** (negative mitzva 209); **3) That a nazirite may not drink wine or a mixture of wine,** not

יַיִן וַאֲפִלּוּ חֹמֶץ שֶׁלָּהֶן (לא תעשה רב). ד) שֶׁלֹּא יֹאכַל עֲנָבִים לַחִים (לא תעשה רג). ה) שֶׁלֹּא יֹאכַל צִמּוּקִים (לא תעשה רד). ו) שֶׁלֹּא יֹאכַל חַרְצַנִּים (לא תעשה רה). ז) שֶׁלֹּא יֹאכַל זָגִין (לא תעשה רו). ח) שֶׁלֹּא יִכָּנֵס לְאֹהֶל הַמֵּת (לא תעשה רח). ט) שֶׁלֹּא יִטַּמֵּא לַמֵּתִים (לא תעשה רז). י) שֶׁיְּגַלַּח עַל הַקָּרְבָּנוֹת כְּשֶׁיַּשְׁלִים נְזִירוּתוֹ אוֹ כְּשֶׁיִּטַּמֵּא (עשה צג).

even in **their** state of **vinegar** (negative mitzva 202); **4) That he may not eat grapes** (negative mitzva 203); **5) That he may not eat raisins** (negative mitzva 204); **6) That he may not eat seeds** of grapes (negative mitzva 205); **7) That he may not eat skins** of grapes (negative mitzva 206); **8) That he may not enter a tent** that is spread over **a corpse** (negative mitzva 208); **9) That he may not become impure** through contact with **the dead** (negative mitzva 207); **10) That he must shave based upon the offerings** he brings **when he completes his naziriteship or after he became impure** (positive mitzva 93).

הִלְכוֹת עֲרָכִין וַחֲרָמִין – יֵשׁ בִּכְלָלָן שֶׁבַע מִצְווֹת, חָמֵשׁ מִצְווֹת עֲשֵׂה וּשְׁתַּיִם מִצְווֹת לֹא תַעֲשֶׂה, וְזֶה הוּא פְּרָטָן: א) לָדוּן בְּעֶרְכֵי אָדָם כַּאֲשֶׁר מְפֹרָשׁ בַּתּוֹרָה, וְזֶה הוּא דִּין עֶרְכֵי אָדָם (עשה קיד). ב) דִּין עֶרְכֵי בְּהֵמָה (עשה קטו). ג) דִּין עֶרְכֵי בָּתִּים (עשה קטז). ד) דִּין עֶרְכֵי שָׂדוֹת (עשה קיז). ה) דִּין מַחֲרִים נְכָסָיו (עשה קמה). ו) שֶׁלֹּא יִמָּכֵר חֵרֶם (לא תעשה קי). ז) שֶׁלֹּא יִגָּאֵל חֵרֶם (לא תעשה קיא).

***Hilkhot Arakhin VaḤaramim* include seven mitzvot: five positive mitzvot and two negative mitzvot. Their enumeration follows: 1) To adjudicate the valuations of persons as detailed in the Torah, and this is the law of the valuations of persons** (positive mitzva 114); **2) The law of the evaluations of animals** (positive mitzva 115); **3) The law of the evaluations of houses** (positive mitzva 116); **4) The law of the evaluations of fields** (positive mitzva 117); **5) The law of one who dedicates his property** (positive mitzva 145); **6) That a proscribed** field **may not be sold** (negative mitzva 110); **7) That a proscribed** field **may not be redeemed** (negative mitzva 111).

נִמְצְאוּ כָּל הַמִּצְווֹת הַנִּכְלָלוֹת בְּסֵפֶר זֶה חָמֵשׁ וְעֶשְׂרִים, עֶשֶׂר מֵהֶם מִצְווֹת עֲשֵׂה וַחֲמֵשׁ עֶשְׂרֵה מִצְווֹת לֹא תַעֲשֶׂה.

Thus, all the mitzvot that are included in this ***Sefer*** are **twenty-five: Ten of them** are **positive mitzvot and fifteen** are **negative mitzvot.**

סֵפֶר זְרָעִים

7. Sefer Zera'im

הִלְכוֹתָיו שֶׁבַע, וְזֶה הוּא סִדּוּרָן: הִלְכוֹת כִּלְאַיִם, הִלְכוֹת מַתְּנוֹת עֲנִיִּים, הִלְכוֹת תְּרוּמוֹת, הִלְכוֹת מַעַשְׂרוֹת, הִלְכוֹת מַעֲשֵׂר שֵׁנִי וְנֶטַע רְבָעִי, הִלְכוֹת בִּכּוּרִים וּשְׁאָר מַתְּנוֹת כְּהֻנָּה שֶׁבַּגְּבוּלִין, הִלְכוֹת שְׁמִטָּה וְיוֹבֵל.

Sefer Zera'im contains **seven *Hilkhot*, in the following order: *Hilkhot Kilayim*** (Laws of Prohibited Mixtures), ***Hilkhot Mattenot Aniyyim*** (Laws of Gifts to the Poor), ***Hilkhot Terumot*** (Laws of *Teruma*), ***Hilkhot Maaser*** (Laws of Tithes), ***Hilkhot Maaser Sheni*** (Laws of the Second Tithe), which also includes the laws of **fourth-year saplings, *Hilkhot Bikkurim*** (Laws of First Fruits), which also includes the laws of **the rest of the gifts of the priesthood in the outlying areas**, and ***Hilkhot Shemitta VeYovel*** (Laws of Sabbatical and Jubilee Years).

הִלְכוֹת כִּלְאַיִם – יֵשׁ בִּכְלָלָן חָמֵשׁ מִצְווֹת לֹא תַעֲשֶׂה, וְזֶה הוּא פְּרָטָן: א) שֶׁלֹּא לִזְרֹעַ זְרָעִים כִּלְאַיִם (לא תעשה רטו). ב) שֶׁלֹּא לִזְרֹעַ תְּבוּאָה אוֹ יָרָק בַּכֶּרֶם (לא תעשה ריו). ג) שֶׁלֹּא

***Hilkhot Kilayim* include five negative mitzvot. Their enumeration follows: 1) Not to sow diverse kinds of seeds** (negative mitzva 215); **2) Not to sow grain or vegetables in a vineyard** (negative mitzva 216); **3) Not to**

לְהַרְבִּיעַ בְּהֵמָה כִּלְאַיִם (לא תעשה ריז). ד) **שֶׁלֹּא לַעֲשׂוֹת מְלָאכָה בְּכִלְאֵי בְּהֵמָה כְּאֶחָד** (לא תעשה ריח). ה) **שֶׁלֹּא לִלְבֹּשׁ כִּלְאַיִם** (לא תעשה מב).

mate diverse kinds of animals (negative mitzva 217); **4) Not to perform labor with diverse kinds of animals together** (negative mitzva 218); **5) Not to wear diverse kinds** of clothing (negative mitzva 42).

הִלְכוֹת מַתְּנוֹת עֲנִיִּים – יֵשׁ בִּכְלָלָן שְׁלֹשׁ עֶשְׂרֵה מִצְוֹת, שֶׁבַע מִצְוֹת עֲשֵׂה וְשֵׁשׁ מִצְוֹת לֹא תַעֲשֶׂה, וְזֶה הוּא פְּרָטָן: א) לְהַנִּיחַ פֵּאָה (עשה קכ). **ב) שֶׁלֹּא יְכַלֶּה הַפֵּאָה** (לא תעשה רי). **ג) לְהַנִּיחַ לֶקֶט** (עשה קכא). **ד) שֶׁלֹּא יְלַקֵּט הַלֶּקֶט** (לא תעשה ריא). **ה) לַעֲזֹב עוֹלֵלוֹת בַּכֶּרֶם** (עשה קכג). **ו) שֶׁלֹּא יְעוֹלֵל הַכֶּרֶם** (לא תעשה ריב). **ז) לַעֲזֹב פֶּרֶט הַכֶּרֶם** (עשה קכד). **ח) שֶׁלֹּא יְלַקֵּט פֶּרֶט הַכֶּרֶם** (לא תעשה ריג). **ט) לְהַנִּיחַ שִׁכְחָה** (עשה קכב). **י) שֶׁלֹּא יָשׁוּב לָקַחַת הַשִּׁכְחָה** (לא תעשה ריד). **יא) לְהַפְרִישׁ מַעֲשֵׂר לַעֲנִיִּים** (עשה קל). **יב) לִתֵּן צְדָקָה כְּמִסַּת יָד** (עשה קצה). **יג) שֶׁלֹּא יְאַמֵּץ לְבָבוֹ עַל הֶעָנִי** (לא תעשה רלב).

Hilkhot Mattenot Aniyyim **include thirteen mitzvot: seven positive mitzvot and six negative mitzvot. Their enumeration follows: 1) To leave** *pe'a,* produce in the corner of the field, which is given to the poor (positive mitzva 120); **2) Not to finish reaping the corner** of one's field (negative mitzva 210); **3) To leave gleanings** (positive mitzva 121); **4) Not to gather the gleanings** (negative mitzva 211); **5) To leave** ***olelot,*** incompletely formed clusters of grapes, **in a vineyard** (positive mitzva 123); **6) Not to harvest a vineyard completely** (negative mitzva 212); **7) To leave the** ***peret,*** individual fallen grapes, **of a vineyard** (positive mitzva 124); **8) Not to gather the** ***peret*** **of a vineyard** (negative mitzva 213); **9) To leave forgotten** produce (positive mitzva 122); **10) Not to return to take forgotten** produce (negative mitzva 214); **11) To separate a tithe for the poor** (positive mitzva 130); **12) To give charity, as one can afford** (positive mitzva 195); **13) Not to harden one's heart against the poor** (negative mitzva 232).

הִלְכוֹת תְּרוּמוֹת – יֵשׁ בִּכְלָלָן שְׁמוֹנֶה מִצְוֹת, שְׁתַּיִם מִצְוֹת עֲשֵׂה וְשֵׁשׁ מִצְוֹת לֹא תַעֲשֶׂה, וְזֶה הוּא פְּרָטָן: א) לְהַפְרִישׁ תְּרוּמָה גְּדוֹלָה (עשה קכו). **ב) לְהַפְרִישׁ תְּרוּמַת מַעֲשֵׂר** (עשה קכט). **ג) שֶׁלֹּא יַקְדִּים תְּרוּמוֹת וּמַעַשְׂרוֹת זֶה לָזֶה אֶלָּא יַפְרִישׁ עַל הַסֵּדֶר** (לא תעשה קנד). **ד) שֶׁלֹּא יֹאכַל זָר תְּרוּמָה** (לא תעשה קלג). **ה) שֶׁלֹּא יֹאכַל אֲפִלּוּ תּוֹשַׁב כֹּהֵן אוֹ שְׂכִירוֹ תְּרוּמָה** (לא תעשה קלד). **ו) שֶׁלֹּא יֹאכַל עָרֵל תְּרוּמָה** (לא תעשה קלה). **ז) שֶׁלֹּא יֹאכַל כֹּהֵן טָמֵא תְּרוּמָה** (לא תעשה קלו). **ח) שֶׁלֹּא תֹאכַל חֲלָלָה תְּרוּמָה וְלֹא מוּרָם מִן הַקֳּדָשִׁים** (לא תעשה קלז).

Hilkhot Terumot **include eight mitzvot: two positive mitzvot and six negative mitzvot. Their enumeration follows: 1) To separate** ***teruma gedola*** (positive mitzva 126); **2) To separate** ***teruma*** **of the tithe** (positive mitzva 129); **3) Not to** separate ***terumot*** **and tithes** incorrectly, the later **one before** the earlier one, but **rather one should separate them in order** (negative mitzva 154); **4) That a non-priest may not eat** ***teruma*** (negative mitzva 133); **5) That not even one who resides with a priest or his hired laborer may eat** ***teruma*** (negative mitzva 134); **6) That an uncircumcised man may not eat** ***teruma*** (negative mitzva 135); **7) That a ritually impure priest may not eat** ***teruma*** (negative mitzva 136); **8) That a** ***ḥalala*** **may not eat** ***teruma,*** **or** the portions **separated from consecrated** offerings (negative mitzva 137).

הִלְכוֹת מַעֲשֵׂר – מִצְוַת עֲשֵׂה אַחַת, וְהִיא לְהַפְרִישׁ מַעֲשֵׂר רִאשׁוֹן בְּכָל שָׁנָה וְשָׁנָה מִשְּׁנֵי הַזְּרִיעָה וְלִתְּנוֹ לַלְוִיִּם (עשה קכז).

Hilkhot Maaser include **one positive mitzva, which is to separate the first tithe in each and every year of the years of sowing** the fields, i.e., except during the Sabbatical and Jubilee Years, **and to give it to the Levites** (positive mitzva 127).

הִלְכוֹת מַעֲשֵׂר שֵׁנִי וְנֶטַע רְבָעִי – יֵשׁ בִּכְלָלָן תֵּשַׁע מִצְווֹת, שָׁלֹשׁ מִצְווֹת עֲשֵׂה וְשֵׁשׁ מִצְווֹת לֹא תַעֲשֶׂה, וְזֶה הוּא פְּרָטָן: א) **לְהַפְרִישׁ מַעֲשֵׂר שֵׁנִי** (עשה קכח). ב) **שֶׁלֹּא לְהוֹצִיא דָּמָיו בִּשְׁאָר צָרְכֵי הָאָדָם חוּץ מֵאֲכִילָה וּשְׁתִיָּה וְסִיכָה** (לא תעשה קנב). ג) **שֶׁלֹּא לְאָכְלוֹ בְּטֻמְאָה** (לא תעשה קן). ד) **שֶׁלֹּא לְאָכְלוֹ בַּאֲנִינוּת** (לא תעשה קנא). ה) **שֶׁלֹּא לֶאֱכֹל מַעֲשֵׂר שֵׁנִי שֶׁל דָּגָן חוּץ לִירוּשָׁלַיִם** (לא תעשה קמא). ו) **שֶׁלֹּא לֶאֱכֹל מַעְשַׂר תִּירוֹשׁ חוּץ לִירוּשָׁלַיִם** (לא תעשה קמב). ז) **שֶׁלֹּא לֶאֱכֹל מַעְשַׂר יִצְהָר חוּץ לִירוּשָׁלַיִם** (לא תעשה קמג). ח) **לִהְיוֹת נֶטַע רְבָעִי כֻּלּוֹ קֹדֶשׁ, וְדִינוֹ לְהֵאָכֵל בִּירוּשָׁלַיִם לִבְעָלָיו כְּמַעֲשֵׂר שֵׁנִי לְכָל דָּבָר** (עשה קיט). ט) **לְהִתְוַדּוֹת וִדּוּי הַמַּעֲשֵׂר** (עשה קלא).

Hilkhot Maaser Sheni **and** the laws of **fourth-year saplings include nine mitzvot: three positive mitzvot and six negative mitzvot. Their enumeration follows: 1) To separate the second tithe** (positive mitzva 128); **2) Not to spend its proceeds on human requirements other than eating, drinking, and smearing** (negative mitzva 152); **3) Not to eat it in** a state of **ritual impurity** (negative mitzva 150); **4) Not to eat it in** a state of **acute mourning** (negative mitzva 151); **5) Not to eat second tithe of grain outside Jerusalem** (negative mitzva 141); **6) Not to eat** second **tithe of wine outside Jerusalem** (negative mitzva 142); **7) Not to eat** second **tithe of oil outside Jerusalem** (negative mitzva 143); **8) That a fourth-year sapling shall be entirely holy, and its law** is that its produce **shall be eaten in Jerusalem by its owner, like second tithe in all respects** (positive mitzva 119); **9) To recite the declaration of tithes** (positive mitzva 131).

הִלְכוֹת בִּכּוּרִים עִם שְׁאָר מַתְּנוֹת כְּהֻנָּה שֶׁבַּגְּבוּלִין – יֵשׁ בִּכְלָלָן תֵּשַׁע מִצְווֹת, שְׁמוֹנֶה מִצְווֹת עֲשֵׂה וְאַחַת מִצְוַת לֹא תַעֲשֶׂה, וְזֶה הוּא פְּרָטָן: א) **לְהַפְרִישׁ בִּכּוּרִים וּלְהַעֲלוֹתָן לַמִּקְדָּשׁ** (עשה קכה). ב) **שֶׁלֹּא יֹאכַל הַכֹּהֵן בִּכּוּרִים חוּץ לִירוּשָׁלַיִם** (לא תעשה קמט). ג) **לִקְרוֹת עֲלֵיהֶן** (עשה קלב). ד) **לְהַפְרִישׁ חַלָּה לַכֹּהֵן** (עשה קלג). ה) **לָתֵת זְרוֹעַ וּלְחָיַיִם וְקֵבָה לַכֹּהֵן** (עשה קמג). ו) **לִתֵּן לוֹ רֵאשִׁית הַגֵּז** (עשה קמד). ז) **לִפְדּוֹת בְּכוֹר הַבֵּן וְלִתֵּן פִּדְיוֹנוֹ לַכֹּהֵן** (עשה פ). ח) **לִפְדּוֹת פֶּטֶר חֲמוֹר וְלִתֵּן פִּדְיוֹנוֹ לַכֹּהֵן** (עשה פא). ט) **לַעֲרֹף פֶּטֶר חֲמוֹר אִם לֹא רָצָה לִפְדּוֹתוֹ** (עשה פב).

Hilkhot Bikkurim and the laws of **the rest of the gifts of the priesthood in outlying areas, include nine mitzvot: eight positive mitzvot and one negative mitzva. Their enumeration follows: 1) To separate first fruits and bring them up to the Temple** (positive mitzva 125); **2) That a priest may not eat first fruits outside Jerusalem** (negative mitzva 149); **3) To read** the passage of the first fruits **over them** (positive mitzva 132); **4) To separate *ḥalla* for a priest** (positive mitzva 133); **5) To give the foreleg, the jaw, and the maw** of domesticated animals **to a priest** (positive mitzva 143); **6) To give** a priest **the first of the sheared** wool (positive mitzva 144); **7) To redeem one's firstborn son and to give** the sum of **his redemption to a priest** (positive mitzva 80); **8) To redeem a firstborn donkey and to give** the sum of **its redemption to a priest** (positive mitzva 81); **9) To break the neck of** that **donkey if one does not wish to redeem it** (positive mitzva 82).

הִלְכוֹת שְׁמִטָּה וְיוֹבֵל – יֵשׁ בִּכְלָלָן שְׁתַּיִם וְעֶשְׂרִים מִצְווֹת, תֵּשַׁע מִצְווֹת עֲשֵׂה וּשְׁלֹשׁ עֶשְׂרֵה מִצְווֹת לֹא תַעֲשֶׂה, וְזֶה הוּא פְּרָטָן: א) **שֶׁתִּשְׁבֹּת הָאָרֶץ מִמְּלַאכְתָּהּ בַּשְּׁבִיעִית** (עשה קלה). ב) **שֶׁלֹּא יַעֲבֹד עֲבוֹדַת הָאָרֶץ בְּשָׁנָה זוֹ** (לא תעשה רכ). ג) **שֶׁלֹּא יַעֲבֹד עֲבוֹדַת הָאִילָן בְּשָׁנָה זוֹ** (לא תעשה רכא). ד) **שֶׁלֹּא יִקְצֹר הַסָּפִיחַ כְּנֶגֶד הַקּוֹצְרִים** (לא תעשה רכב). ה) **שֶׁלֹּא יִבְצֹר הַנְּזִירִים כְּנֶגֶד הַבּוֹצְרִים** (לא תעשה רכג). ו) **שֶׁיַּשְׁמִיט מַה שֶּׁתּוֹצִיא הָאָרֶץ** (עשה קלד). ז) **שֶׁיַּשְׁמִיט כָּל הַלְוָאָתוֹ** (עשה קמא).

Hilkhot Shemitta VeYovel include twenty-two mitzvot: nine positive mitzvot and thirteen negative mitzvot. Their enumeration follows: 1) That the land rest from its labor in the seventh year (positive mitzva 135); 2) Not to perform the labor of the land in this year (negative mitzva 220); 3) Not to perform the labor of trees in this year (negative mitzva 221); 4) Not to reap the aftergrowth in the manner of the harvesters (negative mitzva 222); 5) Not to gather the uncultivated grapes in the manner of the grape harvesters (negative mitzva 223); 6) To renounce ownership over that which the land produces (positive mitzva 134); 7) To release all of one's loans (positive mitzva 141); 8) Not to demand payment of one's

ח) שֶׁלֹּא יִגֹּשׂ וְלֹא יִתְבַּע הַלֹּוֶה (לא תעשה רל). ט) שֶׁלֹּא יִמָּנַע מִלְּהַלְווֹת קֹדֶם הַשְּׁמִטָּה כְּדֵי שֶׁלֹּא יֹאבַד מָמוֹנוֹ (לא תעשה רלא). י) לִסְפֹּר שָׁנִים שֶׁבַע שֶׁבַע (עשה קמ). יא) לְקַדֵּשׁ שְׁנַת חֲמִשִּׁים (עשה קלו). יב) לִתְקֹעַ בַּשּׁוֹפָר בָּעֲשִׂירִי לְתִשְׁרֵי כְּדֵי לָצֵאת עֲבָדִים חָפְשִׁי (עשה קלז). יג) שֶׁלֹּא תֵּעָבֵד אֲדָמָה בְּשָׁנָה זוֹ (לא תעשה רכד). יד) שֶׁלֹּא יִקְצֹר סְפִיחֶיהָ כְּנֶגֶד הַקּוֹצְרִים (לא תעשה רכה). יה) שֶׁלֹּא יִבְצֹר נְזִירֶיהָ כְּנֶגֶד הַבּוֹצְרִים (לא תעשה רכו). יו) לִתֵּן גְּאֻלָּה לָאָרֶץ בְּשָׁנָה זוֹ, וְהוּא דִּין שְׂדֵה אֲחֻזָּה וּשְׂדֵה מִקְנָה (עשה קלח). יז) שֶׁלֹּא תִּמָּכֵר הָאָרֶץ לִצְמִיתוּת (לא תעשה רכז). יח) דִּין בָּתֵּי עָרֵי חוֹמָה (עשה קלט). יט) שֶׁלֹּא יִנְחַל כָּל שֵׁבֶט לֵוִי בְּאֶרֶץ יִשְׂרָאֵל, אֶלָּא נוֹתְנִין לָהֶם עָרִים מַתָּנָה לָשֶׁבֶת בָּהֶם (לא תעשה קסט). כ) שֶׁלֹּא יִקַּח שֵׁבֶט לֵוִי חֵלֶק בַּבִּזָּה (לא תעשה קע). כא) לִתֵּן לַלְוִיִּם עָרִים לָשֶׁבֶת וּמִגְרְשֵׁיהֶם (עשה קפג). כב) שֶׁלֹּא יִמָּכֵר מִגְרַשׁ עָרֵיהֶם, אֶלָּא גּוֹאֲלִין לְעוֹלָם, בֵּין לִפְנֵי הַיּוֹבֵל בֵּין לְאַחַר הַיּוֹבֵל (לא תעשה רכח).

loan or sue the debtor for it (negative mitzva 230); 9) Not to refrain from lending before the Sabbatical Year due to financial worries, so that one does not lose his money (negative mitzva 231); 10) To count the years in sets of seven (positive mitzva 140); 11) To sanctify the fiftieth year (positive mitzva 136); 12) To sound the shofar on the tenth of Tishrei in order to set slaves free (positive mitzva 137); 13) Not to work the land during this year (negative mitzva 224); 14) Not to reap its aftergrowth in the manner of the harvesters (negative mitzva 225); 15) Not to gather its uncultivated grapes in the manner of the grape harvesters (negative mitzva 226); 16) To provide redemption for the land in this year, which is the law of an ancestral field and a purchased field (positive mitzva 138); 17) That the land may not be sold in perpetuity (negative mitzva 227); 18) To observe and adjudicate the law of houses of walled cities (positive mitzva 139); 19) That the entire tribe of Levi shall not inherit in the Land of Israel; rather, they are given cities as a gift for them to reside in them (negative mitzva 169); 20) That the entire tribe of Levi shall not take a share in the plunder taken during the conquest of the Land of Israel (negative mitzva 170); 21) To give to the Levites cities for them to reside in, and their perimeter fields (positive mitzva 183); 22) That the perimeter fields of their cities shall not be sold; rather, the Levites may redeem them forever, whether before the Jubilee Year or after the Jubilee Year (negative mitzva 228).

נִמְצְאוּ כָּל הַמִּצְוֹת הַנִּכְלָלוֹת בְּסֵפֶר זֶה שֶׁבַע וְשִׁשִּׁים, מֵהֶן שְׁלֹשִׁים מִצְוֹת עֲשֵׂה וְשֶׁבַע וּשְׁלֹשִׁים מִצְוֹת לֹא תַעֲשֶׂה.

Thus, all the mitzvot that are included in this *Sefer* are sixty-seven: Thirty of them are **positive mitzvot and thirty-seven** are **negative mitzvot.**

סֵפֶר עֲבוֹדָה

8. Sefer Avoda

הִלְכוֹתָיו תֵּשַׁע, וְזֶה הוּא סִדּוּרָן: הִלְכוֹת בֵּית הַבְּחִירָה, הִלְכוֹת כְּלֵי הַמִּקְדָּשׁ וְהָעוֹבְדִין בּוֹ, הִלְכוֹת בִּיאַת מִקְדָּשׁ, הִלְכוֹת אִסּוּרֵי הַמִּזְבֵּחַ, הִלְכוֹת מַעֲשֵׂה הַקָּרְבָּנוֹת, הִלְכוֹת תְּמִידִים וּמוּסָפִין, הִלְכוֹת פְּסוּלֵי הַמֻּקְדָּשִׁין, הִלְכוֹת עֲבוֹדַת יוֹם הַכִּפּוּרִים, הִלְכוֹת מְעִילָה.

Sefer Avoda contains **nine *Hilkhot*, in the following order: *Hilkhot Beit HaBeḥira*** (Laws of the Temple), ***Hilkhot Kelei HaMikdash*** (Laws of Vessels of the Temple), which also includes the laws of **those who serve in it, *Hilkhot Biat Mikdash*** (Laws of Entry into the Temple), ***Hilkhot Issurei Mizbe'aḥ*** (Laws of [Items] Prohibited on the Altar), ***Hilkhot Maaseh HaKorbanot*** (Laws of Sacrificial Procedure), ***Hilkhot Temidin UMusafin*** (Laws of Daily Offerings and Additional Offerings), ***Hilkhot Pesulei HaMukdashin*** (Laws of Sacrifices that are Rendered Unfit), ***Hilkhot Avodat Yom HaKippurim*** (Laws of the Service of the Day of Atonement), and ***Hilkhot Me'ila*** (Laws of Embezzlement [from the Temple]).

הִלְכוֹת בֵּית הַבְּחִירָה – יֵשׁ בִּכְלָלָן שֵׁשׁ מִצְוֹת, שָׁלֹשׁ מִצְוֹת עֲשֵׂה וְשָׁלֹשׁ מִצְוֹת לֹא תַעֲשֶׂה, וְזֶה הוּא פְּרָטָן: א) לִבְנוֹת מִקְדָּשׁ (עשה כ). ב) שֶׁלֹּא לִבְנוֹת הַמִּזְבֵּחַ גָּזִית (לא תעשה עט). ג) שֶׁלֹּא לַעֲלוֹת בְּמַעֲלוֹת עָלָיו (לא תעשה פ). ד) לְיִרְאָה מִן הַמִּקְדָּשׁ (עשה כא). ה) לִשְׁמֹר אֶת הַמִּקְדָּשׁ סָבִיב (עשה כב). ו) שֶׁלֹּא לְהַשְׁבִּית שְׁמִירַת הַמִּקְדָּשׁ (לא תעשה סז).

***Hilkhot Beit HaBeḥira* include six mitzvot: three positive mitzvot and three negative mitzvot. Their enumeration follows: 1) To build a Temple** (positive mitzva 20); **2) Not to build the altar from hewn stones** (negative mitzva 79); **3) Not to ascend on stairs to** the altar (negative mitzva 80); **4) To revere the Temple** (positive mitzva 21); **5) To keep a watch around the Temple** (positive mitzva 22); **6) Not to remove the Temple watch** (negative mitzva 67).

הִלְכוֹת כְּלֵי הַמִּקְדָּשׁ וְהָעוֹבְדִים בּוֹ – יֵשׁ בִּכְלָלָן אַרְבַּע עֶשְׂרֵה מִצְוֹת, שֵׁשׁ מִצְוֹת עֲשֵׂה וּשְׁמוֹנֶה מִצְוֹת לֹא תַעֲשֶׂה, וְזֶה הוּא פְּרָטָן: א) לַעֲשׂוֹת שֶׁמֶן הַמִּשְׁחָה (עשה לה). ב) שֶׁלֹּא לַעֲשׂוֹת כְּמוֹתוֹ (לא תעשה פג). ג) שֶׁלֹּא לָסוּךְ מִמֶּנּוּ (לא תעשה פד). ד) שֶׁלֹּא לַעֲשׂוֹת כְּמַתְכֹּנֶת הַקְּטֹרֶת (לא תעשה פה). ה) שֶׁלֹּא לְהַקְטִיר עַל מִזְבַּח הַזָּהָב חוּץ מִן הַקְּטֹרֶת (לא תעשה פב). ו) לָשֵׂאת הָאָרוֹן עַל הַכָּתֵף (עשה לד). ז) שֶׁלֹּא יָסוּרוּ הַבַּדִּים מִמֶּנּוּ (לא תעשה פו). ח) שֶׁיַּעֲבֹד הַלֵּוִי בַּמִּקְדָּשׁ (עשה כג). ט) שֶׁלֹּא יַעֲשֶׂה אֶחָד בִּמְלֶאכֶת חֲבֵרוֹ בַּמִּקְדָּשׁ (לא תעשה עב). י) לְקַדֵּשׁ הַכֹּהֵן לַעֲבוֹדָה (עשה לב). יא) שֶׁיִּהְיוּ כָּל הַמִּשְׁמָרוֹת שָׁווֹת בָּרְגָלִים (עשה לו). יב) לִלְבֹּשׁ בִּגְדֵי כְּהֻנָּה לַעֲבוֹדָה (עשה לג). יג) שֶׁלֹּא יִקָּרַע הַמְּעִיל (לא תעשה פח). יד) שֶׁלֹּא יִזַּח הַחֹשֶׁן מֵעַל הָאֵפוֹד (לא תעשה פז).

Hilkhot Kelei HaMikdash, the laws of vessels of the Temple, and those who serve in it, include fourteen mitzvot: six positive mitzvot and eight negative mitzvot. Their enumeration follows: 1) To make the anointing oil (positive mitzva 35); 2) Not to make anointing oil like it for personal use (negative mitzva 83); 3) Not to anoint oneself with it (negative mitzva 84); 4) Not to make incense for personal use according to the formula of the incense (negative mitzva 85); 5) Not to burn anything on the golden altar apart from the incense (negative mitzva 82); 6) To carry the sacred ark on the shoulder (positive mitzva 34); 7) That the staves may not be removed from the Ark (negative mitzva 86); 8) That the Levite should perform his service in the Temple (positive mitzva 23); 9) That one person should not perform the labor of another in the Temple (negative mitzva 72); 10) To sanctify the priest for the Temple service (positive mitzva 32); 11) That all the watches shall be equal on the pilgrimage festivals (positive mitzva 36); 12) That a priest shall don the priestly vestments for the Temple service (positive mitzva 33); 13) That the robe shall not be rent (negative mitzva 88); 14) That the breastplate shall not be detached from upon the ephod (negative mitzva 87).

הִלְכוֹת בִּיאַת הַמִּקְדָּשׁ – יֵשׁ בִּכְלָלָן חֲמֵשׁ עֶשְׂרֵה מִצְוֹת, שְׁתֵּי מִצְוֹת עֲשֵׂה וּשְׁלֹשׁ עֶשְׂרֵה מִצְוֹת לֹא תַעֲשֶׂה, וְזֶה הוּא פְּרָטָן: א) שֶׁלֹּא יִכָּנֵס כֹּהֵן שִׁכּוֹר לַמִּקְדָּשׁ (לא תעשה עג). ב) שֶׁלֹּא יִכָּנֵס לוֹ כֹּהֵן פְּרוּעַ רֹאשׁ (לא תעשה קסג). ג) שֶׁלֹּא יִכָּנֵס לוֹ כֹּהֵן קְרוּעַ בְּגָדִים (לא תעשה קסד). ד) שֶׁלֹּא יִכָּנֵס כֹּהֵן בְּכָל עֵת אֶל הַהֵיכָל (לא תעשה סח). ה) שֶׁלֹּא יֵצֵא כֹּהֵן מִן הַמִּקְדָּשׁ בִּשְׁעַת הָעֲבוֹדָה (לא תעשה קסה). ו) לְשַׁלַּח טְמֵאִים מִן הַמִּקְדָּשׁ (עשה לא). ז) שֶׁלֹּא יִכָּנֵס טָמֵא לַמִּקְדָּשׁ (לא תעשה עז). ח) שֶׁלֹּא יִכָּנֵס טָמֵא לְהַר הַבַּיִת (לא תעשה עח). ט) שֶׁלֹּא יְשַׁמֵּשׁ טָמֵא (לא תעשה עה). י) שֶׁלֹּא

Hilkhot Biat HaMikdash include fifteen mitzvot: two positive mitzvot and thirteen negative mitzvot. Their enumeration follows: 1) That a drunk priest may not enter the Temple (negative mitzva 73); 2) That a priest with long hair may not enter the Temple (negative mitzva 163); 3) That a priest with torn vestments may not enter the Temple (negative mitzva 164); 4) That a priest may not enter the Sanctuary any time he wishes (negative mitzva 68); 5) That a priest may not leave the Temple during the service (negative mitzva 165); 6) To send impure individuals from the Temple (positive mitzva 31); 7) That an impure person may not enter the Temple (negative mitzva 77); 8) That an impure person may not enter the area of the Temple Mount (negative mitzva 78); 9) Not to perform the Temple service when one is ritually impure

יְשַׁמֵּשׁ טְבוּל יוֹם (לא תעשה עו). יא) לְקַדֵּשׁ הָעוֹבֵד יָדָיו וְרַגְלָיו (עשה כד). יב) שֶׁלֹּא יִכָּנֵס בַּעַל מוּם לַהֵיכָל וְלַמִּזְבֵּחַ (לא תעשה סט). יג) שֶׁלֹּא יַעֲבֹד בַּעַל מוּם (לא תעשה ע). יד) שֶׁלֹּא יַעֲבֹד בַּעַל מוּם עוֹבֵר (לא תעשה עא). טו) שֶׁלֹּא יַעֲבֹד זָר (לא תעשה עד).

(negative mitzva 75); 10) Not to perform the Temple service when one is a *tevul yom* [one who immersed that day] (negative mitzva 76); 11) That one who performs the Temple service shall first sanctify his hands and feet (positive mitzva 24); 12) That a blemished person may not enter the Sanctuary or draw near to the altar (negative mitzva 69); 13) That a blemished person may not perform the Temple service (negative mitzva 70); 14) That one with a temporary blemish may not perform the Temple service (negative mitzva 71); 15) That a non-priest may not perform the Temple service (negative mitzva 74).

הִלְכוֹת אִסּוּרֵי מִזְבֵּחַ – יֵשׁ בִּכְלָלָן אַרְבַּע עֶשְׂרֵה מִצְוֹת, אַרְבַּע מִצְוֹת עֲשֵׂה וְעֶשֶׂר מִצְוֹת לֹא תַעֲשֶׂה, וְזֶה הוּא פְּרָטָן: א) לְהַקְרִיב כָּל הַקָּרְבָּנוֹת תְּמִימִין (עשה סא). ב) שֶׁלֹּא לְהַקְדִּישׁ בַּעַל מוּם לַמִּזְבֵּחַ (לא תעשה צא). ג) שֶׁלֹּא יִשָּׁחֵט (לא תעשה צב). ד) שֶׁלֹּא יִזְרֹק דָּמוֹ (לא תעשה צג). ה) שֶׁלֹּא יַקְטִיר חֶלְבּוֹ (לא תעשה צד). ו) שֶׁלֹּא יַקְרִיב בַּעַל מוּם עוֹבֵר (לא תעשה צה). ז) שֶׁלֹּא יִקְרַב בַּעַל מוּם אֲפִלּוּ בְּקָרְבְּנוֹת הַגּוֹיִם (לא תעשה צו). ח) שֶׁלֹּא יַטִּיל מוּם בְּקָדָשִׁים (לא תעשה צז). ט) לִפְדּוֹת פְּסוּלֵי הַמֻּקְדָּשִׁין (עשה פו). י) לְהַקְרִיב מִיּוֹם הַשְּׁמִינִי וָהָלְאָה, וְקֹדֶם זְמַן זֶה הוּא נִקְרָא מְחֻסַּר זְמַן וְאֵין מַקְרִיבִין אוֹתוֹ (עשה ס). יא) שֶׁלֹּא לְהַקְרִיב אֶתְנָן וּמְחִיר (לא תעשה ק). יב) שֶׁלֹּא לְהַקְטִיר שְׂאֹר וּדְבַשׁ (לא תעשה צח). יג) לִמְלֹחַ כָּל הַקָּרְבָּנוֹת (עשה סב). יד) שֶׁלֹּא לְהַשְׁבִּית הַמֶּלַח מֵעַל הַקָּרְבָּנוֹת (לא תעשה צט).

Hilkhot Issurei Mizbe'aḥ include fourteen mitzvot: four positive mitzvot and ten negative mitzvot. Their enumeration follows: 1) To sacrifice all the offerings when they are unblemished (positive mitzva 61); 2) Not to consecrate a blemished animal for the altar (negative mitzva 91); 3) That a blemished animal may not be slaughtered as an offering (negative mitzva 92); 4) That the blood of a blemished animal may not be sprinkled upon the altar (negative mitzva 93); 5) That the fats of a blemished animal may not be burned upon the altar (negative mitzva 94); 6) Not to sacrifice an animal with a temporary blemish (negative mitzva 95); 7) Not to sacrifice a blemished animal even as one of the offerings of gentiles (negative mitzva 96); 8) Not to inflict a blemish upon sacrificial animals (negative mitzva 97); 9) To redeem disqualified consecrated animals (positive mitzva 86); 10) To sacrifice an animal offering only from its eighth day and onward; before that time it is called "an animal whose time has not yet arrived" and one may not sacrifice it (positive mitzva 60); 11) Not to sacrifice something given as the fee of a harlot or the price of a dog (negative mitzva 100); 12) Not to burn leaven or honey upon the altar (negative mitzva 98); 13) To salt all the offerings (positive mitzva 62); 14) Not to withhold salt from the offerings (negative mitzva 99).

הִלְכוֹת מַעֲשֵׂה הַקָּרְבָּנוֹת – יֵשׁ בִּכְלָלָן שָׁלֹשׁ וְעֶשְׂרִים מִצְוֹת, עֶשֶׂר מִצְוֹת עֲשֵׂה וּשְׁלֹשׁ עֶשְׂרֵה מִצְוֹת לֹא תַעֲשֶׂה, וְזֶה הוּא פְּרָטָן: א) לַעֲשׂוֹת הָעוֹלָה כְּמַעֲשֶׂיהָ הַכְּתוּבִים עַל הַסֵּדֶר (עשה סג). ב) שֶׁלֹּא לֶאֱכֹל בְּשַׂר עוֹלָה (לא תעשה קמו). ג) סֵדֶר הַחַטָּאת (עשה סד). ד) שֶׁלֹּא לֶאֱכֹל מִבְּשַׂר חַטָּאת הַפְּנִימִית (לא תעשה קלט). ה) שֶׁלֹּא יַבְדִּיל בְּחַטַּאת הָעוֹף (לא תעשה קיב). ו) סֵדֶר הָאָשָׁם (עשה סה). ז) שֶׁיֹּאכְלוּ הַכֹּהֲנִים בְּשַׂר קָדְשֵׁי קָדָשִׁים

Hilkhot Maaseh HaKorbanot include twenty-three mitzvot: ten positive mitzvot and thirteen negative mitzvot. Their enumeration follows: 1) To perform the sacrifice of the burnt offering in the order of its rites, as they are written (positive mitzva 63); 2) Not to eat the flesh of a burnt offering (negative mitzva 146); 3) The order of the sin offering (positive mitzva 64); 4) Not to eat the flesh of a sin offering brought inside the Sanctuary (negative mitzva 139); 5) Not to separate the head of a bird sin offering from its body (negative mitzva 112); 6) To follow the order of the guilt offering (positive mitzva 65); 7) That the priests shall eat the flesh of the offerings of the most sacred order

בַּמִּקְדָּשׁ (עשה פט). ח) שֶׁלֹּא יֹאכְלוּם חוּץ לָעֲזָרָה (לא תעשה קמה). ט) שֶׁלֹּא יֹאכַל זָר מִקָּדְשֵׁי קָדָשִׁים (לא תעשה קמח). י) סֵדֶר הַשְּׁלָמִים (עשה סו). יא) שֶׁלֹּא לֶאֱכֹל בְּשַׂר קָדָשִׁים קַלִּים קֹדֶם זְרִיקַת דָּמִים (לא תעשה קמז). יב) לַעֲשׂוֹת כָּל מִנְחָה כְּסֵדֶר מַעֲשֶׂיהָ הַכְּתוּבִין בַּתּוֹרָה (עשה סז). יג) שֶׁלֹּא יָשִׂים שֶׁמֶן עַל מִנְחַת חוֹטֵא (לא תעשה קב). יד) שֶׁלֹּא יִתֵּן עָלֶיהָ לְבֹנָה (לא תעשה קג). טו) שֶׁלֹּא תֵּאָכֵל מִנְחַת כֹּהֵן (לא תעשה קלח). יו) שֶׁלֹּא תֵּאָפֶה מִנְחָה חָמֵץ (לא תעשה קכד). יז) שֶׁיֹּאכְלוּ הַכֹּהֲנִים שְׁיָרֵי מְנָחוֹת (עשה פח). יח) שֶׁיָּבִיא כָּל נְדָרָיו וְנִדְבוֹתָיו בְּרֶגֶל שֶׁפָּגַע בּוֹ רִאשׁוֹן (עשה פג). יט) שֶׁלֹּא יְאַחֵר נִדְרוֹ וְנִדְבָתוֹ וּשְׁאָר דְּבָרִים שֶׁהוּא חַיָּב בָּהֶן (לא תעשה קנה). כ) לְהַקְרִיב כָּל הַקָּרְבָּנוֹת בְּבֵית הַבְּחִירָה (עשה פד). כא) לְהָבִיא קָדְשֵׁי חוּצָה לָאָרֶץ לְבֵית הַבְּחִירָה (עשה פה). כב) שֶׁלֹּא לִשְׁחֹט קָרְבָּנוֹת חוּץ לָעֲזָרָה (לא תעשה צ). כג) שֶׁלֹּא לְהַקְרִיב קָרְבָּן חוּץ לָעֲזָרָה (לא תעשה פט).

in the Temple (positive mitzva 89); 8) That they may not eat it outside the Temple courtyard (negative mitzva 145); 9) That a non-priest may not partake of a certain class of offerings, known as the offerings of the most sacred order (negative mitzva 148); 10) To follow the order of the peace offering (positive mitzva 66); 11) Not to eat the flesh of a different class of offerings, known as offerings of lesser sanctity, before the sprinkling of the blood (negative mitzva 147); 12) To perform the sacrifice of every meal offering in the order of its rites, as they are written in the Torah (positive mitzva 67); 13) Not to put oil on the meal offering of a sinner (negative mitzva 102); 14) Not to put frankincense on that offering (negative mitzva 103); 15) That the meal offering of a priest may not be eaten (negative mitzva 138); 16) That a meal offering may not be baked leavened (negative mitzva 124); 17) That the priests shall eat the remainders of meal offerings (positive mitzva 88); 18) That one shall bring all his vows and voluntary offerings on the first pilgrimage festival after his pledge (positive mitzva 83); 19) That one may not delay bringing his vow offering, voluntary offering, and all other items he is obligated to bring (negative mitzva 155); 20) To sacrifice all offerings in the Temple (positive mitzva 84); 21) To bring consecrated items from outside of the Land of Israel to the Temple (positive mitzva 85); 22) Not to slaughter offerings outside the Temple courtyard (negative mitzva 90); 23) Not to sacrifice an offering outside the Temple courtyard (negative mitzva 89).

הִלְכוֹת תְּמִידִין וּמוּסָפִין – יֵשׁ בִּכְלָלָן תְּשַׁע עֶשְׂרֵה מִצְווֹת, שְׁמוֹנֶה עֶשְׂרֵה מִצְווֹת עֲשֵׂה וְאַחַת מִצְוַת לֹא תַעֲשֶׂה, וְזֶה הוּא פְּרָטָן: א) לְהַקְרִיב שְׁנֵי כְבָשִׂים בְּכָל יוֹם עוֹלוֹת (עשה לט). ב) לְהַדְלִיק אֵשׁ עַל הַמִּזְבֵּחַ בְּכָל יוֹם (עשה כט). ג) שֶׁלֹּא לְכַבּוֹתָהּ (לא תעשה פא). ד) לְהָרִים אֶת הַדֶּשֶׁן בְּכָל יוֹם (עשה ל). ה) לְהַקְטִיר קְטֹרֶת בְּכָל יוֹם (עשה כח). ו) לְהַדְלִיק נֵרוֹת בְּכָל יוֹם (עשה כה). ז) שֶׁיַּקְרִיב כֹּהֵן גָּדוֹל מִנְחָה בְּכָל יוֹם, וְהִיא הַנִּקְרֵאת חֲבִתִּין (עשה מ). ח) לְהוֹסִיף שְׁנֵי כְבָשִׂים עוֹלוֹת בַּשַּׁבָּת (עשה מא). ט) לַעֲשׂוֹת לֶחֶם הַפָּנִים (עשה כז). י) מוּסַף רָאשֵׁי חֳדָשִׁים (עשה מב). יא) מוּסַף הַפֶּסַח (עשה מג). יב) לְהַקְרִיב עֹמֶר הַתְּנוּפָה (עשה מד). יג) לִסְפֹּר כָּל אִישׁ וְאִישׁ שִׁבְעָה שָׁבוּעוֹת מִיּוֹם הַקְרָבַת הָעֹמֶר (עשה קסא).

Hilkhot Temidin UMusafin include nineteen mitzvot: eighteen positive mitzvot and one negative mitzva. Their enumeration follows: 1) To sacrifice two lambs every day as burnt offerings (positive mitzva 39); 2) To kindle fire upon the altar every day (positive mitzva 29); 3) Not to extinguish that fire (negative mitzva 81); 4) To remove the ashes every day (positive mitzva 30); 5) To burn incense every day (positive mitzva 28); 6) To light lamps every day (positive mitzva 25); 7) That a High Priest shall sacrifice a meal offering every day, which is called “the meal-offering on a griddle” (positive mitzva 40); 8) To add two lambs as burnt offerings on Shabbat (positive mitzva 41); 9) To perform the rite of the shewbread (positive mitzva 27); 10) To sacrifice the additional offering of *Rashei Ḥodashim* (positive mitzva 42); 11) To sacrifice the additional offering of Passover (positive mitzva 43); 12) To sacrifice the *omer* of the waving (positive mitzva 44); 13) That each and every man shall count seven weeks from the day of the sacrifice of the *omer* (positive mitzva 161); 14) To sacrifice the additional offering of

יד) מוּסַף עֲצֶרֶת (עשה מה). **טו) לְהָבִיא שְׁתֵּי הַלֶּחֶם עִם הַקָּרְבָּנוֹת הַבָּאוֹת בִּגְלַל הַלֶּחֶם בְּיוֹם עֲצֶרֶת** (עשה מו). **יו) מוּסַף רֹאשׁ הַשָּׁנָה** (עשה מז). **יז) מוּסַף יוֹם צוֹם** (עשה מח). **יח) מוּסַף הֶחָג** (עשה נ). **יט) מוּסַף שְׁמִינִי עֲצֶרֶת** (עשה נא).

Shavuot (positive mitzva 45); 15) To bring the two loaves with the offerings that come on account of the loaves on the day of Shavuot (positive mitzva 46); 16) To sacrifice the additional offering of Rosh HaShana (positive mitzva 47); 17) To sacrifice the additional offering of the Yom Kippur fast day (positive mitzva 48); 18) To sacrifice the additional offering of the festival of Sukkot (positive mitzva 50); 19) To sacrifice the additional offering of Shemini Atzeret (positive mitzva 51).

הִלְכוֹת פְּסוּלֵי מֻקְדָּשִׁין – יֵשׁ בִּכְלָלָן שְׁמוֹנֶה מִצְוֹת, שְׁתֵּי מִצְוֹת עֲשֵׂה וְשֵׁשׁ מִצְוֹת לֹא תַעֲשֶׂה, וְזֶה הוּא פְּרָטָן: **א) שֶׁלֹּא לֶאֱכֹל קָדָשִׁים שֶׁנִּפְסְלוּ וְשֶׁהֻטַּל בָּהֶם מוּם** (לא תעשה קמ). **ב) שֶׁלֹּא לֶאֱכֹל פִּגּוּל** (לא תעשה קלב). **ג) שֶׁלֹּא יוֹתִיר קָדָשִׁים לְאַחַר זְמַנָּן** (לא תעשה קכ). **ד) שֶׁלֹּא יֹאכַל נוֹתָר** (לא תעשה קלא). **ה) שֶׁלֹּא יֹאכַל קָדָשִׁים שֶׁנִּטְמְאוּ** (לא תעשה קל). **ו) שֶׁלֹּא יֹאכַל אָדָם שֶׁנִּטְמָא אֶת הַקֳּדָשִׁים** (לא תעשה קכט). **ז) לִשְׂרֹף הַנּוֹתָר** (עשה צא). **ח) לִשְׂרֹף הַטָּמֵא** (עשה צ).

Hilkhot Pesulei HaMukdashin include eight mitzvot: two positive mitzvot and six negative mitzvot. Their enumeration follows: 1) Not to eat sacrificial animals that were disqualified or upon which a blemish was inflicted (negative mitzva 140); 2) Not to eat *piggul* (negative mitzva 132); 3) Not to leave any sacrificial meat uneaten after its time (negative mitzva 120); 4) Not to eat *notar* (negative mitzva 131); 5) Not to eat sacrificial food that was rendered ritually impure (negative mitzva 130); 6) That a person who was rendered ritually impure may not eat sacrificial food (negative mitzva 129); 7) To burn *notar* (positive mitzva 91); 8) To burn ritually impure sacrificial food (positive mitzva 90).

הִלְכוֹת עֲבוֹדַת יוֹם הַכִּפּוּרִים – מִצְוַת עֲשֵׂה אַחַת, וְהִיא **שֶׁיַּעֲשֶׂה מַעֲשֵׂה יוֹם הַכִּפּוּרִים כֻּלּוֹ עַל הַסֵּדֶר כְּמוֹ שֶׁכָּתוּב בְּפָרָשַׁת 'אַחֲרֵי מוֹת': הַקָּרְבָּנוֹת וְהַוִּדּוּיִין וְשִׁלּוּחַ הַשָּׂעִיר וּשְׁאָר הָעֲבוֹדָה** (עשה מט).

Hilkhot Avodat Yom HaKippurim include **one positive mitzva, which is to perform the entire Yom Kippur rite in the order that is written in *Parashat Aḥarei Mot*: the offerings, the confessions, the sending of the goat, and the rest of the service** (positive mitzva 49).

הִלְכוֹת מְעִילָה – יֵשׁ בִּכְלָלָן שָׁלֹשׁ מִצְוֹת, אַחַת מִצְוַת עֲשֵׂה וּשְׁתַּיִם מִצְוֹת לֹא תַעֲשֶׂה, וְזֶה הוּא פְּרָטָן: **א) לְשַׁלֵּם הַמּוֹעֵל אֲשֶׁר חָטָא בְּתוֹסֶפֶת חֹמֶשׁ וְקָרְבָּן, וְזֶה הוּא דִּין הַמּוֹעֵל** (עשה קיח). **ב) שֶׁלֹּא לַעֲבֹד בַּקֳּדָשִׁים** (לא תעשה קיג). **ג) שֶׁלֹּא לָגֹז קָדָשִׁים** (לא תעשה קיד).

Hilkhot Me'ila include three mitzvot: one positive mitzva and two negative mitzvot. Their enumeration follows: 1) That one who misused consecrated property shall pay the amount he misused, and with which he thereby sinned, with the addition of one-fifth, and bring an offering. This is the law of one who misused consecrated property (positive mitzva 118); 2) Not to perform labor with sacrificial animals (negative mitzva 113); 3) Not to shear sacrificial animals (negative mitzva 114).

נִמְצְאוּ כָּל הַמִּצְוֹת הַנִּכְלָלוֹת בְּסֵפֶר זֶה מֵאָה וְשָׁלֹשׁ, מֵהֶם שֶׁבַע וְאַרְבָּעִים מִצְוֹת עֲשֵׂה וְשֵׁשׁ וַחֲמִשִּׁים מִצְוֹת לֹא תַעֲשֶׂה.

Thus, all the mitzvot that are included in this *Sefer* are **one hundred and three: Forty-seven of them** are **positive mitzvot and fifty-six** are **negative mitzvot.**

סֵפֶר הַקָּרְבָּנוֹת
9. Sefer Korbanot

Sefer Korbanot contains six ***Hilkhot*****, in the following order:** ***Hilkhot Korban Pesaḥ*** (Laws of the Paschal Offering), ***Hilkhot Ḥagiga*** (Laws of the Festival Offering), ***Hilkhot Bekhorot*** (Laws of Firstborns), ***Hilkhot Shegagot*** (Laws of Unintentional Transgressions), ***Hilkhot Meḥuserei Kappara*** (Laws for [Those with] Incomplete Atonement), and ***Hilkhot Temura*** (Laws of Substitution [of Sacrifices]).

הִלְכוֹתָיו שֵׁשׁ, וְזֶה הוּא סִדּוּרָן: הִלְכוֹת קָרְבַּן פֶּסַח, הִלְכוֹת חֲגִיגָה, הִלְכוֹת בְּכוֹרוֹת, הִלְכוֹת שְׁגָגוֹת, הִלְכוֹת מְחֻסְּרֵי כַפָּרָה, הִלְכוֹת תְּמוּרָה.

Hilkhot Korban Pesaḥ include sixteen mitzvot: four positive mitzvot and twelve negative mitzvot. Their enumeration follows: 1) To sacrifice the Paschal offering at its time (positive mitzva 55); 2) Not to sacrifice the Paschal offering while in possession of leaven (negative mitzva 115); 3) Not to leave over the sacrificial parts of the Paschal offering (negative mitzva 116); 4) To slaughter the second Paschal offering (positive mitzva 57); 5) To eat the flesh of the Paschal offering with matza and bitter herbs on the night of the fifteenth of the first month (positive mitzva 56); 6) To eat the flesh of the second Paschal offering with matza and bitter herbs on the night of the fifteenth of the second month (positive mitzva 58); 7) Not to eat the Paschal offering half cooked or cooked, instead of roasted (negative mitzva 125); 8) Not to take away any of the flesh of the Paschal offering from the place where the group is eating it (negative mitzva 123); 9) That an apostate may not eat from the Paschal offering (negative mitzva 128); 10) That one may not feed meat from the Paschal offering to a *ger toshav* or a hired laborer (negative mitzva 126); 11) That an uncircumcised man may not eat from the Paschal offering (negative mitzva 127); 12) Not to break a bone from the Paschal offering (negative mitzva 121); 13) Not to break a bone from the second Paschal offering (negative mitzva 122); 14) Not to leave any of the Paschal offering to the morning (negative mitzva 117); 15) Not to leave any of the second Paschal offering to the morning (negative mitzva 119); 16) Not to leave any of the meat of the festival peace offering of the fourteenth of the first month to the morning of the third day (negative mitzva 118).

הִלְכוֹת קָרְבַּן פֶּסַח – יֵשׁ בִּכְלָלָן שֵׁשׁ עֶשְׂרֵה מִצְווֹת, אַרְבַּע מִצְווֹת עֲשֵׂה וּשְׁתֵּים עֶשְׂרֵה מִצְווֹת לֹא תַעֲשֶׂה, וְזֶה הוּא פְּרָטָן: א) לִשְׁחֹט הַפֶּסַח בִּזְמַנּוֹ (עשה נה). **ב) שֶׁלֹּא לִזְבֹּחַ אוֹתוֹ עַל הֶחָמֵץ** (לא תעשה קטו). **ג) שֶׁלֹּא תָלִין אֵמוּרָיו** (לא תעשה קיו). **ד) לִשְׁחֹט פֶּסַח שֵׁנִי** (עשה נז). **ה) לֶאֱכֹל בְּשַׂר הַפֶּסַח עַל מַצָּה וּמָרוֹר בְּלֵילֵי חֲמִשָּׁה עָשָׂר** (עשה נו). **ו) לֶאֱכֹל בְּשַׂר פֶּסַח שֵׁנִי עַל מַצָּה וּמָרוֹר בְּלֵילֵי חֲמִשָּׁה עָשָׂר לַחֹדֶשׁ הַשֵּׁנִי** (עשה נח). **ז) שֶׁלֹּא יֹאכַל נָא וּמְבֻשָּׁל** (לא תעשה קכה). **ח) שֶׁלֹּא יוֹצִיא מִבְּשַׂר הַפֶּסַח חוּץ לַחֲבוּרָה** (לא תעשה קכג). **ט) שֶׁלֹּא יֹאכַל מִמֶּנּוּ מְשֻׁמָּד** (לא תעשה קכח). **י) שֶׁלֹּא יַאֲכִיל מִמֶּנּוּ לְתוֹשָׁב אוֹ שָׂכִיר** (לא תעשה קכו). **יא) שֶׁלֹּא יֹאכַל מִמֶּנּוּ עָרֵל** (לא תעשה קכז). **יב) שֶׁלֹּא יִשְׁבֹּר בּוֹ עֶצֶם** (לא תעשה קכא). **יג) שֶׁלֹּא יִשְׁבֹּר עֶצֶם בְּפֶסַח שֵׁנִי** (לא תעשה קכב). **יד) שֶׁלֹּא יַשְׁאִיר מִמֶּנּוּ לַבֹּקֶר** (לא תעשה קיז). **טו) שֶׁלֹּא יַשְׁאִיר מִפֶּסַח שֵׁנִי לַבֹּקֶר** (לא תעשה קיט). **יו) שֶׁלֹּא יַשְׁאִיר מִבְּשַׂר חֲגִיגַת אַרְבָּעָה עָשָׂר עַד יוֹם שְׁלִישִׁי** (לא תעשה קיח).

Hilkhot Ḥagiga include six mitzvot: four positive mitzvot and two negative mitzvot. Their enumeration follows: 1) To appear before God on the pilgrimage

הִלְכוֹת חֲגִיגָה – יֵשׁ בִּכְלָלָן שֵׁשׁ מִצְווֹת, אַרְבַּע מִצְווֹת עֲשֵׂה וּשְׁתֵּי מִצְווֹת לֹא תַעֲשֶׂה, וְזֶה הוּא פְּרָטָן: א) לְהֵרָאוֹת

פְּנֵי יי (עשה נג). ב) לָחֹג בִּשְׁלֹשָׁה רְגָלִים (עשה נב). ג) לִשְׂמֹחַ בָּרְגָלִים (עשה נד). ד) שֶׁלֹּא יֵרָאֶה רֵיקָם (לא תעשה קנו). ה) שֶׁלֹּא יַעֲזֹב לֵוִי מִלְּשַׂמְּחוֹ וְלִתֵּן לוֹ מַתְּנוֹתָיו בָּרְגָלִים (לא תעשה רכט). ו) לְהַקְהִיל אֶת הָעָם בְּחַג הַסֻּכּוֹת בְּמוֹצָאֵי שְׁמִטָּה (עשה יו).

festivals (positive mitzva 53); 2) To celebrate the three pilgrimage festivals (positive mitzva 52); 3) To rejoice on the pilgrimage festivals (positive mitzva 54); 4) Not to appear empty-handed before God (negative mitzva 156); 5) Not to abandon the Levite, by refraining from gladdening him, and by giving him his gifts on the pilgrimage festivals (negative mitzva 229); 6) To assemble the people on the festival of Sukkot upon the conclusion of the Sabbatical Year (positive mitzva 16).

הִלְכוֹת בְּכוֹרוֹת - יֵשׁ בִּכְלָלָן חָמֵשׁ מִצְווֹת, שְׁתֵּי מִצְווֹת עֲשֵׂה וְשָׁלֹשׁ מִצְווֹת לֹא תַעֲשֶׂה, וְזֶה הוּא פְּרָטָן: א) לְהַפְרִישׁ בְּכוֹרוֹת (עשה עט). ב) שֶׁלֹּא יֹאכַל בְּכוֹר תָּמִים חוּץ לִירוּשָׁלַיִם (לא תעשה קמד). ג) שֶׁלֹּא יִפְדֶּה הַבְּכוֹר (לא תעשה קח). ד) לְהַפְרִישׁ מַעְשַׂר בְּהֵמָה (עשה עח). ה) שֶׁלֹּא יִגְאַל מַעְשַׂר בְּהֵמָה (לא תעשה קט). וְכָלַלְתִּי הַמַּעֲשֵׂר עִם הַבְּכוֹר, לְפִי שֶׁמַּעֲשֵׂה שְׁנֵיהֶם אֶחָד, וְהַכָּתוּב כְּלָלוֹ עִמּוֹ, שֶׁנֶּאֱמַר: "אֶת דָּמָם תִּזְרֹק" (במדבר יח, יז). כָּךְ לָמְדוּ מִפִּי הַשְּׁמוּעָה, שֶׁזֶּה דַּם מַעֲשֵׂר וְדַם בְּכוֹר.

Hilkhot Bekhorot include five mitzvot: two positive mitzvot and three negative mitzvot. Their enumeration follows: 1) To separate firstborn animals (positive mitzva 79); 2) Not to eat an unblemished firstborn animal outside Jerusalem (negative mitzva 144); 3) Not to redeem a firstborn animal (negative mitzva 108); 4) To separate the animal tithe (positive mitzva 78); 5) Not to redeem the animal tithe (negative mitzva 109). I have included the laws of the animal tithe together with the laws of the firstborn animal because they both have the same rite, and the verse itself includes the animal tithe with it, as it is stated: "You shall sprinkle their blood on the altar" (Numbers 18:17), and the Sages learned as follows, on the basis of the Oral tradition, that this is referring both to the blood of the animal tithe and to the blood of a firstborn animal.

הִלְכוֹת שְׁגָגוֹת - יֵשׁ בִּכְלָלָן חָמֵשׁ מִצְווֹת עֲשֵׂה, וְזֶה הוּא פְּרָטָן: א) שֶׁיַּקְרִיב הַיָּחִיד קָרְבַּן חַטָּאת קָבוּעַ עַל שִׁגְגָתוֹ (עשה סט). ב) שֶׁיַּקְרִיב אָשָׁם מִי שֶׁלֹּא נוֹדַע לוֹ אִם חָטָא אִם לֹא חָטָא עַד שֶׁיִּוָּדַע לוֹ וְיָבִיא חַטָּאתוֹ, וְזֶה הוּא הַנִּקְרָא אָשָׁם תָּלוּי (עשה ע). ג) שֶׁיַּקְרִיב הַחוֹטֵא אָשָׁם עַל עֲבֵרוֹת יְדוּעוֹת, וְזֶה הוּא הַנִּקְרָא אָשָׁם וַדַּאי (עשה עא). ד) שֶׁיַּקְרִיב הַחוֹטֵא קָרְבָּן עַל עֲבֵרוֹת יְדוּעוֹת: אִם הָיָה עָשִׁיר - בְּהֵמָה, וְאִם הָיָה עָנִי - עוֹף אוֹ עֲשִׂירִית הָאֵיפָה, וְזֶה הוּא הַנִּקְרָא קָרְבָּן עוֹלֶה וְיוֹרֵד (עשה עב). ה) שֶׁיַּקְרִיבוּ הַסַּנְהֶדְרִין קָרְבָּן אִם טָעוּ וְהוֹרוּ שֶׁלֹּא כַּהֲלָכָה בְּאַחַת מִן הַחֲמוּרוֹת (עשה סח).

Hilkhot Shegagot include five positive mitzvot. Their enumeration follows: 1) That an individual shall sacrifice a fixed sin offering for his unwitting transgression (positive mitzva 69); 2) That one who does not know whether or not he had definitely sinned shall bring a guilt offering, until he becomes aware that he did indeed sin, and then he shall bring his sin offering. This is called a provisional guilt offering (positive mitzva 70); 3) That a sinner shall bring a guilt offering for specific sins. This is called a definite guilt offering (positive mitzva 71); 4) That a sinner shall bring an offering for specific sins: If he is wealthy, he brings an animal; if he is poor, he brings a bird or one-tenth of an ephah. This is called a sliding-scale offering (positive mitzva 72); 5) That the Sanhedrin shall sacrifice an offering if they erred and ruled not in accordance with the halakha, in a case involving one of the severe transgressions (positive mitzva 68).

הִלְכוֹת מְחֻסְּרֵי כַּפָּרָה - יֵשׁ בִּכְלָלָן אַרְבַּע מִצְווֹת עֲשֵׂה, וְזֶה הוּא פְּרָטָן: א) שֶׁתַּקְרִיב הַזָּבָה כְּשֶׁתִּטְהַר קָרְבָּן (עשה עה). ב) שֶׁתַּקְרִיב הַיּוֹלֶדֶת כְּשֶׁתִּטְהַר קָרְבָּן (עשה עו).

Hilkhot Meḥuserei Kappara include four positive mitzvot. Their enumeration follows: 1) That a *zava* shall sacrifice an offering when she is ritually purified (positive mitzva 75); 2) That a woman after childbirth shall sacrifice an offering when she is purified (positive mitzva 76);

ג) שֶׁיַּקְרִיב הַזָּב כְּשֶׁיִּטְהַר קָרְבָּן (עשה עד). ד) שֶׁיַּקְרִיב מְצֹרָע כְּשֶׁיִּטְהַר קָרְבָּן. וְאַחַר שֶׁיַּקְרִיבוּ קָרְבְּנוֹתֵיהֶן – תִּגָּמֵר טָהֳרָתָן (עשה עז).

3) That a *zav* shall sacrifice an offering when he is ritually purified (positive mitzva 74); 4) That a leper shall sacrifice an offering when he is ritually purified. And after they have sacrificed their offerings, their purification shall be complete (positive mitzva 77).

הִלְכוֹת תְּמוּרָה – יֵשׁ בִּכְלָלָן שָׁלֹשׁ מִצְוֹת, אַחַת מִצְוַת עֲשֵׂה וּשְׁתֵּי מִצְוֹת לֹא תַעֲשֶׂה, וְזֶה הוּא פְּרָטָן: א) שֶׁלֹּא יָמִיר (לא תעשה קו). ב) שֶׁתִּהְיֶה הַתְּמוּרָה קֹדֶשׁ אִם הֵמִיר (עשה פז). ג) שֶׁלֹּא יְשַׁנֶּה הַקֳּדָשִׁים מִקְּדֻשָּׁה לִקְדֻשָּׁה (לא תעשה קז).

Hilkhot Temura include three mitzvot: one positive mitzva and two negative mitzvot. Their enumeration follows: 1) That one may not substitute a consecrated animal for another animal (negative mitzva 106); 2) That the substitute shall be sacred, if one did substitute (positive mitzva 87); 3) That one may not change sacrificial animals from one type of sanctity for another sanctity (negative mitzva 107).

נִמְצְאוּ כָּל הַמִּצְוֹת הַנִּכְלָלוֹת בְּסֵפֶר זֶה תֵּשַׁע וּשְׁלֹשִׁים, מֵהֶן עֶשְׂרִים מִצְוֹת עֲשֵׂה וּתְשַׁע עֶשְׂרֵה מִצְוֹת לֹא תַעֲשֶׂה.

Thus, all the mitzvot that are included in this *Sefer* are thirty-nine: Twenty of them are **positive mitzvot and nineteen** are **negative mitzvot.**

סֵפֶר טָהֳרָה

10. Sefer Tahara

הִלְכוֹתָיו שְׁמוֹנֶה, וְזֶה הוּא סִדּוּרָן: הִלְכוֹת טֻמְאַת מֵת, הִלְכוֹת פָּרָה אֲדֻמָּה, הִלְכוֹת טֻמְאַת צָרַעַת, הִלְכוֹת מְטַמְּאֵי מִשְׁכָּב וּמוֹשָׁב, הִלְכוֹת שְׁאָר אֲבוֹת הַטֻּמְאוֹת, הִלְכוֹת טֻמְאַת אֳכָלִים, הִלְכוֹת כֵּלִים, הִלְכוֹת מִקְוָאוֹת.

Sefer Tahara contains **eight *Hilkhot*, in the following order: *Hilkhot Tumat Met*** (Laws of Ritual Impurity of a Corpse), ***Hilkhot Para Aduma*** (Laws of the Red Heifer), ***Hilkhot Tumat Tzaraat*** (Laws of Ritual Impurity of *Tzaraat*), ***Hilkhot Metamei Mishkav UMoshav*** (Laws of Those Who Cause Ritual Impurity by Lying or Sitting), ***Hilkhot She'ar Avot HaTumot*** (Laws of Other Sources of Ritual Impurity), ***Hilkhot Tumat Okhalin*** (Laws of Ritual Impurity of Foods), ***Hilkhot Kelim*** (Laws of Vessels), and ***Hilkhot Mikvaot*** (Laws of Ritual Immersion Pools).

הִלְכוֹת טֻמְאַת מֵת – מִצְוַת עֲשֵׂה אַחַת, וְהִיא דִּין טֻמְאַת מֵת (עשה קז).

Hilkhot Tumat Met include **one positive mitzva, which is the law of** the **ritual impurity of a corpse** (positive mitzva 107).

הִלְכוֹת פָּרָה אֲדֻמָּה – יֵשׁ בִּכְלָלָן שְׁתֵּי מִצְוֹת עֲשֵׂה, רִאשׁוֹנָה – דִּין פָּרָה אֲדֻמָּה (עשה קיג), שְׁנִיָּה – דִּין טֻמְאַת מֵי נִדָּה וְטָהֳרָתָן (עשה קח).

Hilkhot Para Aduma include two positive mitzvot. The first is the law of the red heifer (positive mitzva 113), and the second is the law of the impurity of the water of sprinkling and its purification (positive mitzva 108).

הִלְכוֹת טֻמְאַת צָרַעַת – יֵשׁ בִּכְלָלָן שְׁמוֹנֶה מִצְוֹת, שֵׁשׁ מִצְוֹת עֲשֵׂה וּשְׁתֵּי מִצְוֹת לֹא תַעֲשֶׂה, וְזֶה הוּא פְּרָטָן: א) לְהוֹרוֹת בְּצָרַעַת אָדָם כְּדִינָהּ הַכָּתוּב בַּתּוֹרָה (עשה קא). ב) שֶׁלֹּא יָקֹץ סִימָנֵי טֻמְאָה (לא תעשה שח). ג) שֶׁלֹּא יְגַלַּח הַנֶּתֶק (לא תעשה שז). ד) שֶׁיְּהֵא הַמְּצֹרָע

Hilkhot Tumat Tzaraat include eight mitzvot: six positive mitzvot and two negative mitzvot. Their enumeration follows: 1) To rule in the case of leprosy of a person, in accordance with its law that is written in the Torah (positive mitzva 101); 2) That one may not cut off the signs of the impurity of leprosy (negative mitzva 308); 3) That one may not shave off a leprous scall (negative mitzva 307); 4) That the status of the leper shall be publicized

מְפֻרְסָם בִּקְרִיעַת בְּגָדָיו וּפְרִיעַת רֹאשׁוֹ וַעֲטִיָּה עַל שָׂפָם (עשה קיב). ה) טָהֳרַת צָרַעַת (עשה קי). ו) שֶׁיְּגַלַּח הַמְּצֹרָע אֶת כָּל שְׂעָרוֹ כְּשֶׁיִּטְהַר (עשה קיא). ז) דִּין צָרַעַת הַבֶּגֶד (עשה קב). ח) דִּין צָרַעַת הַבַּיִת (עשה קג).

through the rending of his garments, the growing out of the hair of his head, and a covering on his upper lip (positive mitzva 112); 5) To observe the purification rite of a leper (positive mitzva 110); 6) That a leper must shave off all of his hair when he is purified (positive mitzva 111); 7) The law of the leprosy of garments (positive mitzva 102); 8) The law of the leprosy of houses (positive mitzva 103).

הִלְכוֹת מְטַמְּאֵי מִשְׁכָּב וּמוֹשָׁב – יֵשׁ בִּכְלָלָן אַרְבַּע מִצְוֹת עֲשֵׂה, וְזֶה הוּא פְּרָטָן: א) דִּין טֻמְאַת נִדָּה (עשה צט). ב) דִּין טֻמְאַת יוֹלֶדֶת (עשה ק). ג) דִּין טֻמְאַת זָבָה (עשה קו). ד) דִּין טֻמְאַת זָב (עשה קד).

Hilkhot Metamei Mishkav UMoshav include four positive mitzvot. Their enumeration follows: 1) The law of the impurity of a menstruating woman (positive mitzva 99); 2) The law of the impurity of a woman after childbirth (positive mitzva 100); 3) The law of the impurity of a *zava* (positive mitzva 106); 4) The law of the impurity of a *zav* (positive mitzva 104).

הִלְכוֹת שְׁאָר אֲבוֹת הַטֻּמְאוֹת – יֵשׁ בִּכְלָלָן שָׁלֹשׁ מִצְוֹת עֲשֵׂה, וְזֶה הוּא פְּרָטָן: א) דִּין טֻמְאַת נְבֵלָה (עשה צו). ב) דִּין טֻמְאַת שֶׁרֶץ (עשה צז). ג) דִּין טֻמְאַת שִׁכְבַת זֶרַע (עשה קה). וַעֲבוֹדָה זָרָה מְטַמְּאָה כְּשֶׁרֶץ, וְטֻמְאָתָהּ מִדִּבְרֵי סוֹפְרִים.

Hilkhot She'ar Avot HaTumot include three positive mitzvot. Their enumeration follows: 1) The law of the impurity of an animal carcass (positive mitzva 96); 2) The law of the impurity of a creeping animal (positive mitzva 97); 3) The law of the impurity of semen (positive mitzva 105). In this context, it should be noted that an object of idolatry transmits impurity in the same manner as a creeping animal, but its impurity applies only by rabbinic law.

הִלְכוֹת טֻמְאַת אֳכָלִין – מִצְוַת עֲשֵׂה אַחַת, וְהִיא דִּין טֻמְאַת מַשְׁקִין וַאֲכָלִין וְהֶכְשֵׁרָן (עשה צח).

Hilkhot Tumat Okhalin include **one positive mitzva, which is the law of the ritual impurity of liquids, foods, and** how **they are rendered susceptible to impurity** (positive mitzva 98).

הִלְכוֹת כֵּלִים – עִנְיַן אֵלּוּ הַהֲלָכוֹת לֵידַע כֵּלִים שֶׁמְּקַבְּלִין טֻמְאָה מִכָּל אֵלּוּ הַטֻּמְאוֹת וְכֵלִים שֶׁאֵינָן מִתְטַמְּאִין, וְכֵיצַד מִתְטַמְּאִין הַכֵּלִים וּמְטַמְּאִין.

Hilkhot Kelim: The **subject of these halakhot is the knowledge of** those **vessels that are susceptible to ritual impurity, with regard to all of these impurities, and** the **vessels that do not become impure, and how** different **vessels become impure and transmit impurity.**

הִלְכוֹת מִקְוָאוֹת – מִצְוַת עֲשֵׂה אַחַת, וְהִיא שֶׁיִּטְבֹּל כָּל טָמֵא בְּמֵי מִקְוֶה וְאַחַר כָּךְ יִטְהַר (עשה קט).

Hilkhot Mikvaot include **one positive mitzva, which is that every impure** person **shall be immersed in the water of a ritual bath and subsequently be purified** (positive mitzva 109).

נִמְצְאוּ כָּל הַמִּצְוֹת הַנִּכְלָלוֹת בְּסֵפֶר זֶה עֶשְׂרִים, מֵהֶם שְׁמוֹנֶה עֶשְׂרֵה מִצְוֹת עֲשֵׂה וּשְׁתֵּי מִצְוֹת לֹא תַעֲשֶׂה.

Thus, all the mitzvot that are included in this ***Sefer*** are **twenty: Eighteen of them** are **positive mitzvot and two** are **negative mitzvot.**

יא. סֵפֶר נְזָקִים

11. Sefer Nezakim

Sefer Nezakim contains **five *Hilkhot*, in the following order: *Hilkhot Nizkei Mamon*** (Laws of Damages to Property), ***Hilkhot Geneiva*** (Laws of Theft), ***Hilkhot Gezeila VaAveda*** (Laws of Robbery and Lost Property), ***Hilkhot Ḥovel UMazik*** (Laws of One Who Injures or Damages), and ***Hilkhot Rotze'aḥ UShemirat HaNefesh*** (Laws of the Murderer and the Preservation of Life).

הִלְכוֹתָיו חָמֵשׁ, וְזֶה הוּא סִדּוּרָן: הִלְכוֹת נִזְקֵי מָמוֹן, הִלְכוֹת גְּנֵבָה, הִלְכוֹת גְּזֵלָה וַאֲבֵדָה, הִלְכוֹת חוֹבֵל וּמַזִּיק, הִלְכוֹת רוֹצֵחַ וּשְׁמִירַת נֶפֶשׁ.

***Hilkhot Nizkei Mamon* include four positive mitzvot which detail the four primary categories of things which cause damage. Their enumeration follows: 1) The law of the ox** (positive mitzva 237); **2) The law of grazing,** i.e., the categories of eating and trampling (positive mitzva 240); **3) The law of the pit** (positive mitzva 238); **4) The law of fire** (positive mitzva 241).

הִלְכוֹת נִזְקֵי מָמוֹן – יֵשׁ בִּכְלָלָן אַרְבַּע מִצְוֹת עֲשֵׂה, וְזֶה הוּא פְּרָטָן: א) דִּין הַשּׁוֹר (עשה רלז). **ב) דִּין הַהֶבְעֵר** (עשה רמ). **ג) דִּין הַבּוֹר** (עשה רלח). **ד) דִּין הַבְּעֵרָה** (עשה רמא).

Hilkhot Geneiva include seven mitzvot: two positive mitzvot and five negative mitzvot. Their enumeration follows: 1) Not to steal property (negative mitzva 244); 2) The law of a thief (positive mitzva 239); 3) To have accurate scales with their weights (positive mitzva 208); 4) Not to commit iniquity through measures and weights (negative mitzva 271); 5) That a person may not have different weights and different measures, even if he does not buy and sell with them (negative mitzva 272); 6) Not to move a boundary (negative mitzva 246); 7) Not to kidnap (negative mitzva 243).

הִלְכוֹת גְּנֵבָה – יֵשׁ בִּכְלָלָן שֶׁבַע מִצְוֹת, שְׁתֵּי מִצְוֹת עֲשֵׂה וְחָמֵשׁ מִצְוֹת לֹא תַעֲשֶׂה, וְזֶה הוּא פְּרָטָן: א) שֶׁלֹּא לִגְנֹב מָמוֹן (לא תעשה רמד). **ב) דִּין הַגַּנָּב** (עשה רלט). **ג) לְצַדֵּק הַמֹּאזְנַיִם עִם הַמִּשְׁקָלוֹת** (עשה רח). **ד) שֶׁלֹּא יַעֲשֶׂה עָוֶל בַּמִּדּוֹת וּבַמִּשְׁקָלוֹת** (לא תעשה רעא). **ה) שֶׁלֹּא יִהְיֶה לְאָדָם אֶבֶן וָאֶבֶן, אֵיפָה וְאֵיפָה, אַף עַל פִּי שֶׁאֵינוֹ לוֹקֵחַ וְנוֹתֵן בָּהֶם** (לא תעשה רעב). **ו) שֶׁלֹּא יַסִּיג גְּבוּל** (לא תעשה רמו). **ז) שֶׁלֹּא לִגְנֹב נְפָשׁוֹת** (לא תעשה רמג).

Hilkhot Gezeila VaAveda include seven mitzvot: two positive mitzvot and five negative mitzvot. Their enumeration follows: 1) Not to rob (negative mitzva 245); 2) Not to exploit (negative mitzva 247); 3) Not to covet something that belongs to another and pressure him until he sells it to him (negative mitzva 265); 4) Not to desire that which belongs to another (negative mitzva 266); 5) To restore a stolen item (positive mitzva 194); 6) Not to disregard a lost item (negative mitzva 269); 7) To restore a lost item (positive mitzva 204).

הִלְכוֹת גְּזֵלָה וַאֲבֵדָה – יֵשׁ בִּכְלָלָן שֶׁבַע מִצְוֹת, שְׁתֵּי מִצְוֹת עֲשֵׂה וְחָמֵשׁ מִצְוֹת לֹא תַעֲשֶׂה, וְזֶה הוּא פְּרָטָן: א) שֶׁלֹּא לִגְזֹל (לא תעשה רמה). **ב) שֶׁלֹּא לַעֲשֹׁק** (לא תעשה רמז). **ג) שֶׁלֹּא לַחְמֹד** (לא תעשה רסה). **ד) שֶׁלֹּא לְהִתְאַוּוֹת** (לא תעשה רסו). **ה) לְהָשִׁיב אֶת הַגְּזֵלָה** (עשה קצד). **ו) שֶׁלֹּא יִתְעַלֵּם מִן הָאֲבֵדָה** (לא תעשה רסט). **ז) לְהָשִׁיב הָאֲבֵדָה** (עשה רד).

***Hilkhot Ḥovel UMazik* include one positive mitzva, which is the law of one who injures another, or damages the property of another** (positive mitzva 236).

הִלְכוֹת חוֹבֵל וּמַזִּיק – מִצְוַת עֲשֵׂה אַחַת, וְהִיא דִּין חוֹבֵל בַּחֲבֵרוֹ אוֹ מַזִּיק מָמוֹן חֲבֵרוֹ (עשה רלו).

הִלְכוֹת רוֹצֵחַ וּשְׁמִירַת נֶפֶשׁ – יֵשׁ בִּכְלָלָן שְׁבַע עֶשְׂרֵה מִצְווֹת, שֶׁבַע מִצְווֹת עֲשֵׂה וְעֶשֶׂר מִצְווֹת לֹא תַעֲשֶׂה, וְזֶה הוּא פְּרָטָן: א) שֶׁלֹּא לִרְצֹחַ (לא תעשה רפט). ב) שֶׁלֹּא לִקַּח כֹּפֶר לְנֶפֶשׁ רוֹצֵחַ, אֶלָּא יוּמַת (לא תעשה רצה). ג) לְהַגְלוֹת הָרוֹצֵחַ בִּשְׁגָגָה (עשה רכה). ד) שֶׁלֹּא לִקַּח כֹּפֶר לִמְחֻיַּב גָּלוּת (לא תעשה רצו). ה) שֶׁלֹּא יוּמַת הָרוֹצֵחַ כְּשֶׁיִּרְצַח קֹדֶם עֲמִידָה בַּדִּין (לא תעשה רצב). ו) לְהַצִּיל הַנִּרְדָּף בְּנַפְשׁוֹ שֶׁל רוֹדֵף (עשה רמז). ז) שֶׁלֹּא לָחוּס עַל הָרוֹדֵף (לא תעשה רצג). ח) שֶׁלֹּא לַעֲמֹד עַל דָּם (לא תעשה רצז). ט) לְהַפְרִישׁ עָרֵי מִקְלָט וּלְכַוֵּן לָהֶם הַדֶּרֶךְ (עשה קפב). י) לַעֲרֹף אֶת הָעֶגְלָה בַּנַּחַל (עשה קפא). יא) שֶׁלֹּא יֵעָבֵד בְּאוֹתָהּ קַרְקַע וְלֹא תִזָּרַע (לא תעשה שט). יב) שֶׁלֹּא לָשִׂים דָּמִים (לא תעשה רצח). יג) לַעֲשׂוֹת מַעֲקֶה (עשה קפד). יד) שֶׁלֹּא יַכְשִׁיל תָּמִים בְּדָבָר (לא תעשה רצט). טו) לִפְרֹק עִם מִי שֶׁנִּכְשַׁל בַּדֶּרֶךְ (עשה רב). טז) לִטְעֹן עִמּוֹ (עשה רג). יז) שֶׁלֹּא יַנִּיחֶנּוּ בַּדֶּרֶךְ נִבְהָל בְּמַשָּׂאוֹ וְיֵלֵךְ לוֹ (לא תעשה רע).

Hilkhot Rotze'aḥ UShemirat HaNefesh include seventeen mitzvot: seven positive mitzvot and ten negative mitzvot. Their enumeration follows: 1) Not to murder (negative mitzva 289); 2) Not to take ransom for the life of a murderer; rather, he shall be put to death (negative mitzva 295); 3) To exile the unwitting murderer (positive mitzva 289); 4) Not to take ransom for one who is liable to exile (negative mitzva 296); 5) That a murderer shall not be put to death before he is brought for judgment (negative mitzva 292); 6) To save the pursued even at the expense of the life of the pursuer (positive mitzva 247); 7) Not to have mercy on a pursuer (negative mitzva 293); 8) Not to stand by the blood of one's neighbor (negative mitzva 297); 9) To separate cities of refuge and signpost the way to them (positive mitzva 182); 10) To behead a heifer in a ravine in the appropriate circumstances (positive mitzva 181); 11) That no work be done in that ground, of the ravine, and that it may not be sown (negative mitzva 309); 12) Not to put blood in one's house, i.e., establish a dangerous situation (negative mitzva 298); 13) To make a parapet on the roof of one's house (positive mitzva 184); 14) Not to cause one who is naive about a matter to stumble (negative mitzva 299); 15) To help unload, with someone, his beast of burden that has fallen while walking on the way (positive mitzva 202); 16) To help reload, with someone, his beast of burden that has fallen and arisen (positive mitzva 203); 17) Not to leave him on the way distressed with his animal suffering under its burden, and depart (negative mitzva 270).

נִמְצְאוּ כָּל הַמִּצְווֹת הַנִּכְלָלוֹת בְּסֵפֶר זֶה שֵׁשׁ וּשְׁלֹשִׁים, מֵהֶן שֵׁשׁ עֶשְׂרֵה מִצְווֹת עֲשֵׂה וְעֶשְׂרִים מִצְווֹת לֹא תַעֲשֶׂה.

Thus, all the mitzvot that are included in this ***Sefer*** **are thirty-six: Sixteen of them** are **positive mitzvot and twenty** are **negative mitzvot.**

יב. סֵפֶר קִנְיָן

12. Sefer Kinyan

הִלְכוֹתָיו חָמֵשׁ, וְזֶה הוּא סִדּוּרָן: הִלְכוֹת מְכִירָה, הִלְכוֹת זְכִיָּה וּמַתָּנָה, הִלְכוֹת שְׁכֵנִים, הִלְכוֹת שְׁלוּחִין וְשֻׁתָּפִין, הִלְכוֹת עֲבָדִים.

Sefer Kinyan contains **five** ***Hilkhot*****, in the following order:** ***Hilkhot Mekhira*** (Laws of Sales), ***Hilkhot Zekhiya UMattana*** (Laws of Ownerless Property and Gifts), ***Hilkhot Shekhenim*** (Laws of Neighbors), ***Hilkhot Sheluḥin VeShutafin*** (Laws of Agents and Partners), and ***Hilkhot Avadim*** (Laws of Slaves).

הִלְכוֹת מְכִירָה – יֵשׁ בִּכְלָלָן חָמֵשׁ מִצְווֹת, אַחַת מִצְוַת עֲשֵׂה וְאַרְבַּע מִצְווֹת לֹא תַעֲשֶׂה, וְזֶה הוּא פְּרָטָן: א) דִּין מֶקַח וּמִמְכָּר (עשה רמה). ב) שֶׁלֹּא יוֹנֶה בְּמֶקַח

Hilkhot Mekhira include five mitzvot: one positive mitzva and four negative mitzvot. Their enumeration follows: 1) The law of buying and selling (positive mitzva 245); 2) Not to defraud when buying and selling (negative

וּמִמְכָּר (לא תעשה רנ). ג) **שֶׁלֹּא יוֹנֶה בִּדְבָרִים** (לא תעשה רנא). ד) **שֶׁלֹּא יוֹנֶה גֵּר צֶדֶק בְּמָמוֹנוֹ** (לא תעשה רנג). ה) **שֶׁלֹּא יוֹנֵהוּ בִּדְבָרִים** (לא תעשה רנב).

mitzva 250); 3) Not to verbally mistreat another (negative mitzva 251); 4) Not to mistreat a convert in his finances (negative mitzva 253); 5) Not to verbally mistreat a convert (negative mitzva 252).

הִלְכוֹת זְכִיָּה וּמַתָּנָה – עִנְיַן אֵלּוּ הַהֲלָכוֹת לֵידַע דִּין זוֹכֶה מִן הַהֶפְקֵר הֵיאַךְ יִקְנֶה וּבַמֶּה יִקְנֶה, וְדִין נוֹתֵן מַתָּנָה וּמְקַבֵּל, וְאֵי זוֹ מַתָּנָה חוֹזֶרֶת וְאֵי זוֹ אֵינָהּ חוֹזֶרֶת.

Hilkhot Zekhiya UMattana: There are no special mitzvot in these chapters. Rather, the **subject of these halakhot is to know** the **law of how** one who wishes to **acquire** an item **from** what is established as **ownerless property can take possession** of it, **and by** means of **what** act of acquisition **he takes possession** of it, **and the law of one who gives a gift and one who receives it, and what** type of **gift can be retracted and what** type **cannot be retracted.**

הִלְכוֹת שְׁכֵנִים – עִנְיַן אֵלּוּ הַהֲלָכוֹת לֵידַע דִּין חִלּוּק הַקַּרְקָעוֹת בֵּין הַשֻּׁתָּפִין, וְהַרְחָקַת נִזְקֵי כָּל אֶחָד מֵהֶם מִשְּׁכֵנוֹ וּמִבַּעַל הַמֶּצֶר שֶׁלּוֹ, וְדִין בַּעַל הַמֶּצֶר.

Hilkhot Shekhenim: There are no special mitzvot in these chapters. Rather, the **subject of these halakhot is to know** the **law of the division of land between partners, and for each of them to take precautions so as not to damage his neighbor or one whose** field **borders his** field, **and the law of one whose** field **borders** his own.

הִלְכוֹת שְׁלוּחִין וְשֻׁתָּפִין – עִנְיַן אֵלּוּ הַהֲלָכוֹת לֵידַע דִּין שְׁלוּחוֹ שֶׁל אָדָם וְשֻׁתָּפוֹ, וּמִשְׁפְּטֵיהֶן בְּמִקְחָן וּמִמְכָּרָן וּבְהֶפְסֵדָן וּשְׂכָרָן.

Hilkhot Sheluḥin VeShutafin: There are no special mitzvot in these chapters. Rather, the **subject of these halakhot is to know** the **law of a person's agent and partner, and their legal** status and rights **with regard to their buying and selling, and their losses and profits.**

הִלְכוֹת עֲבָדִים – יֵשׁ בִּכְלָלָן שָׁלֹשׁ עֶשְׂרֵה מִצְווֹת, חָמֵשׁ מִצְווֹת עֲשֵׂה וּשְׁמוֹנֶה מִצְווֹת לֹא תַעֲשֶׂה, וְזֶה הוּא פְּרָטָן: א) **דִּין קִנְיַן עֶבֶד עִבְרִי** (עשה רלב). ב) **שֶׁלֹּא יִמָּכֵר מִמְכֶּרֶת עֶבֶד** (לא תעשה רנח). ג) **שֶׁלֹּא יַעֲבִידֶנּוּ בְּפֶרֶךְ** (לא תעשה רנט). ד) **שֶׁלֹּא נַנִּיחַ גֵּר תּוֹשָׁב לִרְדּוֹת בּוֹ בְּפֶרֶךְ** (לא תעשה רס). ה) **שֶׁלֹּא נַעֲבֹד בּוֹ עֲבוֹדַת עֶבֶד** (לא תעשה רנז). ו) **לְהַעֲנִיק לוֹ בְּצֵאתוֹ חָפְשִׁי** (עשה קצו). ז) **שֶׁלֹּא יֵצֵא רֵיקָם** (לא תעשה רלג). ח) **לִפְדּוֹת אָמָה עִבְרִיָּה** (עשה רלד). ט) **לְיַעֲדָהּ** (עשה רלג). י) **שֶׁלֹּא תִּמָּכֵר** (לא תעשה רסא). יא) **לַעֲבֹד בְּעֶבֶד כְּנַעֲנִי לְעוֹלָם, אֶלָּא אִם הִפִּיל לוֹ אֲדוֹנָיו אֶחָד מֵרָאשֵׁי אֵבָרָיו** (עשה רלה). יב) **שֶׁלֹּא לְהַסְגִּיר עֶבֶד שֶׁבָּרַח מִחוּצָה לָאָרֶץ לְאֶרֶץ יִשְׂרָאֵל** (לא תעשה רנד). יג) **שֶׁלֹּא לְהוֹנוֹת עֶבֶד זֶה הַנִּצָּל אֵלֵינוּ** (לא תעשה רנה).

Hilkhot Avadim include thirteen mitzvot: five positive mitzvot and eight negative mitzvot. Their enumeration follows: 1) The law of the acquisition of a Hebrew slave (positive mitzva 232); 2) That a Hebrew slave may not be sold as a slave (negative mitzva 258); 3) That a Hebrew slave may not be made to perform hard labor (negative mitzva 259); 4) Not to allow a *ger toshav* to oppress a Hebrew slave with hard labor (negative mitzva 260); 5) Not to put a Hebrew slave to work as a Canaanite slave (negative mitzva 257); 6) To give a Hebrew slave a severance gift when he is released (positive mitzva 196); 7) That he may not be released empty-handed (negative mitzva 233); 8) To redeem a Hebrew maidservant (positive mitzva 234); 9) To designate a Hebrew maidservant as a wife for oneself or one's son (positive mitzva 233); 10) That a Hebrew maidservant may not be sold (negative mitzva 261); 11) To enslave a Canaanite slave forever, unless his master caused him to lose one of his extremities (positive mitzva 235); 12) Not to hand over to his master a Canaanite slave who fled from outside of the Land of Israel to the Land (negative mitzva 254); 13) Not to exploit this slave who was spared from his master outside of the Land of Israel and came to us (negative mitzva 255).

נִמְצְאוּ כָּל הַמִּצְוֹת הַנִּכְלָלוֹת בְּסֵפֶר זֶה שְׁמוֹנֶה עֶשְׂרֵה, שֵׁשׁ מֵהֶן מִצְוֹת עֲשֵׂה וּשְׁתֵּים עֶשְׂרֵה מִצְוֹת לֹא תַעֲשֶׂה.

Thus, all the mitzvot that are included in this *Sefer* are eighteen: Six of them are **positive mitzvot and twelve** are **negative mitzvot.**

יג. סֵפֶר מִשְׁפָּטִים

13. Sefer Mishpatim

הִלְכוֹתָיו חָמֵשׁ, וְזֶה הוּא סִדּוּרָן: הִלְכוֹת שְׂכִירוּת, הִלְכוֹת שְׁאֵלָה וּפִקָּדוֹן, הִלְכוֹת מַלְוֶה וְלוֶֹה, הִלְכוֹת טוֹעֵן וְנִטְעָן, הִלְכוֹת נְחָלוֹת.

Sefer Mishpatim contains **five *Hilkhot*, in the following order: *Hilkhot Sekhirut*** (Laws of Hiring), ***Hilkhot She'ela UFikadon*** (Laws of Borrowing and Deposit), ***Hilkhot Malve VeLoveh*** (Laws of Creditor and Debtor), ***Hilkhot Toen VeNitan*** (Laws of Agents and Partners), and ***Hilkhot Naḥalot*** (Laws of Inheritances).

הִלְכוֹת שְׂכִירוּת – יֵשׁ בִּכְלָלָן שֶׁבַע מִצְוֹת, שָׁלֹשׁ מִצְוֹת עֲשֵׂה וְאַרְבַּע מִצְוֹת לֹא תַעֲשֶׂה, וְזֶה הוּא פְּרָטָן: א) דִּין שָׂכִיר וְשׁוֹמֵר שָׂכָר (עשה רמג). **ב) לִתֵּן שְׂכַר שָׂכִיר בְּיוֹמוֹ** (עשה ר). **ג) שֶׁלֹּא יְאַחֵר שְׂכַר שָׂכִיר אַחַר זְמַנּוֹ** (לא תעשה רלח). **ד) שֶׁיֹּאכַל הַשָּׂכִיר מִן הַמְחֻבָּר שֶׁעָשָׂה בּוֹ** (עשה רא). **ה) שֶׁלֹּא יֹאכַל הַשָּׂכִיר מִן הַמְחֻבָּר שֶׁלֹּא בִּשְׁעַת גְּמַר מְלָאכָה** (לא תעשה רסז). **ו) שֶׁלֹּא יוֹלִיךְ הַשָּׂכִיר בְּיָדוֹ יָתֵר עַל מַה שֶּׁאָכַל** (לא תעשה רסח). **ז) שֶׁלֹּא יַחְסֹם שׁוֹר בְּדִישׁוֹ, וְכֵן שְׁאָר הַבְּהֵמָה** (לא תעשה ריט).

Hilkhot Sekhirut include seven mitzvot: three positive mitzvot and four negative mitzvot. Their enumeration follows: 1) The law of a hired laborer and a paid bailee (positive mitzva 243); 2) To give the wage of a hired laborer on its due day (positive mitzva 200); 3) Not to delay the wage of a hired laborer after its due time (negative mitzva 238); 4) That a hired laborer may eat from the attached produce with which he is working (positive mitzva 201); 5) That a hired laborer may not eat from the attached produce when it is not at the time of the completion of labor (negative mitzva 267); 6) That a hired laborer may not take away in his hand more than what he has eaten (negative mitzva 268); 7) Not to muzzle an ox, and likewise other animals, when they are threshing (negative mitzva 219).

הִלְכוֹת שְׁאֵלָה וּפִקָּדוֹן – יֵשׁ בִּכְלָלָן שְׁתֵּי מִצְוֹת עֲשֵׂה, רִאשׁוֹנָה – דִּין הַשּׁוֹאֵל (עשה רמד), **שְׁנִיָּה – דִּין שׁוֹמֵר חִנָּם** (עשה רמב).

Hilkhot She'ela UFikadon include two positive mitzvot. The first is the law of the borrower (positive mitzva 244), and the second is the law of the unpaid bailee (positive mitzva 242).

הִלְכוֹת מַלְוֶה וְלוֶֹה – יֵשׁ בִּכְלָלָן שְׁתֵּים עֶשְׂרֵה מִצְוֹת, אַרְבַּע מִצְוֹת עֲשֵׂה וּשְׁמוֹנֶה מִצְוֹת לֹא תַעֲשֶׂה, וְזֶה הוּא פְּרָטָן: א) לְהַלְווֹת לְעָנִי וָמָךְ (עשה קצז). **ב) שֶׁלֹּא יִגֹּשׂ אוֹתוֹ** (לא תעשה רלד). **ג) לִנְגֹּשׂ אֶת הַנָּכְרִי** (עשה קמב). **ד) שֶׁלֹּא יְמַשְׁכֵּן בַּעַל חוֹב בִּזְרוֹעוֹ** (לא תעשה רלט). **ה) לְהַחֲזִיר הַמַּשְׁכּוֹן לִבְעָלָיו בִּזְמַן שֶׁהוּא צָרִיךְ לוֹ** (עשה קצט). **ו) שֶׁלֹּא יְאַחֵר הַמַּשְׁכּוֹן מִבְּעָלָיו הֶעָנִי בְּעֵת שֶׁהוּא צָרִיךְ לוֹ** (לא תעשה רמ). **ז) שֶׁלֹּא יַחֲבֹל אַלְמָנָה** (לא תעשה רמא). **ח) שֶׁלֹּא יַחֲבֹל**

Hilkhot Malve VeLoveh include twelve mitzvot: four positive mitzvot and eight negative mitzvot. Their enumeration follows: 1) To lend to the poor and destitute (positive mitzva 197); 2) Not to demand payment of a loan from the poor or destitute (negative mitzva 234); 3) To demand payment of a loan from a gentile (positive mitzva 142); 4) That a creditor may not take collateral forcibly (negative mitzva 239); 5) To restore collateral to its owner when he needs it (positive mitzva 199); 6) Not to delay the return of collateral from its owner, if he is a poor person, when he needs it (negative mitzva 240); 7) Not to take an item from a widow as collateral (negative mitzva 241); 8) Not to take as collateral any implements with which

כֵּלִים שֶׁעוֹשִׂין בָּהֶן אֹכֶל נֶפֶשׁ (לא תעשה רמב). ט) שֶׁלֹּא יִתֵּן הַמַּלְוֶה בְּרִבִּית (לא תעשה רלה). י) שֶׁלֹּא יַלְוֶה הַלֹּוֶה בְּרִבִּית (לא תעשה רלו). יא) שֶׁלֹּא יִתְעַסֵּק אָדָם בֵּין מַלְוֶה וְלֹוֶה בְּרִבִּית, לֹא יָעִיד בֵּינֵיהֶם וְלֹא יִכְתֹּב שְׁטָר וְלֹא יַעֲרֹב (לא תעשה רלז). יב) לִלְווֹת מִן הַנָּכְרִי וּלְהַלְווֹתוֹ בְּרִבִּית (עשה קצח).

food is prepared (negative mitzva 242); 9) That a lender may not give a loan at interest (negative mitzva 235); 10) That a borrower may borrow at interest (negative mitzva 236); 11) That a person may not become involved in the dealings between a lender and borrower at interest; he may not testify to the transaction between them, nor write the promissory note nor serve as guarantor (negative mitzva 237); 12) To borrow from a gentile and to lend to him at interest (positive mitzva 198).

הִלְכוֹת טוֹעֵן וְנִטְעָן – מִצְוַת עֲשֵׂה אַחַת, וְהִיא דִּין טוֹעֵן וּמוֹדֶה אוֹ כּוֹפֵר (עשה רמו).

Hilkhot Toen VeNitan include **one positive mitzva, which is the law of one who issues a claim** against another, **and** that person either **admits** to the claim **or denies** it (positive mitzva 246).

הִלְכוֹת נְחָלוֹת – מִצְוַת עֲשֵׂה אַחַת, וְהִיא דִּין סֵדֶר נְחָלוֹת (עשה רמח).

Hilkhot Nahalot include **one positive mitzva, which is the law of the order of inheritances** (positive mitzva 248).

נִמְצְאוּ כָּל הַמִּצְווֹת הַנִּכְלָלוֹת בְּסֵפֶר זֶה שָׁלֹשׁ וְעֶשְׂרִים, מֵהֶן אַחַת עֶשְׂרֵה מִצְווֹת עֲשֵׂה וּשְׁתֵּים עֶשְׂרֵה מִצְווֹת לֹא תַעֲשֶׂה.

Thus, all the mitzvot that are included in this *Sefer* are **twenty-three: Eleven of them** are **positive mitzvot and twelve** are **negative mitzvot.**

יד. סֵפֶר שׁוֹפְטִים

14. Sefer Shofetim

הִלְכוֹתָיו חָמֵשׁ, וְזֶה הוּא סִדּוּרָן: הִלְכוֹת סַנְהֶדְרִין וְהָעֳנָשִׁין הַמְּסוּרִין לָהֶם, הִלְכוֹת עֵדוּת, הִלְכוֹת מַמְרִים, הִלְכוֹת אֵבֶל, הִלְכוֹת מְלָכִים וּמִלְחָמוֹת.

Sefer Shofetim contains **five *Hilkhot*, in the following order: *Hilkhot Sanhedrin*** (Laws of the Sanhedrin), which also includes the laws of **the punishments that are entrusted to them, *Hilkhot Edut*** (Laws of Testimony), ***Hilkhot Mamrim*** (Laws of the Rebellious), ***Hilkhot Evel*** (Laws of Mourning), and ***Hilkhot Melakhim UMilhemoteihem*** (Laws of Kings and War).

הִלְכוֹת סַנְהֶדְרִין וְהָעֳנָשִׁין הַמְּסוּרִין לָהֶם – יֵשׁ בִּכְלָלָן שְׁלֹשִׁים מִצְווֹת, עֶשֶׂר מִצְווֹת עֲשֵׂה וְעֶשְׂרִים מִצְווֹת לֹא תַעֲשֶׂה, וְזֶה הוּא פְּרָטָן: א) לְמַנּוֹת שׁוֹפְטִים (עשה קעו). ב) שֶׁלֹּא לְמַנּוֹת דַּיָּן שֶׁאֵינוֹ יוֹדֵעַ דֶּרֶךְ הַמִּשְׁפָּט (לא תעשה רפד). ג) לִנְטוֹת אַחֲרֵי רַבִּים אִם נֶחְלְקוּ הַשּׁוֹפְטִים (עשה קעה). ד) שֶׁלֹּא לַהֲרֹג אִם רַבּוּ הַמְחַיְּבִין בְּאִישׁ אֶחָד עַד שֶׁיִּהְיוּ יֶתֶר שְׁנַיִם (לא תעשה רפב). ה) שֶׁלֹּא יְלַמֵּד חוֹבָה מִי שֶׁלִּמֵּד זְכוּת בְּדִינֵי נְפָשׁוֹת (לא תעשה רפג). ו) לַהֲרֹג בִּסְקִילָה (עשה רכט). ז) לַהֲרֹג

Hilkhot Sanhedrin, which also includes **the punishments that are entrusted to them, include thirty mitzvot: ten positive mitzvot and twenty negative mitzvot. Their enumeration follows: 1) To appoint judges** (positive mitzva 176); **2) Not to appoint a judge who does not know the way of judgment** (negative mitzva 284); **3) To incline after a majority, if judges disagree** (positive mitzva 175); **4) Not to execute** an accused person **if those condemning** him **are only one man more** than the acquitters, **unless there are two** or more **in the majority** (negative mitzva 282); **5) In cases of capital law, one who has taught** a reason to **acquit** the accused **may not** subsequently **teach** a reason to **condemn** him (negative mitzva 283); **6) To execute** certain guilty individuals **through stoning** (positive mitzva 229); **7) To execute**

בִּשְׂרֵפָה (עשה רכח). **ח) לַהֲרֹג בְּסַיִף** (עשה רכו). **ט) לַהֲרֹג בְּחֶנֶק** (עשה רכז). **י) לִתְלוֹת** (עשה רל). **יא) לִקְבֹּר הַנֶּהֱרָג בְּיוֹם הֲרִיגָתוֹ** (עשה רלא). **יב) שֶׁלֹּא תָלִין נִבְלָתוֹ** (לא תעשה סו). **יג) שֶׁלֹּא לְהַחֲיוֹת מְכַשֵּׁף** (לא תעשה שיא). **יד) לְהַלְקוֹת לָרָשָׁע** (עשה רכד). **טו) שֶׁלֹּא יוֹסִיף בְּהַכָּיַת הַלּוֹקֶה** (לא תעשה ש). **יו) שֶׁלֹּא לַהֲרֹג נָקִי בְּאֻמְדַּן הַדַּעַת** (לא תעשה רצ). **יז) שֶׁלֹּא לַעֲנֹשׁ אָנוּס** (לא תעשה רצד). **יח) שֶׁלֹּא לָחוּס עַל הוֹרֵג חֲבֵרוֹ אוֹ חוֹבֵל בּוֹ** (לא תעשה רעט). **יט) שֶׁלֹּא לְרַחֵם עַל הַדַּל בַּדִּין** (לא תעשה רעז). **כ) שֶׁלֹּא לְהַדֵּר גָּדוֹל בַּדִּין** (לא תעשה רעה). **כא) שֶׁלֹּא לְהַטּוֹת הַדִּין עַל בַּעַל עֲבֵרוֹת אַף עַל פִּי שֶׁהוּא חוֹטֵא** (לא תעשה רעח). **כב) שֶׁלֹּא לְעַוֵּל מִשְׁפָּט** (לא תעשה רעג). **כג) שֶׁלֹּא לְהַטּוֹת מִשְׁפַּט גֵּר יָתוֹם** (לא תעשה רפ). **כד) לִשְׁפֹּט בְּצֶדֶק** (עשה קעז). **כה) שֶׁלֹּא לִירְאָה בַּדִּין מֵאִישׁ זְרוֹעַ** (לא תעשה רעו). **כו) שֶׁלֹּא לִקַּח שֹׁחַד** (לא תעשה רעד). **כז) שֶׁלֹּא לִשָּׂא שֵׁמַע שָׁוְא** (לא תעשה רפא). **כח) שֶׁלֹּא לְקַלֵּל הַדַּיָּנִין** (לא תעשה שטו). **כט) שֶׁלֹּא לְקַלֵּל הַנָּשִׂיא** (לא תעשה שיו). **ל) שֶׁלֹּא לְקַלֵּל אָדָם מִשְּׁאָר בְּנֵי יִשְׂרָאֵל הַכְּשֵׁרִים** (לא תעשה שיז).

certain guilty individuals **through burning** (positive mitzva 228); **8) To execute** certain guilty individuals **by the sword** (positive mitzva 226); **9) To execute** certain guilty individuals **by strangulation** (positive mitzva 227); **10) To hang** certain executed individuals (positive mitzva 230); **11) To bury the executed on the day of his execution** (positive mitzva 231); **12) That his carcass shall not remain overnight** (negative mitzva 66); **13) Not to allow a warlock to live** (negative mitzva 311); **14) To flog the wicked** (positive mitzva 224); **15) Not to add to the lashes of one who is flogged** (negative mitzva 300); **16) Not to execute an innocent person through** mere **speculation** (negative mitzva 290); **17) Not to punish a victim of circumstances beyond his control** (negative mitzva 294); **18) Not to pity one who kills or injures another** (negative mitzva 279); **19) Not to favor a pauper in judgment** (negative mitzva 277); **20) Not to favor an eminent person in judgment** (negative mitzva 275); **21) Not to distort judgment against a transgressor, even though he is a sinner** (negative mitzva 278); **22) Not to perform injustice in judgment** (negative mitzva 273); **23) Not to distort the judging of a convert or an orphan** (negative mitzva 280); **24) To judge with righteousness** (positive mitzva 177); **25) Not to fear a violent man in judgment** (negative mitzva 276); **26) Not to take a bribe** (negative mitzva 274); **27) Not to accept a false report** (negative mitzva 281); **28) Not to curse judges** (negative mitzva 315); **29) Not to curse a *Nasi*** (negative mitzva 316); **30) Not to curse** any **reputable person from the rest of the children of Israel** (negative mitzva 317).

הִלְכוֹת עֵדוּת – יֵשׁ בִּכְלָלָן שְׁמוֹנֶה מִצְוֹת, שָׁלֹשׁ מִצְוֹת עֲשֵׂה וְחָמֵשׁ מִצְוֹת לֹא תַעֲשֶׂה, וְזֶה הוּא פְּרָטָן: א) **לְהָעִיד בְּבֵית דִּין לְמִי שֶׁיּוֹדֵעַ לוֹ עֵדוּת** (עשה קעח). ב) **לִדְרֹשׁ וְלַחֲקֹר הָעֵדִים** (עשה קעט). ג) **שֶׁלֹּא יוֹרֶה הָעֵד בְּדִין זֶה שֶׁהֵעִיד עָלָיו בְּדִינֵי נְפָשׁוֹת** (לא תעשה רצא). ד) **שֶׁלֹּא יָקוּם דָּבָר בְּעֵדוּת אֶחָד** (לא תעשה רפח). ה) **שֶׁלֹּא יָעִיד בַּעַל עֲבֵרָה** (לא תעשה רפו). ו) **שֶׁלֹּא יָעִיד קָרוֹב** (לא תעשה רפז). ז) **שֶׁלֹּא לְהָעִיד בְּשֶׁקֶר** (לא תעשה רפה). ח) **לַעֲשׂוֹת לְעֵד זוֹמֵם כַּאֲשֶׁר זָמַם** (עשה קפ).

Hilkhot Edut include eight mitzvot: three positive mitzvot and five negative mitzvot. Their enumeration follows: 1) That one who knows information relevant for testimony about something should testify to it in court (positive mitzva 178); 2) To inquire of and interrogate a witness (positive mitzva 179); 3) That in cases of capital law a witness may not issue a ruling in this same case regarding which he has testified (negative mitzva 291); 4) That a matter shall not be established by the testimony of one witness (negative mitzva 288); 5) That a transgressor may not give testimony (negative mitzva 286); 6) That a family relative may not give testimony (negative mitzva 287); 7) Not to testify falsely (negative mitzva 285) 8) To do to a conspiring witness as he conspired to do to another (positive mitzva 180).

הִלְכוֹת מַמְרִים - יֵשׁ בִּכְלָלָן תֵּשַׁע מִצְוֹת, שָׁלֹשׁ מִצְוֹת עֲשֵׂה וְשֵׁשׁ מִצְוֹת לֹא תַעֲשֶׂה, וְזֶה הוּא פְּרָטָן: א) לַעֲשׂוֹת עַל פִּי הַתּוֹרָה שֶׁיֹּאמְרוּ בֵּית דִּין הַגָּדוֹל (עשה קעד). ב) שֶׁלֹּא לָסוּר מִדִּבְרֵיהֶם (לא תעשה שיב). ג) שֶׁלֹּא לְהוֹסִיף עַל הַתּוֹרָה, לֹא בַּמִּצְוֹת שֶׁבִּכְתָב וְלֹא בְּפֵרוּשָׁן שֶׁלָּמַדְנוּ מִפִּי הַשְּׁמוּעָה (לא תעשה שיג). ד) שֶׁלֹּא לִגְרֹעַ מִן הַכֹּל (לא תעשה שיד). ה) שֶׁלֹּא לְקַלֵּל אָב וָאֵם (לא תעשה שיח). ו) שֶׁלֹּא לְהַכּוֹת אָב וָאֵם (לא תעשה שיט). ז) לְכַבֵּד אָב וָאֵם (עשה רי). ח) לְיִרְאָה מֵאָב וָאֵם (עשה ריא). ט) שֶׁלֹּא יִהְיֶה הַבֵּן סוֹרֵר וּמוֹרֶה עַל קוֹל אָבִיו וְאִמּוֹ (לא תעשה קצה).

Hilkhot Mamrim include nine mitzvot: three positive mitzvot and six negative mitzvot. Their enumeration follows: 1) To act in accordance with the law that the High Court instructs you to follow (positive mitzva 174); 2) Not to deviate from their statements (negative mitzva 312); 3) Not to add to the Torah, neither with respect to the written mitzvot, nor with respect to their interpretations which we learned on the basis of the Oral tradition (negative mitzva 313); 4) Not to subtract from any of the written mitzvot or their interpretations (negative mitzva 314); 5) Not to curse one's father or mother (negative mitzva 318); 6) Not to strike one's father or mother (negative mitzva 319); 7) To honor one's father and mother (positive mitzva 210); 8) To revere one's father and mother (positive mitzva 211); 9) That a son shall not act stubbornly and rebelliously against the voice of his father and mother (negative mitzva 195).

הִלְכוֹת אֵבֶל - יֵשׁ בִּכְלָלָן אַרְבַּע מִצְוֹת, אַחַת מִצְוַת עֲשֵׂה וְשָׁלֹשׁ מִצְוֹת לֹא תַעֲשֶׂה, וְזֶה הוּא פְּרָטָן: א) לְהִתְאַבֵּל עַל הַקְּרוֹבִים, וַאֲפִלּוּ כֹּהֵן מִתְטַמֵּא וּמִתְאַבֵּל עַל הַקְּרוֹבִים. וְאֵין אָדָם מִתְאַבֵּל עַל הֲרוּגֵי בֵּית דִּין, וּלְפִי זֶה כְּלַלְתִּי הֲלָכוֹת אֵלּוּ בְּסֵפֶר זֶה, שֶׁהֵן מֵעֵין קְבוּרָה בְּיוֹם מִיתָה, שֶׁהִיא מִצְוַת עֲשֵׂה (עשה לז). ב) שֶׁלֹּא יִטַּמֵּא כֹּהֵן גָּדוֹל לַקְּרוֹבִים (לא תעשה קסז). ג) שֶׁלֹּא יִכָּנֵס עִם הַמֵּת בְּאֹהֶל (לא תעשה קסח). ד) שֶׁלֹּא יִטַּמֵּא כֹּהֵן הֶדְיוֹט לְנֶפֶשׁ אָדָם, אֶלָּא לַקְּרוֹבִים בִּלְבַד (לא תעשה קסו).

Hilkhot Evel include four mitzvot: one positive mitzva and three negative mitzvot. Their enumeration follows: 1) To mourn one's family relatives; even a priest becomes ritually impure and mourns his relatives. Since a person does not mourn those executed by the court, I have included these halakhot in this *Sefer*, for they are a kind of extension of the law that a person's burial must be carried out on the day of his death, which is a positive mitzva (positive mitzva 37); 2) That a High Priest may not become impure even for his relatives (negative mitzva 167); 3) That a High Priest may not enter a tent and be there together with a corpse (negative mitzva 168); 4) That an ordinary priest may not become impure for the body of any person, other than for his relatives alone (negative mitzva 166).

הִלְכוֹת מְלָכִים וּמִלְחָמוֹת - יֵשׁ בִּכְלָלָן שָׁלֹשׁ וְעֶשְׂרִים מִצְוֹת, עֶשֶׂר מִצְוֹת עֲשֵׂה וּשְׁלֹשׁ עֶשְׂרֵה מִצְוֹת לֹא תַעֲשֶׂה, וְזֶה הוּא פְּרָטָן: א) לְמַנּוֹת מֶלֶךְ מִיִּשְׂרָאֵל (עשה קעג). ב) שֶׁלֹּא יְמַנֶּה מִקְּהַל גֵּרִים (לא תעשה שסב). ג) שֶׁלֹּא יַרְבֶּה לוֹ נָשִׁים (לא תעשה שסד). ד) שֶׁלֹּא יַרְבֶּה לוֹ סוּסִים (לא תעשה שסג). ה) שֶׁלֹּא יַרְבֶּה לוֹ כֶּסֶף וְזָהָב (לא תעשה שסה). ו) לְהַחֲרִים שִׁבְעָה עֲמָמִים (עשה קפז). ז) שֶׁלֹּא לְהַחֲיוֹת מֵהֶן נְשָׁמָה (לא תעשה מט). ח) לִמְחוֹת זַרְעוֹ שֶׁל עֲמָלֵק (עשה קפח). ט) לִזְכּוֹר מַה שֶּׁעָשָׂה עֲמָלֵק (עשה קפט). י) שֶׁלֹּא

***Hilkhot Melakhim UMilḥemoteihem* include twenty-three mitzvot: ten positive mitzvot and thirteen negative mitzvot. Their enumeration follows: 1) To appoint a king from the Jewish people** (positive mitzva 173); **2) Not to appoint** a king **from the congregation of converts** (negative mitzva 362); **3) That** a king **may not amass wives for himself** (negative mitzva 364); **4) That** a king **may not amass horses for himself** (negative mitzva 363); **5) That** a king **may not amass silver and gold for himself** (negative mitzva 365); **6) To destroy the seven** Canaanite **nations** (positive mitzva 187); **7) Not to keep any person of them alive** (negative mitzva 49); **8) To expunge the memory of Amalek** (positive mitzva 188); **9) To remember what Amalek did** (positive mitzva 189); **10) Not to forget** Amalek's **evil deeds and his lying in**

לִשְׁכֹּחַ מַעֲשָׂיו הָרָעִים וַאֲרִיבָתוֹ בַּדֶּרֶךְ (לא תעשה נט). **יא)** שֶׁלֹּא לִשְׁכֹּן בְּאֶרֶץ מִצְרַיִם (לא תעשה מו). **יב)** לִשְׁלֹחַ שָׁלוֹם לְיוֹשְׁבֵי הָעִיר כְּשֶׁצָּרִים עָלֶיהָ, וְלָדוּן בָּהּ כַּאֲשֶׁר מְפֹרָשׁ בַּתּוֹרָה, אִם תַּשְׁלִים וְאִם לֹא תַּשְׁלִים (עשה קצ). **יג)** שֶׁלֹּא לִדְרֹשׁ שָׁלוֹם מֵעַמּוֹן וּמוֹאָב בִּלְבַד כְּשֶׁצָּרִים עֲלֵיהֶם (לא תעשה נו). **יד)** שֶׁלֹּא לְהַשְׁחִית אִילָנֵי מַאֲכָל בַּמָּצוֹר (לא תעשה נז). **טו)** לְהַתְקִין יָד שֶׁיֵּצְאוּ בּוֹ בַּעֲלֵי הַמַּחֲנֶה לְהִפָּנוֹת בּוֹ (עשה קצב). **יו)** לְהַתְקִין יָתֵד לַחְפֹּר בּוֹ (עשה קצג). **יז)** לִמְשֹׁחַ כֹּהֵן לְדַבֵּר בְּאָזְנֵי אַנְשֵׁי הַצָּבָא בִּשְׁעַת הַמִּלְחָמָה (עשה קצא). **יח)** לִהְיוֹת מְאָרֵס וּבוֹנֶה בִּנְיָן וְנוֹטֵעַ כֶּרֶם שְׂמֵחִים בְּקִנְיָנָם שָׁנָה תְּמִימָה וּמַחֲזִירִין אוֹתָן מִן הַמִּלְחָמָה (עשה ריד). **יט)** שֶׁלֹּא יַעֲבֹר עֲלֵיהֶן דָּבָר וְלֹא יֵצְאוּ אֲפִלּוּ לְצָרְכֵי הָעִיר וְצָרְכֵי הַגְּדוּד וְדוֹמֶה לָהֶן (לא תעשה שי). **כ)** שֶׁלֹּא לַעֲרֹץ וְלַחֲזֹר לְאָחוֹר בִּשְׁעַת מִלְחָמָה (לא תעשה נח). **כא)** דִּין יְפַת תֹּאַר (עשה רכא). **כב)** שֶׁלֹּא תִּמָּכֵר יְפַת תֹּאַר (לא תעשה רסג). **כג)** שֶׁלֹּא יִכְבְּשֶׁנָּה לַעֲבְדוּת אַחַר שֶׁנִּבְעֲלָה (לא תעשה רסד).

ambush on the way (negative mitzva 59); **11) Not to reside in the land of Egypt** (negative mitzva 46); **12) To send** an offer of **peace to the residents of a city when laying siege to it, and to treat it as specified in the Torah,** depending on **whether it makes peace or whether it does not make peace** (positive mitzva 190); **13) Not to seek peace with Amon and Moav alone, when laying siege to them** (negative mitzva 56); **14) Not to destroy fruit-bearing trees in a siege** (negative mitzva 57); **15) To establish a place to which** soldiers **in a camp can go out to defecate** (positive mitzva 192); **16) To prepare a spade with which to dig** and cover one's excrement in that place (positive mitzva 193); **17)** That the **priest who is anointed** for war **should address the members of the army at a time of war** (positive mitzva 191); **18) That one who has betrothed a woman, and one who has built** a new **structure, and one who has planted a vineyard, rejoice in their acquisition** for **a whole year, and that they are returned from war** (positive mitzva 214); **19) That they shall not be obligated in any matter, and not go out even for the requirements of the city or the requirements of the troops, and the like** (negative mitzva 310); **20) Not to fear** the enemy **and retreat during a time of war** (negative mitzva 58); **21)** To follow **the law of a beautiful woman** captured in war (positive mitzva 221); **22) That a beautiful woman** captured in war **may not be sold** (negative mitzva 263); **23) That one may not subjugate** this woman **in slavery after she has engaged in intercourse** (negative mitzva 264).

נִמְצְאוּ כָּל הַמִּצְוֹת הַנִּכְלָלוֹת בְּסֵפֶר זֶה אַרְבַּע וְשִׁבְעִים, מֵהֶן שֶׁבַע וְעֶשְׂרִים מִצְוֹת עֲשֵׂה וְשֶׁבַע וְאַרְבָּעִים מִצְוֹת לֹא תַעֲשֶׂה. וְנִמְצְאוּ כָּל הַהֲלָכוֹת שֶׁל אַרְבָּעָה עָשָׂר סֵפֶר – שָׁלֹשׁ וּשְׁמוֹנִים הֲלָכוֹת.

Thus, all the mitzvot that are included in this *Sefer* are **seventy-four: Twenty-seven of them** are **positive mitzvot and forty-seven** are **negative mitzvot. And all the *Hilkhot*** sections **of** the **fourteen books thus** amount to **eighty-three* *Hilkhot*** sections.

וְעַתָּה אַתְחִיל לְבָאֵר מִשְׁפְּטֵי כָּל מִצְוָה וּמִצְוָה וְכָל הַדִּינִים הַנִּגְלָלִין עִמָּהּ מֵעִנְיָנָהּ עַל סֵדֶר הַהֲלָכוֹת בְּעֶזְרַת שַׁדַּי.

I will now start to clarify the regulations of each and every mitzva, and all the laws that come with it, from its specific **topic, following the orders of the *Hilkhot*** sections, **with the help of the Almighty.**

INSIGHTS OF THE LUBAVITCHER REBBE

***And all the *Hilkhot* sections…thus amount to eighty-three – וְנִמְצְאוּ כָּל הַהֲלָכוֹת...שָׁלֹשׁ וּשְׁמוֹנִים:** Two points of significance can be made regarding the number eighty-three: 1) The Gemara notes (*Bava Kamma* 92b) that the numerical value of the word *maḥala* [sickness] is eighty-three, and it adds that there are eighty-three sicknesses which can all be negated by eating bread dipped in salt in the morning, and drinking a flask of water afterward. On the spiritual plane, bread and water symbolize Torah study, especially halakha. Thus, studying and engaging in the eighty-three *Hilkhot* sections of the Rambam's book can heal eighty-three sicknesses. 2) A full life consists of seventy years ("the days of our lives in it are seventy years" Psalms 90:10), and the Rambam lived for seventy years minus eighty-three days. If the number of *Hilkhot* in his work are added to his days, he lived a full life of seventy years (*Torat Menaḥem*, *Hitvaaduyot*, *Motzaei Zot Ḥanukka* 5746; *Parashat Shemot* 5752).

Steinsaltz
Center

KOREN